SOCIAL WORK
WORK
FIELDS OF PRACTICE

SOCIAL WORK
FIELDS OF PRACTICE

SECOND EDITION

Edited by
Margaret Alston and
Jennifer McKinnon

OXFORD
UNIVERSITY PRESS

OXFORD

UNIVERSITY PRESS

253 Normanby Road, South Melbourne, Victoria 3205, Australia

Oxford University Press is a department of the University of Oxford.
It furthers the University's objective of excellence in research, scholarship,
and education by publishing worldwide in

Oxford New York

Auckland Cape Town Dar es Salaam Hong Kong Karachi
Kuala Lumpur Madrid Melbourne Mexico City Nairobi
New Delhi Shanghai Taipei Toronto

With offices in

Argentina Austria Brazil Chile Czech Republic France Greece
Guatemala Hungary Italy Japan Poland Portugal Singapore
South Korea Switzerland Thailand Turkey Ukraine Vietnam

OXFORD is a trade mark of Oxford University Press
in the UK and in certain other countries

First published 2001
Reprinted 2003, 2004
Second edition published 2005

National Library of Australia
Cataloguing-in-Publication data:

Social work : fields of practice.

2nd ed.
Bibliography.
Includes index.
ISBN 0 19 555047 1.

1. Social service—Australia. I. Alston, Margaret.
II. McKinnon, Jennifer, 1959– .

361.320994

Typeset by OUPANZS
Printed by Sheck Wah Tong Printing Press Ltd, Hong Kong

Contents

Contributors

Margaret Alston (B SocStud, M.Litt, PhD) is Professor of Social Work and Human Services and Director of the Centre for Rural Social Research at Charles Sturt University. She has written widely on rural social issues, rural communities, rural policy, service delivery, and gender. Her social work books include *Research for Social Workers,* co-authored with Wendy Bowles, reprinted in 2003.

Robert Bland is Professor of Social Work at the University of Tasmania, and has a practice background in hospital and community-based mental health. Robert has written extensively in the areas of families and mental illness, social work and mental health, and mental health policy. Recently he has been researching the areas of spirituality and mental illness. He represents the AASW on the Mental Health Council of Australia, is a member of the Mental Health Advisory Group for the AASW, a member of the AASW Practice Standards Committee, and coordinator of the national social work and mental health email network, and is a life member of ARAFMI.

Robin Bowles (BSW(Hons), MSW) Robin began working with refugee survivors of torture and trauma 16 years ago, commencing work at the Service for the Treatment and Rehabilitation of Torture and Trauma Survivors (STARTTS) in October 1988, two months after the service began. Robin's current work is primarily as a psychotherapist and clinical supervisor, and she is currently a trainee in the Adult Psychotherapy Training Program with the NSW Institute of Psychoanalytic Psychotherapy. Her research and practice interests include the interface of culture, politics, trauma, and psychotherapy, and working with interpreters in psychotherapy.

Wendy Bowles is a Senior Lecturer in Social Work at Charles Sturt University and member of the Centre for Rural Social Research. Her teaching and research interests include disability, social work theory and practice, gender, ethics, and rural issues. Recent research and publications include a research textbook written with Margaret Alston: *Research for Social Workers, an introduction to methods*, 2nd edition (2003) and papers on ethics, social work practicum, and rural health and welfare issues. Wendy serves as Chair of her local access committee and is a member of the Management Committee of IDEAS, a disability information service in rural New South Wales.

Elspeth Browne (BA, DipSocStud, AIHA, MSW) has practised in teaching hospitals in Sydney, Brisbane, and London, and has taught at the Universities of Queensland, Sydney, and New South Wales. In 1989, she retired as a Senior Lecturer at the University of New South Wales and returned to part-time hospital practice. She left the hospital in 1998, and is now supervising social workers and undertaking socio-legal consultancies. She has been a long-time member of AASW, holding office in the Queensland and New South Wales branches. Elspeth has chaired the ethics committee for the New South Wales branch, and has published widely in the field of social work in health care.

Brian Cheers (BSW, MSW, PhD) is Associate Professor, Associate Dean (Research), and Director, Centre for Rural and Regional Development at Whyalla Campus of the University of South Australia, and Adjunct Associate Professor with the School of Public Health and Community Medicine at the University of NSW. He has written several books and published widely in international and Australian journals. Brian is a rural and community sociologist. Current research includes measuring community capacity and community strength, rural social care, community impacts of water markets, Indigenous involvement in bush produce industries, governance in natural resource management, and community participation in health.

Jeanette Conway is Convenor of the International Social Work Committee of the Australian Association of Social Workers (AASW), a member of the International Federation of Social Work (IFSW) Asia and Pacific Committee, and Honorary General Secretary of the Commonwealth Organisation for Social Work. For 25 years she belonged to an international order of Catholic nuns who worked in developing countries facilitating the social development of women and children. In the 1980s she coordinated a three-year national study on marriage and family life in Papua New Guinea. Back in Australia she has worked extensively with aged Russian Jewish migrants and their families in Melbourne and until recently ran the field education programme at the School of Social Work at the University of Melbourne.

Michael Darcy (BSW, MAdmin, PhD) worked as a Community Worker in a public housing estate and in local government before joining the University of Western Sydney where he is a member of the Social Justice and Social Change Research Centre and Associate Dean (Research). In the 1990s he was the head of ACOSS's Urban and Regional Development Unit. He has conducted projects on housing issues for AHURI, National and NSW Shelter, NSW Department of Housing and local councils, and published in the international journals *Urban Studies* and *Critical Quarterly*. He was an expert member of the NSW Housing Assistance Plan Advisory Committee, and is currently a Board Member of Shelter NSW.

Elizabeth Fernandez (MSW, PhD) is Senior Lecturer, School of Social Work, at the University of New South Wales teaching courses in Human Behaviour, Child and Family Welfare and Professional Supervision. She is a research affiliate of the UNSW Social Policy Research Centre. She has collaborated with Barnardos Australia on ARC research projects involving the implementation of the UK *Looking After Children* framework and the *Framework for The Assessment of Families of Children in Need* in Australian child welfare. Her research is in the areas of out of home care and child abuse prevention. Elizabeth is the author of *Significant Harm: Unravelling Child Protection Decisions and Substitute Care*

Careers, and is a founding member of the International Association for Outcome-Based Evaluation in Family and Children's Services.

Peta Fitzgibbon is currently the ACT Territory Manager for the departments of Family and Community Service and Health and Ageing. Prior to this Peta worked in the Department of Social Security and more recently Centrelink as a social worker. She was the first National Manager of Social Work Services in Centrelink and then held positions as the National Manager of Youth and Students and then Participation Strategies. Peta gained her Social Work degree from Flinders University and is currently enrolled in her Masters in Social Administration at the University of Queensland.

Stephanie Gilbert (AssocDipCommWelf, BSW(Hons), GradCertEd, MA) has worked at a number of Australian universities in Indigenous Education and Social Work. She has worked in foster care and youth employment and has a long-standing interest in examining the removal of Aboriginal children from their families. Currently working at the University of Newcastle, she has been on the Board of the Australian Association of Social Work for five years and is active locally in the Hunter Branch of the AASW. She has published widely on feminist and Indigenous issues, and also contributed to *Child Welfare Policy: Critical Australian Perspectives*, edited by Jan Mason.

Desley Hargreaves is the National Manager, Social Work and Social Inclusion Services, at Centrelink. A graduate of the University of Queensland, she is a past president of the University of Queensland Social Work Alumni. Her recent employment history has been in Centrelink in Social Work Leadership positions. Prior to that Desley worked in Social Security in Social Work and management positions. Desley has also worked in a range of Commonwealth and state government agencies and non-governmental organisations.

Karen Healy (BSocWk(Hons), PhD) is Associate Professor in the School of Social Work and Applied Human Sciences at the University of Queensland. Karen has practised as a child protection worker, youth worker, and health services worker. She continues to maintain strong links with community services practice and is currently undertaking research on child and family welfare services and social capital creation in geographically diverse communities. Karen has written extensively on social work practice and applied social policy. She is the author of *Social Work Practices* (2000) and *Social Work Theories in Context* (2005).

Jennifer McKinnon (BSW, MSocWk) has a practice background in hospital social work, community health, Indigenous affairs, and mental health. She is an adjunct lecturer at Charles Sturt University, having taught there for over eight years, and has conducted sustainability research projects in Thailand and Europe. She has recently published articles on social sustainability, school social work, and women's well-being, and is currently completing her PhD on the topic of social work and sustainability.

Anthony McMahon (BSW(Hons), MSW, PhD) has worked for a number of years in child welfare and community development in Western Australia. Currently, he is Head of the School of Social Work and Community Welfare at James Cook University, Queensland. He has published books and articles on child welfare, cross-cultural practice, and social policy. His most recent publications have been on well-being indicators for Indigenous children in foster care.

Jan Mason (MA, Dip Ed(tertiary), MSW, PhD) is Professor of Social Work at the University of Western Sydney. She researches broadly in the area of social work, as well as specifically in child welfare, having acquired in-depth knowledge of child welfare through employment in practice and management positions in this area. She edited the book *Child Welfare Policy, Critical Australian Perspectives* (1993), and has published in journals and books on child and family issues. She has recently completed (with others) two ARC linkage projects, one in the area of families and their needs from services, the other on the needs of children in care.

Elizabeth Moore (BSocSci, BSocWk, MA, MLS) lectures at Charles Sturt University, having worked in public sector casework, management, and policy positions, and advising on integrity issues. Since taking up teaching Elizabeth has continued to contribute to juvenile justice policy and practice through Ministerial appointment as an Official Visitor to a youth detention centre, and as a member of the New South Wales Juvenile Justice Advisory Council. Two recent research projects focused on local court services, family violence, and protection orders, and the particular experience of Indigenous women in seeking protection through the court.

Maureen O'Regan (BAVisArts, BSW, MSW) has over 25 years' experience working with marginalised young people and families in a variety of settings, including drug and alcohol withdrawal, sexual assault, youth detention, youth services, a women's hospital, rehabilitation, income security, and local government. She is currently the team leader of the Adolescent Drug and Alcohol Withdrawal Service at the Mater Hospital in Brisbane. Maureen has provided supervision and training to youth workers and social workers and undertaken research projects for various universities, government policy units, and NGOs. Maureen is a member of the Children's Services Tribunal, Queensland Department of Justice.

Manohar Pawar (MSW, PhD) is a senior lecturer at Charles Sturt University, and a key researcher and associate director of the Centre for Rural Social Research. He has also taught at La Trobe University, Melbourne, and the Tata Institute of Social Sciences, Mumbai. Manohar was awarded a Quality of Life Award in 2001 from the ACU, and a Research Excellence Award 2001 from the Faculty of Arts, CSU. He has published several books and refereed journal articles. Some of his own and co-authored published titles include *Community Informal Care and Welfare Systems* (2004), *Data Collecting Methods and Experiences* (ed., 2004), and *International Social Work* (2005).

Richard Roberts (BA, DipEd, BSocStud, PhD) is a Senior Lecturer in the School of Social Work at the University of New South Wales. In his academic and professional career over the last 30 years much of his attention has been given to lesbian and gay issues. During 1991 to 1993 he was an Associate Professor of Social Work at Charles Sturt University,

Riverina. During this time he undertook several research projects on gay men coping with isolation and discrimination in rural areas.

Judith Stubbs (BSW, PhD) practiced for 10 years in local government community development and social planning. She was awarded the NSW Local Government and Shires' Association 'Innovative Planning in Local Government' award in 1994. Following this, she set up a social research and planning consultancy, and recently took up an appointment at the Social Justice and Social Change Research Centre at UWS where she is Adjunct Senior Research Fellow. Judith also holds a post-doctoral research fellowship with UWS in developing participatory approaches to public housing renewal, and is Chairperson of a number of community organisations including the Illawarra Community Legal Centre and the NSW Department of Housing Regional Customer Advisory Council, and is a member of Shelter NSW.

Michael Tansky (MA, BSW) has over 30 years' experience working with marginalised young people, and in associated policy and research areas in the community, public, and university sectors. He is currently the director of Brisbane Youth Service, and has previously worked with Birmingham Social Services (UK) in residential care, the University of Queensland, Queensland University of Technology, the Australian Federation of AIDS Organisations, and the Queensland Departments of Families and Premier and Cabinet. Michael has also conducted research projects for the Commonwealth Office of Youth Affairs, the Australian Federation of AIDS Organisations, Catholic Prison Ministry, and Micah Projects. He has published widely on youth issues.

Judy Taylor (BA, DipSocWk, MSW) is manager of Research and Enterprise, Spencer Gulf Rural Health School in South Australia. She has extensive experience in planning, funding, and developing health and human services and initiatives in rural, regional, and remote areas of Australia. Currently she is researching the development of appropriate primary health care services and undertaking action research with several Aboriginal communities and organisations in rural and remote South Australia. She is on regional health service planning committees and helps plan for the national Primary Health Care Research and Evaluation Development programme. Her publications are primarily about research capacity building and service development in rural, regional, and remote locations.

Michael Wearing (PhD) is Senior Lecturer in Social Work at the University of New South Wales where he specialises in the teaching of social theory, research methods, and social policy. His main areas of interest are comparative social policy, health, and mental health policy, and he has published in variety of sociological and social policy journals and books. His latest book is *Organizations and Management in Social Work*, Sage Publications, jointly authored with Mark Hughes.

David Wiles (BA, BSocAdmin, PhD) has a practice background in aged community care and generalist hospital social work, and teaches Gerontology, Human Services, Social Policy, and Social Work at Edith Cowan University. David also served the Council on the Ageing

(WA) in a wide range of voluntary roles from the 1980s, and worked with schools including Councils and Parents and Citizens committees through the 1990s. He now serves with the Executive Committees of the Academic Staff Association (ASAECU) and the National Tertiary Education Union (NTEU, ECU Branch), to which he was first elected in 2001. David has a number of publications in the field of aged care.

Preface

We are delighted to offer this second edition of *Social Work: Fields of Practice* to the reader. It has enabled us to capitalise on the foundations begun in the first edition and introduce new areas for discussion. For a very long time, many of us who work in the field of social work education had been bemoaning the lack of references on social work practice for the Australian context. We have been well served in Australia with a range of journals offering a high standard of literature on social work theory and practice. However, it seemed to us that what was missing was a broad overview that would give a background to various fields of practice and could be used for a range of purposes.

Our aim in beginning this book was to gather information on different fields of practice in which social work experts are based that would serve as a central reference for both practitioners and students looking for a starting point in or overview of a particular practice field. The process has been educative and empowering, exposing to us (and ultimately to the reader) the depths of research and scholarly activity, and range of exceptional practice among our social work colleagues. Although we each have specialised in particular research and interest areas, the information and analysis provided by the authors of each chapter has rekindled our interest in a range of social work fields. It has reminded us of why we became social workers all those years ago, and has inspired us to look further into particular areas that have grasped our attention. This is exactly the effect we envisaged when the idea for this book was new and dear to our hearts: we certainly hope that readers will get as much from the book as we have done.

We have sought from each author a broad picture of their field of practice or expertise. The task we had set for ourselves and the contributing authors was actually an onerous one. The result is that each chapter represents new knowledge for social work in Australia. This second edition has been fully revised, and includes two new chapters on important fields of social work practice—those of housing and the criminal justice system.

The structure of this book

We have endeavoured to provide a chapter on most major fields of practice of social work. 'Major' is defined as those fields of social work practice that already provide large employment bases for social workers in Australia, and the areas that we expect will open up to social workers in the near future.

Areas covered by the chapters have fallen quite naturally into three sections: Part 1 relates to target groups for social work practice, Part 2 relates to social work practice settings, and Part 3 documents emerging trends and issues in fields of social work practice.

There are seven chapters or target groups in Part 1. Margaret Alston discusses the issues relating to working with women, pointing out that social work professionals and social work clients are largely female, and suggesting that working with women has many layers of meaning. She discusses the development of alternative services for women since the development of the second-wave women's movement in the 1970s.

Richard Roberts notes the importance of including a chapter on working with gay men and lesbians as it indicates that social work professionals have an important role to play in recognising and addressing the issues raised. Yet he notes that social work practice lags behind the ideals of non-discriminatory practice espoused by the profession. This chapter is of critical importance to the development of anti-oppressive practice.

Wendy Bowles's chapter on the disability field points out that the ideology underpinning the disability field has changed significantly over the past 20 years, ensuring that practice in this field has also altered in major ways. Bowles argues that social workers are ideally placed to be allies of the disability movement in the struggles for equity and recognition.

Social work with Indigenous Australians is discussed by Stephanie Gilbert. She notes that such practice must be informed by an understanding of history and a commitment to challenge racism. She argues that practice with Indigenous Australians cannot be prescriptive but must be governed by ideals and reflective practice, and involves great joy and great sadness in coming to terms with the realities of the lived experiences of Indigenous Australians.

Anthony McMahon notes that Australia has become a culturally diverse society and that social work practice must reflect an understanding of anti-oppressive practice. Multiculturalism is a reality in contemporary Australia, and social workers must have a commitment to addressing the issues raised for the diverse groups who have come to be part of the future of this country.

In her chapter on working with families, Jan Mason notes how 'familism'—an unquestioning acceptance of the bourgeois model of the family—has dominated policy and practice in this area. She argues that work with families must be governed by a commitment to challenge rationalist ideologies, to give a voice to the marginalised, and to give prominence to human values.

Karen Healy, Maureen O'Regan, and Michael Tansky, in their chapter on working with young people, outline the vulnerability of young people in Australian society and the vulnerability of non-governmental organisations offering support for young people. They note that youth work is a growing area of practice and urge social workers to adopt anti-oppressive practices when working with young people.

Part 2 deals with work in practice settings, detailing the more obvious areas in which a number of social workers are employed. In her chapter on health settings, for example, Elspeth Browne notes that 60 per cent of social workers are employed in this area, thus pointing to the critical nature of this field to the profession. She notes the need to understand the impact of social conditions on health and the need for equity and access in health service delivery. To achieve fairness she notes that social workers must become 'thorns in the side' of other practitioners.

Robert Bland addresses the complexities of social work in the mental health field, giving attention to the changing policy context and to significant practice issues. He notes that confidentiality and self-determination are coloured by the sometimes competing needs of clients and caregivers, and that workers therefore must act with sensitivity and care when working in this area and be constantly aware of the ethical ambiguities.

Peta Fitzgibbon and Desley Hargreaves discuss the area of income maintenance, pointing to the extraordinary changes in service delivery in this area. They argue that the creation of the corporate body Centrelink and the privatisation of employment services have implications for workers in all fields. The authors address the implications of social and economic participation, mutual obligation, and a more limited role for government in welfare service delivery. They argue that social work in this area will be characterised by entrepreneurialism, social policy development, and research, as well as providing a response to the needs of marginalised people.

Michael Wearing addresses the area of employment services, noting that the welfare state has moved from its original status as the 'wage-earners' welfare state' to that of an almost anti-wage-earner focus with highly targeted provisions. He argues for social work to provide a lead in challenging inequality, poverty, and oppression and in formulating an argument about the social right to work in a society where work is currently characterised by many insecurities.

David Wiles notes that gerontological social work will provide many challenges in the coming years as the population ages. For social workers committed to addressing social conditions and helping the vulnerable there is much to be done in a society moving to foster individual responsibility over community obligation. He urges workers to move out of casework roles to take up the challenge of policy reform, social action, and programme development.

The critical area of child protection is addressed by Elizabeth Fernandez in a wide-ranging discussion of the nature of child abuse, its extent, the policy framework, and workers' roles. She argues that an awareness of the links between the state and family is critical to our understanding of work in this area. Further, she notes that workers as agents of the state must balance conflicting demands of child protection, empowerment of parents, and community expectations.

Michael Darcy and Judith Stubbs provide an overview of the field of housing, noting that access to adequate housing is one of the critical elements of well-being. Yet rising house prices are signaling a new underclass of people unable to own their own home and with reduced access to affordable rental property.

Elizabeth Moore has contributed one of the new chapter titles in this edition—alerting readers to social work practice issues within the criminal justice system. She makes important points on public perceptions of crime versus actual crime rates and the ideological underpinnings of the criminal justice system. Elizabeth then gives readers a comprehensive picture of the various agencies that are involved in the criminal justice system and social work's place within them.

There are many new and emerging fields of practice in social work. Some have arisen out of generalist practice, and have developed as areas of specialisation. Others are still emerging, and do not necessarily have a distinct body of knowledge within the social work profession. Nevertheless, we felt it important to alert potential practitioners to developing fields within which social work knowledge and skills are very relevant. A selection of some of these new and emerging fields forms the basis of Part 3.

Jennifer McKinnon's chapter, 'Social work, Sustainability, and the Environment', offers options for social workers who want to incorporate environmentally friendly practices into their knowledge base. This is based on a broad definition of social justice, and expands on the view that social responsibility and social action are core values at the very heart of social work. She posits the idea that eco-social concerns can inform our practice with individuals, couples, groups, and communities, and that social workers can learn from some of the practices of marginal social groups and movements.

Social work practice in rural and remote areas has never been easy. Brian Cheers and Judy Taylor, writing on social work in rural and remote Australia, detail the harsh realities of practice in isolated areas, but also offer a strategic model for practice as an alternative to the policies and programmes that centre on urban areas and come out of our capital cities. They offer a view of social work and welfare practice that is more responsive to rural and remote issues, and which takes into account geographical realities.

Robin Bowles details social work with refugee survivors of torture and trauma, gives an overview of the development of social work practice in this field, and looks at contemporary practice issues. She identifies practice opportunities at several levels in this field, ranging from project and community work to therapy and management.

Jeanette Conway and Manohar Pawar give us an Australian perspective on the concern within the social work profession about human rights violations and a range of social justice issues around the world in their chapter on international fields of social work practice. They identify a number of opportunities for practice, and detail the links between our professional association in Australia, the AASW, and the international social work groups that, together and separately, aim to improve approaches to human rights around the world.

We have presented a comprehensive overview of contemporary and emerging fields of social work practice in Australia. This material reflects current thinking in the social work profession. The reader is invited to extend their interest by exploring these fields in greater depth. Meanwhile, we look forward to a vibrant and exciting future for social work professionals. We hope that this book adds value to that future.

Margaret Alston
Jennifer McKinnon
Wagga Wagga, November 2004

Acknowledgments

No large, deadline-filled venture can be undertaken without the help, support, and feedback of a great number of people—including those who do not realise at the time that they are helping out by providing a sounding board for ideas or acting as a source of inspiration. There are far too many people involved for us to name, but suffice to say that our colleagues and friends have helped us enormously and we are most grateful to them for listening to us, and particularly for their feedback about the first edition.

Lucy McLoughlin at OUP has been a fabulous project manager. She has kept us on track as well as offering very valuable ideas. Pete Cruttenden, our editor, has likewise been wonderful to work with, and has turned the text into a much more readable document.

Finally, our families have lived with us through the anxious moments that characterise any major project, and we thank them for their support and their patience. Here's to you Phil, Louise, Mark, Megan, and Catherine; George, Peter, Stephanie, and Felicity; and to HSCs, weddings, house moves, and the normal crises of everyday life!

1

CONTEXT OF CONTEMPORARY SOCIAL WORK PRACTICE

Margaret Alston and Jennifer McKinnon

Social work has been at something of a crossroads since economic orthodoxy became dominant in the 1980s and beyond, and while the way ahead is exciting, it is also very challenging. Socio-political changes have brought about a climate that makes social work's liberal-democratic and humanistic values rather unfashionable, yet the time has never been better for the kinds of interventions that social workers make so well; times of crisis are, indeed, times of change. The aim of this book is to give an overview of various fields of social work practice in Australia. We are aware that many social work texts originate in the United Kingdom or the United States of America, and while there are similarities to which Australian social workers can relate, there has long been a need to examine the breadth of social work practice in a way that acknowledges its uniquely Australian aspects.

In this book we present many fields of social work practice prominent in Australia. We are not attempting to include all fields—that would be impossible. What we have sought to do is give an overview of the fields in which the majority of social workers are employed, and in this way provide student social workers with the 'flavour' of each field. Social workers are employed now in a range of settings, largely within government structures at federal, state, and local levels, but also within a great many non-governmental organisations. The roles of social workers range from individual casework to group work and community work, from research and policy analysis to programme development, and from management to advising Government Ministers. In this introduction we give background information on the history of social work and the current socio-political climate in Australia, and we look at what the future might hold for social work practice in this country. This sets the stage for the information offered by each of the specialist contributors throughout the remainder of the text.

History of social work

The profession of social work in Western nations had its beginnings in a variety of different settings in the United Kingdom and the United States. In examining these origins we can see the genesis of the ongoing debate about different styles of social work practice. In nineteenth-century post-Dickensian Great Britain, for example, the Charity Organizations Society (COS) developed. While members of the COS worked with the poor, their work focused on persuading the poor to accept their circumstances and adjust to their poverty. Poverty was generally seen as the result of personal failings, and the work of the COS was aimed at helping individuals to overcome their deficiencies.

By contrast, the Settlement Movement arose in Chicago in the late nineteenth century, led by Jane Addams who later was awarded the 1931 Nobel Peace Prize. Addams established a vast social organisation centred on Hull House, a settlement house in the poorest district of Chicago, which was a focal point for work with immigrant families. The ideology of the settlement house was that 'young and old alike, in fact all who ask, receive a helping hand' (Koht 1931), reflecting a view that society was not providing for the basic needs of its most vulnerable members.

The methods of the two movements signify an underlying political standpoint. Members of the COS acted in a way that encapsulated classical liberal ideology: victims were blamed for their position in society, and a distinction was made between the 'deserving' and 'undeserving' poor. The Settlement Movement, on the other hand, emphasised social democratic values and processes, and promoted inclusion, egalitarianism, and a fairer distribution of resources.

It would be unfair, though, to say that these two movements represented the sum of charitable works in these regions. From its beginnings, social work had an ethos of service and a growing awareness of the interplay between individuals and societies that could lead to accidental disadvantage. There was not such a clear philosophical dichotomy in practice. A liberal philosophical tradition moved workers to teach the poor better skills, and to develop more responsive and better-coordinated services. Unmet needs of the poor needed to be better articulated, and in some ways social workers became the go-betweens who articulated these needs (Thorpe & Petruchenia 1985). Clement Attlee, the British prime minister, made clear in 1920 that the rightful role of the social worker at that time included both community work and advising on social policy, along with traditional casework (Osburn 1999).

The philosophical underpinning of the COS and the Settlement Movement, though, illustrates the divide between various forms of social work over the past 150 years. Social work practitioners and educators have tended either to emphasise the treatment and cure of individual problems and deficiencies (individual casework) or to promote understanding of structural inequities and the importance of social reform (radical and structural approaches).

The COS and the Settlement Movement exemplify the way that the development of social work from diverse traditions has led to a continuing debate about 'traditional' versus 'radical' social work. There is some agreement among contemporary practitioners that, over recent decades, social work has assumed responsibility for both individual and structural interventions as the different approaches have gradually converged (Fook 1993; Trainor 1996), and as the radical social critique of the 1960s and 1970s has been incorporated into practice.

There is a strong tradition of social work in many Eastern and South American countries. In India, for example, a social work profession has developed from a long tradition of community activism among untrained social carers. Although many schools of social work in India teach from a Western tradition, there has not necessarily been the dichotomy that has influenced approaches to social work in the West. Rather, social workers have always focused on social action at the interface of individual and structural problems. The current code of ethics for Indian social workers emphasises the responsibility that social workers have to work towards overall social justice goals, as well as doing what they can to ameliorate the circumstances of the poorer and more vulnerable members of society.

The Australian context

Middle-class and influential women were active in the early years of the Australian colonies in defining the needs of the poor. For example, Anna King, the wife of Governor King of New South Wales, established the Parramatta Female Factory in 1804 to provide housing and work training for neglected and deserted female children. Colonial Australia also was affected by the welfare measures for migrants and employment reforms introduced by Caroline Chisholm in New South Wales around this time, and from 1887 the COS was active in Melbourne. People doing 'social work' in the early years tended to be unpaid middle-class women of good standing, while in hospitals, almoners provided advice, counselling, and assistance to patients.

McMahon (2003) makes the point that neither the Settlement Movement nor the COS was ever particularly successful in Australia, though there is a strong history of social activism, particularly among women, which pre-dates the formation of professional social work associations. Between 1800 and 1850, colonial men and women were active in at least eighteen separate philanthropic and moral reform causes in Australia, with much of this work carried out by Catholic religious sisterhoods (McMahon 2003). This work included the establishment of basic social services including free schools and hospitals, refuges, and accommodation, as well as services for working women—all achieved long before the beginnings of the Australian welfare state (McMahon 2003).

One prominent early social activist was Louisa Lawson who, among others, established the Womanhood Suffrage League in 1891, with the purpose of not only gaining the right to vote but also creating a better and more just society. McMahon (2003) also credits social activists in women's associations and industry with being instrumental in the establishment of social work in New South Wales, while others claim that the push for formal training of social workers came initially from the medical field, which perceived a need to train hospital almoners.

Training boards were set up in Sydney, Melbourne, and Adelaide to provide courses for social workers in a joint venture with hospitals and universities. It was not until 1940 that Australian social workers were able to receive degree-level training when it was offered at Sydney University. Other Australian universities gradually introduced social work courses, many of which focused on the training of almoners and on issues of youth delinquency and criminality. Before the formation of the Australian Association of Social Workers (AASW) in 1946, universities made decisions about the necessary tasks of practice and the training that was needed.

The social work profession is linked around the globe by the International Federation of Social Workers. Codes of ethics vary little from country to country, and the values that underpin social work practice have a universal similarity. However, there is a need to acknowledge that context affects practice, so that interaction between social workers and those who use social work services is unique to the peculiar culture and location.

Australia as an island-nation has a cultural heritage and geographical qualities that are unlike those anywhere else in the world. Though colonisation has had a devastating effect on the Indigenous population, the struggle for coexistence and for reconciliation has, in part, defined and continues to define Australian culture. Working with Indigenous people requires the worker to be aware of Indigenous peoples' experience, and to follow the principles of anti-oppressive practice.

Australian culture has also been richly affected by its history of immigration of people from non-English-speaking backgrounds. This nation has been highly successful, by world standards, in providing a place where people from many countries and cultures can live peacefully together. Being a 'multicultural' nation carries with it a responsibility for us all to be respectful and aware of peoples' experiences, particularly the experience of those from the non-dominant culture.

Australia's location—far from its colonist settler nation, and nestled on the rim of the Asia–Pacific region—brings a unique quality to social work practice in this country. It is believed that the wide open spaces create a need for personal space in those who live here, but more important for social workers are other factors related to rural and remote regions. Although a large proportion of Australia's population now lives in cities, particularly on the coastal rim, those in more isolated and sparsely populated areas still have a need for high-quality social services. The tyranny of distance demands creativity and determination if social justice is to be attained across vast lands, as well as an understanding of the intricacies of practice for social workers who live and work among the small communities they serve.

The Australian Association of Social Workers

The AASW was formed in 1946 at the federal level, although a number of state branches existed before this. The AASW is a member of the International Federation of Social

Workers (IFSW), which has a representative at the United Nations. In this way, the AASW has the ability to give input and be consulted on international issues. From its beginning, one of the AASW's stated goals has been to establish social work as a credible and recognised profession, and to create the structures of professionalism: professional education and accreditation, a code of ethics, and development of competency standards for practice.

The AASW, as a professional association, monitors practice standards, provides continuing education, and promotes the objectives of social work. Thus, the AASW hopes to fulfil its aim of assisting social workers to improve and be accountable for their practice. The AASW Code of Ethics (AASW 2002) outlines guiding principles for social work practice, and is binding on all members.

Socio-political context of practice

The social work profession has always had a steadfast commitment to ideals of social justice and a respect for human rights. While social work has not swayed from these underlying values, it is noteworthy that the context for practice has changed significantly over time, and will continue to change, causing periodic radical shifts in the ideologies, structures, and processes of welfare delivery. Governments come and go, and consequent ideological changes are reflected in the way the issues of marginalised people are addressed. A brief examination of the socio-political context in which social work practice occurs illustrates the dramatic changes that have occurred in the past three decades in Australian society, as the country has moved from being one of the most egalitarian industrialised nations (Webster 1995) to one where there is a growing differential between the most affluent and the poorest Australians (Hamilton 2003). This allows us to outline the limitations and opportunities that will shape social work in the twenty-first century.

In Australia and much of the Western world, political and ideological shifts have led to the emergence and dominance of a New Right ideology based on economic principles and market supremacy. This ideology underpins the economic rationalist or neo-conservative approach that has come to dominate the politics of the Western world and has resulted in major changes to the way Western societies deal with their most vulnerable members. Australia, for example, has moved from a system where income-security entitlements were based in many cases on universalist principles to a residualist system in which these entitlements are means-tested and go to the most 'deserving'. For social workers working with vulnerable groups, the consequence of this philosophical shift has been an increasingly bureaucratic and oppressive work environment. This has led, as Ife (1997b, p. ix) suggests, to 'a sense of outrage' at the apparent uncaring and punitive nature of declining welfare structures and policies. Many social workers feel they are a voice in the wilderness as social justice and human rights issues increasingly appear to be ignored by the state, by governments, and by the community.

The decline of the welfare state

The shift in government welfare policy can be traced through the twentieth century: the welfare state grew at a fast rate, becoming uncoordinated and disorganised, matching changes in the commitment of governments to the disadvantaged. Until the 1930s, the non-interventionist policies of British economist Adam Smith dominated government thinking about welfare and the poor, who were considered the responsibility of charitable organisations rather than governments. However, the interventionist policies of economist John Maynard Keynes gained popularity in Australia following World War II, as governments noted their obligation to care for those who suffered because of the failure of the market economy. The welfare state developed in Western countries as a result of awareness of the problems inherent in the flawed capitalist system, and concerns about the casualties of capitalism. Essentially, the welfare state was designed to redistribute income through the taxation and social security systems to alleviate poverty and ensure the well-being of citizens. It was a significant recognition of collective responsibility for the needs of the most vulnerable community members. Importantly, social work developed as a profession during this period of rapid growth in the welfare state. Jordan (1997) argues, somewhat contentiously, that social work is, in fact, a product of capitalism as it only develops under systems in which economic individualism is the norm, and deals with the products of such regimes. While this issue is debatable, it is certainly the case that social and political structures strongly affect social work practice.

The popularity of Keynesian economics declined in the 1970s when governments could not contain 'stagflation' (concurrent rises in unemployment and inflation), and policy makers subsequently adopted the ideas of Milton Friedman. Friedman favoured non-intervention by governments, preferring to let market forces dictate economic growth and life-chances. He argued, somewhat erroneously, that the welfare state's pursuit of equality had destroyed individual freedom (Rees 1991). Nevertheless, Friedman's antipathy to the welfare state, which he considered an unnecessary governmental prop that corrupted the market economy, was also cultivated by politicians and bureaucrats keen to increase productivity. In Australia, both major political parties adopted these ideas in the 1980s, resulting in a rapid retreat from universalist principles of welfare entitlements, a sharp distinction between the deserving and undeserving poor, a more punitive approach to social security, a rapid escalation of inequality in Australian society, and a growing gap between rich and poor. As Ife (1988) suggests, a consequence of the crisis in the welfare state is that social workers can no longer assume that altruism and compassion, or indeed social justice, will be accepted by politicians, the media, and the electorate as legitimate qualities of the state.

The welfare state is unravelling as the nation is drawn irresistibly into a global economy. While globalisation and the decline of the welfare state occurred under Labor governments during the 1980s and 1990s, these processes accelerated under the subsequent Liberal–National regime. A strong supporter of Friedman's ideas in its quest for minimalist government, the Howard Liberal government, elected in 1996 and re-elected in 1998, 2001, and 2004, has reduced its involvement in many areas including welfare, content to let the market hold sway. In the process, welfare has come to be viewed less as a responsibility of the state, or a right of citizens (and certainly not as compensation for capitalism), and more as a contract involving mutual obligations between recipients and the state. Thus, for example, the unemployed must submit to work tests and, in some cases, undertake 'work for the dole' schemes, despite the fact that the government has withdrawn its commitment to full employment. The prime minister, John Howard, terms this position 'modern conservatism' (Howard 1999b, p. 1), which, he argues, 'supports the full realisation of individual potential as well as the reality of social obligation'. However, Valentine (1999) suggests that the state has effectively moved away from its commitment to acting for and on behalf of the people, favouring economic over social gains.

The implicit faith of governments in the market is largely unjustified when we examine figures relating to poverty in Australia. As a direct result of the shift in welfare policy, poverty in Australia has escalated. Between 1973 and 1996 the number of Australians living below the poverty line increased from 5 per cent to 11.2 per cent (King 1998), with over two million Australians (including 556,000 children) living in poverty (ACOSS 1998). Since this study, a report by the National Centre for Social and Economic Modelling (NATSEM) (Hardy et al. 2001) has revealed that in 2001 the percentage of Australians living in poverty had risen to 13 per cent of adults and 15 per cent of children (Harding et al. 2001). The widening gulf between rich and poor is evidenced by the fact that the top 20 per cent of Australian incomes is more than ten times that of the bottom 20 per cent (ACOSS 1998). Yet welfare agencies face extraordinary problems dealing with the increase in poverty with many turning away an increased number of disadvantaged Australians (ACOSS 1998). It appears that the government has passed much of the state's responsibility for disadvantaged members of society to non-governmental agencies, without adequate funding and resourcing. Meanwhile, Australia is facing a major crisis as a result of its ageing population. By 2010, when the baby-boomer generation moves into old age, the need for a secure system to deal with the vulnerable aged will be critical.

Discourse of disadvantage

The discourse in government policy and rhetoric about disadvantage has changed, and this is worth noting as government discourse tends to shape and reflect community response. The discourse has shifted perceptibly in the past three decades from one framed by social democrats—resonant with terms such as social justice, access, equity, and rights of citizenship—to one framed by economists and managers, focusing on profit, the market, managerialism, privatisation of services, quality assurance, accountability, and mutual obligation. In transforming the language that shapes welfare policy, the government and community have moved away from their commitment to supporting the less well-off, also signalling a shift from a strong sense of social cohesion to one of social disunity and disharmony.

For social workers, who have taken their professional identity from their position within the welfare state, the rapid changes in welfare structures, policy, and discourse have led to dilemmas about the future and about professional identity. Workers committed to a discourse that enshrines social justice and human rights principles find the new language alienating. Social work takes place at the interface where the most vulnerable meet law and the state, and social workers have been able to mediate policy (Jordan 1997). With the rise of a market-focused discourse, social work has found its position destabilised by new messages.

What is clear, however, is that policy makers are becoming increasingly alert to the inherent problems in a market approach to welfare underpinned with a philosophy of individualism. In the United Kingdom and the United States, for example, alternative voices have championed a Third Way discourse that charts a course between market dominance and collective responsibility, spurred by the growing numbers of people joining the ranks of the dispossessed and socially excluded. However, the problem for Third Way exponents is that they maintain their support for market dominance, finding solutions for poverty in economic and jobs growth. Third Way proponents have been captives of economic orthodoxy struggling to find the language and strategies to deal with the disadvantaged within the strictures of neo-liberal policy responses. However, there are new voices emerging, as there must be in the face of growing societal stratification. Clive Hamilton (2003, p. xiv), for example, drawing on Aristotle's idea of Eudemonia, outlines a new vision he terms eudemonism (with emphasis on the long second e): a society where people can work on strategies that improve their own and society's well-being. His 'post-growth society' (2003, p. 205) is one in which countries choose to reduce their work, production, and consumption, effectively 'downshifting' in a pursuit of better quality of life for all rather than unfettered growth at any cost. In such a society governments would focus on society and community activities rather than economic growth, improving access to education, reducing work hours, and addressing poverty and social exclusion.

Hamilton's work provides a challenge to reigning orthodoxy and reminds us that there are alternative ways that potentially provide stronger social coherence and reduced societal dysfunction. Given the inherent problems associated with neo-conservative policies, such new visions will gain credence, and for social workers a reframed society will provide ample opportunities to play a critical role in developing new visions and goals.

Market principles in service delivery

In the meantime, the language of managerialism, which has infiltrated society generally, inevitably has affected welfare service delivery, effectively reshaping the way social care needs are addressed (Chevannes 2002). Rees (1995a) defines managerialism as an ideology that claims efficient management can solve most problems, and that private-sector practices can be transferred to public-sector service delivery. Rees terms such claims 'fraudulent fiction' because the public-sector service industry has become less about the delivery of services to the public and more about the management of scarce resources.

It can be argued that managerialism has led to greater productivity, efficiency, and autonomy within the welfare sector. However, the human costs of new managerialist practices are high, and include tacit acceptance of high unemployment rates, erosion of working conditions, less job security, longer work hours, anti-unionism, stress, loss of morale, and bullying by management (Rees 1995c; Rees 1995b). For workers in the welfare field, it also creates friction between workers and service users. Hough (1995) argues that the emphasis on decision-making by workers rather than on notions of partnership, on restrictiveness rather than support, and on client-control rather than sharing, has led to greater use of compulsory measures against clients, and to more social distance between workers and service users. Salvaris (1995) also notes that more extreme costs of smaller government and managerialism include loss of democratic principles, civil rights, and the independence of public servants.

Thus, at the same time as marginalised people have found their circumstances framed in economic terms, social work services have also been exposed to market principles. With the introduction of National Competition Policy to government service delivery, welfare services equally are expected to operate along managerialist lines and to be competitive and accountable. Many services previously run by government have been competitively tendered to non-governmental organisations, resulting in a community service industry that is being reshaped as a 'quasi-market' (McDonald 1999) where costs are shifted from the government to the organisation and the consumer (Cheers & Taylor 2001). The privatisation of welfare services, and the expectation that they will be run for profit under fee-for-service arrangements, forces a new slant on services to the disadvantaged, and necessarily changes the work environment for social workers. Under the National Competition Policy, the responsibility for assisting the disadvantaged has shifted from the community to individuals and families, focusing the burden of caring work on women—the traditional family carers (Valentine 1999).

With the introduction of new managerialist practices, workers in welfare organisations find themselves being accountable to managers who may have little conception of the type of service offered by social workers. This has changed the complexion of welfare practice in many agencies and departments, as workers deal with new accountability procedures and reporting mechanisms. Further, social workers may be subject to short-term employment contracts based on tenuous funding, be expected to adopt management practices and solicit fees, and be accountable to management for their services. There is no doubt, as McDonald (1999) notes, that the changing policy context is reshaping professional behaviour and, with it, user outcomes.

In this environment, the debate about how much social workers have become involved in social control, and how much they are now expected to carry out regulatory and surveillance work for the New Right, is an aspect of practice that is deeply disturbing to individual social workers. While the community has a right to expect public services to be run with minimal waste and inefficiency, it would appear that the pursuit of social justice is made more difficult when social workers are expected to work under market principles. As commercial relations dominate, many social workers must fight for community-inclusive policies, empowerment of the disadvantaged, and egalitarian principles.

Yet there are opportunities for social workers in the current free-enterprise environment. For example, Cleak (1995), writing about health care, points out that social workers are ideally placed to be case managers for the disadvantaged, to provide alternative models of care through private practice arrangements or community agency structures, to carry out health promotion activities, to specialise in areas such as short-term crisis intervention, to act as advisers and consultants in programmes that promote holistic health care, to offer alternatives to the dominant medical model of care, and to become central players caring for patients moving from short-stay hospital care to the community. The new operating environment gives social workers the opportunity to redefine their position in the health and welfare sector, to reshape their practice and structures, to become more effective practitioners, and to move from being a voice in the wilderness to becoming more effective advocates for the disadvantaged.

Nonetheless, it may be that the current system based on market principles is not sustainable in its present form. Welfare groups, such as the Australian Council of Social Services (ACOSS), and church groups are becoming more vocal about the plight of the disadvantaged. The new vision offered by writers such as Hamilton (2003) and others gives a direction for advocates of social change. No doubt policies will continue to change as they have done during the past 50 years. Social workers have an opportunity to be central to changes developed for the benefit of society, to be forthright in asserting that human development is at least as important as economic development, and to insist that the enhancement of human and social capital must be a priority of the state.

Gender, power, and diversity

Although each of us may have a vision for a model society, we must be particularly cognisant of the implications of gender, power, and diversity in Australian society if we are not to make the mistake of imposing our ideals upon those on whose behalf we are working. Gender, for example, is of paramount significance in an occupation that is dominated by female workers in a society where the feminisation of poverty is a recognised factor (Baldock & Cass 1988; Gimenez 1999). Equally significant are the changes to gender roles evident in society. Women are entering the workforce in large numbers into full-time and part-time positions in which enterprise bargaining has eroded conditions for many workers (Rees 1995c, p. 19), and has resulted in an increasing disparity in wage rates for males and females (Summers 2003). The necessary shift in gender relations, as a result of changed work practices, is an important aspect of Australian society. At the same time, Bittman (1991) and Summers (2003) remind us that women are still largely responsible for society's domestic and caring work. For social workers an understanding of gender implications is a necessary part of practice.

Of equal importance is the issue of power—who has it, who does not, how it operates—and how power relations might be disrupted. Social workers, whose code of ethics refers to the need to empower clients, need to ask: 'empower clients to do what?' Are we urging the most powerless to be empowered 'to fit in' to an inequitable society? Or are we genuinely trying to implement significant shifts in the functioning of power relations? Further, is our own conceptualisation of power consistent with that of our clients, or are we imposing our own values and representations on those with limited power to resist? Unless we understand the political implications of empowerment in differing contexts, we are in danger of reproducing inequitable relationships. Yet much of social work's discourse on welfare and empowerment is apolitical: this must be addressed if we are to bring about change and be effective advocates.

As workers we must understand the nature of power, and be aware, as Foucault (1980) suggests, of the link between power, discourse, and the creation of knowledge. Currently, those with political power are shaping a discourse of disadvantage that penalises and targets the vulnerable as somehow unworthy. Further, as Lukes (1974) notes, those in positions of authority are able to shape the interests of the powerless so that they view their disadvantage as acceptable. Social workers are in a position to empower disadvantaged groups to articulate their interests in differing socio-political circumstances and to change society's acceptance of a markedly stratified society. Power is a complicated concept, but we note that inequitable power relations are open to disruption. As Foucault (1986) suggests, power circulates and is multi-faceted, and as such we can choose to disrupt relations in a number of areas, from our immediate working environment to the wider policy and political sphere, by speaking out against disadvantage and inequitable policy, and by influencing and taking control of the discourse.

Of further significance in our work is the issue of culture and cultural diversity. In 1994, 22 per cent of women and 23 per cent of men living in Australia were born overseas and, of these, 13 per cent of women and 14 per cent of men were from a non-English-speaking background (Office of the Status of Women 1995). We live in a rich multicultural society that also potentially offers Indigenous Australians a central and valued place in society. Yet we should note the disharmony created by the failure of Prime Minister John Howard to apologise to Indigenous people following the release of the 1998 stolen generations report, despite urging from the community. We cannot ignore the strategic rise in the late 1990s of 'Hansonism' and the One Nation Party (now largely defunct), a reactionary group espousing policies of intolerance and racial disharmony. We are aware of the United Nations' call for Australia to account for human rights abuses to Indigenous people, and we note the ugly statements about race made by prominent citizens. Australia has become culturally divided and less tolerant, and this is a disturbing and frightening, but very real, aspect of Australian society, and therefore of social work practice.

Finally, we cannot underestimate the increasing divide between urban and rural Australians. The high rate of poverty, the lower standards of health and well-being, and the loss of services, jobs, and hope in the bush have caused major social problems, including a disturbing rise in suicides and family violence. In February 1999, the Federal Minister for Transport and Regional Services, John Anderson, noted that Australia was in danger of becoming two nations as urban and rural Australia become increasingly divided: 'The sense of alienation, of being left behind, of no longer being recognised and respected for the contribution to the nation being made, is deep and palpable in much of rural and regional Australia today' (Anderson 1999).

As we frame a vision for the future of social work we need to be aware that our vision must incorporate a reshaping of society. Our current socio-political context has ensured that society has become more conservative, economic rationalist policies dominate, new managerialism reigns, and individualist and market principles prevail. Further, the welfare state is in decline, the poor are blamed for their poverty, the discourse of disadvantage is punitive and lacks a sense of community, social justice and human rights principles have been discounted, and gender, power, culture, and rurality are all critical indicators of inequity. We are also conscious that social workers operate in a postmodern world encompassing diversity in its many forms, despite the environment in which we practice, and are acutely aware of the tensions that arise between the values and practices of social work training and increasingly conservative community attitudes. Social workers must ensure that our vision takes none of this for granted.

Social work in the twenty-first century

Meanwhile, as inequities escalate and as the welfare state declines, the profession is experiencing a 'social work crisis' (Mullaly 1997). In the twenty-first century, social work needs a vision that inspires practitioners to work for change in society, to address inequities, and to become vocal advocates of the disadvantaged. Without such a vision social workers are in danger of accepting the social order as given, and of falling into the role of implementers of New Right policies and agents of social control. It may appear that it is hardly an appropriate time to formulate a radical social work vision when conservative rationalist policies are so much in the ascendancy. Yet perhaps this is an ideal time: current policies based on economic objectives are unfair, offensive, and manifestly unjust. There is little doubt that the flaws in the current system will become even more evident as time passes, and that governments will be forced by the weight of community pressure and social movements to intervene. Because of increasing resistance and mounting inequalities, governments inevitably will be called upon to provide increased support for the most vulnerable. It is essential that social workers formulate a vision that allows them to take a lead in reshaping the structures and policies of the future welfare state, thus playing a part in developing the types of egalitarian, open structures that reduce opportunities for bias, racism, and prejudice, and which build social capital.

Social policy commentators, such as Bettina Cass (Steketee 1999, p. 2) and Clive Hamilton (2003), have spoken out about the need to integrate social and economic objectives. Social policy activists, such as Eva Cox in Australia, Robert Putnam in the United States, and John Ralston Saul and the late Robert Theobald in Canada, have brought to prominence ideas about the importance of social capital and humanity in the face of widespread New Right philosophies. All have encouraged the view that the community, the state, and governments should be more interested in quality of life and life-satisfaction indicators than in economic indicators. Cox (1995a) and Putnam et al. (1993), in particular, talk of 'social capital' as the store of trust, goodwill, and cooperation between people in the workplace, voluntary organisations, the neighbourhood, and all levels of government. Cox argues that governments, whatever their political persuasion, have a responsibility to encourage civic structures, including social policies, new technologies, and workplace cultures, which enhance social capital.

By contrast, 'social exclusion' refers to the processes that exclude people from systems and institutions that integrate people into society. A person can become socially excluded through no fault of their own despite their wish to participate in society. For social workers, enhancing social capital and addressing the interests of the growing numbers of socially excluded people are important factors of our work. So, too, is a critique of policies and structures that impact negatively on the socially excluded. Social workers have a role to play in bringing such ideas into mainstream discourse. For example, the individual social worker can define an ideological position that guides their practice and their approach to values and structures that confront them. While there is no unitary social work position or mandatory ideological stance, social workers can shape a position with which they are comfortable: one that is based on the professional code of ethics, and encompasses a commitment to social justice, protection of human rights, and a respect for all people. We take note of Cox's (1993) warning that previous calls for social justice required adjustments at the individual rather than societal level, and therefore legitimated the existing rationalist paradigm. We agree that any new model must be based on mutuality and obligation, and target the state to provide the support and framework for collective survival.

Mullaly (1995) argues that the dominant values for social work must be humanism and egalitarianism supported by the qualities of respect, self-determination, and acceptance. Such issues have framed Western social work practice from its genesis in the poor areas of the United Kingdom, the United States, and Australia. A renewed commitment to these ideals at the individual level ensures that the social work profession will continue to fight for systems, structures, and practices that are just and equitable, and that oppose discrimination against the disadvantaged.

In reframing social work practice, Ife (1997b) urges us to bring radical social work in from the margins. Radical action arguably has been marginalised by the profession's need to maintain its status in a conservative environment, and by the need to work within structures and systems of authority and control. Ife (1997b) notes that it is not such an extreme idea to suggest that social work becomes more radical, as the profession is, by its very nature, radical. Social workers have always worked for a society free from oppression, based on ideas of equity and social justice. Such an agenda in itself is radical in the current political environment, and if acted upon will redress some of the inequities of the New Right.

In adopting this stance, social workers, in the words of Ife (1997b), will legitimise the voices of the marginalised, that have been silenced by the dominance of economic orthodoxy. In recent times, we have heard much from the economically powerful who continue to call for unfettered market policies and greater restrictions on the disadvantaged, including low-paid workers. We have heard far less from those who have suffered from such policies: the socially excluded, the unemployed, the working poor, families, young people, and the aged. One of the key roles of workers will be to assist disadvantaged groups to find their own voice in current debates about policy and its consequences.

Skills, knowledge, and values

The AASW code requires that members uphold the following nine principles of practice:

- having a commitment to social justice
- taking responsibility for developing knowledge

- working with the employing organisation as a member of the AASW
- respecting privacy and confidentiality
- fostering client self-determination
- giving priority to service obligations
- maintaining the integrity of the profession and professional competence
- adhering to high standards of professional conduct.

A set of practice standards is also enunciated for members of the association.

Social workers are relatively atypical in having a systemic understanding of social relations: the interaction between one's own thoughts, feelings, and behaviour; between the individual and the family; and between individuals, families, organisations, and society. Humanistic values, and the ability to understand people in the context of their environment and to undertake multidimensional assessments, is an important part of the social worker's practice in such a challenging and changing world. Systemic understandings are invaluable in working with people and groups at all these levels, as are the interpersonal communication skills and the empowerment approach that underpins social work practice.

Social workers primarily will use this set of skills and knowledge to create systems that are more consultative and inclusive of individuals and groups. Such an approach requires the ability to work sensitively and progressively with individuals, couples, families, and groups, and to translate the wisdom gained from everyday interactions into changes at a structural level when this is required. The link between private troubles and public issues has long informed social work understandings and practice principles.

Acting to change discourses and power relations

Cox (1995a) and Hamilton (2003) argue that we need a utopian view in order to progress, making sure that our structures of power are always open to question and challenge. One significant way of empowering the disadvantaged, and of disrupting inequitable power relations, is for social workers to begin influencing and taking control of the discourse that guides discussions on social policy in this country. Social workers might do this most effectively in their agencies, in their communities, and in their day-to-day interactions. A discourse that highlights human rights, social justice, community, social cohesion, support for marginalised people, and collective responsibility would do much to shape a more cohesive society.

Of equal significance is the need for the profession to join with social movements that are actively rejecting dominant discourses and creating their own paradigms based on the pursuit of social justice and a more sustainable society. These include: the anti-globalisation movement; the women's movement and various women's action groups; environmental groups and political parties such as the Greens; Aboriginal groups working for reconciliation and quality of life for Indigenous people; the disabilities movement; grey-power movements; ethnic groups; ACOSS; and human rights groups. These movements have found a voice, and are active in creating a new vision for society based on principles that dovetail with those of social work.

In many cases, successful social campaigns have utilised social-marketing principles to get their message across, and to build community support. These campaigns create empowering partnerships with affected groups by: focusing on community aspirations; devising strategies that account for the 'how to' of education, and community mobilisation; building partnerships that require trust and maturity on both sides; and using imagination as an essential ingredient in devising a better future. Such strategies are well within the skill and knowledge range of social workers.

Social workers must return to their community base, working closely with Australians at the grass-roots level in support of a system of mutuality and respect. Here the social work profession will find the energy and commitment to reinvigorate its pursuit of social justice and human rights principles.

The profession is ideally placed to help change the shape of Australian society by addressing discourses, values, and structures that divide the community. There is much work to be done, but we can look forward to a brighter future in the new millennium.

Part 1

Working with Particular Groups and Communities of Interest

2

WORKING WITH WOMEN

Margaret Alston

Chapter objectives

- To provide an understanding of gender in the client–worker relationship and the workplace
- To provide an understanding of gender, power, and ideology in social work and social policy
- To examine the nature of the gendered welfare state
- To allow an awareness of women's services
- To note the differences between mainstream and women's services

Introduction

Australian society is fundamentally gendered: Men dominate public positions of power and authority, while women undertake much of society's caring and nurturing work. The profession of social work is also a curiously gendered occupation (Martin & Healy 1993; Ryan & Martyn 1997; Weeks 2003), having in part developed from the efforts of predominantly middle-class nineteenth-century women to provide charity for the poor. The continuing dominance of women within social work, at least at the lower levels of the profession, is explained, perhaps, by the fact that social work is seen as an extension of women's caring role. This chapter explores the gendering inherent in the social work profession, including that within the relationships between social work professionals and women as clients. Women account for a large proportion of social work clientele: a situation arising from the 'feminisation of poverty' (Hanmer & Statham 1999; Shaver 1998; Neave 1995; Clarke 1988) or the 'gender poverty gap' (Casper et al. 1993) and the predominance of women among single-parent households. The many carers and volunteers, who form the vast army of unpaid contributors to the welfare of society, also are predominantly women. Yet the gendering of the client base is matched by the gendered profile of the profession. Women form a significant part of the frontline social work workforce (Dominelli 2002), including 75 per cent of the Australian social work population and 89 per cent of new graduates into the profession (Weeks 2003). Therefore, social work often entails women working with women, and when we discuss working with women we embrace the links between service users, women workers, and women generally (Hanmer & Statham 1999). For social workers the implications of gender in the personal, professional, and political context in which we work is significant.

This chapter notes the way gender, power, and ideology have influenced the shaping of practice and policy; the way the welfare state and social policy have defined women; and the way gender has influenced social work practice with women and the type of services offered. The development of women's services and feminist practice have fundamentally challenged traditional notions of women and their place in society and these are discussed. Finally, the future of women's services in an era of a backlash against women is noted.

It is important to understand that any discussion of women as an undifferentiated group is naive and simplistic. Women who are Aboriginal, disabled, older, younger, lesbian, from a non-English-speaking background, or who live in a rural or remote area will experience unique challenges and may experience multiple disadvantages. Within the limits of this chapter it is impossible to explore all issues affecting different groups of women. However the development of women-centred practice demands that we not ignore the commonalities between women and that we centralise women's issues in our practice. Readers should nonetheless note the complex nature of the diversity of women and extend their reading accordingly.

Historical overview

Women-centred services have a long history in post-colonial Australia. Early services were developed for female convicts sent to Australia following white settlement in 1788. Notable facilitators of services to women were Elizabeth Fry and Caroline Chisholm. In 1812, Fry discovered the appalling conditions of female convicts held in British jails and proceeded to visit all transport ships carrying convict women to Australia. Through her efforts children were allowed to be transported with their mothers and, from 1815, women and children were sent on separate ships to male convicts. Fry corresponded with Samuel Marsden, the magistrate of New South Wales, and was instrumental in establishing hostels in the new colony. Weeks (1994, p. 30) notes that Elizabeth Fry 'had in common with later feminists a capacity to organise and work together with other women; a commitment to consulting with the women most in need ... and a tireless energy for persistently lobbying the authorities'.

Caroline Chisholm, an immigrant to Australia, became alarmed at the plight of disadvantaged immigrant women in and around Sydney in the 1830s. Many of these women had nowhere to live and sought refuge at night in the Domain where they were exposed to constant harassment and assault (Summers 1994). In 1841 she opened a female immigrants' home, providing shelter and facilitating the employment of women. In 1843 she travelled to England to arrange transport to the colony for the wives of emancipated convicts and for the children of convicts. Thus began a National Colonisation Scheme to bring 'respectable' immigrants to Australia (Summers 1994).

What distinguishes these and other similar nineteenth-century services from more recent women's services is the philosophy on which the services were based. Fry and Chisholm were middle-class women motivated by the desire to provide charity. Despite being activists for women, they were not feminists in the twentieth-century tradition. Weeks (1994) refers to them as 'maternal feminists' because of their acceptance of different and secondary roles for women. Their efforts were not founded on a desire to empower women or to achieve equity. In fact, charity was dispensed to ensure that women's choices were limited. Summers (1994) describes how women were restricted to roles of 'damned whores or God's police': reprehensible characters or moral guardians. Thus, nineteenth-century charitable institutions assisted women to be the latter through becoming wives and mothers. Ideals of good womanhood and good motherhood drove these religiously motivated efforts, which were also designed to ensure control of social class (Weeks 1994). Daniels and Murnane (1989) argue that the women's services that developed during this period were both refuges and places of punishment for those who failed the 'respectability test': 'When a woman applied for relief, an enquiry was made, usually by the local police, into her character, background and sexual relationships' (Daniels & Murnane 1989, p. 46). According to Summers (1994), as a result of limited opportunities, nineteenth-century women were economically dependent and culturally impotent.

Second-wave feminism of the late 1960s brought a resurgence of effort for women by feminists and, as a result, women's services in more recent times have been based on feminist principles and philosophy (Thomson 1996). The establishment of targeted women's services in the 1970s represented a challenge to existing mainstream services, which were seen by feminist women as inappropriate because of the ideals they espoused about women's place.

The 1970s were a period of enormous growth of women's services. The 1972–75 Federal Labor Government, under then Prime Minister Gough Whitlam, introduced a major reform agenda that included the appointment of the first women's adviser to the prime minister, Elizabeth Reid, and the setting up of the women's affairs section in the Department of the Prime Minister and Cabinet, the precursor to the Office of the Status of Women. During the 1970s grass-roots activism arose and community organisations, such as the influential Women's Electoral Lobby (WEL), were developed. Critical links were established between community activists, women's organisations, and women in politics and the bureaucracy: links that created a climate of intense social change. Perhaps for the first time, violence against women was recognised as a public issue and the first women's refuges—Elsie in Sydney and the Women's Liberation Halfway House in Melbourne—were opened by volunteers. The International Year of Women in 1975 provided a timely focus on women's issues and a funding source for women's refuges was established.

Women's services have developed across every state and territory in Australia since the 1970s and include women's centres, refuges and shelters, information and referral services, working women's centres, health centres, rape crisis and sexual assault centres, Indigenous women's centres, services for women from non-English-speaking backgrounds, and various outreach services.

Services, such as refuges and women's centres, have developed with a firm agenda to provide safety for women, to facilitate social change, to challenge traditional stereotypes, to centralise service users, to support women's right to self-determination, to recognise women's material and financial needs, to improve access to services, to incorporate participatory decision-making, to link the personal with the political, and to achieve equity for women (Weeks 2003, 1994). Women's services actively create women's space and culture, and Weeks (1996) argues that women-specific services are therefore 'sites of social citizenship'. However, the trade-off has always been that they are poorly funded: Workers often put in many hours of unpaid work and volunteers form a major part of the staffing profile.

Practice issues

Gender, power, and ideology

Gender, power, and ideology are critical elements of the client–worker relationship, particularly in relation to women. The concept of gender was used by early second-wave feminists such as Oakley (1981), Millet (1970), and Janeway (1971) to differentiate between biological differences (sex) and the social aspects of femininity and masculinity (gender), which are socially constructed. Distinguishing between sex and gender demonstrates how inequities between men and women are not biologically determined and can be reconstituted. More recently, post-structuralist feminists have noted that while men and women experience life differently, male bodies have been more highly valued in patriarchal societies. Gender is a fundamental issue affecting not only the lives and circumstances of women in a social work relationship, but also in shaping social policy that so critically influences the lives of women. Social policy, for example, supports a position of women as secondary and, while devaluing society's caring work, 70 per cent of which is done by women (Bittman 1991), nevertheless builds on the assumption that women will perform this work in an unpaid capacity with minimal social support. At the same time women are increasingly to be found in the workforce, and this includes over half of all married women (ABS 2004), suggesting that many Australian women are carrying significant unpaid and paid workloads.

While gender has been critical to the way women both practice and experience the social work relationship, equally important are power and ideology. Harris (1997) defines power as 'having the capacity to act in such a way as to control others'. This simplistic definition ignores the nature of power as a process, but nevertheless captures the critical elements that explain why women have less power both personally and politically. In a society where men hold many of the most powerful positions, women's inferior status and the invisibility of their caring work is rarely challenged. It is important to note that women, both as workers and clients, may have limited access to positions in which they might influence policies that affect their lives and workplaces, thus internalising a sense of powerlessness. While clients may be relatively powerless in the worker–client relationship, social workers are in a more powerful position (Larbalestier 1996), often drawing power from legislation; for example, in the child protection and mental health areas. In this capacity they act as agents of the state. As a result they may, indeed, have the 'capacity to act in such a way as to control others'. For clients, the social work relationship is rarely equitable despite the commitment of the social work profession to empowerment. An understanding of the implications of power differentials in the wider society as well as in the social work relationship is a critical feature of practice with women.

Equally, we cannot overlook the link between gender and power. As Mullender (1997) notes, linking gender and power exposes the fact that social work, like society, privileges a male perspective and downplays women's powerlessness and invisibility. Social work has traditionally undertaken society's housekeeping work, reinforcing existing mores and stereotyping women. In fact, it could be argued that social work processes have, in some instances, fundamentally compromised women's rights: for example, involvement in the stolen generation (Dodds 1997), in negotiating the adoption of children of unmarried mothers in the 1960s (Dodds 1997), and in having persistently punitive attitudes to women experiencing violence (Maynard 1985; Pryke & Thomas 1998). This indicates that some social workers have reinforced a particularly biased view of women: exploiting the relatively powerless position of women, and acting as agents of social control in reinforcing social policy that discriminates heavily against women's rights to care for their children or to protect themselves against violence.

It is also important to note the link between ideology and power. Ideologies are filters through which individuals interpret their social world, and those in dominant positions define ideologies that favour their own interests at the expense of others. Women's sense of powerlessness has been reinforced by dominant ideologies that shape the discourses of everyday life. For example, dominant ideologies have allowed certain ideas to persist such as the view that women are located within the private world of the home and that men are the legitimate inhabitants of the public world. Caring is portrayed as a gendered activity related fundamentally to the way women's roles are construed (Alston 2000; Bursian 1995; Munford 1995). When society's resources are being distributed, ideals of motherhood and the family maintain women in a marginalised position, and have also resulted in policies that restrict women's life-chances.

Equally, we cannot ignore the fact that women as workers are subject to ideologies and power relations that operate in society, their agencies, and their personal lives. Social work involves caring—viewed as natural for women in this female-dominated profession—and is thus given little recognition. Writing in the 1970s, Adams (1971) defined this as the 'compassion trap', a situation that traps women at the frontline level of the profession into working without due regard to their own professional enhancement and without critical analysis of the role of social work in maintaining an inequitable society. Women are not well represented in management or policy positions. Hanmer and Statham (1999) note that it is predominantly men who manage women workers and it is men making policy for the predominantly women who use the services.

Gendered ideologies heavily influence the treatment of female clients in a social work relationship. There is ongoing evidence that social workers overlook or downplay violence against women, seeking to hold women responsible for keeping the family together (Pryke & Thomas 1998; Maynard 1985). Social workers may fail to assess the full implications of presenting problems, and also act as reinforcers of stereotypes if they have an unconditional acceptance of dominant ideologies. As Larbalestier (1996) suggests, workers must challenge stereotypes and critically appraise and resist dominant ideologies and discourses.

In concluding this discussion of gender, power, and ideology, it is worth reiterating that women as clients have their lives shaped by gendered ideologies that influence not only social policies but also the treatment of women within the systems, institutions, and professions that make up our society. The agents of institutions, such as social workers, wield power to control the lives of society's members. As professionals, social workers must critique the ideologies and power structures that shape the way they conduct their practice and, as Dominelli (2002, p. 35) notes, 'draw on feminist solidarities and insights to create an emancipatory welfare'.

Gendered social policy

Before examining the women-centred services that have developed since the 1970s, it is important, firstly, to consider the way the state, through social policy, reinforces a secondary position for women and, hence, the way social workers interact with women. The welfare state developed as a system of government support using the social security and taxation systems. Although the welfare state was developed with the best of intentions, it is run in the context of gendered ideologies and was based on the following assumptions: women largely were responsible for caring work and unpaid work in the home, thus subsidising the waged-labour market; men were in paid employment; and the state only supported women when there was no male relative to do so. As a result the welfare state enshrines patriarchal values and does not privilege the interests of women. Based on a centralised industrial system, the welfare state has been described by Castles (1985) as 'a wage earners' welfare state' and by Bryson (1992) as a 'white male wage earners' welfare state' because it is grounded in the labour market. For example, the Harvester judgment in 1907 enshrined the notion of a family wage for men and led to women's wages being set at approximately 50 per cent of male wages. Throughout the twentieth century, activist women worked—largely unsuccessfully—to overturn this judgment, seeking equal wages. Not until 1958 were moves made towards equal pay and, in the new millennium, women's average wages still fall short of those of men. In a capitalist system where life-chances and influence in society are very much determined by economic prosperity and labour market participation, women have been severely disadvantaged by a welfare state based on an inequitable industrial and wage system and characterised by labour market segmentation.

Because women are considered to be dependent either on a male relative or on the state, the welfare state has impeded equity by reinforcing women's traditional and unequal roles through social policy. Social policy on behalf of women has been limited, focused on children, and shaped by a particular moral and/or ideological perception of women. For example, the first social security payment to women, the baby bonus (Roe 1983), was based on implicit ideals of dependent and deserving womanhood. Introduced in 1912, it was followed in the 1920s by child endowment and widows' pensions, and these remained the only explicit payments for women until the decision in 1973 by the Whitlam Federal Government to introduce a supporting mothers' benefit. While this created a sense of moral outrage among conservatives, it did remove the stigma of having children outside marriage and allowed many women to keep their babies. Yet, despite this benefit, single parent families headed by women are among the most vulnerable in society and are at greatest risk of poverty.

Summers (1994) suggests that the social security system in Australia is a monumental testament to our systematic refusal to grant women economic independence. For women, the welfare state has, indeed, been a double-edged sword—on the one hand ensuring a measure of economic security, but on the other facilitating a secondary and dependent position for women.

Since the 1980s, the welfare state has been under pressure as governments withdraw from the marketplace, leaving volunteers and churches to play a greater role. Privatisation of services also has led to a greater reliance on the family to provide support and has facilitated a move away from collective responsibility for the most vulnerable. Implied in this change is the gendered assumption that women will increase their caring roles in the family and in their communities, and that our capitalist society will continue to be underpinned by the unpaid efforts of women. Women's implied dependence is being reformulated, while their caring work is rendered crucial but invisible. At the same time, however, there is little support for those in caring roles. Childcare services have been restructured, reducing access for many women, and availability of respite services to assist with the care of aged and disabled relatives falls well short of demand. Because women generally are hampered by lower wages and the expectation that they will care for the vulnerable, their position in society is undermined and their sense of powerlessness increases.

It is essential for social workers to analyse the way policy incorporates and facilitates gendered power relations and ideologies if they are to avoid oppressing women as clients by failing to recognise that structural pressures rather than individual failings make women vulnerable. As Wearing (1986, pp. 33–4) argues, 'it is only when we begin to address the issues relating to women's subordinate position in Australian society that we can come to some sort of understanding of some of the symptoms such as poverty and low self-esteem, that are presented daily by women to social workers'. And yet, as Weeks (2003) and Allan (2004) note, the 1990s and beyond has brought a strong backlash against women and a resurgence of mother-blaming to the policy arena. Often women are blamed for circumstances (for example, being single mothers) where men should carry an equal responsibility for relationship breakdown. In a period of neo-conservative backlash it seems women are too easy a target.

It is not surprising that many workers have adopted a feminist framework in recent times, allowing an understanding of the importance of gender in practice, giving them a framework from which to critique the position of women, and encouraging the development of women-centred services and practices. Yet as Hanmer and Statham (1999) note, all workers 'need to find ways of working with women that address their unequal power, status, privileges, and options', not just those espousing overtly feminist ideals.

Adopting a feminist position in social work practice necessarily politicises the client–worker relationship as the worker becomes more attuned to the structures and processes affecting their clients and works for social change. Feminist social workers centralise the concept of gender and are, therefore, able to reflect on the way the political context impacts on women's personal experiences. Thus the disadvantages experienced by women, the punitive social security arrangements, the feminisation of poverty, and the lack of recognition of caring work are understood to reflect women's less influential position in society. Social workers through their work with women understand the 'ugly secrets' surrounding the abuse of women and children (Dominelli 2002, p. 36) and have the capacity to therefore turn private issues into public policy through radical social work action.

Women-centred services

As Weeks (2003, p. 112; 1994, p. 36) notes, feminist women's services are 'run for and by women, and are either community-based or autonomous units of an auspice organization, usually a non-government organization'. Women's services have been developed by feminists in recognition not only of the oppression of women but also as a response to the inappropriate services offered by some mainstream organisations, or the lack of services for women experiencing issues such as violence. Weeks (2003, pp. 107–9) notes that feminist practice rests on a feminist analysis of social issues and:

- makes links between the personal and the political
- focuses action on changing structural conditions rather than helping women to adjust to social situations that disadvantage
- works towards women's emotional well-being
- within organisational structures delivers appropriate services for women's needs.

Weeks (1994, pp. 62–6) also suggests that feminists have criticised mainstream services for a number of reasons, including that they: focus on individual problems and give insufficient attention to context; tend to blame the victim; have hierarchical service-delivery models; apply the medical model to social issues; separate the personal from the political; make women's issues invisible when directing services to families and children; blame mothers for what happens within families; endorse a narrow range of acceptable behaviour for women; reinforce sex-role stereotypes; ignore women's experiences; and are blind to gender.

In 1999 (Weeks 2003) conducted a survey of Australian women's services, including refuges, sexual assault centres, women's health centres, women's housing services, women's legal services and multipurpose women's centres. Weeks found that since the 1990s services have given less emphasis to feminist analysis, but have worked to provide information, education, counselling, advocacy, group work, and outreach services.

What is clear is that women's services have yet to achieve the legitimacy that allows greater certainty in service delivery. Perhaps women's services have made powerful enemies among conservative politicians, who may view them as threatening traditional family structures, and among some in the medical profession who may believe that offering free pap smears, contraception advice, and pregnancy testing is a threat to the profession's control over women's bodies. For social workers working with women, women's services are in stark contrast to mainstream and traditional services because of the challenge they pose to ideologies about women, and because they confront issues of power and control.

For workers seeking to adopt a centralised place for women in their practice, the following principles are based on those adopted by Hanmer and Statham (1999, p. 140). Those aspiring to feminist-centred practice must:

- be aware of feminist principles that underpin women-centred practice
- make practice methods women-centred
- link women service users with agencies that focus on women and their needs
- increase resources for women personally and in the agency and community
- ensure that women are engaged in the decision-making structures of the agency and the evaluation of services
- examine how local supports and infrastructure affects women
- ensure that you have a code of non-sexist, women-centred practice.

Delivering social work services to women: the issues

Mainstream or feminist?

One of the most significant issues in a social work relationship when working with women is whether the agency through which services are delivered is a mainstream or feminist (women-centred) one. They differ markedly in their approach to women as clients. The challenge for workers in mainstream services is to ensure that the needs of women are centralised and not lost within the broader context of family practice.

Failing to recognise the needs of women

In delivering social work services to women, social workers must be mindful of a number of political, professional, and personal issues. One of the most critical political issues is that women have independent needs not necessarily related to their roles within the family or as carers of children, the aged, and the disabled. The social work profession, particularly in mainstream services, has been guilty of accepting stereotyped portrayals of women, of facilitating the persistence of these stereotypes, and of responding in unhelpful or oppressive ways (Pryke & Thomas 1998). Unconditionally accepting a subservient position for women leads to the subsumption of women's individual needs into the conglomerate of 'family' needs, where they inevitably get lost. Fundamental issues of disadvantage, such as violence against women, workplace inequities, and women's more precarious economic position, therefore are not prioritised, and this may even result in blaming women for the failings of others. Without critically appraising the impact of gender, inequitable power relations, and ideologies on the wider society and individual clients, workers will not only fail to recognise the needs of women but also be blind to the way the state and the vast array of institutional structures, such as in legal, business, and bureaucratic infrastructures, effectively keep many women in a state of dependence and poverty.

The ideology and philosophy of the service
Service delivery to women is very much guided by the ideologies and philosophy of the agency through which the service is offered. In contrast to women-centred services, many non-governmental organisations are church-based; hence, they have a particular moral philosophy that impacts not only on the way women are viewed but also on the type of service offered. The increasing influence of non-governmental community organisations may result in a hardening of attitudes about women's secondary status, and service delivery may continue to reinforce women's dependency. For workers, the challenge is to analyse critically the ideological filters in the wider political landscape, in the agency, and in one's own practice that affect how services are developed, and to acknowledge that the oppression of women is multilayered. If workers are to challenge this oppression through their critique of ideologies that marginalise women, they must be willing to remove themselves from the ranks of the oppressors.

Access and equity

A lack of access and equity in service delivery has major implications for women as clients. Women have been particularly ill-served by economic rationalist policies that have resulted in reduced government intervention, budget cuts, and privatisation of services. Funding changes have impacted on services such as refuges and have introduced a variety of theoretical and political perspectives that undermine the original feminist intention. Further, women from non-English-speaking backgrounds and Indigenous and rural women are particularly disadvantaged in relation to access to women's services. The position of women is made more precarious if social workers fail to facilitate women-friendly policies and enhanced service delivery.

The impact of violence

Violence experienced by women in intimate relationships is a critical area where women's needs have been discounted. The only national study of violence against women was conducted by the Australian Bureau of Statistics in 1996. It found that 6.2 per cent of women had experienced male violence in the previous 12 months, and yet, while violence is a major issue for many women, a significant proportion of society fails to perceive such violence as a crime (Office of the Status of Women 1995; Public Policy Research Centre 1988). Social workers who work with women and who are influenced by the attitudes of society may neglect or downplay the impact of violence on the women with whom they come in contact, intimating that women who experience violence are somehow flawed or are tolerant of the violence they experience (Pryke & Thomas 1998). Further, social workers may fail to recognise the very real problems women face when seeking legal assistance to deal with violence (Australian Law Reform Commission 1993) or when escaping violence (Alston 1997).

The centralisation of family care

The centralisation of family care is worth particular note as the downgrading of the welfare state is placing unreasonable demands on women within families, restricting their ability to have an independent working life. The withdrawal of government from welfare service delivery is underpinned by the assumption that families will take over the care previously offered by the state. There are significant implications for women of reduced government involvement in service delivery.

Ethical issues

Social workers working with women face a number of ethical issues: chief among these is the need to recognise inequity in the wider landscape and to address these fundamental problems at a broad political level, as well as at the level of the individual client. How this knowledge of inequity is incorporated into practice remains a contentious issue for workers and is dependent on the broader political context: the impact of ideologies, rationalist policies, staffing shortages, and underfunding; the reliance on volunteers; and less than satisfactory working conditions. It is also dependent on whether the agency is a mainstream or feminist one, and what philosophical or religious context it has. The personal context—the philosophies of the worker and the constraints these place on them—is also important. Yet, despite these constraints, social workers are obliged through their code of ethics to work for social change and for the empowerment of disadvantaged groups and this includes women.

Female workers have also failed to conceptualise their own practice issues as feminist concerns because the 'compassion trap' has convinced them that their work is an extension of their caring roles, and that industrial action may adversely affect clients. Thus, workers have been reluctant to pursue claims for enhanced professional status and working conditions. Consequently, many feel that hardship, low rates of pay, exploitation through working long hours in substandard conditions, a reliance on volunteers, the lack of a strong professional identity, and the lack of female managers are all part of the structure of a profession that reflects its gendered societal context. For social work to move on as a profession, workers must acknowledge their own biases and prejudices and advocate for an improved professional identity. If the female-dominated social work profession is to have an impact on the status of female clients, and on the shape of service delivery to women, it must begin by examining its own situation and asking why female dominance has created inherent professional disadvantage.

The future for women's services

The future of women's services is clouded by a neo-conservative backlash against women in society more generally and by a falling commitment to feminist concerns. Women are being blamed quite scandalously for various issues such as the falling birth rate, the crisis of masculinity, juvenile crime, and the rising number of single mothers. Certain taxation initiatives and a crisis in childcare provision suggest that policy makers see it as more desirable for women to leave the workforce to raise their children, unless they are single mothers, in which case they are expected to economically participate in society in some way. The changing policy environment, which has resulted in the adoption of neo-liberal policies championing reduced government intervention in the marketplace, new managerialism in service organisation, the privatisation of services, and a move to user-pays, reduces the ability of workers to actively address the issues of women. Women's services have had to fall into line with neo-liberal policy expectations and the demands of conservative (largely male) policy makers or lose their funding base. The future for women's services is clouded by falling societal support for women's equality and by a renewed focus on 'family-centred' policy development. What remains unchanged, however, is the commitment of a significant number of social workers to women-centred practice based on feminist principles and support for social justice, equity, access, and social change. These women will ensure that women-centred practice remains a significant focus for the social work profession.

Ethics in context

1   A social worker is employed in a welfare agency run under the auspice of a church organisation. A young woman approaches the worker asking for advice about a pregnancy termination. What are the competing pressures on the social worker in relation to agency context and professional ethics? How does gender and ideology impact on the perception of the issue and the advice given?

2   A social worker is employed in a school environment. A distressed young woman approaches the worker one morning seeking the 'morning after' pill. The young woman is 14 years old. This case raises a number of issues including the following:
   - the stress of the young woman
   - the involvement/non-involvement of the young woman's parents
   - confidentiality
   - the young woman's name will be on her parents' Medicare card and she may be unable to consult a medical practitioner without this
   - services may be at a distance from the school and school child protection rules prevent you taking the young woman in your car to the women's health service.
How would you deal with this young woman?

Review questions

1 What do we mean by 'gender' and how does it differ from 'sex'?
2 Why is gender important in the social work relationship and the workplace?
3 How do gendered ideologies influence social policy?
4 What evidence is there that the welfare state is gendered?
5 Outline a short history of women's services in Australia.
6 What are the differences between mainstream and women's services?
7 What principles underpin women-centred practice?

3

SOCIAL WORK WITH GAY MEN AND LESBIANS

Richard Roberts

Chapter objectives

- To review the personal and structural challenges faced by gay men and lesbians
- To review key aspects of social work knowledge relating to practice with gay men and lesbians

- To help students consider some ethical challenges of working with this client group

Introduction

Shortly after I started teaching social work in 1978, I was approached by a gay student distressed that he had been told by a staff member—herself a lesbian—that the only way to get through the social work course was to be 'less obvious' and to 'play down being gay'. I remember the conversation over 20 years later, recalling the outrage I felt on behalf of the student. I also remember pondering what such an attitude might mean for me, starting my career as a junior untenured academic.

In that same year I marched down George Street, Sydney, with a small group of protesters celebrating the Stonewall Riots, which had occurred in New York in 1969, shouting 'stop the police attacks on gays, women, and blacks!', and demanding recognition for gay men and lesbians. The subsequent events—demonstrations, police violence, arrests, jailings, and, finally, decriminalisation of male homosexuality in New South Wales in May 1984, following a private member's bill of then Premier Neville Wran (Carbery 1995)—are now part of our history. Those who took part in the demonstrations in June 1978 have become known as the '78ers' (see www.mardigras.com.au). These events marked the beginning of what has become the Sydney Gay and Lesbian Mardi Gras parade and festival: an event now attended by over half a million people who watch the parade of 200 entries, and 40,000 people who attend the annual Mardi Gras party and Sleaze Ball (Wherrett 1999). The combined income for the city is estimated at $100 million. The changes over this 22-year period reflect the coming of age of the modern gay rights movement in Australia and attest to the developing pride of and recognition for gay men and lesbians.

However, to be 'out' on George Street, Sydney, and in the community was one thing; to be 'out' on campus, and to expect that a social work curriculum might reflect issues relevant to gay men and lesbians was quite another!

In discussing social work with gay men and lesbians in the present, and considering the challenges for this decade and beyond we need to consider the broader context of social movements such as those involving gay men and lesbians, their impact on social workers, and the politics that shape social work education.

At the outset it needs to be acknowledged that this is one of the few textbooks on Australian social work. It is significant, therefore, that it includes a chapter on working with gay men and lesbians. This inclusion is recognition that social work has a contribution to make in this field. As Berkman and Zinberg (1997) report, there is a dearth of literature on this topic and, therefore, we have to rely too heavily on North American literature.

It is important to recognise that 'gay' means more than acting in a 'homosexual way'. Whereas 'homosexual' refers primarily to behaviour, 'gay' describes the identification with a lifestyle and an identity—it is much more than a particular sexual act. Garnets and Kimmel (1993) note that the term 'homosexual' is often associated with its medical and legal history, and to some is associated with deviance. 'Gay' is a word appropriated by those belonging to and identifying with this community; it is a term of choice. It should also be noted that some literature—for example, in HIV/AIDS prevention—uses the expression 'men who have sex with men' (MSM) to describe men who have sex with other men but do not identify as gay (Department of Health and Family Services 1997). This is to make a distinction between describing behaviour and making reference to an identity. For example, some heterosexually identified men have sex with other men but they would not identify as gay (Altman 1992a).

The term 'non-heterosexuals' is used in order to be inclusive to cover all those who do not fit into heterosexual norms. As such, the term includes gay men and lesbians, and transgender and bisexual people. In making reference to 'gay men and lesbians' I do not wish to imply that the issues are necessarily the same for women and men—far from it—but to emphasise the inclusion of women with men, and to juxtapose gay men and lesbians alongside heterosexuals.

Since the early 1980s, HIV and AIDS have impacted heavily on the gay and lesbian communities. Abelove et al. (1993, p. 654) highlight that the lesbian and gay communities have 'given much of our energy, intellectual energy included, to fighting AIDS'. Furthermore, as Altman (1992b, p. 69) notes, 'the impact of the epidemic on the existing gay community has, of course, been profound' and 'virtually no member of the gay community has been untouched by this epidemic'. I have made a choice not to deal with this as an issue in this chapter, yet in no way wish to marginalise HIV/AIDS and its impact. It is important to deal with the impact of HIV/AIDS as a topic in its own right.

I have chosen to consider social work from a multidimensional perspective (O'Connor et al. 1995; Meyer 1995; Roberts 1990; Compton & Galaway 1989; Middleman & Goldberg 1972); hence, I will cover selective aspects of working with gay men and lesbians as they pertain to a broad social work domain. The chapter has a personal flavour reflecting my experience as a social work academic and clinician for nearly 30 years. I begin with a number of key underlying propositions.

Practice issues

First, in reviewing a history of social work with gay men and lesbians it is important to note that social workers have always worked with these people as clients, but in most cases, and until relatively recently, their sexual orientation has gone unobserved or been ignored. Unlike being male or female, or having a particular skin colour, sexual orientation can be quite invisible. It can be easily confused with gender roles and gender traits. Sexual behaviour, related either to sexual orientation or atypical gender behaviour (Roberts 2001), can attract approbation despite provisions to the contrary in professional codes of ethics. It can be a source of shame for both social worker and client. It is just as easy and convenient for some homosexually inclined social workers to remain 'in the closet' for fear of discrimination as it is for their clients. Hence, the rhetoric of social work about non-discriminatory practice has not been mirrored by appropriate action within the profession, and this has affected both social workers and clients.

The National Association of Social Workers (1997, p. 202) in the United States reports that 'it should be noted that even within the profession, lesbian, gay and bisexual social workers do not necessarily feel safe to openly and publicly declare their sexual orientation'. Appleby and Anastas (1998, p. 32) state that 'unfortunately, the most recent studies continue to suggest that negative attitudes toward homosexuality and homosexual clients persist among some social workers and social work students' (see, for example, Berkman & Zinberg 1997; Reiter 1991; Wisniewski & Toomey 1987; Gramick 1983).

In any consideration of social work with gay men and lesbians, the 'politics of the closet' (Sedgwick 1990), for both client and worker, needs to be paramount in order to appreciate how that relationship, and hence the work to be undertaken, will be constructed. In many respects, 'the closet' represents a point of focus for both client and social worker. It is the positioning of each person in relation to 'the closet' that will determine the extent to which issues of sexual orientation can be used positively or negatively to define the relationship, and hence the effectiveness of any negotiated interventions for change.

Second, it is often forgotten that the social fabric is richly textured by diversity (Thompson 1985). Social work has been tardy to recognise that differences in sexual orientation provide a significant part of the richness of the social fabric. This is not remarkable given the influence of some approaches to social work, which 'psychologise' human behaviour, and the influence of such instruments of social control as the Diagnostic and Statistical Manual (DSM) (see Roach Anleu 1998). The influence of this heterosexual hegemony has inhibited the legitimation of the needs of non-heterosexuals, kept many gay and lesbian social workers from identifying as such, and kept gay and lesbian issues off research and policy agendas.

Third, it can be argued that structuralist aetiology and strategies have less value today when placed alongside postmodern approaches to delineating communities that are defined apart from the 'mainstream' (see, for example, Pease & Fook 1999). Gay and lesbian communities have their own rich diversity: we are both rich and poor, advantaged and disadvantaged; we require the same social protection as other community members and access to social service provisions as the rest of society; we identify with and belong to different socio-economic classes; and we have the same needs as others, as well as our own special needs. Some of us live in cities, others in the bush. In this sense, gay men and lesbians do not form a homogeneous class of people. To talk about the power of the 'pink dollar' or 'homosexual market' (Clark 1993), for example, is to hide the poverty that exists in some sectors of the gay and lesbian communities (Irwin et al. 1995). To treat issues from an exclusively urban perspective is to neglect the politics of the bush (Roberts 1992, 1993, 1994, 1995). 'Context' and 'meaning' are significant in understanding diverse individuals, groups, and communities: merely looking at socio-economic structures as divorced from meaning and context offers only limited insight into the array and complexity of social work interventions that can be used.

Fourth, social work is a multifaceted enterprise, focusing on the person-in-environment interface. Social work with any particular group of people must involve a consideration of different aspects of practice, from working with the individual person through casework, counselling, and psychotherapy to working with groups and communities, as well as under-taking research and developing social policy. A code of ethics championing social justice can be invoked as a guide to the 'ends' to be achieved, and this can set the challenges for the profession with this particular social group. While such an extravagant domain will always be curtailed in practice, both micro- and macro-level approaches need to be used, with the focus on the micro-level practice contextualised by an appreciation of larger issues, and vice versa.

The need to work with and alongside individuals, groups, and communities, which may be at different stages of their development and dealing with different realities, has long been part of social work's modus operandi. For example, a young person growing up in a rural area of Australia may find 'coming out' a traumatic time, to the point where she or he considers suicide a better option (Hershberger et al. 1997). This situation may require intensive inter-personal support to aid the adjustment required to survive this transition (Anderson 1998). On the other hand, a group of affluent, well-educated, urban 'out' professionals may require assistance in developing local community networks to lobby for the right to have or to foster children, equal rights for superannuation beneficiaries, and so on (Gay and Lesbian Rights Lobby of NSW 1994). Any attempt to work with and for the gay and lesbian communities necessitates an understanding of the marked differences that exist within these communities.

Fifth, any discussion of social work with gay men and lesbians must be seen against a background in which homophobia and heterosexism are pervasive (see, for example, Sidoti

1999; Mason & Tomsen 1997; Gay Men and Lesbians Against Discrimination 1994; Wotherspoon 1991; Roberts 1989a, 1989b). A deconstruction of these concepts is useful, although such a project will take some time. In the meantime, it is important to realise that despite the rhetoric of social work, many social workers remain homophobic and heterosexist, either knowingly or unwittingly. Many have never had their heterosexist values and attitudes challenged, so they press on unaware of the effects of their values in promoting heterosexuality, thereby oppressing non-heterosexuals. Some social workers have not been able to manage the conflict between their personal values and a professional code of ethics (Faria 1997; Berkman & Zinberg 1997). Furthermore, social work must also be considered in a context of institutional homophobia (Blumenfeld 1992) in institutions such as religion, law, psychiatry, and psychology, and the mass media, as noted by Herek (1993). Even where anti-discrimination and anti-vilification legislation has been enacted, such as in New South Wales, the operational institutional response of most organisations lags behind legislative provision (Morgan 1999).

Sixth, in order for social workers to work with gay men and lesbians, obviously they need to know about them. Social workers claim not to impose their values on clients, and claim they access social science knowledge in order to make assessments. Nevertheless, there is constant reference to the social worker's own life experience, at least to fill in the gaps in this knowledge. While this practice is hazardous when dealing with clients who are similar in some respects to the social worker, it is perilous when dealing with individuals and groups whose socialisation and experience has been vastly different from the social worker. It is necessary not only to make enquiries about these clients' lifestyles but also to know something from research. In assessing need, for example, it is dangerous and certainly disadvantageous, in many respects, to clients to rely on 'felt' and 'expressed' need without assessing this alongside 'comparative' and 'normative' need (Bradshaw 1981). By contrast with heterosexuals, social science research about gay men and lesbians remains relatively sparse.

Seventh, we must understand and be sensitive to the 'code' that many gay and lesbian clients may use. Because of their experiences of discrimination, many may be unable to be explicit about who they are and their relationships. A fundamental part of the social worker's job is to give permission for gay or lesbian clients to disclose who they are if that is their wish. The use of the terms 'friend' or 'partner', for example, can indicate many types of relationship. It is the social worker's responsibility to establish what this means for the client.

The direction and challenge for social work

Working in the community
At the macro level, social workers are engaged in social policy positions, undertaking research, and working with community organisations. In these roles social workers are strategically placed to help frame and implement social justice goals for the profession. Some important areas are outlined below.

Equality before the law—the fight continues

Many social workers will recall learning about so-called 'sexual deviations', including homo-sexuality, in studies of abnormal psychology (Kisker 1964). Hopefully, contemporary students are not confronted still by this value-laden rhetoric posturing as social science and professional research. However, heterosexist ideology dominates the curricula in social work education (Morrow 1996). Constructing homosexuality as 'deviant' (Ballard 1992) helped to reinforce the position adopted by the law and orthodox religions to problematise and stigmatise non-heterosexuals. While in the last 10 or so years homosexuality has been decriminalised, many people are still suffering from the stigma of this victimless crime.

Having lived in fear of being found out for so long, many individuals have adopted ways of living to cope with the draconian practices of police as agents provocateurs, for example. For many of these people the change in the legal status of homosexual behaviour has made little difference because their elaborate subterfuges for hiding their clandestine acts are too heavily entrenched. Even though the law has changed, many people of all ages still create elaborate pretexts to hide their sexual preferences. In this way, the not-so-subtle difference between decriminalisation and legalisation is acted out. Neither the law nor the community positively portrays difference in sexual orientation as 'equal but different'. Indeed, many of the reforms to legislation in relation to sexual orientation have been brought about as an expedient way of containing the spread of HIV, rather than promoting human rights.

That minority groups in general, and non-heterosexuals in particular, are considered second-class citizens is ably demonstrated when heterosexual social workers are astonished that gay men and lesbians demand equality before the law: to have the same rights as hetero-sexuals to marry and to form intimate relationships recognised in law, to bear and to rear children, to receive the same partners' benefits as their heterosexual counterparts from super-annuation funds, and so on (Millbank 1999). The New South Wales branch of the Australian Association of Social Workers, in a submission to the New South Wales Legislative Council Standing Committee on the Social Issues Inquiry into the proposed amendments (now law in New South Wales) to de facto relationship laws to recognise same sex partnerships, stated:

> Social workers are uniquely situated in serving lesbians and gay men in NSW. Our work is with individuals, partnerships and families and their interactions with society and institu-tions. It is from these perspectives that we are in a position, as professional social workers, to directly note the discrimination that same sex partners encounter in day to day living in NSW. The impact of this inequity is that inherent individual worth and the dignity of lesbian and gay relationships is not recognised, resulting in unrealised human potential, poor community and social well-being for people in same sex relationships (AASW 1998).

It may strike discord in some to talk about 'heterosexual social workers', as if sexual ori-entation is not remarkable in any client–social worker relationship. Unfortunately, social work in this century is only just coming to grips with the position that non-heterosexuals can lead fully functioning, productive, and fulfilling lives outside a 'deviant' paradigm.

Social science has been used, and in some cases is still being used, to marginalise (Rubin 1993). It's time that social science research is put into the service of helping non-heterosexuals achieve their rightful place in the community.

Safe and fulfilling participation in community life

Gay men and lesbians are everywhere. Some choose to be 'out' and to live and work in communities where there is an obvious presence of other gay men and lesbians. Others choose to integrate into the community at large, and may live either 'in' or 'out' of the closet in suburbia or in rural areas. For some people a whole lifestyle will be constructed around their sexuality; others, however, will choose to structure their lives so that their sexual orientation has a less prominent place alongside the many other parts of their lives. Some will be able to participate as fully as they like in their community; others will participate only to the extent that they can hide their difference.

We do know, however, that violence perpetrated against gay men and lesbians is alarmingly high (see, for example, Mason & Tomsen 1997; Cox 1994, 1990; NSW Police Service 1995; Lesbian & Gay Community Action of South Australia 1994; Schembri 1992). This violence takes different forms: from street violence and murder in the inner city to the name-calling and abuse in the suburbs and rural areas (Roberts 1995). Whatever its form, we know that it has a devastating effect on many gay men and lesbians. As Garnets et al. (1993, p. 583) note, following anti-gay violence one's 'homosexuality becomes directly linked to the heightened sense of vulnerability that normally follows victimisation. One's homosexual orientation consequently may be experienced as a source of pain and punishment rather than intimacy, love and community'. The damage to self-concept and self-esteem and the disproportionately high suicide rate among young gay men in rural areas attest to the fact that violence, through word and deed, takes a toll on gay men and lesbians everywhere, affecting their ability to lead productive lives (Ruthchild 1997) and thwarting their participation in and contribution to the life of the community.

Homophobia in the school is well entrenched (Adams 1997; Roberts 1996; Griffin 1994). This is particularly the case in some religious schools that seek exemption from the provisions of anti-discrimination acts. Unless individual schools choose to adopt anti-homophobia policies and to progressively re-educate students, they will remain breeding grounds for prejudice and discrimination. Smith (1993, p. 101) summarises this: 'Schools are virtual cauldrons of homophobic sentiment, as witnessed by everything from the graffiti in the bathrooms and the put-downs yelled on the playground, to the heterosexist bias of most texts and the firing of teachers on no other basis than that they are not heterosexual.' Griffin (1997, p. 112) reports that in New South Wales in 1990 there was a 'murder of a homosexual man by students from a Sydney school and the unsolved murder of a homosexual teacher from the same school'. Some non-heterosexual young people who know they are different do not survive the system and drop out early (Garofalo et al. 1998; Du Rant et al. 1998).

Social work needs to work with groups of gay men and lesbians to strengthen their ability to achieve their aspirations and goals. Social workers also need to work with the community at large to tackle homophobia and prejudice, contributing, for instance, to projects like the NSW Lesbian and Gay Anti-Violence Project Community United Against Violence Campaign, or the YWCA's Annual Week Without Violence activities.

Housing for young and old

While gay men and lesbians of means are able to make a choice about where to live, some, particularly in the more vulnerable age groups, do not have the resources to make these choices. Many young people on coming out to their parents are evicted from their homes, known as 'pushout' (Taylor 1994). Many who no longer wish to cope with a hostile or unsupportive environment move to find a haven elsewhere and some end up homeless, drifting around the inner city (Irwin et al. 1995). Refuges and specialist accommodation, such as 2010 (Twenty-Ten Association Inc. in Glebe, New South Wales), have been established to provide for the needs of these young people. However, similar projects need to be established in other locations. Social workers working in institutions, such as residential care and boarding schools, need to be aware of the needs of young people (Mallon 1997).

As the generation of gay men and lesbians who have adapted to being 'out' ages, the demand for gay and lesbian retirement facilities will increase. Such projects are under way in some North American cities: for example, the 'Our Towns Village' development in Northern California. The implication for practice is that gay men and lesbians, as part of the community, need to be able to define their needs around their social networks and histories. To assume that a person who has lived in a viable gay community most of his or her life will be able to adapt to conventional retirement housing is fraught with problems. Such 'new' needs must be approached with sensitivity and imagination if quality of life is going to be fully achieved for lesbians and gay men.

Recognising the rights of individuals to serve in community organisations

As it is gradually recognised in both law and custom that gay men and lesbians are part of the social fabric and have rights to work in all types of employment and serve within social institutions, organisational change to accommodate this needs to be initiated and consolidated. This process is being helped by the public coming out of eminent people such as High Court judges, members of parliament, leaders of religious organisations, and people at all levels of bureaucracy, in the professions, and in trades. Further, such disclosure by eminent people assists lesbian and gay youth in the development of positive self-esteem and acceptance of their homosexuality. As Durby says, such role models 'demonstrate self-acceptance and positive values about themselves and others' (1994, p. 10).

While anti-discrimination legislation has been passed in institutions such as the Australian armed forces and police services, practice lags behind legislative change and regulation. The same could be said about the application of anti-discrimination legislation, such as the New South Wales anti-discrimination and anti-vilification laws. Chapman notes that for lesbians and gay men the impact of these laws has been disappointing: '[these] statutes, as currently in force, lack the ability to disrupt and displace systemic heterosexism' (1997, p. 59). An important role for social workers is to monitor the operation of those newly created equal opportunity provisions, and to assist in their application and implementation. A key role here is to provide education and training, and to assist in the mediation process where this is required.

Working with individuals

Social workers must assess the importance of sexual orientation to the situations of clients for which assistance is sought. The sexuality of heterosexuals living in a heterosexist society is almost always taken for granted. In other words, the representations of heterosexuality around them enable them to fit in and to enjoy the benefits of those social arrangements geared to promote heterosexuality. For the gay man or lesbian, this heterosexist context challenges them and must be dealt with in one way or another. It is, therefore, essential that social workers become aware of how a client's problem is the result of the client having to cope with a heterosexist context or whether that context is merely the 'backdrop' for other problems. In either case, the client's non-heterosexuality is remarkable, and as such must be considered during the assessment process.

Many of the problematic situations that arise for gay men and lesbians are the result of heterosexist and homophobic structures (Deutsch 1995). An optimistic appraisal of social change in Australian society suggests that many discriminatory structures are slowly being replaced by more inclusive ones. However, while these social-change movements are becoming established, it is important to remember that many people still suffer the adverse effects of a hostile environment, and that many social institutions are slow to reflect the most recent legislative and regulatory changes.

While acknowledging that gay men and lesbians access social work for many different reasons of which their sexuality may or may not play a primary role, I will focus here on the common issues that should be taken into account, regardless of the nature of the presenting problems.

Coming out

Coming out is a process relevant only to those who are different from the mainstream as it occurs when a person decides that it is right to make a public declaration of his or her difference—in this case, being gay or lesbian. Not all people who engage in non-heterosexual behaviour choose to make this known, and these people are often perceived as being in the closet. This can be a powerful and pejorative label used for those who find it too difficult or unnecessary to be public about their difference. People in this situation may seek counselling either to assist in changing their homosexual behaviour or to be supported in their choice to keep their sexual desires and behaviour private. Some people can tolerate 'multiple realities' in terms of their sexuality, and can orchestrate different parts of their lives in a harmonious way; for others, the subterfuge and level of control needed to live one life while apparently conforming to dominant expectations as heterosexuals occurs at great personal cost.

It is generally agreed that orchestrated change in sexual orientation is not possible (Appleby & Anastas 1998). While people have been assisted to control their behaviours—particularly where these behaviours have caused unwanted and undesired outcomes—it must be remembered that actual behaviour is only one component of a sexual repertoire. It has proved impossible to shift markedly one's sexual desires and fantasies. Current practice would encourage clients to accept their acknowledged thoughts, feelings, and fantasies related to their sexuality. For most, a healthy outcome is to give expression to these thoughts and feelings, and to do so is to enable the client to achieve some level of 'coming out'.

The coming out process is well documented. As Minton & McDonald (1985) outline, there have been a number of theoretical analyses and empirical studies of homosexual identity formation. Practitioners should be aware of the process not only for the client, but also for the client's family and significant others. In some cases it may be necessary to involve a client's 'family of orientation' and 'family of procreation', as well as significant others, in this process. In other cases, it may be necessary and expedient to help the client build up his or her own self-concept and 'other' support networks before involving families and others (Mallon 1994). It must be appreciated that for many the reactions of their significant others—from total acceptance to total rejection—may be many and varied. The degree of hostility and even violence that is experienced by some people who come out should not be underestimated. It is therefore prudent for a person to establish a support network before coming out and to find a supportive context for the event itself. Even within the context of a gay couple, relationship strains can result when one partner is 'out' and the other not, or when there are differing degrees of 'gay identity'.

On the positive side, it should be remembered that successful management of the coming out process is a sign of strength in an individual or couple. In reviewing the challenges that this process poses for many people, especially those seeking social work intervention, it is easy to overlook how the strength and resources needed to come out can be used to solve problems in other areas of clients' lives.

Self-esteem
'Normal' developmental milestones are well documented in social science literature (Santrock 1985). However, as Garnets and Kimmel (1993) state, understanding of this for the non-heterosexual person is only just emerging. The hostile environment still faced by young people, especially during the sexual reawakening associated with puberty and adolescence, often impedes the 'normal' course of homosexual identity formation. This often results in the development of a poor self-concept and self-esteem, perhaps resulting, in the worst cases, in depression, failure to realise academic and social potential, school drop out, or even suicide.

Of those who manage to survive the 'storm and stress' years, young gay and lesbian people may not receive the normal support from their peers for experimentation. This may delay the adolescent period for a longer chronological period (Johnson 1996), possibly resulting in adolescent-type experimentation later in life, including involvement in the dance-party circuit and substance use. Such rituals sometimes allow for a re-working of adolescent experience in a more supportive environment.

This contextual understanding is essential in making assessments of gay men and lesbians, because regardless of their age when seeking assistance an assessment of their feelings of self-worth, their ability to utilise supports, and the stage of their sexual identity formation will give some insight into the ways they can be enabled to realise their current aspirations and goals.

Intimacy and relationships

Basic to any understanding of these concepts and their relevance in working with gay men and lesbians is an appreciation that the so-called rules established by heterosexual women and men may or may not be relevant to gay men or lesbians. Because of heterosexual hegemony, many of the norms of intimacy and relationships remain unquestioned by heterosexuals. It is erroneous to believe that they have relevance to all. This can lead to exciting challenges as well as many frustrations as new rules have to be negotiated.

In gay and lesbian sexuality there is a far greater opportunity to explore sexual expression unfettered by a discourse of reproduction and its control (Rofes 1996). This means that sexual exploration can move away from the focus on erogenous body parts associated with reproduction, and different types of sexual expression can be explored, removed from time, place, and, importantly, intimacy as a pre-condition. This sexual expression can result in the use of popular sex-on-premises venues, where public sex and sexual fetishes can be explored. The opportunity for such diversity in sexual expression can bring with it many challenges.

Driggs & Finn (1991) note that this has important ramifications for the management of intimacy, and personal and community relationships. For the heterosexual, there are role models everywhere in the media, and in social and family networks. For non-heterosexuals, such public and diverse role models and ways of doing things are only starting to emerge. Those who feel uncomfortable in acting outside perceived expectations may feel considerable turmoil. For some people, there are heavy pressures to meet the goal of monogamy (or serial monogamy) in their relationships with their partners. To realise this goal in the context of a community of considerable sexual permissiveness, or even to change from one set of perceived expectations to another, puts considerable stress on relationships. This is often compounded by the need for protection from transmission of sexually transmitted diseases and HIV.

Violence in lesbian and gay relationships increasingly has been documented. There is evidence that violence in lesbian and gay relationships occurs in a similar proportion to that found in heterosexual relationships (see, for example, Waldner-Haugrud et al. 1997; Duthu 1996; NSW Violence in Lesbian and Gay Relationships Committee 1995; Island & Letellier 1991). Social workers may be called upon to assist people to develop exit plans from relationships, and offer legal advocacy to assist people to get apprehended violence orders and provide counselling for recovery from abuse perpetrated within relationships.

The goal of intervention in these and related relationship issues should be to facilitate awareness in the client of the ways in which his or her expectations have been formed and to challenge the norms that cause conflict for them. Just as any client will bring his or her set of values to counselling, so too will the gay or lesbian client, and they should be assisted to negotiate behaviour and its impact on relationships in accord with their values and beliefs. However, the significant difference in working with gay men and lesbians is that some of those values and beliefs have been formed within a heterosexist context. Therefore, the client needs to be helped to understand this and supported to challenge norms that are inappropriate or that stifle the development of practices relevant to contemporary gay men and lesbians.

For some this challenge proves too great and results in subterfuge, or construction of multiple realities. Some couples, for example, are able to negotiate 'open relationships' or rules that help enhance their relationship. The concept of 'negotiated safety' in HIV-transmission prevention uses a similar dynamic (Crawford et al. 1998). In some cases it is the 'permission' of the 'other' (the social worker, for example) that leads to the successful negotiation of appropriate rules and expectations for the relationship, rather than the arbitrary adoption of orthodox norms. Clinical experience reaffirms that many potential models can be used. It is not the particular choice that is the concern of the social worker, but rather the process and negotiation by which the rules are constructed that is the fundamental part of this type of intervention.

Being 'different' within the community

The gay and lesbian communities are highly diverse, comprising different values, behaviours, and norms, and containing their own sets of prejudices and oppressive practices. It is often assumed that discrimination and oppression would not exist in a minority group. This is not the case. Appleby & Anastas (1998) argue that racism, ageism, sexism, and other 'isms' are also part and parcel of the fabric of the broader gay and lesbian communities. Added to this is the divide between urban gays and lesbians and those living in rural areas. Indeed, a closer scrutiny of 'the community' reveals that many diverse groups have quite different degrees of 'connectedness' (Pallotta-Chiarolli 1998). After all, sexual orientation is only one component of a person's life—'other' parts may reflect the person's age, class, affiliations, work, recreation, and so on. It is not surprising, therefore, to find almost a replica of broader social, work, and recreational groups in similar groupings of gay men and lesbians.

For the social worker, it is important to determine from the client where she or he fits in terms of these potential groupings. There may not be an easy fit between some of these groups: for example, between young men with an inner-city lifestyle and other gay male couples living in homes in the suburbs or country, or in isolated rural districts. There may not be much in common between younger and older gay men. It may not be easy for older men, as their interests and proclivities change, to find an appropriate support network. Gay men and lesbians may not have much in common: the differences between gay men and lesbians and the different networks and communities they access may lead to discrimination within these community structures. This is a 'double jeopardy' for gay men and lesbians who feel the rejection from heterosexist practices, as well as from other gay men and lesbians.

A gay identity for some may mean that age barriers are transcended and may allow for inter-generational friendships. The role of 'mentors' within the community is a well-recognised one in which older men and women help 'newcomers' to become acquainted with networks and community resources.

Osborn (1996, p. 86) states that in many cases gay men and lesbians have decided to form 'families of choice' that do in truth embody the best, most basic 'family value' of all—

love. This may be because they have similar interests and affiliations, but also for some because they have been rejected by their families of birth, in which 'our experience as exiles from our families of origin has taught us how to be free from the strictures of convention that can too often narrow human potential' (Osborn 1996, p. 87). Social workers need to be sensitive to these unorthodox family connections to be able to establish the meaning of these ties for their clients. It is often these families of choice to which gay men and lesbians will turn to get help and support in times of need.

Social work education and professional associations

While the AASW Code of Ethics (AASW 2002) prescribes a goal of social justice and advocates non-discriminatory practice—including not discriminating against a person on the basis of their sexual orientation—practice lags behind these aspirations. Gay and lesbian issues have not been well integrated into social work curricula. A one-off lecture on gay and lesbian issues will not address the heterosexism weaved both obviously and subtly throughout the remainder of a four-year undergraduate course. If the Code of Ethics is to be honoured and practice changed to reflect the needs of gay men and lesbians, then content that is more systematic needs to be included in programmes. Likewise, special interest groups need to be formed within the professional associations. Seventeen years ago I suggested the formation of a gay and lesbian task force within a branch of the AASW (Roberts 1987a, 1987b). Such a group has not yet formed.

The future for social work

A multidimensional approach to social work forces the practitioner to look for interrelationships between social contexts and individual behaviours, as well as searching for aetiologies taking into account both the individual and his or her social context. This complex interplay challenges both the researcher and practitioner. However, to look only within the individual for cause and remedy is dangerous and inaccurate. Nowhere is this more apparent than for a member of a subgroup with a stigmatised and marginalised history. While that context is gradually changing for the better (for example, with gradual law reform), for gay men and lesbians this historical social context still influences both self-esteem and life chances. The challenge for the practitioner is to understand an individual person's behaviour within its social context and its relevance for cause and remedy. Neo-conservative influences on practice can dislocate this nexus and place far too much optimism on the potential of the individual for change.

Full equality before the law now forms part of the agenda for many gay and lesbian reform platforms (see, for example, GLRL 2004b; GLRL Victoria 2004; Moore 2004). The achievement of an equal age of consent in New South Wales in 2003 (Roberts & Maplestone 2001, GLRL 2004a) is representative of legislative demands to ensure that gay men and lesbians and their partners and families are given the same rights and responsibilities before the law as their heterosexual counterparts. This includes law reform in the areas of superannuation benefits, recognition of de facto partnerships and relationships, parenting, adoption, and fostering. While reforming the law and its regulations to bring about same-sex equality is a goal in itself, of equal importance is the concomitant potent message that same-sex relationships and rights are to be valued in the same way as heterosexual relationships and rights, and that anything less than equality in law will continue to favour heterosexuality as more desirable and superior.

The legal recognition of same-sex partnership and the rights of gay and lesbians couples to parent will become matters of increasing debate. Within the community some gay men and lesbians argue that 'marriage' rights should be extended to non-heterosexual couples. Others, however, maintain that rather than pursuing a challenge to the institution of heterosexual 'marriage' and its accompanying ideology, a more strategic path is to focus the debate on law reform that focuses on equality in secular de facto relationships.

Parenting of children by same-sex couples has proceeded in practice far beyond the legal frameworks available for its regulation, including protocols for dispute resolution (Millbank & GLRL 2002). Through IVF by donor, private adoption, and fostering, lesbians and gay men have already established themselves as good parents and appropriate parent role models (Millbank 2002; Patterson 2002; Tasker 2002; Buxton 1999). In the cases where the donor is a known gay man and where co-parenting arrangements are sought between say a lesbian couple and a gay male couple, the legal frameworks governing such arrangements need to be developed to protect the rights of all parties, including those of the child. Failure of the law to be proactive in this regard, and the need to resort to legal remedies to settle disputes where such protocols are just emerging, has already resulted in tragedy and hardship for Australian families involving lesbian and gay male couples (Age 2002; SMH 2002; FamCA 2002; NZH 2003).

While discrimination and harassment continue to be felt, some noticeable changes in the use of public space and the integration with other sections of the community can also be observed. Dating from before the gay rights confrontations of the late 1970s, the need for gay men and lesbians to have their own public space was much in evidence with parts of large cities designated as 'typically gay'. Part of the reason for this was the need for 'safe space' in which to socialise and a need for a separate space in which gay culture could develop. While some of these traditional areas still exist, the trend for gay men and lesbians to mix with other subcultures, particularly young and 'queer' identified subcultures, has become increasingly apparent in larger urban areas. This may represent an abatement of harassment and discrimination, but it also may mark the greater acceptance of gay culture by the mainstream, particularly the young, inner-city crowd. Such acceptance may be seen in the context of changing public images such as those portrayed in national television shows such as *Queer Eye for the Straight Guy* and *The Block*.

With the advent of greater integration with the community at large, as well as the continuing need to stay in the closet for some gay men and lesbians, the problem of 'invisibility' will continue to challenge social work practice. Those populations most affected will be those where heterosexual type assumptions can more easily be applied and where pressure from older stereotypes can be influential. For example, many older gay men and lesbians may well become invisible and hence their needs marginalised where such stereotypes as 'gay being associated with being young' prevail. Likewise, parents might be assumed to be heterosexual and hence their special needs not met. While structural deficits and exclusions will act to deprive some people of services and facilities, these lacks may also impact negatively on the self-image and self-concept of those affected.

While scant research exists, body image and its impact on self-concept and self-esteem will continue to be part of some counselling scenarios for some gay and lesbian clients (Atkins 1998; Shernoff 2002; Stout 2001). For example, the trend to hyper-masculinisation and the search for the 'body perfect'—with associated obsessive gym use and, in some cases, the use of anabolic steroids to enhance this process—is of concern. Likewise, the overuse of chemicals to enhance the dance party experience may be indicative not only of the search for the delayed adolescence that can now occur under more propitious circumstances (Johnson 1996), but also may, in fact, be indicative of low self-esteem, problems in forming and maintaining fulfilling relationships, and generally escaping from what might appear a life full of opportunity for some young people. While there is no conclusive evidence to support such theorising, one must try to understand what motivates such a young person to take these risks.

One possibility is the impact of loneliness. This theme permeates much clinical work across age groups and is a quality that can only be understood by the impact of contemporary social forces rather than isolation from people in general (Martin & D'Augelli 2003; Grossman et al. 2001). The widespread use of the Internet for a range of communication needs (from e-communication through to dating and sex online) on the surface might be seen as indicative of gregariousness and more possibilities for meeting others (Egan 2000). On the other hand, its increased use might also be indicative of a growing social isolation and inability of some people to initiate intimacy with others in real life rather than 'cyberlife' (Strombeck 2003; Tikkanen & Ross 2003). This needs much further research. However, leaving aside cyber communication and relationships, there is growing anecdotal and clinical evidence of the impact of loneliness because of perceived differences and felt ostracism, even within sexual subcultures themselves. The resolution of this issue will continue to challenge practitioners at the interpersonal dynamics level as well as provision of community facilities and supports to ameliorate the impact of this phenomenon.

A conservative estimate is that there are more than 1.7 million gay men and lesbians in Australia. Many more people will experience sexual and other intimate relationships with members of the same sex at some point during their lives. Social workers will make contact with many of these people with or without knowing about their sexual lives. For social workers to make the most effective contribution to these people and their communities they must start to deconstruct the manner in which heterosexist hegemony continues to make many of these people invisible. Social workers must begin to learn about the lifestyles and the ways these people are able to cope with and, in many cases, overcome a hostile environment.

Ethics in context

The *AASW Code of Ethics* (2002) asserts in 4.1.2 a 'commitment to social justice' and that 'social workers will act without prejudice, seeking to prevent and eliminate negative discrimination' based on a number of grounds including 'sexual preference'. Given this professional requirement, consider the following:

- What challenges will face a social worker who holds a personal belief system that disapproves of same-sex relationships?
- Is it enough for a social worker to help an individual client adjust to a hostile and discriminatory environment, without trying to change that environment?

Review questions

1 What are some strengths of a multidimensional approach when applied to social work practice with gay men and lesbians?
2 In what ways has equality been achieved for gay men and lesbians and has the job been completed?

Acknowledgment

I wish to thank Anthony Schembri (currently Area Clinical Director, Allied Health and Clinical Support, Sydney South West Health, Sydney) for his research assistance for the first edition of this chapter.

4

SOCIAL WORK AND PEOPLE WITH DISABILITIES

Wendy Bowles

Chapter objectives

- To explore the meaning of the term 'disability' and the ways disability is measured
- To examine conflicting models or approaches to disability that shape the disability field in Australia

- To consider issues for social work practice in the disability field

Introduction

Since the early 1970s, people with disabilities and their supporters have been struggling to transform our understanding of disability. In the process, they have turned the disability field on its head. In the early 1970s the disability field was barely recognised as a field of practice—somehow people with disabilities and those involved with them were hidden away from the public eye in large institutions or charitable organisations. Disability was seen as a personal tragedy, an unfortunate event that removed people from the mainstream of life. Today, in contrast, people with disabilities are moving back into the community. As Patrick Foley, a man with quadriplegia[1] in a country town commented recently:

> When I had my accident nearly thirty years ago, I was put in a nursing home in Sydney with other young people like me. I was told that basically my life was over. Now I am in living in my own house in this country town, where I want to be. I am involved in my kids' school and life, I can go down the street when I want and do what I want to do. Sure there are plenty of things that still need improving. I can't get into most of the shops around here and have to wait outside till someone notices me on the footpath and comes to see what I want.

But at least I have my own life and I am part of the community even with all the blocks that stop me from doing a lot I could do.

Patrick Foley, West Wyalong resident, member Blandshire Access Committee, May 2004

Patrick is back in the community, but he still cannot access the goods and services that others take for granted. Clearly there is still much to be done in the disability field, even though these days disability is an international human rights issue (United Nations 2004) and many countries have introduced disability rights laws (Kanter 2003). In Australia the *Disability Services Act* 1986 and the *Disability Discrimination Act* 1992 proclaim that people with disabilities are citizens with the same rights and responsibilities to participate in their communities as other people. The disability field is now recognised as one of the important social and political issues in Australia. People with disabilities and the issues that affect them have become the topic for national statistics and studies, Commonwealth–state service agreements, and huge budgets. Nowadays it is publicly acknowledged that 'disability is something that affects most people in the population, to varying degrees and at different life stages' (AIHW 2003a).

However, as United Nations Secretary-General Kofi Annan recently explained in his message to the opening of the third session of the Ad Hoc Committee on a Comprehensive and Integral Convention on Protection and Promotion of the Rights and Dignity of Persons with Disabilities (United Nations 2004):

… as has become clear to us, more needs to be done. Societies have continued to create disabling barriers; persons with disabilities have continued to suffer from discrimination and lower standards of living. That is why, last year, after two years of deliberations, the international community recognized the need for an international convention, of an equal standard to other major conventions, to correct this injustice.

This chapter introduces the complex field of practice that is the Australian disability field today. First, we examine how the concept of disability is understood, and the conflicts in understanding disability that make it such a struggle to improve conditions for people with disabilities. Some of the current practice issues for social workers are discussed. Finally some ethical dilemmas, as well as the future for social work, are examined.

What is disability?

Disability is a complex phenomenon, involving several dimensions. We need to include these dimensions when we try to understand, define, or measure disability.

In May 2001 the World Health Organization (WHO) adopted a multidimensional definition of disability called the International Classification of Functioning, Disability and Health (ICF). This definition highlights the importance of the environment and social and political forces in defining disability, as well as problems within people's bodies—termed impairments. In this definition, disability is understood as a dynamic interaction between health conditions and environmental and personal factors. It includes people's body structures and functions, their activities, the life areas they participate in, and the factors in their environment that affect their experiences (WHO 2001, p. 6). The ICF is now one of the two major international classifications of health and health-related information, the other being the ICD (International Classification of Diseases and Related Health Problems) (AIHW 2003).

The Australian Institute of Health and Welfare (AIHW) summarises the WHO definition thus (AIHW 2003, p. 332):

> Disability is the umbrella term for any or all of: a limitation in body structure or function, a limitation in activities, or a restriction in participation. The key components of disability are defined as follows:
>
> - Body functions are the physiological functions of body systems (including psychological functions).
> - Body structures are anatomical parts of the body such as organs, limbs, and their components.
> - Impairments are problems in body function or structure, such as significant deviation or loss.
> - Activity is the execution of a task or action by an individual.
> - Participation is involvement in a life situation.
> - Activity limitations are difficulties an individual may have in executing activities.
> - Participation restrictions are problems an individual may experience in involvement in life situations.
>
> Environmental factors make up the physical, social, and attitudinal environment in which people live and conduct their lives. These are recorded either as facilitators or barriers (both on a five-point scale) to indicate the effect they have on the person's functioning.

The AIHW (2003) points out that the ICF is a very useful definition in Australia, because not only does it include environmental considerations and the importance of being able to participate when we define disability, but it also provides a framework within which a wide range of information about disability can be assembled and used. With this definition, the mainstream disability field joins disability activists and theorists such as Morris (1991, 1993, 2001), Barnes et al. (1999), Crow (1996), Oliver (1992), Newell (1996), and Bickenbach (1993) in proclaiming that human rights are central to understanding disability.

For example, the fact that Patrick Foley is prevented from getting into his local shops can be included in defining his disability, as a participation restriction. This means that policy makers have to consider Patrick's lack of access as part of his disability, which in turn implies that they now have responsibility to do something about it. While this is a new way of looking at disability for non-disabled workers and policy makers in the disability field, people with disabilities have long considered environmental barriers to be the major part of their disability. As an Australian lawyer who uses a wheelchair once commented: 'I am so much less disabled in America, where I can get into most public buildings and catch public transport on my own.'

Australians with disabilities

In 1998 the Australian Bureau of Statistics (ABS) conducted its latest survey of *Disability, Ageing and Carers, Australia* (ABS 1999b). Ever since the first survey was conducted in 1981, the proportion of Australians with disabilities has been increasing (ABS 1999b). This is due partly to the ageing of the population (especially the baby-boomers) and the fact that older people have more disabilities, partly to changes in the way disability is measured and reported, and partly to emerging new features of disability in younger age groups (AIHW 2003a).

In 1998, 19.3 per cent of Australians (3,610,300 people) reported that they had one or more of 17 impairments, limitations, or restrictions, which had lasted or were likely to last for six months or more and which restricted everyday activities; 14.6 per cent of the population under the age of 65 reported having a disability; and 4 per cent of the population aged under 65 had a severe or profound core activity restriction, which means that they needed help with self-care, mobility, or communication.

In Australia there are four main groupings of disability, which include not only impairments (problems in body structure and function) but also activity limitations and participation restrictions. The four groups are (AIHW 2003a):

- physical and/or diverse disability—a very varied category including acquired brain injury as a subcategory, with a huge range of physical impairments, activity limitations, and participation restrictions
- speech and/or sensory disability—including impairments related to seeing, hearing, and communicating
- psychiatric disability—involving clinically recognisable symptoms and behaviour patterns relating to distress or impairment of mental functions
- intellectual and/or learning disability—associated with impairment of intellectual functions, with limitations in a range of daily activities and participation restrictions in various areas of life.

Estimates of the numbers of people in these disability groups vary depending on how disability is measured (AIHW 2003a). For example, we could simply count people's 'main disabling condition' (the single condition that causes them the most problems). This method counts every person with a disability once, and is the way the 19.3 per cent figure is calculated. However, this does not take account of the fact that many people have more than one disability. Other estimates include all the disabling conditions that people experience, then progressively 'filter out' more and more people till only those who encounter the most severe or profound restrictions associated with their disabling condition remain. The AIHW (2003) describes four different estimates of the numbers of people with disabilities, using this method.

Table 4.1, based on figures from the AIHW (2003), shows how estimates of the percentages of Australians in the various disability groups vary, depending on how disability is measured. The first two columns of figures show firstly the percentages of all Australians who reported having a disability and then those under 65 years of age, including all disabling conditions. The next two columns report the most 'filtered' estimates, when only those with severe or profound restrictions are included (those who need help with self-care, mobility, or communication). Whichever way disability is counted, the most prevalent group is the physical and/or diverse group.

Table 4.1 Percentages of Australians with various disabilities

Disability groups	Australians— all disabling conditions	Australians under 65 yrs (all disabling conditions)	Australians with a severed or profound restriction (all disabling conditions)	Australians under 65 yrs with a severe or profound restriction (all disabling conditions)
Physical disability	16.2	11.6	5.2	3.2
Acquired brain injury	1.1	1.0	0.6	0.5
Intellectual disability	2.7	2.3	1.6	1.1
Sensory and/ or speech	7.5	4.2	2.8	1.3
Psychiatric	4.1	3.1	2.1	1.3

Source: AIHW (2003, p. 382).

About 2.3 million Australians provide informal assistance to those who need help because of disability or ageing (family and friends provide most of the assistance to people with disabilities). Of these, 19 per cent (450,900 people) are primary carers who provide most help with personal activities to a person with a disability (Department of Family and Community Services 1999a).

Subgroups within the Australian population, such as migrants and Indigenous people, differ substantially in their experience of disability from the general population. Although, as yet, there are no accurate national data on Indigenous people's experience of disability (ABS, AIHW & DHFS 1998), it is expected that the rate of disability among Indigenous people is higher than that of the general population. This is due to the higher rates of disabling conditions caused by injury and respiratory and circulatory disease found among Indigenous Australians (Madden 1998).

In summary, the figures in this section show that disability affects a large proportion of Australians; not only the large numbers who actually experience disability but also a similarly large group of carers—mostly women and mostly unpaid—who give their time caring for people with disabilities. When family, friends, and other supporters of people with disabilities also are considered, disability is clearly an important issue for a large proportion of Australians.

Historical overview—a tale of conflicting models

The different dimensions captured in the ICF relate to three quite different models, or underlying beliefs, about disability that have emerged historically. Each model affects the way people with disabilities are seen and treated. Understanding these models and the differences between them is crucial if social workers are to be effective in their work in the disability field.

The three models of disability discussed in this chapter draw on Bickenbach's (1993) framework of disability approaches, as well as Oliver's (1990, 1996) and others' explanations of the social model (for example, Morris 2001; Barnes et al. 1999; Crow 1996). The three models are:

- the individual–medical model (based on the concept of impairment)
- the welfare or policy model (based on the concept of activity limitations)
- the social–political model (based on the notion of participation restriction).

The individual–medical model

The earliest model to be apparent in Australia, the individual–medical model, was a response to the moral approach to disability and human difference that had previously dominated attitudes and perceptions (Curra 1994; Bickenbach 1993). In the moral approach, individuals were held responsible for their disabilities or differences. Vestiges of the moral approach linger today: for example, in condemnatory attitudes to people with HIV/AIDS (Draper 1995).

The medical model was a significant shift in thinking from the moral approach. Individuals were no longer held responsible for their medical conditions, but were seen instead as hapless victims in need of expert help to assist them to recover. In New South Wales, the medical model in relation to disability was in evidence fairly soon after colonisation (Madden et al. 1993; Dickey 1987).

De Jong (1983) and others (Bickenbach 1993; Wolinsky 1988) describe how, once it is accepted that disability is permanent (that is, not a temporary state that expert doctors can cure and from which obedient patients do everything in their power to recover), people with disabilities slip into the 'impaired role'. In this role, individuals are exempted from all normal social roles and responsibilities, such as employment, and from other ordinary social expectations, such as forming partnerships and raising families. Ultimately, in this role, people with disabilities are exempted from responsibility not only for their condition but also for their whole lives. They are accorded a type of second-class citizenship, characterised by a child-like status in which others make decisions for them.

The confining of people in large institutions, consequently depriving them of ordinary social relationships and roles, is an example of how people with disabilities are viewed in this medical model.

In a further distortion of these perceptions, it tends to be accepted that not only the condition but also the actual existence of the person with the disability is undesirable (Sayce &

Perkins 2002; Newell 2002). Examples include abortion solely on the grounds that the child might have a disability, euthanasia for people with disabilities on the grounds of poor 'quality of life', and genetic engineering. Recent advances in genetics have caused a storm of ethical debate over the implications of knowing about genetic impairments during pregnancy, and even in relation to denying people medical insurance. The fact that there is such hot debate about whether it is justifiable to prevent life or end it solely on the grounds of having a disability shows the power of the individual–medical model and the impaired role that flows from it today.

Social work under the medical model has generally been restricted to a role that is secondary to medical intervention. As people with disabilities were seen as helpless victims, so the role of social workers tended to involve counselling people to 'accept' their disability, counselling families who were about to place children with disabilities in long-term care, and working in institutions (running social groups, arranging family contacts, and assisting in financial issues, for example). The key features of social work practice within the individual–medical model are the focus on 'caring' for or changing the person with a disability, and accepting the external environment as a given. For example, a social worker working from the medical model in a school environment might run groups for pupils with disabilities to increase their self-esteem, rather than running groups for the 'able-bodied' students to challenge discriminatory attitudes.

Under the individual–medical model, people with disabilities are viewed as victims with special needs, which results in a 'charity approach' to disability: people with disabilities are deserving and passive recipients of services. In Australia, until the 1970s and early 1980s, the major service providers for people with disabilities tended to be disability-specific public charities, which were partly funded by government (Parmenter et al. 1994; Madden et al. 1993).

These large charities were responsible for sheltered employment, accommodation, and education for children with disabilities, and often employed social workers. They increased rapidly throughout Australia in the post–World War II period, especially during the 1960s and 1970s under the federal government's funding programme. Parmenter et al. (1994, p. 76) comment that this rapid increase occurred under 'the combination of the welfare and charity models'. The welfare model, also known as the economic or policy model, was growing in parallel with the medical model as the welfare state developed in Australia.

The welfare or policy model
This model, termed the welfare model (Parmenter et al. 1994), or economic or policy model (Bickenbach 1993), developed with the growth of the welfare state and the need for rehabilitation of returned war veterans (Madden et al. 1993). For the first time, disability had to be seen as a social problem that required social solutions—not just a medical impairment that forever stopped any hope of a 'normal' life. This change in approach to disability focuses on the notion of 'activity limitation' in the ICF. It emphasises educational, vocational, and community support for people with disabilities, and goals of 'independence' and employment (Madden et al. 1993; Bickenbach 1993).

After World War I, in 1919 the Repatriation Commission in Australia provided funds and other means of support to ex-servicemen, including vocational training schemes. By the 1950s, a major objective of support services across Australia for adults with disabilities was to offer employment and training for employment. Large vocational and residential services flourished throughout the 1960s and 1970s, as noted above.

Within the welfare model, 'patients' became 'clients' and service approaches emphasised a more holistic approach. Multidisciplinary teams, which advocated working with the whole person in their environment, were vitally important to the rehabilitation process (Heller at al. 1989). Social workers, rehabilitation counsellors, speech pathologists, and occupational therapists flourished under this model, with its emphasis on improving individual functioning.

Under the influence of the welfare model, social workers and other professionals took a more primary role with their newly labelled 'clients'. Social workers, as part of multidisciplinary teams, offered a range of services such as education for independent living; groups on relationships and sexuality, self-esteem, and assertiveness; and training in communication and work-preparation skills. Many of the activities undertaken as part of the individual–medical model—running social groups, advocating for people with disabilities and their families, and counselling of families—remained important. However, the focus of social work intervention was on assisting people with disabilities towards 'independence', rather than 'caring' for them and their families, as had been the case under the individual–medical model.

An important aspect of the welfare model is the notion that disability is an administrative category (Oliver 1990; Stone 1984). In Australia, following the depression of the 1890s, cash social services, such as pensions, had been advocated as a cheaper alternative to institutionalisation or charity as a means of addressing disadvantage (Madden et al. 1993). The first invalid and age pensions were introduced by the Commonwealth in 1908 and had been introduced even earlier in New South Wales. Throughout the early and mid twentieth century, additional income-security schemes for adults and children with disabilities were funded.

Today the largest income-support payments are the Disability Support Pension (with almost 660,000 recipients, costing $6.4 billion in 2001–02), the Disability Pension for returned war veterans (almost 160,000 recipients, costing $1.2 billion), and the Carer Allowance (almost 300,000 recipients when carers of children and adults are combined, costing $645.7 million in 2001–02) (AIHW 2003a, p. 350).

Several inherent conflicts within the welfare model have resulted in critiques of this approach. One of the criticisms of this model from the disability movement is that able-bodied 'professional' perceptions dominate concepts such as 'independence'. For example, professionals may emphasise the need for a person with a disability to continue to use crutches and callipers to try to 'walk', whereas it may be much easier for the person to use a wheelchair—they can keep up with able-bodied friends in the street, can carry things, and so on.

With the rising numbers of people claiming disability benefits around the world, the welfare model's tendency to view disability as being an economic problem is becoming more powerful. The OECD suggests reshaping disability policy around 'a framework of mutual obligations' (OECD 2003), and for some years now Australian governments have been focusing on getting people off benefits and back into open employment. The recent Commonwealth government programme, *Australians Working Together* (FACS 2004) and the discussion paper *Building a Simpler System to Help Jobless Families* (FACS 2002), together with the McClure Report, *Participation Support for a More Equitable Society* (FACS 2000), are examples of an attempt to implement an inclusive practice for all Australians, regardless of their abilities.

It is important to remember that people with disabilities have lobbied for many years to be included in the community and receive income commensurate with their ability to work. However, it is equally important to remember that once disability is reduced to a matter of cost-benefit analysis, fundamental conflicts arise. For example, what happens if it is more cost-effective to remove 'unemployables' from the labour market than to bring them into it? Participation is not a right under this model; it is contingent upon efficiency.

In the same way that the concept of 'independence' in the welfare model is reduced to the individual–medical perspective, so several authors have shown how the welfare model ultimately falls back on individualist notions of disability in other areas such as employment (Chadwick 1994; Bickenbach 1993; Oliver 1990). While in theory the welfare model has the capacity to incorporate both the individual and the environment, in fact the focus has remained solely on the individual, or adapting people with disabilities to existing workplace environments (Chadwick 1994). In Australia this tendency has continued despite seemingly progressive legislation and policy change, which appears to have been driven by the third approach to disability, the social–political model.

The social–political model

In part, the rise of the social–political or human rights approach to disability is due to the persistent failure of both the individual–medical model and the welfare model to take into account the effects of the social environment in creating disability. Because these models do not acknowledge the impact of the social environment, they are unable to 'see' or address social and economic solutions to overcome the disadvantage that having a disability causes.

The social–political model arose in conjunction with worldwide protests from people with disabilities who formed the growing disability movement (Parmenter et al. 1994; Swain et al. 1993; Oliver 1990, 1996a; Crewe & Zola 1983). While it has become highly influential in the disability field today, and has led to rights-based disability legislation and policies around the world, this approach actually includes many different ideas and priorities, which are hotly contested (Newell 1996; Meekosha 2000).

Two key points make the social–political model a radical shift in perspective from the individual–medical and welfare models. Firstly, the social–political model emphasises the role of the socio-economic environment in producing disability, thus portraying people with disabilities as a minority group. For example, Morris (2001) argues that disability is oppression and discrimination, and that the term itself refers to 'the disabling barriers of unequal access and negative attitudes'. Secondly, this model asserts the rights of people with disabilities to be in charge of decisions and policy about their lives and to be independent, active citizens at all levels in society; speaking with their own voices rather than being dependent recipients of services dominated by able-bodied interests and perspectives (Swain et al. 1993; Oliver 1990). Today, the social–political model is represented in the 'participation restriction' dimension of the ICF.

The social–political model presents two important challenges to the disability field in regard to policy and service provision, which affect how social workers work. The first challenge involves a shift in focus from perceiving and dealing with disability merely as a problem within a 'faulty' individual to intervening in the disabling environment. The second challenge involves a radical shift in the traditional power relationship between people with disabilities and the services and service personnel with whom they are involved.

An example of the first challenge—a shift to a focus on the social environment—is provided by Parsons's (1994) work on advocacy. He identifies the trap whereby advocacy agencies continue to work within the individual–medical model by trying to prove that people with disabilities can achieve and compete within the existing system. By doing only this, he argues, workers and advocates are legitimising an inherently unjust system that excludes and disadvantages people with disabilities. In contrast, he challenges advocates to work towards making the place of people with disabilities in the community one of importance and power. For example, does the school social worker (discussed under the individual–medical model above) spend his or her time running social skills groups for students with disabilities, or instead hold groups for all pupils, raising awareness about discriminatory attitudes that lead to the social exclusion of the students with disabilities in the first place?

The second challenge of the social–political model (a shift in power relations between people with disabilities and professionals to the more equal relationship of allies or colleagues, in which the interests and opinions of the person with a disability are central) resonates with social work's emphasis on self-determination. Instead of counselling people to 'accept' their disability and the losses associated with it, social workers are challenged to join the struggle for equal rights alongside people with disabilities, and to fight with them in overturning the barriers that block their full participation in society.

In Australia, the social–political model had its beginning in the late 1960s and early 1970s with the rise of the disability rights movement and its call to bring people with disabilities out of the institutions in which they were segregated, enabling them to be part of the ordinary community to live, work, and go to school (Parmenter et al. 1994; Madden et al. 1993).

The United Nations International Year of Disabled Persons in 1981, with its themes of full participation and equality, was the catalyst for an upsurge in community activism and government responses (Ozdowski 2002). In 1983, the Commonwealth initiated the Handicapped Persons Review. The subsequent report, *New Directions* (Department of Community Services 1985), then the *Disability Services Act* 1986 (Australian Parliament 1986), were the landmarks of major change in disability policy, adopting the language of rights and equity, and echoing many of the elements of the social–political model (Baume & Kay 1995; Parmenter et al. 1994; Butow 1994; Madden et al. 1993). The *Disability Discrimination Act* 1992 gave people with disabilities 'enforceable rights to deal with discrimination' (Ozdowski 2002) although, as the Acting Disability Discrimination Commissioner comments: 'The record of achievements since 1993 can be summed up as encouraging, but uneven and incomplete' (Ozdowski 2002).

Like the other two models, the social–political model has had its share of criticism. Several authors, particularly those who write from a feminist perspective within the disability movement, criticise a sole reliance on the social–political model, calling instead for a more complex understanding of disability that recognises the importance of impairment (Cocks 1998; Shakespeare 1996; Crow 1996; French 1993; Bickenbach 1993; Morris 1991, 2001). As Crow argues so powerfully (1996, pp. 58–60):

> Our insistence that disadvantage and exclusion are the results of discrimination and prejudice, and our criticisms of the medical model of disability, have made us wary of acknowledging our experiences of impairment ... External disabling barriers may create social and economic disadvantage but our subjective experience of our bodies is also an integral part of our every-day reality. What we need is to find a way to integrate impairment into our whole experience and sense of ourselves ... As a movement, we need to be informed about disability and impairment in all their diversity if our campaigns are to be open to all disabled people ... Our current approach to the social model is the ultimate irony: in tackling only one side of our situation we disable ourselves.

It is important then to understand disability as a complex, multidimensional phenomenon: an 'unstable mixture' (Bickenbach 1993) of the three models described. No single model on its own can provide an adequate account of disability—hence the multidimensional nature of the ICF itself. Social workers must be able to recognise the influence of the different models in various layers of policy and practice, and in their own attitudes, as well as recognising the strengths and dangers inherent in each, if they are to be effective allies in furthering the interests of people with disabilities. It is the conflict between the models that poses so many dilemmas for social workers and service providers in the disability field today.

Practice issues

Since disability affects almost everyone at some stage of their life, and Australian disability policy prioritises access to generic services by people with disabilities (CSTDA 2003), understanding this complex social issue is important for all social workers. Not only is it likely that they will have to deal with it wherever they work, but most probably disability will be part of their own lives at some time.

Whether they work in specialist disability services, or in the generic services that people with disabilities are being encouraged to use, social workers find themselves having to negotiate conflicting perceptions and demands from the three models of disability outlined above. At the most basic level, these assumptions even affect who we talk to. Does the social worker, like many people, only look at and speak to the able-bodied people accompanying the person with a disability during an interview (in the distortion of the individual–medical model that depicts the person as so defective they can't speak for themselves or understand communication)? Or do they go to the other extreme and ignore or discount anything the carers might say (in a distortion of the social–political model)?

Most services and policies are based on human rights rhetoric, yet there is always the pressure from the welfare model to cut costs, 'do more with less', and operate from a 'mutual obligations' framework. Although much has improved for some people with disabilities, such as in part of Patrick's story in the Introduction, there are still large areas of unmet need. In these situations, it becomes meaningless to speak of cost efficiencies, and human rights seem unattainable. For example, in June 2004 a Sydney mother pleaded guilty to the manslaughter of her son, aged 10 (SMH 2004a). The newspaper asks 'Who should share the blame when a depressed mother is driven to kill her severely autistic son?' (SMH 2004b). Various media reports that week told the story of 'a system so stretched that the wait for care can be up to two years', detailing the fruitless search for respite and other support services that led to such despair and tragedy in this family (SMH 2004a).

It was official in 2001 that 12,500 people who needed accommodation or respite services were unable to get them (AIHW 2003). There are similar shortfalls for other services such as employment support and community access programmes. How many individuals and families suffer the same stress as the family who hit the headlines in Sydney?

In a recent *Special Report to Parliament*, the New South Wales Ombudsman (2004) reported that ineffective implementation of policy led to inadequate services that 'unduly aggravated' the 'significant stress' experienced by families with children with disabilities. At times, according to this damning report, the support services referred to in departmental policies simply do not exist. Social workers working in this environment clearly need to have good advocacy and organisational skills, as well as people skills, if they are to be effective in the battle to improve conditions for people with disabilities. Nowhere is the relationship between 'private troubles and public issues' more clear than in social work practice in the disability field.

Ethical issues

In addition to the ethical issues raised in the previous section relating to lack of services and resources, social work practice in the disability field is a minefield of ethical issues, particularly with the increased genetic technology and the possibility of discrimination based on a person's real or perceived genetic status (AIHW 2003). Disability activists argue that it is ignorance and wrong assumptions about the value of life with a disability, as well as lack of resources, that lead to decisions to prevent the birth of children with disabilities (Newell 2002).

Ethics in context

1 Maria is a woman aged 25 with Down's Syndrome who is pregnant and looking forward to having a baby. Her mother approaches the social worker asking for information about abortion services, because she does not believe Maria will be able to mother her child, and Maria's mother, a woman in her early 80s, says she cannot raise a child at her age.

2 A father seeks help from a social worker to have his 7-year-old child Jordan placed in care permanently. He is worried that the demands of Jordan's care place too great a strain on the family, particularly his wife and their other two children. While his wife will not want to have Jordan placed permanently, and thinks he has the same right as their other children to be part of their family, the father believes it would be in the best interests of all if his son is removed. He hopes the social worker can make a 'firm offer' so that the decision will have to be made.

The future for social work

Accepting that disability is a human rights issue, and that people with disabilities have the same rights as others to be citizens in our society, is just the beginning. If we are to create a community where diversity is valued and interdependence accepted, there is a huge amount of work to be done to dismantle the barriers (both physical and attitudinal) that for so long have excluded people with disabilities. In addition, as the number of people with disabilities increases, and with it the size and complexity of the support services needed to assist people to be genuinely part of their communities, so will the need for social workers, with and without disabilities, rise.

Social work's mission and toolkit have the potential to make a valuable contribution to the disability field. Social workers have a focus on human worth and dignity, and social justice (AASW 2002). Similarly their perspective of 'person in environment', and ability to engage with social issues using a multilayered approach (working systemically at policy and organisational levels, as well as individually with people and families) should make them strong and effective allies with the disability movement. It is up to the profession to realise this challenge and move into the twenty-first century in partnership with people with disabilities, with hope and determination.

Review questions

1 What solutions could be argued for the two ethical dilemmas listed above, from the individual–medical model, the welfare model, and the social–political model of disability?

2 Take a walk along a street with shops close to where you live. Can someone in a wheelchair get in and out without assistance? What is the access like inside the

shops? What strategies could a social worker in a local government setting use to begin working on this issue?

3   Think about the people with whom you come into contact—the doctors, teachers, shopkeepers, and service workers (such as waiters, publicans, and entertainment workers). If close to 20 per cent of the Australian population has a disability, and people with disabilities are fully integrated into our community, around one in five of the people listed should have a disability. Is that your experience? If, in your experience, the proportion seems to be lower, how do you account for the lack of people with disabilities in these positions?

Acknowledgements

The author wishes to thank Gail Gardner and Diana Palmer for reading drafts of this revised chapter and providing many valuable suggestions.

Notes

1   Quadriplegia is an impairment caused by the severing of the spinal cord. In Patrick's case, the level of damage was very high—level C5/6. Patrick's reliance on an electric wheelchair for mobility means that he faces many barriers in the environment that restrict his participation in day-to-day activities.

5

SOCIAL WORK WITH INDIGENOUS AUSTRALIANS

Stephanie Gilbert

Chapter objectives

- To introduce the main factors influencing relations between Aboriginal people and Torres Strait Islanders and the wider Australian society
- To introduce some main characteristics of Aboriginal and Torres Strait Islander Australia

- To reinforce awareness that self-reflection is central to good and effective social work practice

Introduction

Working with Aboriginal and Torres Strait Islander people poses a great challenge to the social work profession. There is little doubt that Aboriginal and Torres Strait Islander people hold a unique position in the nation's history and psyche. There is an increasing body of information that we, as social workers, can draw on to understand our practice with Aboriginal and Torres Strait Islander people and within their respective communities. Much of the material available prior to the 1970s was based in the disciplines of history and anthropology and, as such, was very much focused on understanding cultural aspects of the lives of Aboriginal and Torres Strait Islander people.

Gradually we see an increasing amount of material discussing the issues relevant to our practice. This chapter addresses both practice and ethic issues with a view to explaining the position and experience of Aboriginal and Torres Strait Islander people in Australia. It draws on some of the material available in fields such as youth work and child protection. Unfortunately, we are yet to see many issues like ageing or crisis intervention with Aboriginal and Torres Strait Islander people dealt with in any serious way in Australian social work publications.

While Aboriginal and Torres Strait Islander communities are neither heterogeneous nor uniform, some of their commonalities and their implications for practising social work will be drawn together in this chapter. The chapter is premised on the belief that social workers cannot expect to work effectively with Indigenous communities without a sound knowledge of the history of Australia and the experiences of Aboriginal and Torres Strait Islander people with government authorities. Working with Aboriginal people and Torres Strait Islanders requires soul-searching, forgiveness, and preparedness to challenge our potential for racism. At both an individual and societal level it may also requires a rethinking of our history.

A review of social work practice with Aboriginal and Torres Strait Islander people

History of contact

To understand the types of experiences Aboriginal and Torres Strait Islander people bring to their interactions with social workers, we must understand the forms of contact since 1788. By the time social work became known as such in Australia, Aboriginal people had already been living under the colonising regime for over 120 years. Jones (1996) describes how the colony of New South Wales started with two social problems: convicts and Aboriginal people—and that Aboriginal people have remained as a perceived problem to this day.

Before the development of social work in the 1920s, 'communities of caring' had existed in Australia, including those of missionaries and the anti-slavery movements. Evidence of these activities exists, for instance, in Acts passed in the colonies. For example, in 1849 in New South Wales the *Act to Provide Care of Infants Convicted of Felony or Misdemeanour* was passed. Records held by church groups and missionaries also contain evidence of the role they played in fulfilling these acts (HREOC 1997).

Aboriginal people first encountered welfare personnel early in the history of the new colonies of New South Wales and Victoria, and by Federation had been dealt with by them for up to 100 years. For instance, in 1814, Governor Macquarie set up the Native Institution, a dormitory school where Aboriginal children could be educated. When that closed in 1823, the students were sent to the Black Town Native Institution, which then closed in 1829. In 1816, Macquarie instituted meetings with Aboriginal people where blankets could be distributed and traded, and 'Kings' (important men) were given breastplates (Parbury 1986). These types of interactions continued through the following decades.

By Federation, when Australia first started looking seriously at social policy, Aboriginal people in all colonies on the continent had been dispossessed of their lands and many had been moved to missions. They suffered constant abuses of their human rights and had control of their children removed. Dispossession, carried out by 'the Welfare', the police, and Protectors (a group of individuals or Boards legislated in each state to 'care' for Aboriginal people), was a constant theme in their lives (Parbury 1986).

Markus (1994) argues that until the 1930s there were few Australians who dissented from the racial theory of Social Darwinism, popularised in the late 1800s, which described

Europeans as 'different and superior to all non-European peoples', suggesting that the 'hegemony of these ideas was close to complete' (p. 111).

The following quote, written by Professor Baldwin Spencer in 1927, is an illustration of Markus's point:

> Australia is the present home and refuge of creatures, often crude and quaint, that have elsewhere passed away and given place to higher forms. This applies equally to the aboriginal as to the platypus and kangaroo. Just as the platypus, laying its eggs and feebly suckling its young, reveals a mammal in the making, so does the aboriginal show us, at least in broad outline, what early man must have been like (Markus 1994, p. 111).

Protection and segregation policies enacted for Aboriginal people in the early 1900s also entrenched beliefs about Social Darwinism. These common perceptions clashed with Australians' view of themselves as a just and humane people, and yet there clearly existed a double standard in the administration of law and policy. This double standard for Aboriginal and Torres Strait Islander people resulted in death through malnutrition, untreated disease, and general lack of care. The newly founded social work profession made little difference to either the dominant ideologies of the time or the already deeply entrenched treatment of Aboriginal people. Social workers were participants in this process of dispossession and oppression, sometimes only by default. Social workers have also continued to hold central roles in areas such as child protection and health services, where great injustices have been carried out against Aboriginal and Torres Strait Islander people.

In all states and territories in Australia, governments in the late 1800s and the 1900s set up missions, reserves, and institutions specifically for controlling Aboriginal people and their movements. Brock (1993) argues these places played a necessary role in the survival of their inhabitants. During the years that segregation and protection policies were at the forefront of social thought (circa 1890 to 1950), missions and reserves served to 'smooth the dying pillow' of full-blooded Aboriginal people on their way to evolution's end. During the time of assimilationist policies (post-1940), institutions, reserves, and missions were perceived as more akin to halfway houses for Aboriginal people making their way to being responsible citizens of Australia. The reserves and missions offered some protection from the racism of non-Aboriginal society, as well as providing rations, and some training and education in European skills. Unfortunately, later missions became increasingly restrictive, and they had a negative impact on the Aboriginal people associated with them. This negative impact tends to dominate the telling of those times (Brock 1993).

Social policy and legislative change

Jones (1996) argues that Australians have tended to be uninterested in broad social movements designed to create a more just society. Australian social policy in the earlier parts of this century shows the internal contradictions and flaws in the system that allowed Aboriginal and Torres Strait Islander people, and other low income Australians, to live with poverty, inequality, and a general lack of social justice. Social work has attempted to keep social justice principles at its core, with varying levels of success. Overwhelmingly, though, social policy designed to assist or control Aboriginal people and Torres Strait Islanders has failed. Previous policies have encouraged dependency on welfare relationships, and no current policy appears to create social and economic independence effectively. Indeed, Jones (1996) argues that the treatment of Indigenous Australians appears to be the best example of Australia's incompetence in social policy.

During the Hawke and Keating era of federal politics (1983–96), some wins in the High Court appeared to signal an end to the tyrannical treatment of Aboriginal and Torres Strait Islander people. The first important High Court win was in relation to the Murray Islands in the Torres Strait. Five plaintiffs—Eddie (Koiki) Mabo, James Rice, Sam Passi, Celia Salee, and Dave Passi—rejected the ownership of Mer (Murray Island) by the State of Queensland and fought their case through to the High Court. It is unfortunate that during this long case a number of the plaintiffs died before the High Court decision was handed down in June 1992. In this landmark decision, the High Court overturned the legal notion of *terra nullius*: that the country was empty of people when Cook landed and claimed it for England. The decision also had major implications for mainland Aboriginal people who had been battling the doctrine of *terra nullius*. Prior cases put by Aboriginal people, such as the Gove Land Rights case (*Milirrpum v. Nabalco Pty Ltd and The Commonwealth of Australia* 1971), had been lost upon the basis of *terra nullius*.

After the loss of the Gove Land Rights case in the 1970s, concerns of Indigenous people about land became marginalised from the national political agenda. The 'Mabo et al. case' presented a real opportunity for Aboriginal people's land concerns to return to the centre of national politics. Some political leaders became more outspoken in their disavowal of past treatment of Aboriginal people and their recognition of the need for Reconciliation: 'Mabo will serve as a significant signpost in the history of Australian race relations' (Markus 1994, p. 175).

Chesterman and Galligan (1997) posit that while there has been little improvement in the life situation and health of Aboriginal people in the past quarter of a century, politically there have been significant changes in the conception of rights of Aboriginal and Torres Strait Islander people in that time. Lowitja O'Donoghue, former chairperson of the Aboriginal and Torres Strait Islander Commission, identifies two overarching themes to the struggle of Aboriginal people. The first is citizenship rights, including the right to be treated the same as other Australians, to receive the same benefits, and to be provided with the same level of services (Chesterman & Galligan 1997). The second type of rights O'Donoghue identifies as collective rights for Indigenous people, which are owed to Aboriginal people as distinct people and as the original occupiers of this land.

Chesterman and Galligan (1997) argue that during the quarter of a century leading to the year 2000, Commonwealth and state restrictions on Aboriginal people's citizenship rights were abandoned. The idea of rights for Indigenous people that exist over and above their rights as Australians, however, remains contentious. This area of rights seems to raise the ire of some Australian citizens, including social workers. These rights have been gained through political protest combining with changing public attitudes, and key institutional changes such as the Mabo and Wik High Court decisions (Chesterman & Galligan 1997).

In 1996, Pauline Hanson, an independent politician, who was elected to represent the Oxley electorate in the Federal Parliament, set a new tone in Australian politics. In the run-up to the election, and in her maiden speech, Hanson argued that Aboriginal people received more benefits than non-Aboriginal people: 'I am fed up to the back teeth with the inequalities that are being promoted by the government and paid for by the taxpayers under the assumption that Aboriginals are the most disadvantaged people in Australia' (Hanson 1996). Her stance generated massive media debate, and allowed overt racism, which had simmered through Paul Keating's time in office, to surface. In late 1996, supporters of Hanson created the Pauline Hanson Support Movement, which converted to the Pauline Hanson One Nation Party in April of 1997. This party encouraged many anti-Aboriginal and Torres Strait Islander views to be espoused in the mainstream media. By the October 1998 federal election, the party had lost their grip on public opinion, and Hanson lost her election battle for the seat of Blair. However, public debate about the rights of Aboriginal people, spurred on by the One Nation Party, continues to resound.

The Wik decision (December 1996) was another important decision of the High Court, and aroused debate led by One Nation supporters. The Wik decision held that 'pastoral leases did not extinguish native title recognizing that pastoral leases do not convey rights of exclusive possession; and that the rights of Aboriginal people can co-exist with the rights of pastoral leaseholders, but where there is a conflict between those rights, the pastoralists' rights prevail' (AASW 1997c, pp. 15–16). The reaction of the Prime Minister, John Howard, to this decision came in the form of a ten-point plan to amend the 1993 *Native Title Act*. This plan was a particularly virulent example of the type of power and control for which the Howard government will be remembered. It is also indicative of the control exercised over Aboriginal people. The major aim of the ten-point plan was to close the gap for Native Title claimants opened by the Wik decision. It also signalled a denial of those Indigenous rights identified by O'Donoghue.

In Aboriginal and Torres Strait Islander communities, among others, there was a discernible loss of confidence in Howard's government, and its ability to act positively on behalf of Indigenous Australians. This was in spite of the fact that many conservative Aboriginal and Torres Strait Islander people forgave the Prime Minister for not taking stronger steps to censure Pauline Hanson's One Nation Party. Mr Howard's actions with the ten-point plan, then later with his refusal to apologise to the 'stolen generations', signalled an apparent affiliation with the beliefs of Hanson's One Nation Party. Aboriginal and Torres Strait Islander people had again become the 'legitimately disempowered' of this nation.

Perhaps the only light at the end of this very dark tunnel was Prime Minister Howard's apparent change in tack when, on 26 August 1999, he decided that the Federal Government ought to recommit to the process of Reconciliation. In his motion he said:

That this House … recognises the importance of understanding the shared history of indigenous and non-indigenous Australians and the need to acknowledge openly the wrongs and injustices of Australia's past … [and] expresses its deep and sincere regret that indigenous Australians suffered injustices under the practices of past generations, and for the hurt and trauma that many Indigenous people continue to feel as a consequence of those practices (Howard 1999a, pp. 1–2).

While this is not the apology members of the 'stolen generation' and many other Aboriginal and Torres Strait Islander people had sought, it signalled that conservatives had moved closer to recognising the rights Lowitja O'Donoghue earlier identified.

During the late 1990s, there was denigration and defunding of Aboriginal and Torres Strait Islander services—services that had been started after political action in the 1970s. These services, such as Aboriginal medical services and childcare agencies, were designed to be culturally appropriate, and to provide services for Aboriginal and Torres Strait Islander people by Aboriginal and Torres Strait Islander people. Attempts were made—and in some places were successful—to 'mainstream' the services for Indigenous people into departments designed to serve the whole population. Economic rationalists have posited a number of reasons to justify these actions, including the misuse of funds by Aboriginal agencies. The economic rationalist's argument is that Aboriginal and Torres Strait Islander agencies are offering services that are already available in the wider community. This viewpoint clearly denied the cultural differences argued by Aboriginal and Torres Strait Islanders people. It also failed to recognise that Aboriginal and Torres Strait Islander agencies have had major hurdles to overcome to offer services to their communities: their actions are constantly checked by funding bodies, media, and 'interested parties'; the funding structures for services are inappropriate; the needs, values, and desires of funding bodies are prioritised over community needs; and Aboriginal people are comparatively inexperienced in offering these services.

When the attack on native title is combined with existing racism and the defunding of Aboriginal and Torres Strait Islander services, we begin to get a sense of a poor community experiencing considerable disempowerment. Anderson (1997, p. 105) notes that '59 per cent of Aboriginal people receive an income of $12000 per annum or less, with only 11 per cent actually receiving over $25000 a year'. For social workers, this means that the Aboriginal and Torres Strait Islander clients they see generally will be poor and socially disadvantaged with few resources at their disposal.

On 15 April 2004, the Howard Government announced a desire to close down the Aboriginal and Torres Strait Islander Commission (ATSIC) and its associated agency, Aboriginal and Torres Strait Islander Services (ATSIS). Their desire was to transfer responsibility for ATSIC–ATSIS programmes and services to mainstream agencies from 1 July 2004. The representative structures would stay in place until 30 June 2005 to be replaced by an National Indigenous Council and Office of Indigenous Policy Coordination appointed by Government.

The legislation to enable this was introduced to Parliament in late May 2004. In June of that year, Senate referred it to a Select Committee on the Administration of Indigenous Affairs to report in October 2004. What remains clear is that in the face of government machinations, Aboriginal and Torres Strait Islander people retain concern over their self-determination, particularly where they perceive they have very little ability to influence public and government perceptions (ATSIC 2004).

Practice issues

Social work with Aboriginal and Torres Strait Islander people occurs across Australia in differing workplaces. These can include services for child protection, tenancy advocacy, hospital social work, and many others. There are places for social workers in Aboriginal and Torres Strait Islander communities and community agencies, as well as in mainstream agencies that serve these communities. There are positions for social workers, for instance, at Thursday Island Hospital, which services the northern peninsula region of Queensland and all of the Torres Strait. In some places in Australia, working with Aboriginal and Torres Strait Islander people will mean that the social worker will need to become accustomed to working with people who speak a number of languages, whether it be Torres Strait pidgin or one of the many mainland languages. Many communities speak an Aboriginal language as their first language. In many cases, the social worker will experience all the challenges of working in rural or remote areas, combined with a lack of resources akin to social work practices in the Developing World.

Aboriginal and Torres Strait Islander people continue to be perceived by many in Australia as different from other Australians, having distinct, specific problems uncommon to other groups. Perhaps what most shapes perceptions of Aboriginal people is the position Aboriginal people hold in the Australian psyche. Some speak of Aboriginal and Torres Strait Islander people with deep-seated feelings of guilt, and some with words of anger. Either position is unhelpful when working with Aboriginal and Torres Strait Islander people (Pollard 1988).

In September 2002, the *Australian Social Work* journal published Anthony McMahon's content and critical discourse analysis of the journal itself over its 50-year existence. His particular focus of analysis was the articles focusing on 'research, policy and practices with Indigenous and immigrant Australians' (p. 173). McMahon shows that the articles fit three types: research reports, descriptions of policy, and social work practice. He advances three themes in his critical discourse analysis. The first he argues is that although social workers are working with Aboriginal people there is little written analysis of that practice in the journal. His second argument was that articles involving Aboriginal people 'reflect social policies rather than challenge them' (p. 174). McMahon suggests the articles are generally less positive when reporting on research, but practice-based articles where the authors were based in situ were able to recognise 'politics of resistance, agency and power' in Aboriginal lives (p. 174). He suggests that 'central to the identity of Australian social work must be the voices of all those who make up the profession' (Gaha in McMahon 2002, p. 179).

Other journals reflect the same sort of delineation in their articles dealing with Aboriginal Australians. In *Children Australia* a brief search found a couple of articles dealing with the removal of Aboriginal children from their families. Briskman's (2001) main focus was to look a the actions of churches and their agencies since their participation in the National Inquiry into the Separation of Aboriginal and Torres Strait Islander Children from their Families. This article focused mainly on the Minajalku Project, which was a research project that 'aimed to assist in clarifying the role of the churches and agencies in the removal and placement practices in Victoria' (p. 5). Social work practice is noted for its contribution to labels used to judge people. She says labels were used for Aboriginal people such as 'neglect, drunkenness, immorality and abuse' (p. 7).

In another article in *Children Australia*, Swain (2002) looked at child welfare in Australia. She makes the point that often studies on the treatment of Aboriginal children in Australia have been isolated from the wider child welfare system. The end result of policies in the child welfare area, though, 'impacted both on individual lives and the national identity' (p. 8).

Pastor (1997) in *Northern Radius* points out that in spite of social work rhetoric about wanting to service Aborigines and to operate effectively, cultural blindness often dominates. She says the negative attitudes about Aboriginal people are fed by the idea that the cultural differences of Aborigines are in effect cultural deficiencies. This view is due to a lack of recognition that there is a difference in the first place or to a perception that mainstream culture is logical and right.

Greer and Breckenridge (1992) says workers with Aboriginal communities must learn what are culturally appropriate interventions for community issues such as family violence. Non-Aboriginal workers must 'recognise the effects of institutionalised racism and their own institutionalised racisms' (Greer 1992, p. 194).

In *Working with Indigenous Australians* Dudgeon (2000, p. 249) says 'history teaches us that it is important to gain a background knowledge of Indigenous history and contemporary issues to understand not only the client but also one's own situatedness in culture and society'. We must understand who we are in our practice and the limitations social work itself may have for resolving Aboriginal and Torres Strait Islander community and personal issues.

Ethics in context

How does a practitioner with Aboriginal and Torres Strait Islander clients avoid racist or colour-blind practice?

The future for social work

In 1997, the Australian Council of Social Services (ACOSS) apologised on behalf of many social welfare organisations, including the Australian Association of Social Workers, to those Aboriginal and Torres Strait Islander children identified in the Inquiry into the Separation of Aboriginal and Torres Strait Islander Children From Their Families. The inquiry reported on the large number of Aboriginal and Torres Strait Islander children who had been taken from their families. The *Bringing Them Home* report identified the many actions undertaken to control Aboriginal people and their children. These actions appeared to have two broad aims: first, to provide children with the benefit of a European education, and second, to inculcate the diligent subservience thought desirable in servants and the working class. In the ACOSS apology issued in a press release in 1997 it was said:

> Collectively, we feel a particular sense of responsibility for the consequences of these racist policies (identified by the Inquiry) because their implementation required the active involvement of community welfare organisations. We unreservedly and wholeheartedly apologise to the individuals, families and communities who have suffered such pain and grief from these terrible acts of injustice.

As Kevin Gilbert (in Markus 1994, p. 203) so aptly stated, 'Aboriginal Australia underwent a rape of the soul so profound that the blight continues in the minds of most blacks today … The real horror story of Aboriginal Australia today is locked in police files and child welfare reports. It is a story of private misery and degradation, caused by a complex chain of historical circumstance, that continues into the present.' Paternalistic attitudes, so blatant in the early years of invasion, continue to filter through the structures of society, including the provision of welfare services.

It is important in the telling of this story that all are represented fairly. Many people have dissented from the dominant social thought throughout colonised Australia's past. These include those who stood with the anti-slavery lobby, those who stood up for the humanity of Aboriginal people, those who petitioned for better conditions for Aboriginal people, those who supported the Aboriginal people in the Day of Mourning in 1938, those who supported Aboriginal people in the fight for the 1967 Referendum, those who marched at the Commonwealth Games in 1986, those who marched in the 1988 Bicentennial protests, those who signed a sorry book, and those who continue to support the process of Reconciliation. These actions are crucial to sustain our society. Social work has a place in ameliorating the suffering of Aboriginal and Torres Strait Islander people.

We have recognised that social and welfare workers, and those known by such labels, have been in positions of control over Aboriginal and Torres Strait Islander people. The evidence also leads us to believe that social workers accepted popular Darwinist thought, and other doctrines, which have harmed the lives of many Aboriginal and Torres Strait Islander people. So, where to from here?

Over the past decade there have been attempts to resolve the tensions of the past. In the early 1990s, Prime Minister Paul Keating signalled a willingness to acknowledge the wrongs of the past. In his historic speech at Redfern Park, December 1992, he said:

> We took the traditional lands and smashed the traditional way of life. We brought the diseases.
> The alcohol. We committed the murders. We took the children from their mothers. We prac-

tised discrimination and exclusion … It might help us if we non-Aboriginal Australians imagined ourselves dispossessed of land we had lived on for 50,000 years, and then imagined ourselves told that it had never been ours. Imagine if ours was the oldest culture in the world and we were told it was worthless. Imagine if we had resisted settlement, suffered and died in defence of our land, and then were told in history books that we had given up without a fight … Imagine if we had suffered the injustice and then were blamed for it (Markus 1994, p. 221).

When the Honourable Sir William Deane, Governor-General of Australia, opened the 1997 AASW Conference in Canberra he said the future of our nation lies in the true reconciliation between Australia's Aboriginal people and the nation of which they form such an important part: 'We will not succeed until the nation has properly addressed and made significant progress towards resolving the current plight of the Aboriginal people in relation to both spiritual and practical matters' (AASW 1997a, p. 3).

The future for social work—as posited by Imelda Dodds in her 1997 Norma Parker Address—is to further ways to 'actively extend our understanding as professionals and as Australians' and to make a full commitment to reconciling all people of our country with each other (AASW 1997b, p. 4). This is our nation's agenda, but it is also ours as social workers and as individuals. Reconciliation does require practical and real steps to decrease the disadvantage Indigenous Australians experience. After all, Aboriginal and Torres Strait Islander people remain the 'poorest, unhealthiest, least employed, worst housed and most imprisoned Australians' (Council for Aboriginal Reconciliation 1997, p. 3).

In 1999, Jo Gaha, then President of the Australian Association of Social Workers, argued that social workers were poised to become a significant voice in social policy and human rights. She encouraged us to not forget that what is personal is also political, that what is individual is social, and that our personal practice of empowerment must be linked to actions designed to empower all people across the nation. This is the way forward for social work:

> Social work is the profession committed to the pursuit of social justice, to the enhancement of the quality of life and the development of the full potential of each individual, group and community in society. Social workers pursue these goals by working to address the barriers, inequalities, and injustices that exist in society, and by active involvement in situations of personal distress and crisis. This is done by working with individuals towards the realisation of their intellectual, physical and emotional potential, and by working with individuals, groups and communities in the pursuit and achievement of equitable access to social economic and political resources (AASW 1997a, p. 3).

This definition, by the Australian Association of Social Workers, states the role of the social worker clearly. Each social worker's commitment and practice must be measured against this definition. Aboriginal and Torres Strait Islander people have not had equitable access to social, economic, and political resources. Social work in this field is overwhelmingly based in the pursuit of these resources. At its very foundation is the unequal power relationship between Indigenous and non-Indigenous people.

The AASW has asked schools of social work in universities to ensure that social work students develop an understanding of the history of Indigenous Australians (AASW 1998). To work effectively in this area, the obligation of social workers must go even further than that. Bland, quoted by Gaha (1999), argues that clients and relatives want an acknowledgment of their lived experience from social workers. It is the human contact, the respect, and understanding that the worker conveys that is crucial. This is what Aboriginal and Torres Strait Islander clients must experience if the relationship is to be successful. If this requires the worker to revisit their beliefs, values, and understanding of Australian history, then they must take this on as their challenge. Not to do so will result in an encounter in which the social worker may believe that the client is defensive, obtuse, resistant, or shut off, and may not see that the problem could be their own.

Since the 1997 release of the *Bringing Them Home* report and consequent outcomes, the AASW has continued to work on addressing its commitment to Indigenous people through the development of an acknowledgement statement. Recognition of the past relationship between Australia's Indigenous people and social work is included in this statement, as well as what this might look like in the future. Clearly this remains an ongoing challenge for the AASW as well as for the rest of Australia.

This chapter has not been prescriptive about how to work with Aboriginal and Torres Strait Islander people because working well with these communities relies more upon a commitment to particular ideals and reflective practice than on prescriptive behaviours. None of us wants to repeat the mistake of denying Indigenous Australians their rights, or practising racism. A competent social worker is one who has examined their beliefs and value system: we must attempt to understand how racism works, and how we can challenge its existence at both an individual and societal level. We must seek how best to empower our clients. Social workers working with Aboriginal and Torres Strait Islander people can experience great joy and great sorrow. Unless you experience personally the lives that Aboriginal and Torres Strait Islander people live, you cannot begin to understand the glory and the despair of being part of or working with the oldest living culture in the world.

Review questions

1   How do you think a committed practitioner can make a difference in this field?
2   Dudgeon (2000, p. 249) says 'history teaches us that it is important to gain a background knowledge of Indigenous history and contemporary issues to understand not only the client but also one's own situatedness in culture and society'. What do you know about your own situatedness and how it impacts on your practice?

6

SOCIAL WORK PRACTICE IN AN ETHNICALLY AND CULTURALLY DIVERSE AUSTRALIA

Anthony McMahon

Chapter objectives

- To demonstrate that social work practice in Australia takes place within an explicitly multicultural society
- To show that culturally sensitive and anti-racist approaches are necessary to guide practice

- To reinforce that social workers are obliged to 'develop appropriate intervention strategies that take into account the racial, social, cultural, historical and environmental influences of culturally different clients' (AASW 2002)

Introduction

Australia is a country with a history of ethnic and cultural diversity. The development of our cosmopolitan society is generally accepted as being a good thing despite occasional panics about particular groups of immigrants and refugees. All of us have been fashioned by our own racial and ethnic circumstances; each of us has cultural, ethnic, and racial backgrounds that have formed and shaped our experiences, knowledge, and values, and, inevitably, will shape our social work practice. Without denying some class and racial tensions, most sectors of Australian society appreciate the dynamism of our cosmopolitan society:

> Socially, migration has contributed to the emergence of Australia as one of the most cosmopolitan and dynamic societies in the world. It has meant the introduction of more than 100 languages into Australian life, while English remains the common language. It has also resulted in the growth of community language schools, ethnic media, businesses, diverse religious and cultural activities and variety in foods, restaurants, fashion, art and architecture (DFAT 2004a).

As a consequence, all social workers in Australia must be able to work effectively with clients from cultural groups other than their own. No social worker in contemporary Australia is able to work exclusively with members of their own cultural group.

Multicultural Australia: 'We are one but we are many'

Australia is officially a multicultural country. Government policies since the 1970s have urged citizens to acknowledge and value the cultural diversity of Australian society (Doyle 2001; Jupp 1989). While the idea of a culturally diverse Australia has not been welcomed in all circles (see instances in Jamrozik et al. 1995), pragmatically:

> [A] commitment to multiculturalism stems from the simple observable fact that the cultural backgrounds of Australians are varied, that a high proportion were born overseas and that the Australia of today is quite different in terms of diversity of origins from the Australia of 50 years ago (Jupp 1989, p. 1).

Officially, multiculturalism is a philosophy permeating government policy and therefore fundamental to social work practice:

> Australian multiculturalism is the philosophy, underlying Government policy and programs, that recognises, accepts, respects and celebrates our cultural diversity. It embraces the heritage of Indigenous Australians, early European settlement, our Australian-grown customs and those of the diverse range of migrants now coming to this country.
>
> The freedom of all Australians to express and share their cultural values is dependent on their abiding by mutual civic obligations. All Australians are expected to have an overriding loyalty to Australia and its people, and to respect the basic structures and principles under-writing our democratic society. These are the Constitution, parliamentary democracy, freedom of speech and religion, English as the national language, the rule of law, acceptance, and equality (DIMIA 2004a).

Australian multiculturalism, therefore, attempts to create an acceptance of ethnic and cultural diversity within an Anglo-centric structure. This it does by putting forward four principles to regulate behaviour and sets out the benefits we can expect from a culturally diverse Australia.

This vision is reflected in the four principles that underpin multicultural policy:

- Responsibilities of all—all Australians have a civic duty to support those basic structures and principles of Australian society that guarantee us our freedom and equality, and enable diversity in our society to flourish.
- Respect for each person—subject to the law, all Australians have the right to express their own culture and beliefs, and have a reciprocal obligation to respect the right of others to do the same.
- Fairness for each person—all Australians are entitled to equality of treatment and opportunity. Social equity allows us all to contribute to the social, political, and economic life of Australia.
- Benefits for all—all Australians benefit from productive diversity; that is, the significant cultural, social, and economic dividends arising from the diversity of our population. Diversity works for all Australians (DIMIA 2003, p. 6).

Australian multiculturalism is essentially an assimilationalist programme of tolerance within a framework that values a diversity of cultures so long as they fit within the frameworks of responsibility, respect, and fairness. There is little place in this definition for what Lechte and Bottomley (1993) call the 'interweaving' of contemporary Australian multiculturalism where a new Australia culture is being created that is more than the addition of 'foreignness' into or onto an essential Britishness. An example of this interweaving is the description of a wedding in North Queensland where cultural motifs important to the families and to the region are interwoven to celebrate a marriage:

> In the first week of the new Australian century, I attended a wedding in Townsville. The marriage was between a young woman of Irish Catholic background and a young Aboriginal man. Her parents are academics, and they had brought up their children in the Kimberly and the USA before moving to Townsville—Celtic people of the world and Australians through and through. His family was from Palm Island, tropical paradise and, not so long ago, hellish concentration camp. He had played rugby league for the North Queensland Cowboys, then become a plumber. Both were now students at the university, the young woman studying business and the young man medicine. These achievements went barely remarked in the many speeches. This is Australia, and achievement sometimes come easily. The cultural heritages were interwoven: clapsticks and brolga dancing; larrikin exuberance and Irish irreverence; all mixed with lace and flowers and pale blue bridesmaids. This is Australia, a place of sometimes easy diversity.
>
> Marriage vows, white dresses, tiered wedding cakes. And other Australian touches, like the bonbonnieres—those fancy little parcels of sugared almonds traditionally distributed at Greek and Italian weddings as a symbol of fertility. No, not Greek or Italian any longer, but near-universal in North Queensland, where the migrants in the sugar industry have turned something exotic and strange into something ordinary and touching. Something for everybody.
>
> This is Australia, one hundred years after Federation (Kalantzis 2001).

Australian multiculturalism, then, much like social work practice, is a way of being in the world articulated through social practices (Lechte & Bottomley 1993). Like all social practices, Australian multiculturalism and the examples of cultural diversity that it values are at least a two-way experience: Australia is not a melting pot where all cultures change to become one or a mosaic where different cultures keep their separateness; it is more a tossed salad where both unity and diversity are valued at the same time.

Asylum seekers

> For those who've come across the seas,
> We've boundless plains to share.

Advance Australia Fair

This generally benign acceptance of immigrants and multiculturalism is not reflected in Australian responses to people who flee to Australia and seek asylum. Refugees are those who have been found to have fled their country because of, or through fear of, persecution. Asylum seekers are those who have come directly to Australia and applied for refugee status here rather than apply for asylum in their own or neighbouring countries, often for excellent reasons. Mandatory detention of those the Department of Immigration and Multicultural and Indigenous Affairs (DIMIA) calls 'unauthorised arrivals' was begun by the Labor Government in 1992 and has received continued support from the major political parties and most of the Australian people since. Government responses to unauthorised arrivals have been detention, demonisation, and deportation.

At the time of writing, according to DIMIA, there were 943 people in detention in the six detention centres in Australia, including 42 children (DIMIA 2004b). Most of the detainees are from Iraq or Afghanistan, where fighting and violence are ongoing. A further 82 people are in detention on Nauru (DFAT 2004b) as part of the Australian Government's policy of keeping asylum seekers offshore so that they cannot access Australian legal and welfare resources. Sixteen of these are children. One human rights group puts the number of children in detention, including on Nauru, at 92 (Baxterwatch 2004).

The mandatory detention of refugees seeking asylum, especially the detention of children, has been a controversial policy in Australia and has provoked condemnatory comment from professional associations of doctors, psychiatrists, and social workers. There are numerous reports of detainees suffering depression and anxiety, and engaging in self-harm including mutilation and suicide. The inevitability of health and mental health problems caused by detention itself is especially problematic for children in detention. When this is government policy, it amounts to child abuse and a number of commentators have identified it as such (Goddard & Briskman 2004). In general, though, while a number of social justice commentators, welfare agencies, and rural communities are supportive of asylum seekers, Australians generally are largely unsympathetic to unauthorised arrivals and favour their indefinite detention, despite the well-documented harm they suffer in long-term detention.

Practice issues

Because the Australian social welfare system has 'evolved in a monocultural tradition, unable to cope adequately with a multicultural society' (Jamrozik & Boland 1989, p. 218), an inadequacy that Australian social work shares (McMahon 2002), there is a need to use a range of different approaches when working in cross-cultural situations. The two main approaches to incorporating cultural diversity into social work practice have been an emphasis on cultural sensitivity and on anti-racist practice. The culturally sensitive approach, called ethnic-sensitive practice (Devore & Schlesinger 1981; Schlesinger & Devore 1995) or working with 'people of color' (Lum 1996) in the United States, aims to reduce misunderstandings, miscommunication, and bias in the worker's relationship with the client. The anti-racist approach (Dominelli 1997a), and its corollaries anti-oppressive (Gil 1998; Mullaly 2002) and anti-discriminatory practice (Thompson 1997), focus on structural and/or historical disadvantages, particularly those embedded in gender, class, race, and ethnic identities and positions. Together, these two broad approaches of cultural sensitivity and anti-racism attempt to address one of the central tenets of social work practice: working with the person or group within their environment.

Within each of these broader approaches there are a number of models that can guide social work practice. A good, brief summary of some of these models can be found in Cope et al. (1994a) and they are summarised and added to here.

Cultural sensitivity models

Taking culturally sensitive practice first, we can identify four models of practice, each with its own advantages and limitations. Cultural sensitivity models of practice are comparable to the current understanding of the policy of Australian multiculturalism and appear to be the preferred option of the Australian Association of Social Workers (AASW 2002).

The first is the ethno-specific model in which 'each culture is considered to be a fixed thing, a set of particular attitudes, values, beliefs and behaviours shared by its members' (Cope et al. 1994b, p. 20). Characteristic of this model is a focus on differences between cultural groups, an emphasis on homogeneity within groups, and a stereotypical description of particular cultures. Examples of this model include ethnically specific welfare agencies and writings that attempt to describe the typical ethnic family (see Hartley 1995). Some of the advantages of this model are that it provides knowledge of specific cultural practices, customs, and values, and enables the worker to communicate more effectively and appropriately with members of a particular cultural group. At the same time, there are also some disadvantages of the ethno-specific model, which can stereotypically portray cultures as fixed and static rather than dynamic and open to change, and may disregard individual differences among people of a particular culture.

The second cultural sensitivity model, very popular in the literature, is the psychological or interpersonal approach that attempts 'to understand another's beliefs and behaviours in terms of that person's culture. [It] is promoted through self-exploration of one's own values, beliefs and attitudes' (Cope et al. 1994a, p. 30). Understanding culture is seen as understanding the other's personal feelings and attitudes, and being reflective about one's own biases and perceptions. This reflection can be uncomfortable for the worker as they confront their own prejudices. The psychological or interpersonal model emphasises empathy, raises the worker's awareness of cultural difference, and helps the worker apply interpersonal skills to assist others who are culturally different from themselves. However, the model tends to focus on individual deficits rather than strengths, and often sees cultural interaction as only happening at the moment of encounter between individual people.

The third cultural sensitivity model is the linguistic or communication approach which has 'a focus on what is said and how it is said, which can be useful when there are specific language problems in the setting' (Cope et al. 1994b, p. 27). This model examines the dynamics of communication in cross-cultural interactions (see Irwin 1996; Pauwels 1995). The model focuses on breakdowns and misunderstandings in communication and language, and sensitises the worker to communicate effectively with non-English speakers. Typically, proponents of this model provide workers with communication strategies for effective communication, including non-verbal aspects of communication. A strength of this model is the emphasis on the relationship of language to culture, but the model does presume that language difficulties are only about words when, in fact, success or failure in cross-cultural communication may really be about the nature and context of the information itself.

The fourth cultural sensitivity model is that of productive diversity. Productive diversity is one of the four principal objectives of the federal government's multicultural policy (DIMIA 2004c): 'The overall aim of the PD program is to encourage and support business to harness and capitalise on the talents of language and cultural diversity in the workplace and the community.' The productive diversity approach values cultural diversity as a productive resource. It values members of ethnic and cultural groups for their language skills, cultural knowledge, access to networks, and the insights they have into accessing hard-to-reach consumers. Productive diversity moves away from the monocultural tradition of Australian workplaces. In social work practice, this model values the language and cultural skills of workers who are from different cultural groups: work colleagues often benefit from a broader approach to practice and to problem solving. On the other hand, workers chosen for their links with particular communities can feel they are being used tokenistically, particularly when they are only valued in relation to their ability to access a particular cultural group.

Anti-racist models

While cultural sensitivity models of cross-cultural practice concentrate on sensitising or changing the perception and behaviours of the worker, anti-racist models attempt to challenge oppressive systematic and structural realities that impact on people's lives. Anti-racist practice is based on a specific social justice perspective that 'attempts to change those institutional arrangements, social processes, and social practices that work together to benefit the dominant group at the expense of subordinate groups' (Mullaly 2002, p. 193). Writings on anti-racist practice give some prominence to cultural sensitivity and awareness of racism, but the major emphasis is on 'tackling racism' (Dominelli 1997a) at institutional and organisational levels. There are three main approaches to anti-racist social work practice.

The first model, anti-oppressive practice, confronts the institutional or underlying causes of racism, racist policies, and racist behaviour. Usually, this is a collective action where people develop a critical consciousness of the reasons for their oppression as a preparation for some form of action for social change (Freire 1970). The goal is to liberate both the oppressed and the oppressors through new forms of non-oppressive social relationships. Gil (1998) calls this form of social work practice 'structural transformation', which he describes as 'spreading critical consciousness concerning societal realities, and facilitating involvement of social workers and people they serve, in social movements to overcome the root causes of injustice and oppression' (Gil 1998, p. 69). Exponents of this model work with those who suffer under racist situations to challenge those situations and the policies that give rise to them. Because this model challenges racism and those who benefit from it, whether they are aware of that or not, it is often tiring and confrontational work and a lot of energy is expended on developing and maintaining group processes. Workers who work solely from this perspective can often become alienated from their colleagues and organisations. In addition, there is criticism of this model of practice in its claims of the high moral ground and its sometimes negative effects on service users (Wilson & Beresford 2000).

The second model, which is more an educational perspective than a practice method, is the socio-historical approach, which 'is about facts ... the facts are historical as well as descriptive and are used to label people' (Cope et al. 1994a, p. 35). Attention is focused on factual knowledge (history, demography) for the purpose of outlining the oppressive social and historical contexts in which some cultural groups are enmeshed. This model challenges monocultural explanations of society and makes workers aware of the history and conditions of disadvantaged groups in society. Exponents of this model set out to show the social and political connections between cultural groups and their (often disadvantaged) place in society. Because this is a didactic, top-down model and attempts to set the context for understanding prior to attempting to change attitudes, it may alienate workers by presenting harsh facts they find difficult to deal with personally or are unable to respond to adequately. In addition, a stress on history and social disadvantage may seem remote to many people, particularly when there is an emphasis on historical injustices that may appear far removed from current situations.

The third model, the equal opportunity (EEO) or anti-discrimination model, is a legal model about following rules 'to give members of all cultures a fair go' (Cope et al. 1994b, p. 41). This model focuses on the civil rights of people in regard to access, equity, and freedom from discrimination: discrimination is any act or practice or omission that makes distinctions between individuals and/or groups so as to advantage unfairly one over the other. The EEO approach provides workers with legal and administrative knowledge about anti-discrimination, makes workers aware of the social and organisational norms underlying anti-discriminatory policies and regulations, provides workers with procedures and strategies to activate EEO procedures and supports anti-discrimination with the force of law or regulation, whether individuals accept the principles or not. On the other hand, as a practice method, the EEO approach can create resistance in people because it is a legal threat rather than an accepted internal norm. This model emphasises the letter of the law and threatens rather than persuades.

Ethical issues

The main ethical issue facing Australian society and Australian social work in working in culturally diverse situations is the indefinite detention of asylum seekers, especially children. The harm being done is well documented. Furthermore, the use of mandatory detention as a deterrent is the abuse of some people so that other asylum seekers will not think of coming to Australia. The reason this is wrong is that it means doing harm to people so that a so-called 'good' (that is, less asylum seekers coming to Australia) might eventuate.

There are other ethical issues in social work practice in an ethnically and culturally diverse Australia. One could mention the power differential between social workers and consumers of social services, but this is an issue in all relationships between social workers and clients, and not only in regard to practice with culturally diverse populations. We could also mention the monocultural approach to service provision in multicultural Australia (Jamrozik & Boland 1989), an approach that fails to 'develop appropriate intervention strategies that take into account the racial, social, cultural, historical and environmental influences of culturally different clients' (AASW 2002, p. 26). Service provision includes the inadequacy of many theories of counselling and therapy to describe, explain, predict, and suggest appropriate interventions with clients of diverse cultural backgrounds (Sue et al. 1996).

More germane are the attitudes of some workers and agencies that refugees and immigrants are in Australia now, and therefore no special skills, knowledge, or attitudes are required to provide services to them. I trust that the practice section above challenges that view. Yet, this self-centred view pervades practice when workers and agencies indulge in stereotypes, ignore religious and cultural traditions, and think that a narrow form of unreflecting practice that is comfortable for the worker is appropriate for practice in a multicultural Australia. Although the same deficiency is apparent in non-white workers, Lum (1996, p. 295) quotes 'five areas of deficiency in the relationship between ethnic client and white social worker':

- the worker's inability to comprehend the social, economic, and cultural customs of the client
- the worker's lack of awareness of his or her own feelings regarding race or class
- minimal research on the particulars of behavior in other cultures
- use of theoretical constructs designed by and for whites to treat people of color
- culturally deficient clinical training that does not communicate a culturally sensitive helping perspective.

The ethical response to these deficiencies is highlighted in the *Australian Association of Social Workers Code of Ethics* where it sets out the guidelines for culturally sensitive practice (AASW 2002. p. 26).

Ethics in context

1   You are working with a refugee family where physical violence has been reported in regard to the teenage daughter. The family believe in familial respect and obedience to the parents, especially the father of the family. One solution is to remove the young woman to a refuge. Another solution is to accept the violence as part of their culture. A third solution is to have the police charge the father and the eldest son and remove them from the family. A fourth solution is to work through the family structure and resolve the situation within the family. How do you protect the daughter? How do you support the family?

2 You are counselling a client who does not speak English very well. She has said little about her problem but is always on time for your meetings. The client is very attentive to what you say and agrees with your suggestions about what she should do but she says that her problem is God's will. She first wishes to involve a minister from her church to exorcise her of evil spirits and wants you, as her counsellor, to be part of the ceremony. You are not comfortable about this as the idea of evil spirits and exorcisms are contrary to your own beliefs. Yet, you are the only counsellor she will talk to and you feel that, after the exorcism, she can make real progress. What should you do and what will be the consequences of your decision?

The future for social work

While Australian life, and therefore social work practice, is still operating within an official policy of multiculturalism, we are almost in a post-multicultural period. In general, our cultural and ethnic diversity is not the pure strain it was in its various homelands; we have made adaptations to our customs and beliefs while still holding them dear, if only, for many, in a nostalgic rather than practical sense. The old 1950s term 'cosmopolitan' is enjoying a comeback and some commentators prefer it to multiculturalism. This inter-ethnic adaptation or hybridity is a 'third space' (Bhabha 1994) that is more than an amalgamation of the cultural values of immigrants' homelands and an imagined Australian-ness. It is the constant creating of new blended self-identities (see the example of the Townsville wedding described earlier). As Luke and Luke (1998) argue: 'Interracial families are a focal site for the construction of identities and practices of "new ethnicities". As such, the description and analysis of such families may require theoretical and practical models and vocabularies beyond those offered by post-war literature on immigration and multiculturalism' (pp. 748–9). The challenge for social work is not to be looking back at what was but to look forward to what is being produced and reproduced in contemporary Australia.

One practice issue that is becoming prominent in Australia is the increasing importance of religion and spirituality (Lindsay 2002). Social work practice has often seen religious and spiritual values as relevant but obstructive beliefs in those of differing cultural backgrounds. They were sometimes seen as an obstacle to be negotiated rather than of central significance in working with others. With the rise of fundamentalism in Christianity, Judaism, and Islam, the challenge is going to be to develop social work practice that can respect and respectfully challenge value positions that will continue to become more hard edged, insular, and exclusionary.

Finally, the future is going to be the same as the past: 'In their direct service, and community, organisational and social policy work, social workers will need to promote a deeper understanding and appreciation of cultural and racial diversity as they develop an anti-oppressive practice. The challenge, like effective social work practice itself, remains somewhat elusive, but worthy of endless and tireless effort' (Doyle 2001, p. 68).

Review questions

1   Compare and contrast culturally sensitive practice and anti-racist practice. What are the basic culturally sensitive behaviours that workers need to employ in their practice and in the organisations where they work? What are the basic anti-racist behaviours that workers need to employ in their practice and in the organisations where they work? When is it appropriate to use these different approaches?

2   Who are you? What is the historical background of your family or families? How do you describe your own ethnicity and/or racial background? In what situations is your background important to you? (For example, foods, child-rearing practices, celebrations, care of elderly, whom you should marry, etc.). What are the concepts and values that workers need to know to work with you and your family?

7

SOCIAL WORK WITH FAMILIES

Jan Mason

Chapter objectives

- To provide an understanding that social work with families can be practised either to support the status quo or promote social change

- To note that inequalities within families and between families in society are basic to tensions experienced by individuals in socially disadvantaged families

Introduction

The term 'social work with families' is used in the literature to describe those social work interventions and services where the focus is on the family (see, for example, Zastrow 1995). Batten et al. (1991) noted the lack of Australian literature on social work with families. Within Australia, this field has been influenced by trends in England and the United States, as evidenced in the extent to which texts from these two countries have dominated in teaching social work with families in Australian social work courses.

Fundamental to many social work interventions with families is an assumption that the family is an interacting and interdependent system, so that 'problems' for any family member are typically understood as being related to the dynamics within that person's family (Zastrow 1995). This assumption has been most explicit in, but not limited to, social casework and therapeutic interventions with families.

An alternative approach to social work with families considers the family as a social construction, with the interactions of family members being influenced by the structural context in which they are located. Interventions based on this assumption occur in what is described as 'radical' social work (Ife 1997b; Fook 1986, 1993). These interventions may be carried out in casework and therapy, or in community development and other activities directed to social change.

In Australia, most social work with families has been and is provided through organisations, either government or non-government. The trend to private social work practice with families may be increasing in Australia, but is not currently a major form of social work practice. It introduces to the practice of social work with families parameters that differ from more traditional practice in terms of the practitioner–client relationship, and is not discussed in this chapter.

Historical overview

Historically, social work with families in Australia, as elsewhere in the English-speaking world, has its foundations in the late-nineteenth-century professional discourse that focused on the family as a major social institution requiring intervention by the state and its experts. During this period, social work, like other social behavioural disciplines, marked out the family as its province for intervention (Gilding 1991).

As a field of professional enterprise, social work with families has reflected the contradictions and ambiguities inherent in social policy in capitalist states (Batten et al. 1991). Indeed, it has been a key discursive space for both promoting and challenging the construction of 'normal' families and socially acceptable forms of parenthood within the dominant discourse.

This historical overview provides a brief description of some aspects of the development of social policies associated with the promotion of 'normal' families through 'familism'. It also outlines the discourse that challenges these policies. Examples are provided of social work practice in Australia in which familism has been dominant, and also of more radical practice. Implicit in the following overview is the understanding that examples of practice within each discourse may have been occurring concurrently at any time in history, although one discourse dominated.

Familism and social work with families

Social work practice within the historically dominant construction of 'normal' families has focused on the problems or pathology of parents—usually mothers. Here two interrelated concepts have been fundamental: familism and 'familisation'.

The concept of familism, as defined by Barrett & Mackintosh (1982), implies the 'naturalness' of what is considered the traditional bourgeois family, with the breadwinner husband supported by a wife who is responsible for the maintenance of the home and care of children—children being a crucial element of the nuclear family. This concept, dominant in capitalist societies, 'operates as a principle of social organisation at both the domestic and public level, especially in the field of social care … it is the standard against which all forms are measured and, importantly, judged' (Dalley 1988, pp. 20–1). Inherent in the application of this concept is the subordination of women to men in interpersonal relations, and the associated inequities in terms of the division of labour and distribution of resources.

Women's 'natural' caring responsibilities have included the care and socialisation of children, and care and maintenance in the home of others requiring care, such as the elderly and the disabled (Baines et al. 1991; Dalley 1988).

Familism and the development of the 'ideal' family in Australia have been traced by Burns & Goodnow (1985) to colonial policies of the late nineteenth century. For example, in New South Wales, Caroline Chisholm devised a scheme where single immigrant women were placed in domestic service in rural areas with the explicit aim of breaking up the bachelors' quarters, and with the 'dearest hope that the girls will marry and become the mothers of happy families' (Kiddle 1950, p. 61, quoted in Burns & Goodnow 1985, p. 21). By Federation, familism, which consisted of the man leaving the home for 'business' and the woman being involved in 'domestic occupations', including raising children, was well established. It was given impetus in 1907 by a policy decision that established the basic or minimum wage as a family wage, paid to the husband for his labour, but calculated at an amount to enable him to support his wife and for their children to live in 'frugal comfort' (Burns & Goodnow 1985, p. 22). Women's wages were set at a rate below those for men, on the basis that they did not have to support families. This differential continued in wage setting until the 1970s (Senate Economic Committee 1996).

As women have, in the late twentieth century, increasingly moved out of the home and achieved some economic independence in the marketplace, familism can be seen still to dominate, although in a somewhat different form. Women have moved from a position of subordination in domestic pursuits to a similar position within public patriarchy, whereby they are 'firmly embedded in class relations, which are themselves male dominated' (Bryson 1992, p. 197). In recent years women's responsibility as the main carers of children, particularly in middle- and low income groups, has continued and indeed increased, particularly as access to affordable childcare has become more difficult (Brennan 1999). While current policies have contributed to an increase in childcare places and the childcare benefit, the number of places has not kept pace with demand, costs have exceeded the amount of benefit provided, and the locations of childcare are determined on a commercial basis, meaning they are often not available to those in socio-economically disadvantaged locations. It remains the case that, 'for many Australian families there is still no choice—childcare is either too expensive or simply not available in their area' (NABCS 2003).

The ideological fusion of childhood within the institution of the family, described by the term 'familisation', identifies the way in which childhood is constructed in relation to the family, so that the 'family prevails as the social unit with reference to which childhood is conceptualized' (Makrinotti 1994, p. 268). This fusion of children in the family obstructs the public visibility of childhood as a social entity, so children exist only as minors or dependants. As a consequence of this, social policies for children are typically subsumed into other policies (Makrinotti 1994, p. 275). For example, in the Australian context, Wilkinson (1993) has noted how children's interests are presumed to be the same as the interests of their parents in deliberations relating to child custody in the Family Court. Fusing children within the family on the basis of their dependency on adults hides the issues of children's lesser status within and outside families and the fact that children experience their dependency as weakness, in that they lack opportunities for autonomy and adults can force them to do what they consider is in children's best interests (Mason & Falloon 2001; Shamgar-Handleman 1994). Policies and practices designed for children's issues separate from the family (as in child-abuse policies) tend to occur only in situations in which they or their parents are defined as pathological. In such instances, policies and practice are designed to monitor and reform families, create substitute families on the basis of how closely they approximate the ideal nuclear family, or reform the children and return them to their families.

Implementing the concept of familism through punitive policies towards those people who do not live in 'ideal' families, and are likely to be labelled deviant, has contributed to social work practices that have marginalised childless couples, non-heterosexual groups, and extended families such as occur in Aboriginal communities. Examples of punitive practices have been those implemented in areas of child welfare. Adoption and fostering practices in 'redistributing' children from sole-parent or economically disadvantaged families to more 'normal' middle-class families have frequently had the effect of marginalising and causing further trauma to those already disadvantaged in society on bases of gender, race, ethnicity, class, and age (Mason 1993). Child welfare interventions in which social workers have participated have frequently oppressed women, while men have been ignored on the basis that they are not present in families, or where present are not very useful or too difficult to deal with (MacKinnon 1998; Mason & Noble-Spruell 1993). Child welfare workers also have been part of child protection policies that in imposing Western concepts of familism on Aboriginal families have separated children from families, causing abuse and devastation to the children, their families, and broader communities (Bird 1998).

While these interventions typically have been justified as being in the best interests of children, there are many accounts of children whose experiences have challenged the validity of this justification (Bird 1998; Owen 1996; Mason 1993, Mason & Gibson 2004). Foster care practices, in emphasising the placement of children with 'normal' families, have maintained children's subordination within families and vulnerability to further abuse, as highlighted by contemporary allegations of widespread physical and sexual abuse of children in the Queensland foster care system (SMH 2003).

Social justice for families and social work practice

Within Australian social policy and social work practice, there has been an alternative, sometimes complementary, approach to interventions with families. This approach, which has sought to redistribute power to those on the margin, has been based on the more subordinate discourse of social justice. It has been evident in those social policies for families that have contributed to income redistribution and facilitated the provision of resources to disadvantaged families or to individuals oppressed by assumptions about nuclear families. Here, the provision of benefits to sole parents and the availability of refuges to women suffering domestic violence have been significant.

The theoretical basis for this alternative form of social work practice with families has been derived from critical and post-structural analysis. Emphasis has been on individual subjectivities and on social inequalities based on gender, race, class, and age. Further highlighted has been the significance of the power inequalities that typify social relationships, including those between professional and client. Social work practice within this discourse is based on concepts of empowerment and attempts to link the personal with the political (Ife 1997b, p. 180). It has as central tenets the importance of consciousness-raising and collaborative forms of practice in which social worker and clients together frame their understandings of issues and of desired outcomes (Ife 1997b). Radical social work with families is practised with individuals or groups who define themselves as family. Historically, social work practice influenced by this discourse has been about 'straddling the split' between the objective status imposed by the state on individuals in families and the subjective states of these individuals (Horne 1997). Social workers working with those who have been labelled abusing parents, victims of abuse, relinquishing mothers, or adopted children have frequently been aware of the subjective experiences of individuals in terms of 'pain, suffering, need, love, hate' (Horne 1997). For social workers, acknowledging the realities of individual subjectivities has meant recognising the diversity between and within Australian families, the structural and organisational influences on them, and the significance of the personal for family members. It has also meant acknowledging that clients, as well as professionals, have knowledge and skills, and that social work practice is about sharing these. This sharing becomes a challenge for social workers in practice with adults whose values and experiences differ from their own. It is even more of a challenge when working with children, whose knowledge and ability to contribute to decision-making processes tends to be discounted by adults in general.

Social workers who have intervened with families from within this discourse characteristically have utilised strategies to promote social change, such as community work and organisational change. An important example of structural social work practice with families, which deliberately sought to improve the material and financial position of families, was that implemented by the Brotherhood of St Laurence in the 1970s and 1980s. The Brotherhood's Family Centre Project was designed to find ways of working with families on low incomes by first providing the practical resources they needed, such as income, housing, education, and employment, while simultaneously involving them as participants in the service itself and in the broader community (Carter 1990). The implementation of this project highlighted the dilemma of how to transfer power from professional social workers to those families with whom they work.

A more recent example of such practice is that undertaken by social workers with residents of a public-housing estate at Waterloo in inner Sydney. Living in an area characterised by 'general social fragility', many of the families experienced social disadvantage with high unemployment, low levels of home ownership, and low household income. Social workers worked with these families and other residents to identify strategies to address aspects of their disadvantage, including the removal of alienating features of the physical environment and barriers to employment (Vinson 1996).

An example of an attempt to bring about organisational change based on client–practitioner collaboration was that instigated by Wesley Dalmar Child and Family Services Agency, in conjunction with the University of Western Sydney. In this project the views of members of families—men, women, and children who had used Wesley Dalmar services—were sought on how services could most appropriately meet their needs. Findings from this project are now guiding the organisation in developing policies for improved service delivery (Wesley Dalmar 2004).

Structural analysis has also been applied to direct practice with families. Within Australia, the work of Beecher (1986), and more particularly of Fook (1986, 1993), has been important in promoting methods of working with families and individuals through family casework and therapy, based on the values and techniques derived from radical and feminist theory. In outlining strategies to challenge gender assumptions and other inequalities within families, they have challenged implicitly the influence of familism, while promoting techniques for working with the social context in which families exist (Fook 1993, 1986; Beecher 1986).

The application of structural theory to direct work with families is evident in an example of practice outlined by MacKinnon (1998). She describes how, within a therapeutic framework of an Australian child and family services agency, practitioners worked with family members in situations in which child abuse had been alleged to understand and respond to their subjectivities, and relate them to gender and class analysis. Crucial to hearing the stories of family members was an understanding of the significance of violence and issues of powerlessness in their lives, and the relevance of these issues to the structuring of therapist–client relationships (MacKinnon 1998).

Social work practice with families that has directly challenged the familisation of children and young people has occurred more recently than other forms of structural practice. It is recognisable in the descriptions of the work of some feminist social workers and other child advocates. Feminists, in highlighting the gendered nature of child sexual abuse and urging that primacy be given to the testimony of children, have supported the rights of children to be taken seriously as people, independent of their status in families (Latham 1992).

Social workers have been among those professionals who have advocated for and implemented processes to ensure that the voices of children are heard through agencies such as the New South Wales Community Services Commission. This agency implemented strategies to facilitate children having a say in decisions about their welfare (CSC 1993–94, 1995–96).

Practice issues for social workers working with families

The major issues currently facing practitioners working with families are similar to those that historically have characterised this area of work. Workers practise in a context in which contradictory discourses influence the delivery of social welfare services. However, the tension between the values of social justice and familism are now particularly explicit. This marked tension is occurring within Australian social policy as attempts are made to respond to global influences, first for greater recognition and extension of human rights principles, particularly in relation to children, and second for privatisation of welfare and of other associated economic rationalist strategies, which are part of the increasing 'residualisation' of welfare policy. This tension is played out in practice around issues of inequality, unemployment, and poverty, which are increasingly marginalising some families.

The emphasis on human rights

An increased emphasis on human rights principles has great relevance for social work practice. It is expected to be even more influential as such principles become further enshrined in international and, sometimes, domestic legislation. Yeatman (2000, p. 1499) notes that 'the institutionalisation of human rights after 1945 onwards represents a new set of positive demands of the governing authorities of states, namely, that they accord respect to the principle of human dignity … because they are human beings'. Legislation encoding human rights principles affecting social work practice with families includes anti-discrimination, Family Court, and child protection laws. For example, the New South Wales *Children and Young Persons (Care and Protection) Act* 1998 includes a clause (s.13 (1a)) recognising the rights of Aboriginal and Torres Strait Islander children who need out-of-home care to be placed in their 'extended family or kinship group'. Similarly, Carrick describes how challenges to laws governing reproductive technologies—by decisions made under laws prohibiting discrimination against unmarried women, de facto couples, and lesbians—have contributed to the weakening of norms fundamental to the patriarchal nuclear family structure (Burbidge 1998).

For social work with families, potentially the most revolutionary application of human rights principles is that encoded within the United Nations *Convention on the Rights of the Child* (1989). The extension to children of entitlements to be treated as 'beings' with rights—in particular, the right to be heard—has important implications for treating children as individuals, not just dependants. Acknowledgment of these entitlements provides an important tool for social workers in their advocacy for children.

The Convention's recognition of the right of children to participate in decision-making on issues concerning their welfare (clauses 12 & 13) can be considered to pose a direct challenge to practices of social workers making decisions in the 'best interests' of children, while not taking their expressed points of view into account. The reported experiences in the United Kingdom of implementing social work strategies to support rights for children are sobering. Here, the hoped-for progress in empowering children and young people to have greater say in decisions about their lives has not necessarily followed legislation and policies directed at this goal. Brown (1995), Director of the National Society for the Prevention of Cruelty to Children (NSPCC), has noted that it is difficult for practitioners to involve children as decision-makers when their professional training has taught them that they have the expertise to make decisions for their clients. He claims that to involve children in decision-making will require 'a fundamental change in our attitudes and in the culture of our institutions'. This has been borne out by Australian research. A recent attempt by Scarba services of The Benevolent Society to introduce child participation into its services for the treatment of families in child protection situations highlighted the advantages but also the obstacles to involving children as participants. It was found that to involve children in this way requires both systemic changes and the acquisition by workers of specific skills in engaging children (Mason & Michaux in press).

Privatisation and the increasing reliance on residual social policy measures

The contemporary emphasis by governments on privatising the development and delivery of social welfare services, as part of the increasing residualisation of welfare policy, impacts on the context in which social workers intervene with families.

Privatisation has meant a move away from collective responsibility for the provision of welfare and a renewed emphasis on the family as provider of support and welfare (Baldock 1994), re-emphasising the value of familism. In shifting responsibility for care from government to families, women's responsibilities for the aged and younger members of their families, as well as people with disabilities, have increased (Burbidge 1998; Baldock 1994). A report of the Commonwealth Department of Human Service and Health in 1995 estimated that 74 per cent of care to disabled and elderly people to assist them to remain in their homes is provided by informal carers (Bittman & Rice 1999). In 1998 Australian Bureau of Statistics figures showed that 90 per cent of people with disabilities who needed and were provided with care received assistance from informal carers, while only 49 per cent received assistance from formal organisations and 23 per cent from government organisations. Many received both formal and informal care (ABS 1999b, table 13). The reliance on women as informal carers is indicated by the fact that 70 per cent of those providing informal care were women (ABS 1998, table 36).

At the same time as women are assuming responsibility for providing welfare to other family members, their dependency on the patriarchal family structure has been reinforced by policy developments that move responsibility from the state back on to the family so that women with children must rely on their ex-partners for income support (Baldock 1994). This trend has been exemplified in the Child Support Scheme of 1988–89, which increased the extent to which women must rely on their ex-partners.

Other policy developments of recent decades, in placing responsibility with families for the support and control of young people at increasingly older ages, have had serious implications for young people as well as their families. These policies include replacing unemployment benefits for people aged 16–20 years and student assistance for students up to the age of 24 with Youth Allowance, which is subject to a parental means test. As Hartley and Wolcott (1994) point out, underlying these and other youth and family policies of the

Commonwealth are assumptions about families providing emotional and financial support for their children until at least 18, but more often to 25, and until they are capable of supporting themselves. Such policies, while increasing surveillance over families to ensure the production and maintenance of the 'good' child and future citizen, are also in marked opposition to policies that seek to promote the rights and thereby autonomy of young people.

An evaluation of the impact of the Youth Allowance is relevant here. While describing the 'overall response' to the scheme as 'positive', it stated that the extension of parental means testing to unemployed young people aged 18–20 years was seen to conflict with community expectations about young people and the age at which they become independent (DFCS 1999b). Further, the report noted that parents expressed resentment at having to be responsible for their children beyond age 18, while young people wanting to leave the family home due to family breakdown were concerned about the implications for them.

The fact that Aboriginal young men were reported as being concerned with policies whose effects increased their dependency on their families (DFCS 1999b) has particular implications for the continued oppression of Aboriginal families. These implications are highlighted when considered in the context of other policies that seek to enforce family control over young people: two examples of these policies are the New South Wales *Children (Parental Responsibility) Act* 1994, which Burbidge (1998) has criticised for recriminalising welfare issues; and the Western Australia policy extending the power of police to pick up young people in 'moral danger' on the street and take them to their place of residence (Burbidge 1998). The differential impact of such legislation on Aboriginal youth has been highlighted by a report of the Aboriginal Justice Advisory Council that noted 'disastrous' effects for Aboriginal children of the implementation of the *Children (Parental Responsibility) Act*. This is exemplified in an increase in the proportion of Aboriginal people incarcerated in juvenile justice centres in New South Wales from 25 per cent in January 1996 to 36 per cent in January 1998 (SMH 1999). The extension of techniques for surveillance of families, and potential removal of children to places of reform when parents are assessed as failing to 'control' them, is a characteristic of contemporary Australian society that poses dilemmas for social workers working with marginalised families.

Families in poverty

The growth in residual social policy measures, as well as what Perry and Henman (2002) refer to as global labour market changes, and entrenched unemployment in households, particularly for those with low skills or disabilities, is resulting in a growing income disparity in Australia. Saunders (2003) shows that the average income of the country's richest 20 per cent of households in 2000–01 was about nine times that of its poorest 20 per cent (adjusted for household size it was five times). In 2000, one in every eight Australians lived in income poverty, and the risk of being in poverty was higher for children than adults, with 14.9 per cent of children and 12.3 per cent of adults being in poverty (Harding et al. 2001). This disparity affects interactions between and within families, and contributes significantly to problems of the families who currently comprise much of the clientele of social workers.

More specifically, the impact of poverty on families affected by lack of jobs is likely to be greatest where there are dependants. Families of Aboriginals, sole parent (women-headed) families, and families of recent migrants, especially those from non-English-speaking backgrounds, have been particularly severely affected by this phenomenon (Fincher & Nieuwenhuysen 1998). The ways in which unemployment, poverty, and associated disadvantage impact on some families of recent immigrants from non-English-speaking backgrounds exemplify the issues social workers confront in their work with families. The children of this particular population have been found in studies (see, for example, Taylor & MacDonald 1994) to be over-represented among those living in poverty and, in comparison with others in the population, to be disadvantaged by their parents' lack of English and education, their mothers' lack of social supports, and the fact that they live in rental and high-rise estate accommodation. The widespread unemployment and the associated trend to breakdown in these families have been found to contribute to 'street-frequenting behaviour' and homelessness among some of the young people in these communities (Frederico et al. 1997).

The privatisation of such problems into families for whom disadvantage is most severe requires of social workers who work with these families a capacity to implement innovative strategies explicitly designed to promote principles of social justice at both the micro and macro levels.

Ethical issues

In working with families within a social justice framework, the reflective practitioner is challenging policies that oppress individuals in relationships within families, and within the broader social and political context in which families exist. In challenging practices and policies that stereotype certain constellations of individuals as 'problem' families, or marginalise and render mute individuals within families, practitioners must inevitably focus on issues of power and raise questions about values at the core of ethical practice.

Central to these questions for practitioners working with individual members of families are power inequalities between the worker as professional and the 'others': families marginalised within the broader socio-political context. Frequently, within these families also are inequalities based on gender and age, so that men's subjectivities may have more legitimacy than those of women, while children's subjectivities are typically discounted as of lesser legitimacy than those of adults.

To practise ethical social work with families, reflexivity is the tool for achieving insight into the translation of theory into practice. Reflexivity requires practitioners to examine how their values and political and social positioning influence the way they use their claims to specialist knowledge and expertise. In accepting that neither their frameworks of knowledge nor their interactions with clients occur in a neutral context, practitioners can recognise and work to decrease the power inequalities between themselves and those families and individuals with whom they work.

> ## *Ethics in context*
>
> **1** A child in a family you are working with, around this child's behaviour, tells you he does not consider his stepmother part of the family and does not want her present in casework sessions with his father and sister. How do you proceed?
>
> **2** You are a female social worker who identifies with the woman in a family where the man is also having difficulty in coping. How do you hear and respond to him?

The future for social work

The future for social workers in the twenty-first century is likely to be assured. This prediction is based on the assessment (see, for example, Austin 1997) that the connection between individuals and their families and the social context in which they live will continue to be at the heart of many of the problems experienced by families impacted by social and technological change and marked social inequality. Additionally, as the result of policies discussed in this chapter, direct social work with families to deal with the financial and emotional strains is likely to continue to be part of government strategies.

A consequence of the way in which privatisation and residualist policies hold families accountable for their 'own' miseries and the miseries and problems of individual members has been the growth in mediation, counselling, and conflict-resolution services, including services 'to deal with parent–child conflict, juvenile delinquency, industrial conflict, marriage guidance and financial counselling for people in poverty' (Baldock 1994, p. 113). These methods of practice with families, when practised in a radical framework, can be empowering to those involved in them. However, it has been forecast that as mediation and dispute resolution increasingly become the tools of economic rationalist management philosophy, it will be more difficult to practise radical and activist forms of social work (De Maria 1992).

Additionally, there are serious implications for social workers in the focus of policies on parental and family responsibility and accompanying surveillance mechanisms. For example, as police, juvenile justice, and street-level bureaucrats are increasingly asked to monitor and enforce social control, dilemmas will increase for social workers who struggle to ameliorate the pain of individuals in families in the context of unemployment and social inequalities. Consequently, social workers will need to be vigilant in order to assess the extent to which seemingly empowering practices actually do so. For example, the current emphasis on 'strengths-based' methods of working with families seems to provide a marked improvement in contrast to deficit-based approaches as a way of working with clients. However, such practices may actually disadvantage clients if they limit workers' options for responding to client vulnerabilities and dependencies with practical and emotional supports.

The abilities that social work education can emphasise in helping place social workers as leaders in confronting economic rationalist policies have been identified by Ife (1997b) as including the skill to articulate the link between the public and the private, and between individual disadvantage and social context. Important for social workers in furthering a social justice agenda in the future will be their willingness to facilitate the voices of those most disadvantaged being heard in the public arena, and their capacity to form alliances with other groups struggling to develop strategies that give prominence to human values (Ife 1997b).

Review questions

1   What are the issues in providing supports required by vulnerable families to enable them to cope effectively with their emotional and practical problems, when your agency has limited resources and requires you to put boundaries around the assistance you provide to particular families?

2   How do you hear the needs and aspirations of individual family members when these conflict and when they are coming from unequal positions of power within their family?

3   How do you constructively use your own negative and positive experiences of family to inform your practice with other families?

Acknowledgments

I am grateful to Leanne Craze for assistance in researching this chapter and to Julia Perry for contributions to the chapter revisions.

8

WORKING WITH YOUNG PEOPLE

Karen Healy, Maureen O'Regan, and Michael Tansky

Chapter objectives

- To define what is a vulnerable young person
- To outline the history of youth work in Australia

- To show how theories for practice can be used to promote social justice with young people
- To discuss ethical issues in youth work practice

Introduction

Social and community service agencies engage with young people to address a broad range of needs and issues. In this chapter we refer to young people as those aged between 12 and 25 years and we focus on young people who are vulnerable to abuse and exploitation. We refer to abuse as psychological, emotional, sexual, and physical maltreatment, while we use the term 'exploitation' to denote the use of young people's vulnerability to coerce them to engage in practices that they would not choose of their own free will. Opportunistic prostitution, where the young person provides sexual favours in exchange for basic needs—such as food, accommodation, or dependent drugs—is one example of the kinds of exploitation to which vulnerable young people may be subject.

We begin with an overview of the issues contributing to the vulnerability of this group of young people and then we outline a brief history of youth work practice in Australia. We consider an example of direct work with a vulnerable young person drawing on social work theories to develop specific responses. Finally, we discuss trends and issues for the future.

Vulnerable young people—who are they?

Many young people who come into contact with social and community services are vulnerable to abuse and exploitation for a range of reasons. The most common reasons include family violence or family breakdown, poverty, social isolation, drug and alcohol dependence, and mental illness. Some groups of young people are especially vulnerable to abuse and exploitation; these include Indigenous young people, disabled young people, and also young people from single parent families, culturally and linguistically diverse communities, and from socio-economically disadvantaged areas (AIHW 2003b).

Indigenous young people experience much higher rates of vulnerability, on a range of health and welfare indicators, compared with non-Indigenous young people. Indigenous young people have significantly lower rates of participation in education, lower educational attainment, and poorer literacy than other young people (AIHW 2003, p. 324). In addition, the death rate for Indigenous young people is 144 per 100,000. This is almost three times the rate of that for non-Indigenous young people whose death rate is 52 per 100,000 (AIHW 2003, p. 331). Moreover, 38 per cent of deaths among Indigenous young people are due to suicide whereas only 6 per cent of deaths among non-Indigenous young people can be attributed to this cause (AIHW 2003b, p. 334).

Effective youth work practice requires us to establish a purposeful working relationship with the young person while also recognising the social, cultural, and economic conditions that contribute to the issues facing the young person.

Historical overview—youth work services in Australia

Youth work has a long history that has antecedents stretching back to the British *Poor Law Act* of 1536 when children between the ages of 5 and 14 who were found begging were apprenticed into the labour force. Up until the middle of the nineteenth century, children and young people up to the age of 21 remained subject to flogging, imprisonment, transportation, and hanging, in the same way as adults. By the end of the nineteenth century, working class young people were associated with delinquency. The so-called rise in 'delinquency' was accounted for by 'a rise of non-indictable offences—playing football in the streets, loitering and public bathing' (Blanch 1979, p. 103). Modern youth work finds its roots in those early attempts to provide informal youth subcultures of the street with 'counter-attractions' in the form of alternative morally acceptable leisure pursuits (Davies & Gibson 1967, pp. 47–8).

Of course, long before British colonisation of Australia, Aboriginal people had their own traditions and ceremonies for initiating children into adulthood. As Tom Petrie observed in the 1830s near the settlement of Brisbane, when Aboriginal boys turned 12–15 years, they were initiated through a three- to four-week ceremony into young men. In recognition of their new status, their names were changed. The initiation involved the separation of the boys from their parents and supervision by men from another clan, who gave them instructions relating to proper conduct, particularly in relation to silence. The boys' resolve was tested day after day, culminating in a ritualised ceremonial fight, which initiated the 'kippas' as men. (Petrie 1963, pp. 37–43). Petrie provides no information about girls' transition to womanhood. Cross-culturally, however, it is well understood that kin, community, customs, and ceremony all played a role in guiding the child's transition to adulthood.

British occupation dramatically disrupted Indigenous traditions. From the very beginning of the penal colony to the early twentieth century, Indigenous children and young people were kidnapped from their families and communities and exploited for free labour as servants and farm workers (HREOC 1997, p. 27). Today, the substantial over-representation of Indigenous young people in child protection and juvenile justice systems reflects the lack of adequate policy and programme strategies for this youth population.

At various points throughout Australia's modern history concerns about youth subcultures has risen to prominence in public policy and within the community more generally. Following the Great Depression and World War II there were periods of official and media 'panic' about youth subcultures (Brake 1980, p. 61). There were waves of concern about Bodgies and Widgies in the 1950s, and motorbike gangs, hippies, and deviants in the 1960s.

Until the 1970s, provision of services for vulnerable young people, such as homeless youth, was provided mainly by church welfare agencies, with little if any government funding (Chesterman 1988, p. 7). In 1974, the Whitlam administration funded the Homeless Persons' Assistance Program, which included a handful of youth services. In 1979, the Commonwealth and states agreed to jointly fund the Youth Services Scheme to provide emergency accommodation, and referral and information services to people under 18 years of age. In addition, the Commonwealth funded the Community Youth Support Scheme (CYSS), which offered literacy and numeracy, leisure and art and craft activities, and employment preparation programmes for unemployed young people.

A range of government inquiries throughout the 1980s led to increased public awareness of, and responsiveness to, vulnerable young people. In 1985, the Supported Accommodation Assistance Program (SAAP) was initiated and included homeless young people aged 12–25 years, and their dependants, as one of its target groups. This spearheaded an unprecedented increase in the number and quality of youth services, including some Aboriginal youth services, across the country. The growth in services to homeless young people was accompanied by the professionalisation of youth work practice in Australia. Increasingly, employers looked for staff who could articulate social justice values, a practice framework, relationship boundaries with clients, and an understanding of structural issues impacting on young people. Students trained in social work and social science entered youth work in growing numbers. As an additional support measure for homeless young people, the Commonwealth introduced the Young Homeless Allowance in 1986. In 1989, The Burdekin Report *Our Homeless Children* (Burdekin 1989) was instrumental in focusing national attention on youth homelessness and resulted in a doubling of accommodation capacity, expansion of the Youth Homeless Allowance, and the funding of youth health services.

Despite all the inquiries and reports since the 1980s, homelessness remains entrenched in Australia. As both the 1996 and 2001 Census found, over 100,000 Australians are homeless on any one night. Of these, 46,000 are under the age of 25, and 25,000 are aged between 12 and 18 years. Nearly 20 per cent of those sleeping on the streets and in parks are Indigenous, yet they only make up 2 per cent of the population.

Practice issues

Youth work practice is now incredibly diverse. Among youth workers there is strong recognition of the diverse identifications and needs of young people. Youth workers use a range of practice approaches to engage and work with vulnerable groups of young people. Outreach models, such as detached youth work whereby the worker engages with young people in the places they congregate rather than in an official agency environment, are important for making connections with marginalised young people. Youth workers also provide support and leadership to young people in youth shelters, accommodation services, schools, drug and alcohol services, and when employed by statutory juvenile justice and child protection agencies.

Youth workers are also involved in community education processes with young people. For example, youth workers have been at the forefront of creative community health initiatives aimed at reducing the harms associated with high-risk drug use and sexual behaviour. Another area of youth work practice is the promotion of community development responses that both improve young people's access to resources, such as housing, or their options for social support, such as peer-support networks. Participation models also provide powerful opportunities for young people to experience the responsibilities of organising arts and cultural activities with their peers, thereby enhancing their self-confidence to pursue their aspirations. Youth participation requires youth worker support to build partnerships with other peers and organisations in their community. This model is currently being actively encouraged and funded by the Foundation for Young Australians and some state youth bureaux.

The question of who is responsible for meeting the social, emotional, and material needs of young people is contested terrain. Over the past decade, government policy at a Commonwealth level has increasingly emphasised the responsibility of families for meeting young people's needs. For example, Commonwealth income support arrangements have made young students dependent on their parents until they reach the age of 25. Young people looking for work remain dependent on parental support until they reach the age of 21. Only young people whose parents are on very low incomes are eligible for the maximum rates of Youth Allowance, unless they can prove that they meet stringent criteria relating to family breakdown, serious risk, or have earned certain levels of income for a prescribed period since leaving school. This renewed emphasis on family responsibility has exacerbated the vulnerability of those young people whose families are unable to meet these responsibilities.

Working with young people—developing practice responses

Social workers working with young people must use approaches that bring into focus the social, cultural, and economic conditions that contribute to abuse and vulnerability of some subgroups of adolescents. Without this 'bigger picture', youth workers risk offering assistance that, at best, addresses immediate problems but does little to intervene in the ongoing vulnerability of the young person. Two practice perspectives that are of use here are the ecosystems and the anti-oppressive practice perspectives. The ecosystem perspective draws attention to the role of family, community, and institutional supports in service users lives. In addition, the anti-oppressive perspective shows how cultural and structural oppressions shape service users' lives.

Like other forms of social work practice, engaging with the client and working effectively with them requires us to understand where the client 'is at'. In youth work practice, it is important for workers to understand the particular issues and challenges associated with adolescent personal development. In post-industrial countries like Australia, adolescence is often a time of experimentation as one establishes one's adult identity (Berk 2002, p. 390). Young people who are vulnerable to abuse and exploitation are likely to lack a network of adult carers who can support them through this developmental phase. Youth workers can play a critical role in providing support and reducing harm to young people through this developmental phase. One way youth workers can do this is by providing clear and accurate information about reducing the harms associated with drug and alcohol use or sex. Another way is to resource and support young people to deliver or participate in peer support and peer education processes about issues that matter to them, such as well-informed sexual health and safe drug use.

See this chapter's case study, which considers how these perspectives can inform social work practice with young people.

Ruby

Two outreach youth workers met Ruby in an inner-city park where she was inhaling paint from a Coke bottle with six other young people. The group are friends and cousins from the same outer suburban community. Ruby is a 14-year-old Indigenous Australian. She has some contact with her Mum—but not with her Dad. Ruby has never met her Dad but does know *he's a white-fella*.

Ruby and her friends sleep under a city bridge. None of them have any income, and together or alone they steal purses, break into cars, and shoplift. Ruby gets some money from her maternal grandmother who lives in an inner-city hostel. But Ruby feels bad about taking money from her grandma, who is weak from emphysema and never has much to spare.

By providing food and information the youth workers have managed to engage the interest of Ruby and her friends in the park. They also provide access to a health service along with showers, toilets, and a free change of clothes back at their office base. Ruby has a persistent cough and saw a doctor who works part-time at the youth service. She likes all these workers because they'll give her *a feed* and not ask too many questions. The police always ask a lot of questions and take the paint off her. This makes Ruby wild.

Case Study

Ruby's stepfather sexually abused her from the age of nine. The abuse continued until Ruby told her Mum at the age of 11. But Ruby's Mum refused to believe her and a big argument between them resulted in Ruby's ejection from home. Ruby's Mum and younger sister still live with the stepfather. Now Ruby is worried about her sister but can't say anything to her Mum—even though they are back on talking terms. Ruby visits her Mum sporadically—never mentioning the abuse and never visiting if her stepfather is home.

Ruby sniffs spray-paint most days. She'll also smoke pot and cigarettes, and inject speed if it's available. Other homeless friends first introduced Ruby to injecting drug use at the age of 13. She still prefers someone else to inject her, but says she's not really into speed.

Before the abuse, and the fight with her Mum, Ruby was relatively settled at school. But her fear and rage undermined her interest and capacity to cooperate at school. Finally, in Year 7, Ruby was suspended for two weeks after screaming abuse at a teacher who chastised her for being late. Ruby never returned to school and never made the transition to high school.

The youth workers know that Ruby and some friends have been attacked and raped by older homeless men. This explains recent changes in Ruby's demeanour and her escalating substance abuse. Prior to the rapes Ruby had displayed a lively sense of humour and talent for graffiti art—the only real distraction from her chroming. However, since the rapes, Ruby has been very withdrawn and her cough is much worse.

The youth workers have decided that they must do something about:

- stopping the attacks on these girls
- reducing the toxic effects of paint and other substances on the young people
- strengthening Ruby and her friend's chances of protecting themselves
- reducing their risk of pregnancy and infection with hepatitis C and sexually transmitted diseases.

Although the above concerns were identified by the youth workers as issues to act on, they may not be ones where Ruby and her friends want support. It is imperative that the youth workers consult with Ruby and her friends about what they want to do to change what is happening for them. This process requires strong and effective communication skills on the part of the workers, and an explicit interest in the group's—and its individuals'—strengths and resources. These strengths and resources, along with the workers' capacities, will need to be harnessed to improve the group's safety and promote their ongoing welfare. It becomes tricky for workers when young people downplay the risks they are exposed to or resist any action toward change if it threatens their own sense of control—including their power to continue to chrome. In these instances youth workers, acting to prevent further harm to Ruby and her friends, will have to balance a number of competing values. These include:

- respect for the individual and their right to self-determination versus the workers' duty of care to a 14-year-old homeless teenager
- Ruby's right to confidentiality versus duty of care to act to protect a 14-year-old homeless teenager from further harm
- Ruby's right to understand the worker's role and any actions taken that will impact on her rights and welfare.

In making these practice decisions workers must be clear about their role and its responsibilities and have a clear sense of Ruby's rights and needs both developmentally and in relation to the special circumstances relating to her homelessness. These include a responsibility to provide basic practical assistance, advocacy and support, information, and, if necessary, action to ensure the safety of children and young people who are homeless and without adults to care for them.

Developing a practice response

We will use ecosystems and anti-oppressive approaches to develop a framework for understanding and responding to Ruby's situation. The ecosystems approach draws attention to the 'transactions' between Ruby and her social environment, and the ultimate aim is to enhance the 'fit' between the person and their social arrangements (Germain & Gitterman 1996, p. 8). The ecosystems approach recognises that a range of systems impact on service users' lives including: micro systems (home and family networks); mezzo systems (neighbourhood and peer networks); and macro systems (major welfare and economic systems).

Viewing Ruby's situation from an ecosystems perspective we can see both strengths and weaknesses in social systems that impact upon her life. At the micro systems level of home or family networks, a culturally sensitive approach demands that we recognise kinship relationships beyond the nuclear family unit. With this broader focus we can see that Ruby has a moderately supportive relationship with her grandmother and an ambivalent relationship with her mother. She has an antagonistic relationship with her stepfather due to sexual abuse and a lack of relationship with her birth father. A focus on improving the relationship between Ruby and her mother may be one way of promoting Ruby's safety and well-being. One way of improving these relationships would be to engage Ruby and her mother and grandmother in mediation or a restorative justice process about Ruby's experiences of abuse in the family home (see Strang & Braithwaite 2002). The role of the youth worker here would be to enlist the assistance of an Indigenous family work or family mediation service, and to continue to actively support Ruby. Youth work support can enable Ruby's participation in this process and ensure Ruby's voice is heard alongside the concerns and wishes of her mother and grandmother. The family worker is then free to engage the mother and grandmother, prepare for their coming together with Ruby, and facilitate a solution-focused process where all are empowered to participate.

This case study also raises concerns about the safety of Ruby's younger sister who remains at home. As workers with young people we would be under an ethical, and perhaps a legal, obligation to report this concern to a relevant child protection agency. In order to ensure that our approach is culturally sensitive we would continue to work with an Indigenous child and family service to determine how best to deal with this concern. This work requires active partnership with both the Indigenous services and the child protection agency to ensure appropriate and effective action is taken (see Briskman 2003).

At the level of neighbourhood and peer systems, we can see that Ruby does not have a neighbourhood network, in part because of the abuse she experienced and the need to leave her family home. Her relationship with her school was also poor. On the other hand, Ruby does have strong peer relationships and a positive relationship with the youth service. Youth workers can work with both Ruby and her friends to discuss issues of vulnerability and to develop safety strategies that are appropriate and acceptable to the group. The youth workers may be able to work with the peer group to: rebuild links with their communities and schools; reduce the harm associated with solvent use, poor hygiene, and unsafe sex; enhance their talents and skills; and identify appropriate accommodation options with them. Again, the youth workers should seek to engage Indigenous services to develop culturally appropriate safe accommodation options for Ruby and her friends.

Over the past decade, ecosystems approaches have increasingly recognised the importance of understanding the macro context of service-users' lives (Germain & Gitterman 1996). In analysing this level of Ruby's ecosystem, we can see that Ruby is a member of an oppressed minority group; that is, Indigenous Australians. Ruby's continuing vulnerability to violence and self-harm reflects the failure of a range of human service systems to adequately respond to her situation. For example, Ruby, like many Indigenous young people, has left the school system prematurely and there are few options for her reintegration into formal education. Similarly, Ruby's vulnerability to violence, as a homeless person, reflects a lack of safe and appropriate housing options for young people who, like Ruby, are distanced from their kinship networks (see Briskman 2003).

An anti-oppressive framework can be usefully combined with the ecosystems perspective to bring into focus the cultural and structural oppression to which Ruby is subject. Thompson (1997), an anti-oppressive theorist, argues that culture 'represents the interests and influence of society as reflected in the social values and cultural norms we internalize via the process of socialization'. Anti-oppressive approaches require social workers to constantly reflect on the ways in which the structures associated with capitalism, patriarchy, and imperialism contribute to, and interact with, personal and cultural oppression. Using an anti-oppressive lens we draw attention to the ways in which the services we provide could be reformed to be more culturally appropriate and accessible to Ruby and her peers. We might also engage in a process of exploring, with Ruby, her cultural heritage and the potential for greater connection with a heritage the dominant culture has denied her. The local

Aboriginal Elders may be able to offer opportunities for Ruby and her friends to understand and be proud of their cultural heritage. Finally, we might reflect on the extent to which our own cultural heritage, whatever that might be, is a point of connection or a barrier in our work with Ruby.

Ethics in context

What we do as youth workers must reflect:

- what the young person wants to do, to talk about, or to change
- what we understand could promote the safety and well-being of the young person, particularly if that young person is functioning in the world without adult carers and is under the age of 15 (or over 15 and functioning in a manner that indicates developmental delays and/or mental distress).

This can make the youth work task complex and challenging, especially if action is called for prior to the establishment of a good rapport and a clear agreement. In such cases it may be wise to ensure another worker is available to offer support. For instance, if child protection and other health and safety issues are immediately apparent, the worker may need to act in advance of establishing that rapport. Or, having established strong connection they may need to act contrary to a young person's injunction to *not worry about it*. For example, Ruby's friend may have told you about the homeless men attacking the group and told you not to tell anyone. Such a promise cannot be made when strong action—for example, police intervention—may be required to prevent further attacks. Or Ruby may have disclosed her fears for her sister and then told you not to do anything. Again, despite the risk of losing trust with Ruby, the worker is obliged to clearly explain their job and its responsibilities. Paradoxically, workers who respectfully counter such requests with clear explanations of how they will discreetly and respectfully manage these concerns can experience a strengthened connection with the vulnerable young person, who clearly understands where they stand and what they can realistically expect from this adult support person. Support and leadership are two core elements of the youth work role and must remain integrated in practice. Youth workers are not friends. But they can be friendly in approach and must be clear in their intent.

The future of social work practice

The future for small to medium community-managed youth services is bleak. They are under attack from the government as well as large national corporate church-based agencies and a new breed of for-profit agencies competing for government contracts.

Governments are replacing grant processes with purchasing policies, tendering processes, and contract management that favour the large corporate and private operators with lower overheads. Large church welfare organisations now employ business managers and are less inclined to publicly criticise government policies. The large corporate and private contractors are expanding and competing with each other for a greater share of the welfare 'market'. They see growth potential in taking business from the thousands of smaller community-based agencies.

With the demise of recurrent funding and its replacement with competitive tendering, funds are being 'mainstreamed' or re-channelled from the community sector to the corporate and private sectors. This presents a challenge for social workers who will be employed or contracted across all four sectors and pitted in competition with each other.

An associated challenge is the replacement of social justice values, which have guided many youth services, with business values that emphasise efficiency, cost control, cash flow, competition, expansion, and centralised control. One unintended consequence of the application of government purchasing policy to the delivery of welfare services is the commodification of children and young people. Children and young people in the youth justice and child protection systems now have dollar signs attached to them. Services are bid for in a commercial marketplace in which cost-effectiveness, rather than service values, can become primary factors influencing service provision. A further negative consequence of commercialisation is that social workers in youth work may find their capacity to 'speak out' against government policy is constrained, especially in services financially reliant on government tenders.

Social workers in youth work practice must carefully consider the scope and purpose of their roles. Throughout this chapter we have argued for critical and holistic responses to vulnerable young people. More effective, holistic responses to the needs of young people require strong analysis and adequate resources to services—particularly to enable youth workers to do more than provide immediate practical assistance, support, and information. In this chapter, we have shown that social justice remains an important guiding value for social work with vulnerable young people and that, today, we face more challenges than ever in realising this value.

Review questions

1 Why is social justice an important value in practice with young people?
2 What theories for practice are useful for youth work practice with young people?
3 What are the main challenges for youth workers today in realising the value of social justice in their practice?

Part 2

Social Work Practice Settings

9

SOCIAL WORK IN HEALTH CARE SETTINGS

Elspeth Browne

Chapter objectives

- To introduce this field of practice: its history, its changing character, ethical issues, and future
- To discuss the complexities of the field and social work's place within it
- To identify the challenges faced by social work in the field

Introduction

This chapter is a general introduction to the nature of social work in health care settings. Health care is something of a misnomer, of course, because most of these settings—for example, hospitals—care for the ill, not the healthy. About 60 per cent of qualified social workers are employed in the health field in Australia, in general and specialist hospitals (children's, maternity, psychiatric) and in community health centres. Mental health services are excluded from this chapter as they are dealt with elsewhere in this book.

As far as the community is concerned, it is rare for social workers in Australia to be attached to general medical practices. More usually, social workers are employed in community health centres. Social workers are also employed in the private hospital system; sometimes salaried, sometimes on a 'shared service' basis with an allied public hospital, and sometimes on a fee-for-service basis. The main focus of this chapter, however, will be on social work in public hospitals, in which the majority of workers in this field are found.

Health is the business of all social workers, since health service delivery in the developed world is one part of a comprehensive welfare system designed to meet a broad range of needs; for example, education, income security, or housing. Health care is one need common to all members of society. Furthermore, morbidity and mortality rates are indicators of overall social well-being. Even if social workers are not employed in the 'illness system', they need to have some grasp of the determinants of health and illness. We need to know how social conditions impact on health, how illness affects people and their social well-being, and how to access the illness system and make sense of its sometimes labyrinthine character on behalf of our clients. As part of our general social welfare arrangements, health services suffer many of the problems of distribution, equity, and access that are a continuing issue for all welfare services. Social workers committed to principles of social justice must be as concerned about equity in the health system as they are in other services.

The system of health service delivery is extremely complex. It ranges from primary care delivered by general practitioners through to highly sophisticated procedures carried out by tertiary institutions (acute specialist teaching hospitals). It is also extremely costly and labour-intensive. Its funding arrangements are a constant source of political and community concern and debate. Because of the complexity of the system, it is not possible to deal with some matters in great detail. This chapter is only an introduction and interested readers are encouraged to explore the subject further.

A short history of social work in health care settings

Hospitals in the Western world began life as welfare agencies, established in medieval times by religious orders for the care of the needy who had no one to look after them when sick, frail, or disabled. Long before the advent of the social work profession, there was an established tradition of health care provided by charities and religious orders in which the medical profession played little, if any, part. Shelter and nursing care were their functions. Nurses—either religious or, more commonly, poorly educated poor women—tended the ill, until nursing was professionalised from the middle of the nineteenth century.

Medical practitioners, however, became increasingly interested in hospitals as education became more scientific. Hospital patients offered a wealth of clinical experience for medical practitioners and students. Qualified practitioners gave their services in an honorary capacity and, in return, received exposure to a clinical practice not readily available from their paying customers, providing a rich educational experience for their students (George & Davis 1998).

Medicine eventually brought with it a scientific understanding of the working of the human body, of sepsis and anaesthesia, enabling care and particularly surgical practice that had not been previously possible. Consequently, by the latter part of the nineteenth century, hospitals had become highly specialised organisations for the care of all—rich or poor. This created administrative questions as to who would have entitlement to care, given these organisations started life as voluntary charitable institutions. Sociological knowledge combined with scientific medicine contributed to an increased understanding of the social determinants of health status, in particular quality of housing, nutrition, water supply, and waste disposal.

Not surprisingly, these influences resulted in the employment of professional social workers in the United Kingdom in 1895, and in the United States in 1905. The first trained social worker—known as an 'almoner' in the British hospital system—was Mary Stewart, appointed in 1895 to the Royal Free Hospital in London with the brief 'to prevent the abuse of the hospital by those who could afford to pay, to refer those in need of relief to the Poor Law, and to recommend to all who could afford to do so to join a Provident Dispensary' (Moberly Bell 1961, p. 28). In other words, her task was to sort the 'deserving' from the 'undeserving'—a far cry from the social worker's role in a universal health care system, open to all regardless of ability to pay.

From the time of colonisation, the development of the modern hospital in Australia largely reflected developments in the United Kingdom, but with some important differences. In the first instance, medical care was provided entirely by the colonial administration for convicts and the military, as part of the overall provision of services, which included food and shelter. The First Fleet carried with it naval surgeons, and the first hospital, the Sydney Dispensary (now Sydney Hospital), was established in 1816. It was funded by the proceeds of the government-controlled rum trade, hence its popular name: the Rum Hospital. The administration felt no obligation to provide for people other than those for whom it had direct responsibility, namely the convicts, and their warders. Once convicts who had served their sentence had been freed, and with the arrival of free settlers and private medical practitioners, provision for others became a community concern. Hospitals established by religious orders, and by the voluntary effort of philanthropic citizens, became more commonplace. The funding of health care shifted, to some extent, from the public purse to funding by donation, provident societies (the forerunner of health insurance), and fees paid by those who could afford them.

Professional social work in these institutions was a relative latecomer. However, concern for the poor and the general needs of the sick were acknowledged. Epps (1918), commenting on the first Australian social service department—established at Sydney's Royal Prince Alfred Hospital, then the largest general hospital—wrote of the hospital's most recent achievement:

> This, which is the first instance of this type of hospital work in a general hospital in Australasia, carries out most important duties, as affecting the patient in his or her private life, as distinct from treatment. By this means, patients are assisted to meet difficulties in their home-life, such as the care of their families in their absence, and many matters of their private affairs are adjusted; while after they leave hospital, they are assisted by advice, and in various ways, to overcome obstacles which have surrounded them. The hospital thus becomes more than a mere place for curative or operative work; it enables people who could not otherwise leave their homes to come to the hospital, and it helps them to obtain afterwards the full advantages of the treatment received (p. 86).

Epps's statement in broad terms bears some resemblance to the role of the social worker in health care today, although little to Mary Stewart's Royal Free Hospital brief more than 20 years earlier.

Education for professional social work came later, in part arising from the contingencies of the 1930s depression, when it was believed that assisting the needy required a more systematic and professional approach (Lawrence 1965). Interestingly, this approach was generated in the first instance in the field of medical social work. In 1929, Agnes McIntyre came to the Melbourne Hospital from St Thomas's Hospital, London, not only to set up the first almoner department in Australia but also to establish medical social work education. She was the first directress of training at the Victorian Institute of Hospital Almoners, Australia's first training body for social workers (O'Brien & Turner 1979).

In Sydney, training for general social work preceded specialist medical social work education. The New South Wales Institute of Hospital Almoners was established in 1936, to a large extent out of dissatisfaction with the generalist social work training available in New South Wales at that time, which, it was claimed, was insufficient for work in the specialised health care settings (Browne 1996).

These institutes were the only organisations to offer training in medical social work. Begun after the completion of a two-year diploma in social work, this training was regarded as an essential qualification for work in hospitals. Gradually, as new social work programmes developed in other Australian states, the emphasis shifted to generic education in preference to training by specific field. The Victorian institute closed its doors in 1950, followed by its New South Wales counterpart in 1957. By this time, education for health care practice was being absorbed into university social work programmes. As O'Brien and Turner (1979) commented, the director of the University of Melbourne's Social Studies department 'stressed the need for social work education and practice to emphasise the core or generic elements in social work regardless of setting, though acknowledging the differences in methods used and the special features of host agencies' (p. 12).

Social work in community health settings eventuated in the 1970s. With a few notable exceptions—such as 'well baby' clinics or family planning—community health centres were not established until the Whitlam Government (1972–75) seized this initiative. From the outset, they were conceived as multidisciplinary centres offering a range of health-related services, such as counselling, community nursing, physiotherapy, and other allied health services.

What, then, is the role of social work in contemporary health care settings? In many respects it has not altered greatly from Epps's definition. Social workers:

- assess the social circumstances of clients, establish the extent to which these have contributed to ill health, and alleviate these conditions
- plan adequate care in the community once people have been discharged from hospital
- attend to those matters that may interfere with health care
- ameliorate the social distress, including that of family and friends, caused by illness, disability, frailty, and death.

The methods employed are common to all social work interventions:

- interpersonal helping through casework and social group work
- advocacy and community development
- administration, social policy development, and research.

These interventions vary in emphasis, depending on where the social worker practises, but all are fundamental to social work practice in health care settings.

Practice issues

Hospitals may have started life as welfare organisations, but today they characterise their primary function as diagnosis and treatment of illness. Social work within such a health care service is a function often described as secondary to medical and nursing care. It is claimed that, in a secondary setting, workers do not have the same degree of control over referrals, the nature of their work, or their workplace as they would in a primary setting. Payne (1996) has argued, however, that since all social work (other than private practice) is carried out in agencies, it is affected by the organisational context. Nowhere is this more apparent than in hospitals, with their grounding in the so-called medical model, which is often seen as antithetical to social work based on a psychosocial model of practice.

The context clearly raises a number of practice issues:

- technology and concomitant patient care issues
- the changing face of illness, demographic change, and the medicalisation of social phenomena
- funding of costly technological and labour-intensive services with consequent administrative demands for accountability
- ethical dilemmas raised by these factors.

The impact of technology

The delivery of health care in the latter half of the twentieth century has been marked by technological change. Advances such as the transplantation of organs may be awe-inspiring, but the real miracles are the many procedures such as laser and 'keyhole' surgery that save people months of debilitation, pain, and dislocation.

Technological change and scientific medicine have brought many benefits; however, they place pressure on patients, their families, and on social workers. Length of stay in hospitals has shortened significantly. In consequence, social workers often must intervene quickly to ensure that their clients will be discharged to a safe environment, and to deal with the practical and emotional matters arising from illness. There is little time to move at the client's pace when a woman is confronted with making a hasty decision for mastectomy, followed by discharge a day or two after surgery. People leave hospital 'quicker and sicker', and are dependent on others for ongoing care. Social work intervention becomes one of crisis management, and hospital social workers know that they must refer their patients elsewhere for more long-term support and counselling. This creates significant issues of social justice where community support is minimal or non-existent.

The highly specialised nature of the contemporary hospital also has consequences for how people fare in this system. Patients may be perceived as simply 'an orthopaedic problem' or 'a heart case', not human beings, and although health care rhetoric assumes a holistic approach, in reality this may not be the case. Social work challenges these perceptions by taking account of patients' personal attributes, immediate contexts, and wider environments.

The specialised work in such settings inevitably involves a wide range of specialist professionals. The sick are subjected not only to doctors and nurses but also to a confusing procession of pathologists, radiologists, physiotherapists, dietitians, discharge planners, occupational therapists, and various others, depending on the nature of their condition and the location of their care. Furthermore, other medical teams may be consulted along the way, each with particular interest and expertise in one part of the patient's anatomy or functioning. Finally, shift work means a constant turnover of nurses, and therefore a constant change in fragile care relationships and continuity of care.

This demands a high level of teamwork and communication and, if this is less than effective, sometimes results in blurring of inter-professional boundaries, tension, and conflict. More particularly, patients are bewildered and distressed, and often ill-informed about the staff and their respective roles, let alone their medical condition, care, and treatment. Social workers with their interpersonal skills have a role to play in interpreting and mitigating, as much as possible, this alien environment, often taken for granted by those who work in it.

Changing social, demographic, and illness patterns

In tandem with technological change has come demographic change. Improvement in nutrition and basic hygiene, as well as mass immunisation programmes, has resulted in a decline in infant mortality. More people in the Western world today live out their 'three score years and ten' and beyond.

Other dramatic social changes, such as universal education, income security for the aged, and women's rights, generated a steady decline in family size throughout the twentieth century. In consequence, people over the age of 65 constitute a larger proportion of the Australian population than used to be the case, with the 'old old' becoming the fastest growing sector of the population. When the 'baby boomers' (those born between 1946 and the mid 1960s) start to turn 65 from 2010, assuming birth rates and immigration remain stable, the elderly will constitute about one in four of the population.

The consequences of these trends for the health care system are already exercising the minds of policy makers. In an ordinary life cycle, our use of health care services is highest at birth and at death, with the elderly more likely to use the whole range of health services— hospitals, general practitioners, community services, pharmaceutical, and subacute services such as hostels and nursing homes—than any other age group. Health care arrangements, with the exception of obstetric and paediatric services, serve an older clientele with most users being the 'old old'.

Older people, however, do not fit neatly into a system geared to the high technology specialisation of the modern hospital. Their medical problems often are multi-systemic, affecting more than one physiological system. Their expectations of the system are based on an understanding established decades earlier. Their care in the community is often complicated by changed social conditions, where women, traditionally carers, are unavailable due to work commitments. Social workers in health care today are likely to be engaged in ameliorating the circumstance of older people in the community and ensuring access to decent care.

While older people are the major users of health care, the demographic change is something to be celebrated, since it indicates a better state of health in society overall. Palmer and Short (1989) argue that health care personnel have an 'overly negative view', and that older people should not be regarded as a burden. While older people are the more frequent users of service, most older people, in fact, will not need the most costly types of health care delivery (Palmer & Short 1989).

More troubling is the health status and lack of equity of Aboriginal Australians, who suffer rates of morbidity and mortality that are a disgrace in a developed country (George & Davis 1998). Aboriginal people have not benefited from the social changes that have improved health in the twentieth century. They are the victims of poor nutrition, poor housing, inadequate water supply and waste disposal, and the diseases of social alienation, such as violence and abuse of both legal and illicit drugs (Bates & Linder-Pelz 1990). Writers such as Bates, Linder-Pelz, George, and Davis note that for many Aboriginal people, Western methods of health care are inadequate or inappropriate. Their disadvantage may be further compounded by life in isolated communities with limited access to care. Perhaps Aboriginal health status will improve only when Indigenous people are able to assert more control over their social circumstance and destinies, through strengthening of basic human rights.

Another demographic factor that has had an impact on health care has been the influx of immigrants after World War II, particularly those of non-English-speaking backgrounds. Apart from language problems, culture sometimes may be a significant barrier to health care. Social workers need to be sensitive to cultural difference, to be aware of their own cultural bias, and to be able to use health service interpreters effectively to ensure access to care (Ferguson 1991; Barker 1991).

Technological and demographic changes are only part of the dynamic changes in health care that social workers have accommodated. Social change—particularly the changing place of women in Australian society, perhaps the most significant change of all—has made a contribution. While the demand for obstetric services may be lower today, the demand for quality, particularly women's control of the circumstances of childbirth, has grown. First-time mothers are now older, and have sometimes required assistance with conception, perhaps needing counselling support to deal with infertility issues. Furthermore, the trend towards the one-child family means that there is a fear of litigation among obstetricians should a less than perfect infant result, especially for an older mother. The rate of caesarean section has increased in consequence. Early discharge sometimes leaves women unsupported at home, with more need for community support that, in earlier times, may have been provided by family.

Social workers are acutely aware of diminishing family support in care of the frail aged, but other age groups also need support. Caring has been almost solely the role of women, but their availability to carry out this role is increasingly circumscribed, with little acknowledgment on the part of government in terms of policies. Health care policies press for early discharge, and shortened length of stay in hospitals, without providing the concomitant community support to make this an effective health care strategy.

Women's independence has also contributed to the growing incidence of single parent-hood. This issue was once regarded as a matter of concern for the community, and for social workers, in particular, if adoption were planned. This is rarely an issue for social workers today, unless there are other issues, such as relationship problems, parenting difficulties, financial need, and suchlike.

Women have taken a more active role in the wider society, and their health status in terms of life expectancy has improved relative to that of men. However, according to George and Davis (1998), women experience particular risks: those of poverty and violence (par-ticularly sexual abuse). Social workers have an established role in responding to sexual abuse and violence against women, cases that almost always come to the attention of the health system in the first instance.

The ageing process itself has had an impact on women. Women can expect to outlive men by some years. One social consequence is that men may be cared for by their partners until death, while women find themselves alone when aged, frail, or disabled. As social workers know, it is women who most often need alternative accommodation in old age.

Patterns of illness have changed. New diseases have replaced illnesses such as tuberculo-sis, poliomyelitis, or rheumatic fever that used to require protracted and disruptive care and treatment. Phenomena such as AIDS, child abuse, occupational overuse syndrome, sudden infant death, post-traumatic stress disorder, and abuse of illicit drugs have emerged in their place. Some are the result of behavioural change; some (like sudden infant death) increase in importance as other causes of mortality have disappeared; some are long-standing, but have been redefined as issues because of changing community standards; some are the direct result of technological change. Some, such as drug abuse, involve the most marginalised people in Australian society—the young unemployed, the homeless, the alienated—whom the wider society chooses to ignore. Political debate centres on whether drug abuse is a legal or health issue, with little recognition of its social origins.

Whatever the phenomenon and its cause, all illness presents a crisis. This is brought into sharp relief in emergency departments and intensive care units, where social workers are in increasing demand to support the distressed, to provide information and interpretation, and to liaise with family and services, such as the police. As already mentioned, social workers are central to sexual assault care services, where the traumatised need support and care, as well as assistance with the legal system. Similarly, social workers are centrally involved in cases where children present with non-accidental injuries, discussed in more detail later.

Funding and accountability in the health care system

The major debate today focuses not on health issues, and least of all their social causes and consequences, but on the costs of providing a health service. Much publicity has focused on underfunding, and the 'crisis' in the universal health service system (Medicare), with little attention shown to Australia's comparative success internationally at keeping health costs down, maintaining access to services, while producing good mortality and morbidity data (Leeder 1999; Metherell 1999).

The system is largely funded through the public purse (Sax 1990). In the prevailing climate of economic rationalism and managerialism, the costs of a highly labour-intensive and technology-dependent service, which requires constant monitoring, justification, and accountability, are questioned (Davis 1995). Limits to resources result in competing interests, rationing of service, and closure of services.

In a publicly funded system, social workers, like other health professionals, are caught up in the demands of providing and documenting a quality service through total quality management and quality improvement programmes, while accounting for every minute by sophisticated computerised data collection. They can sometimes feel that their clinical work is in conflict with administrative demands.

Yet these administrative and accountability requirements can be used to support the case for an increase in resources. The accreditation mechanisms of the Australian Council on Health Care Standards demand the visibility of social work service. Social workers are consulted and represented on committees at the level of area health boards to ward and team committees in the workplace. Perhaps, as the system with its biomedical dominance becomes more answerable, either because of litigation or the move to evidence-based medicine, it may begin to take stock of psychosocial as well as biological outcomes, client satisfaction, and demands for patient autonomy and rights. As Khadra (1998) asked, in his chilling description of patienthood: 'What price compassion?'

Ethical issues

Resource limitations, rationing, and distribution inevitably pose questions of social justice and ethics. Social workers have to prioritise their work, making choices about whose needs must come first, often doing more with less. In targeting particular groups for service, they know that some may not have their needs met adequately.

In this dilemma, social work is not alone. George and Davis (1998) discuss the implications of medical technology for genetic engineering, right to life, in-vitro fertilisation, and life support, claiming that scientific medicine increasingly has had to justify intervention (particularly costly ones with questionable patient benefit) in terms of social consequences. Social workers may often be consulted on these matters: for example, to find out the views of family when questions of life support are being decided.

On a more day-to-day basis, social workers have their own professional ethical dilemmas to contend with. Lawrence (1999) argues that, because professionals have power and influence in society, 'it is especially important that they conform to ethically justifiable standards'. For social workers, these standards are outlined in the AASW Code of Ethics (2000a), which emphasises the primacy of the client's interests.

While this may appear simple enough, because social workers in health care deal with a complex array of demands (organisational, societal, and familial, as well as those of the client), conflict between interests, and resolving this conflict, is a constant challenge. By way of example, a hospital administrator, conscious of efficiency and budget limitations, demands the immediate discharge of an elderly patient. The patient's doctor also wants the bed cleared in order to admit another patient in urgent need of medical attention. The patient wants to go home, but lives alone and needs assistance with personal care, meals, domestic tasks, and shopping. Community support may not be available for some time. The patient's family cannot decide who, if any, among them will be able to care for the patient.

Sometimes social workers may become so embroiled in organisational demands and familial problems that they lose sight of who the clients are, especially if clients are infants or elderly people with dementia, brain damage, or who are unconscious or unable to express their own needs. Respecting client autonomy is often not possible, but the social worker must serve the client's interests, the more so when there is conflict between the autonomy of the client and the worker's duty of care.

In some cases, the superficially simple concept of 'client' is obscured by policies that refer to the patient as a 'customer' (Schembri 1995), and that require workers to give equal consideration to co-workers, the organisation, family, and community, including taxpayers, as 'customers' of the health care system. Social workers need to be clear-headed about who their clients are if they are to practise ethically.

Health services have not been spared the widespread movement to corporatisation of public services in Australia. This raises particular ethical problems for social workers. The values of the corporation and its handmaiden, managerialism, often do not sit easily with social work values. The measure of outcomes as a measure of efficiency does not always accord with social work's value of respect for individual rights, for client empowerment and self-determination. A hospital administrator may insist that a patient be discharged to a nursing home in order to meet length of stay criteria, regardless of his or her wishes, financial circumstances, or family convenience. Social justice and economic rationalism may be in conflict (Browne & Davidson 2004).

Lawrence (1999) developed a model whereby the professional might assess ethical conduct. Much depends on who defines the situation, who responds, the criteria for decision-making, who implements the decision, and with what result. At each stage in the process the 'why' must be assessed; in other words, ethical behaviour is defined by values.

Social work values, encoded by the AASW and defining the focus of the profession, encompass social justice, and respect for people, service, integrity, and competence. Some workers experience difficulty in health settings when they must deal with, and respect, people whose values conflict with their own. Comprehensive health care must serve all comers: people with racist, or sexist positions, for example, or people whose culture accepts behaviours that some may find reprehensible. Some find it difficult to respect people whose behaviours—for instance, smoking, overeating, drug and alcohol abuse, unsafe sex—have caused their illness or disability. Not being judgmental is a constant challenge.

Respecting the client's confidences can also be difficult, particularly when there are legal implications. Social workers do not have privilege in the courts, and must argue a case in court to maintain confidence if contempt of court is to be avoided. More frequent, however, is the question of what to record in medical notes, and how to convey to the client that there are limits to confidentiality, particularly when maintaining confidence is not in the interests of the patient.

Finally, social workers have an obligation to advocate on behalf of their clients or for a group of disadvantaged clients. This is sometimes difficult to do individually, as most social workers in the health field are public servants, bound by the rules of the service that do not allow employees to be publicly critical. Here, social workers may make the needs of clients known through their professional organisation or other outside bodies as appropriate. Lobbying for change through membership of groups of concerned citizens is often effective.

Returning to the case of the elderly person's discharge plan outlined above, one long-term goal may be to apply political pressure to government through outside organisations for adequate funding of services. To achieve a desirable outcome for clients, then, requires research, data collection, and well-supported arguments, all necessary parts of ethical social work practice.

Ethics in context

1 An elderly person is ready for discharge from hospital, insists on going home but needs care and the carer is alcoholic and thought to be abusive. No community assistance is immediately available. What are your first steps in this situation?

2 The partner of your client tells you something in confidence that she doesn't want the client to know but which is integral to the care, health, and well-being of your client. How will you deal with this information?

The future for social work

That the delivery of health care is rapidly changing is, by now, apparent. It is an extremely dynamic and challenging field of practice, in which professional Australian social workers have worked for more than 70 years. Furthermore, the professionalised nature of health care delivery has largely ensured that those employed in it are properly qualified for the job. Even so, much of what drives social work today has changed very little in that time: the aims and objectives, and the profession's values and ethical position have barely altered. What then is its future?

Patford (1999), citing the Council of Australian Governments' (COAG) reform agenda for health, notes the key objectives: to shift health care policy away from institutions, to encourage health promotion and preventive programmes, to expand choice for consumers, to reduce reliance on expensive medical services, and to foster service integration. With British and particularly North American models to draw on, policy makers appear determined to cut health costs by reducing access to and length of stay in the most expensive part of the system, namely hospitals. In this scenario, social workers increasingly may be employed in the community, keeping people out of hospitals and ensuring they are cared for away from costly institutions.

To some extent this is already occurring, with management and clinical tools such as casemix, pre-admission clinics, clinical pathways, discharge planning, and early discharge programmes, in all of which social workers have had a part to play. Social workers are also firmly established in the community, although perhaps not in the numbers that will ensure the brave new world of the 'hospital in the home'.

Here is the paradox: Is the health care system reverting to its medieval form, in which the well-to-do will be properly cared for at home, and only those without care will have relatively protracted periods of hospitalisation? If family members, namely women, are not available to care for the sick and people do not have the means to purchase home care, to what extent will community service arrangements be adequately funded to support health care objectives? Will the physically sick, frail, and disabled be deinstitutionalised, to be forced to fare as those with mental health problems?

The social worker is often used as a troubleshooter, and sometimes as a necessary thorn in the side or conscience of health bureaucrats and other health professionals, reminding them of social obligations, patient rights, and ethical practice. These may not be comfortable roles to perform, but are necessary if patient needs are to be met.

Patford (1999) also points out that social workers face some competition for these roles, particularly from nurse counsellors and psychologists. Social workers need to be more assertive in articulating their functions, and they need to demonstrate their worth through research, documentation, and evaluation of outcomes. Their expertise is not necessarily self-evident. They also need to be more assertive in carving out new roles, especially in such areas as preventive work and health promotion.

Finally, wherever social work is used in health practice—in hospitals, subacute care, in the community—difficult social conditions of unemployment, poverty, stress, family breakdown, alienation, and violence will contribute to higher morbidity. Social workers have a role outside the health system in social action and in social movements (Peterson 1994). In this respect, social work has a long tradition of grappling with these and similar issues both inside and outside the health field.

Review questions

1   In some health service systems, social workers work entirely in the community accepting referrals from hospital staff, private medical practitioners, and others. What are the advantages and disadvantages of such a system?

2   While funding health care seems to be a major pre-occupation of policy makers, access to health services in a timely way is the pre-occupation of the sick, injured, disabled, and chronically ill. In Australia, what do you think are the major barriers to access?

Acknowledgments

I am indebted to the Directors of Social Work in Teaching Hospitals (New South Wales), and particularly to Jill Davidson of The St George Hospital, for their helpful suggestions and comments.

10

SOCIAL WORK PRACTICE IN MENTAL HEALTH

Robert Bland

Chapter objectives

- To provide an overview of the practice of social work within the field of mental health in Australia
- To outline the ethical considerations for practitioners in this field
- To highlight issues related to clients, consumers, and families in the mental health system

Introduction

Social work has a long history of practice and innovation in the mental health area (Aviram 1997). This history extends through a diversity of hospital and community based work settings, involving a range of practice modalities in individual, group, family, and community work, including policy development and management. As well as working in adult mental health, social workers are employed in areas of child and adolescent mental health, specialised aged care settings, and with specific population groups such as Indigenous Australians and ethnic communities. While it is possible to describe broad aspects of social work practice, each of these areas has its own specialised knowledge base, practice competencies, and challenges for practice.

If mental health is defined broadly to include individual well-being, self-esteem, and healthy relationships, then social workers are involved in mental health work in every work setting. A more useful focus for this chapter is to consider social work practice in the area of mental illness and disorder. This is a pragmatic as well as a principled focus. It reflects the core business of the range of treatment and rehabilitation settings where social workers are employed, but it is a reminder that people with mental illness and their families represent the most disadvantaged and vulnerable end of the mental health spectrum. For this group the impact of illness or disorder on sense of self, relationships, family welfare, life chances, income security, and broader quality of life (the areas of primary concern for social work) is most severe.

This chapter is divided into three broad sections, beginning with an attempt to capture the complexity of practice in the area by defining the domain of social work in mental health. Section two considers important developments in the policy context for practice by examining the National Mental Health Plans and the emergence of consumer and carer perspectives on service development and professional practice. Section three considers the current practice issues for social workers in the mental health area.

The domain of social work practice

The domain of social work in mental health is that of the social context and social consequences of mental illness and mental disorder. The purpose of practice is to restore individual, family, and community well-being, to promote the development of each individual's power and control over their lives, and to promote principles of social justice. Social work practice occurs at the interface between the individual and the environment: social work activity begins with the individual, and extends to the contexts of family, social networks, community, and the broader society.

Social context
At the level of 'social context', social work is concerned with the way each individual's social environment shapes their experience of mental illness. Its concerns include issues of individual personality, vulnerability and resilience, family functioning, strengths and stressors, support networks, culture, community, class, ethnicity, and gender. Beyond the intrapsychic aspects of ego functioning, self-esteem, and meaning making, and interpersonal aspects of family functioning and personal relationships, its concerns include broader social issues of economic well-being, employment, and housing.

Social consequences
At the level of 'social consequences', social work is concerned with the impact of mental illness on the individual, the family and personal relationships, and the broader community, including the impact on sense of self, life chances, and family well-being, and on economic security, employment, and housing. Social work is concerned with the interface between mental illness and broader health and welfare issues such as child protection and domestic violence.

Social justice
At the level of 'social justice', social work is concerned with issues of stigma and discrimination, of political freedoms and civil rights, of promoting access to necessary treatment and support services, and of promoting consumer and carer rights to participation and choice in mental health services. It is concerned with making all human services more accessible and responsive to the specific needs and wishes of people with mental illness, and their family carers.

Underpinning this model of the domain of social work in mental illness are a number of key values. As well as the core social work values of respect for the individual, self-determination, and confidentiality, there are values that relate specifically to the mental health area. Social workers recognise the complexity of human experience, and try to see beyond the limits of illness, diagnosis, and treatment labels. Accordingly, social workers recognise that people are much more than an illness or diagnostic label, and that individuals have broad human needs beyond specific treatment needs. Similarly, social workers stress the 'personhood' rather than the 'patienthood' of individuals who are consumers of mental health services. Social workers recognise the importance of family and friendship relationships beyond concepts of 'carer'.

Social workers recognise the importance of working in respectful partnerships with consumers and family carers. These respectful partnerships are marked by efforts to ensure consumer and carer participation and choice in decision-making and self-determination, as well as mutuality in assessment and action planning. Partnership and mutuality are values that extend to working with social work colleagues.

Social workers are sensitive to the impact of illness, treatment, and stigma on the experience of people with mental illness and their family carers. Social work practice seeks to address issues of equity, access, participation, and power directly with individuals and families, and at the broader systems levels where discrimination and stigma may operate at a structural level. Human qualities of empathy, compassion, and hopefulness are central to social work practice. Other values are a sensitivity to process, and principles of mutuality, respect, honesty, and integrity in day-to-day work practices.

The context for practice

The policy context for practice

Developments in mental health policy in the last 10 years have provided an exciting context of change and challenge for social worker practice. These changes began when the Eisen and Wolfenden report (1988), which began as a review of Commonwealth funding of mental health, finally recommended a proactive role for the Commonwealth in what had formerly been an area of state responsibility. In order to promote mental health services at a national level, the report recommendations included adoption of a national mental health policy, direct funding of state mental health programmes, and a framework for ongoing Commonwealth coordination of service developments including the possibility of uniform mental health legislation.

The Mental Health Discussion Paper presented to the Australian Health Ministers Advisory Council (AHMAC 1990) in October 1989 incorporated the substantive findings of the Eisen and Wolfenden report, and formed the basis for the *National Mental Health Policy* (Australian Health Ministers 1992), which was finally adopted in 1992. The principles outlined in this report have subsequently provided the policy framework for all aspects of mental health activity—programme and service delivery, legal developments, research, and teaching.

These underlying principles are as follows:

- Services should be provided in a multifaceted and multidisciplinary manner.
- People with mental disorders have potential for personal growth and the right to opportunities to support this growth.
- People with mental disorder should have the same civil, political, economic, social, and cultural rights as everyone else in the community.
- The community and individual have a justifiable right to protection.
- Positive consumer outcomes are the first priority in mental health policy and service delivery.
- Priority should be given to people with severe mental illness and disability.
- Services should encourage consumer participation in decision-making.
- Positive outcomes depend on well-trained staff and strong support for carers and advocates.

The policy covered such issues as consumer rights, the relationship between mental health services and the general health sector, service mix, promotion and prevention, primary care services, carers, non-governmental organisations, mental health workforce, legislation, research and evaluation, standards, and monitoring and accountability.

The *National Mental Health Policy*, and subsequent policy developments such as the *National Standards for Mental Health Services* (AHMAC 1996), the *Second National Mental Health Plan* (Australian Health Ministers 1998) and the *National Mental Health Plan 2003–2008* (Australian Health Ministers 2003), have encouraged a broad approach to mental health issues and there is a clear recognition of the importance of the social context and social consequences of mental illness. Subsequent policy developments have extended the radical principles of the original policy to consolidate the importance of the concept of 'partnership' among service providers, service consumers, and family carers. There is a specific emphasis on incorporating consumer involvement in all aspects of service development, service provision, research, and evaluation, and the training of the mental health workforce. Achieving such partnership arrangements in fact, rather than in principle, is probably the greatest challenge to the professions who staff the mental health services. It is the sort of challenge that social work has traditionally embraced and enjoyed.

Consumer and carer issues

A central feature of mental health policy and service development in the last decade has been an emerging recognition of the importance of consumer and carer perspectives in all areas of mental health activity. This is formally established in the National Mental Health Plan, and restated in subsequent reviews and developments of the policy. The family self-help and advocacy movement developed quite separately from the consumer movement, and the needs and demands of carers and consumers have distinct differences and well as similarities (Bland 1995). Their common interests are based on the need to challenge the dominance of the service provider definitions of the experience of mental illness, to be heard and respected by service providers, and to be included in the various activities of service planning, implementation, and evaluation.

Consumer and carer participation in all areas is based on two key principles:

- Participation is a right—By this argument, the recipients of services have a right to be fully involved in planning, delivering, and evaluating those services.
- Participation ensures better services—By this argument, consumer and carer participation in services is a way of improving services. Participation will strengthen accountability mechanisms and ensure increased responsiveness of mental health services to the needs of consumers and carers.

Formal support for the promotion of the voices of consumers and carers has come through a range of sources. As part of the National Mental Health Strategy, the Commonwealth and state governments established formal advisory bodies made up of consumer and carer appointees. These were known as Consumer Advisory Groups (CAGS) at the state level, and NCAG (National Community Advisory Group) at the federal level. These advisory bodies served to bring consumer and carer interests to the highest levels of decision-making and policy development. From 1998, NCAG was replaced by the Mental Health Council of Australia, a body representing a diversity of mental health interest groups. Formal articulation of the rights of carers and consumers has been expressed in the *Mental Health Statement of Rights and Responsibilities* (Australian Health Ministers 1991) and reinforced in all subsequent policy documents making up the National Mental Health Strategy. This policy guarantees consumer rights to participation, as far as possible, in decision-making around all aspects of mental health activity. Rights of carers are similarly defined.

These developments have been enhanced by a number of consumer-based projects emphasising the establishment of structures for including consumer involvement, and encouraging training for consumers in advocacy. The Lemon Tree Project (VMIAC 1997), and other activity of the Victorian Mental Illness Advisory Council, has provided a theoretical and practical basis to the consumer advocacy movement. Writers such as Epstein (Epstein & Shaw 1997) have developed the concepts of consumer empowerment beyond slogans to detailed statements of the activities and processes of consumer participation. The Community Development Project (Spice Consulting), an initiative of the National Mental Health Strategy, has developed an extremely useful consumer guide to advocacy known as *The Kit—A Guide to the Advocacy We Choose to Do* (Spice Consulting 1998). This project has summarised much of the knowledge and skill base of the consumer advocacy movement and is intended as a DIY guide for consumer and carer advocates.

The concept of partnership among consumers, service providers, and family carers has been developed through the annual activities of The Mental Health Services Conference (THEMHS). These annual conferences have reinforced the importance of drawing professionals, consumers, and carers together in order to get the best services for consumers and carers, and the best education for mental health professionals. While success has been achieved in key areas of policy development, service provision, and education and training, it has been less successfully applied to mental health research (Bland 1995).

The importance of engaging carers and consumers in developing practice is reflected in the methodology of the Social Work and Mental Health Competencies Project (Bland et al. 1999). The project team involved consumers and carers, as well as practising social workers, in the process of reflecting on the range of social work activity. Consumers and carers were clear in their understanding of what makes a good social worker:

- knowledge of psychiatric disorders, their treatment, and prognosis
- medication and side effects
- the mental health legislation and assisting carers involved in the involuntary hospital admissions of family members
- community resources including special benefits and accommodation.

Consumers and carers saw social workers as being the liaison person between them and the treating psychiatrist and multidisciplinary team. Carers, in particular, requested that social workers be trained to assertively approach psychiatrists to obtain relevant information on how best to support their mentally ill relatives. They acknowledged the need for confidentiality, but stated this should be in the context of an appropriate duty of care towards the client and their family.

Underlying consumer and carer concerns was the very clear plea that social workers in the mental health services treat consumers and carers with dignity, and that they listen to their issues and concerns. It was often the common, basic courtesies that were most appreciated. These included phone calls being returned; a non-judgmental attitude; being treated with respect, as an intelligent human being; and being listened to. Social workers who showed warmth and empathy, who were both assertive and firm, but who were able to help clients identify and appropriately address their individual issues, were particularly appreciated.

The project identified a number of specific consumer and carer based principles for social work practice. In summary, social workers must:

- treat consumers and carers with respect and dignity, empathy, kindness, and compassion
- extend to their clients the common courtesies appreciated by society as a whole
- honour the individual's abilities and strengths, and encourage them to set realistic goals and work towards achieving them
- acknowledge the person's individuality and their unique place in their family and in the community
- have the basic skills of assertiveness, reflective listening, advocacy, and conflict resolution to enable them to make the most positive contribution to a person's life
- listen to the concerns of carers and learn to balance consumer confidentiality with their duty of care for consumers and their carers
- actively participate in the multidisciplinary teams and liaise between the consumer, carer, and treating psychiatrist
- be open to feedback from consumers and carers to ensure that individual needs and desires are appropriately addressed
- appreciate their value and the importance of their role in mental health services.

The principles identified by consumers and carers are consistent with social work practice principles. They appear deceptively simple but represent a powerful reminder to social workers that basic human qualities are essential for effective helping. The 'Competencies Project' as it has become known, was recently re-endorsed by the AASW (2003) as forming the basis for social work involvement in the *National Practice Standards for the Mental Health Workforce* (Australian Health Ministers Advisory Council 2003) and other projects within the broader education and training initiatives of the Commonwealth government.

Issues for practice

This section will consider a number of key areas for practice. These include the need for a model of practice to include medical, social, and human aspects of mental illness, welfare aspects of practice, social work in multidisciplinary settings, and ethical issues for practice.

Towards a model for practice

Social work has traditionally sought to emphasise the social and personal aspects of mental illness and disorder, rejecting the simple disease models of mental illness as narrow and somehow dehumanising. In the mental hospitals, community clinics, therapeutic communities, housing and rehabilitation projects, and in working with families of children with disorders, social workers have stressed the need to look beyond medical definitions of problems, to locate people in a social context, and to work with a person and not an illness. Without the capacity for prescribing medication or other invasive treatments, social workers have sought to assist through the purposeful application of relationships with people, in counselling, group work, family therapy, and through community work.

In the past, this emphasis on social aspects of mental health problems has been accompanied by a deep suspicion of a 'medical model' of mental illness. This very confusing term has many meanings (Knight 1998). At one level it means that a wide range of deviant or unusual behaviour is defined as 'illness' requiring medical intervention. Thus, not only are clearly organic conditions such as behavioural disturbance associated with brain tumours seen as illness, but so, too, are schizophrenia, depressions, and even differences in sexual behaviour, or responses to extreme personal stress. By this model, treatment begins with a thorough process of assessment and diagnosis, followed by medical intervention, typically with drugs. Critics of the medical model claim that the emphasis is on the illness, and not the person, and on the power of the medical system at the expense of the power of the consumer of services (Engel 1977).

A second interpretation of 'medical model' refers to the distribution of power and authority in the treatment services. When some social workers complain about the 'medical model' they sometimes mean that medical doctors have most of the power in the system, and that the opinions of the social worker do not carry as much authority.

Social workers have been strongly influenced by social models of health, including the labelling theories of Scheff and others (Scheff 1966), and have often applied sociological or psychogenic theories to explain mental disorder. Beels and McFarlane (1982), in an analysis of changing conceptions of mental disorder over time, describe the three decades following World War II as a time of 'radical environmentalism'. Alternative non-medical explanations of the nature and cause of such mental disorders as schizophrenia were popular at this time and strongly influenced mental health workers including social workers. These radical theories suggested that mental disorder in the individual was based on a response to an intolerable environment, usually disordered family relationships (Hatfield 1987).

The research evidence of the last 30 years shows the importance of adopting a multidimensional understanding of the nature and cause of mental disorder: what is known as a *bio-psychosocial* model of disorder (Australian Health Ministers 1992). This model recognises the complex interaction of biological, psychological, and environmental factors that lead to the development and expression of mental disorder. In schizophrenia, for example, research has shown not only the importance of genetic and biochemical factors in the development of the illness but also the importance of social factors in promoting recovery and preventing relapse (Falloon et al. 1984). The broader impact of the disorder on the life circumstances of the person and their family is also part of the important social component of the condition. Other disorders, such as postnatal depression, are similarly complex in origin and construction. Given this complexity, both simple disease models of disorder and social models of disorder are inadequate and unhelpful. These conceptual issues are well developed in the opening chapters of the recently published text *Mental Health in Australia* (Meadows & Singh 2001).

The extent to which all of the professional disciplines in mental health have adopted a common conceptual framework of mental disorder for practice is reflected in the final report of the Deakin Consultancy project *Education and Training Partnerships in Mental Health* (Deakin Human Services 1999) conducted as part of the National Mental Health Strategy. The report details the common areas of knowledge, skills, and values that inform the practice of psychiatry, occupational therapy, social work, mental health nursing, and clinical psychology. For example, all disciplines share a knowledge of the causes, epidemiology, and treatment of mental illness, as well as a knowledge of the historical, cultural, social, and political contexts for mental health and the treatment of mental illness. Social workers retain a focus on the social context and consequences of mental illness and disorder, but their practice is based on this shared understanding of the bio-psychosocial dimensions of mental health.

In summary, social workers employed in mental health settings are confronted with the need to develop a model for practice that is both respectful and critical of the medical model. They need to understand the biomedical discourse and appreciate the way that discourse shapes the knowledge base for practice for all disciplines, including their own. At the same time they need to be critical of the limits of the model to define and describe disorder and response, and its impact on people diagnosed with mental illness, and also be sensitive to the issues of power and marginality that are fundamental to the mental health field.

In recent years the debate between social and medical models of mental illness has largely been overtaken by a growing challenge to mental health workers to adopt a more human approach to practice. This challenge is developed elsewhere in this chapter in discussing the rise of the consumer and carer movements, but central to it is the recognition that workers should value the lived experience of people with mental illness as a starting point for practice. The approach stresses the humanity of the worker as well as the consumer and family carers. Concepts like recovery, hope, and spirituality are increasingly recognised as basic to working in the mental health area (Bland & Darlington 2002).

Welfare dimensions of practice in mental illness

An enduring tension in social work practice in mental health has been the extent to which practitioners are concerned with clinical and counselling issues, or with the broader social welfare aspects of income security, work, and housing. There has been a tendency for social workers to see therapeutic work as more important, or perhaps more exciting or 'professional' than welfare work (Segal & Baumohl 1981; Bland & O'Neil 1990). There are, however, good reasons for focusing on the broader welfare issues for practice.

The limited research literature available suggests a strong link between long-term mental illness and poverty (Eisen & Wolfenden 1988). Bland and O'Neil (1990) suggest that the enduring welfare issues for people with mental illness include income security, housing, stigma, and powerlessness. Many people with schizophrenic illness find it difficult to find and sustain employment, and rely on disability pensions as their only source of income, often for many years. As a result they experience long-term poverty based on low fixed incomes. Often this financial burden is shared by family members. Parents may continue to provide a home for adult children with mental illness, thus reducing costs of housing but at the expense of diminished independence and quality of life for all concerned. Where people on disability support are living in private rental or 'board and care' situations, they are generally paying a high proportion of their low fixed income as rent or board. This leaves very little disposable income, and little opportunity to save to move out to more independent living. In these circumstances, housing projects that seek to link people with more affordable long-term housing become an essential part of rehabilitation. Social work involvement in developing and administering such projects represents a significant area of professional practice.

Despite the general blurring of professional roles within the treatment team, social workers are generally seen as having the responsibility for the broader welfare needs of the consumer (Black 1984). For many people, long-term adjustment to illness and disorder, and indeed the process of recovery itself, depends on development of effective social supports and resources. People need good housing, work, and income security in order to feel secure and stay well. Beyond this therapeutic imperative, such benefits are part of their broader rights as citizens. Retaining an appropriate emphasis on welfare aspects of mental illness remains an essential part of the social work role, and it is essential, both in terms of the needs and rights of people with mental illness, that this role is properly exercised.

Practice in a multidisciplinary setting

An enduring issue for social work practice is that of defining and defending the role of social work within the multidisciplinary team. A variation on this theme has been the tendency in recent years for mental health services to adopt generic position descriptions for staff, rather than discipline specific positions. It is now just as likely for services to advertise for case-managers or project officers as it is for them to advertise for social workers or nurses. This 'a-disciplinary' approach to staffing creates both opportunities and threats for social workers.

The Deakin consultancy on the education and training of the mental health professions (Deakin Human Services 1999) identified core knowledge, skills, and values held by the five disciplines: nursing, occupational therapy, clinical psychology, social work, and psychiatry. These core areas were augmented by discipline-specific skills and knowledge. The project recognised that competition for authority in mental health among the professions was ongoing and intense. Significantly, social work was seen as having a generic professional training, and, unlike medicine, nursing and psychology, required only a basic degree as preparation for practice. Social work's generic training, and its connection to the broader welfare system, was seen as a strength for the discipline, but the comparatively limited exposure to mental health content in undergraduate teaching was seen as threatening the ability of the profession to compete for authority within the multidisciplinary context.

This issue is addressed by the *Social Work and Mental Health Competencies Project* (Bland et al. 1999). In their conclusions, the authors of the report recommend that the professional association and the Schools of Social Work within the universities work towards increasing the opportunities for postgraduate education in the area of social work and mental health. They further recommend that social workers are clear and articulate about the social work role in mental health, and its importance in any comprehensive mix of services for consumers and family carers.

Recent Commonwealth initiatives in education and training, particularly the *National Practice Standards for the Mental Health Workforce* (Australian Health Ministers Advisory Council 2003) and the currently active Implementation Committee for this project, have identified the need for the social work profession to address more systematically the teaching of mental health skills and content in undergraduate programmes around the country.

Clearly the traditional areas of concern for social work as outlined in this chapter are likely to continue to be central to the welfare of people with mental illness and their families. The task for social work as a profession within the contested domain of mental health may be twofold: ensuring competence based on a detailed knowledge base, skills, and values; and promoting the importance of the broader human and social aspects of mental illness. Establishing partnerships with consumers and carers around these issues will be one important strategy for helping to shape the mental health agenda more broadly—beyond narrow issues of illness and treatment.

Ethical issues for practice

Social work practice in mental health has traditionally confronted a number of ethical issues. As well as the need to adopt a knowledge, skills, and value base appropriate to the demands of the workplace, social work continues to struggle with broader issues of the social control component of practice, and with balancing the needs of people with mental illness with the needs of their families.

Social control

Mental health social workers are frequently given special powers under mental health legislation, and are part of the broader debate in mental health about the appropriate legal arrangements to provide treatment for people against their will (Kirk & Einbinder 1994). This complex debate is based on the extent to which people with mental illness can choose to refuse treatment. In recent years, family advocates have suggested that processes that protect individual civil rights may compromise not only the rights of individuals to proper and speedy treatment but also the rights of family carers to support and protection (Lefley 1993).

Individual social workers will resolve these ethical dilemmas on a case-by-case basis. A number of simple principles should be applied. Firstly, the legal context for practice must be clearly understood by the individual social worker so that the civil rights of people with mental illness are fully protected. It is important that individuals, and their families, are fully informed of the legal processes that govern their options. Secondly, the social worker should adopt a critical analysis of each practice situation, so that the competing needs and rights of all the participants are considered. Difficult decisions are sometimes required, and it is essential that these are made after careful reflection, rather than in response to agency demands. Thirdly, it is important that the social worker has access to professional consultation in steering an informed path through the difficulties.

The issue of social control needs to be understood within the broader issue of powerlessness experienced by people with mental illness. The value base for practice, previously discussed, emphasises the importance of social workers practising in such a way that restores, as much as possible, the individual's control over all aspects of their lives. Advocacy for the rights of clients and their families remains a central area of practice for social work.

Ethics in context

You have been working with a 17-year-old client who has confided that she is secretly intending to self-harm. Her family, with whom she lives, is unaware of this. In what ways do you work with this person and/or family to address this issue? To what extent are you prepared to override client confidentiality considerations if you think the person is at considerable risk of self-harm?

Balancing the needs of consumers and family members

Because social workers adopt a broad approach to practice they may be aware of the potential for conflict between the needs and rights of individual consumers, and the needs and rights of other family members. Principles of confidentiality and self-determination are potentially threatened when the wishes of individual consumers and their family carers are in conflict (Szmukler 1998). Szmukler suggests a number of circumstances in which a worker might feel obliged to break client confidentiality in order to protect the welfare of family carers. For example, the worker may become aware of client delusions that may threaten the welfare of family members. Caregivers may wish to intervene quickly to force treatment for a resistant family member. Conflict may occur when consumers may want to continue to live at home, despite the wishes of family carers who may feel trapped in the caregiving role. Social workers have to be able to deal with the ethical ambiguity of these situations, weighing up the rights and needs of the various parties, and acting carefully and with respect for people involved.

An emerging area of practice is that at the interface of mental illness and child and family welfare. Social workers in child protection are often confronted with assessing the capacity of parents who may have a mental illness (Birchall 1999), and the practice issues revolve around supporting the parental role, and respecting the self-determination of parents while at the same time protecting the welfare of their dependent children.

Conclusions

Significant developments in mental health policy, and the emergence of consumer and carer issues in all aspects of the provision of mental health services, have created a challenging context in which social work in mental health is practised. The aspects of the social context and consequences of mental illness, areas basic to the domain of social work practice, are recognised as central to mental health services. Yet significant competition for authority among the mental health professions remains a challenge for social work, and raises issues of the undergraduate and ongoing education of social workers.

Review questions

1 How would you define 'mental health'?
2 What are some strategies used by social workers to balance the needs of consumers and/or families with legislative and agency and/or organisational considerations?
3 Does good social work practice in the mental health field occur from within or without the 'medical model'?

11

SOCIAL WORK IN THE CHANGING FIELD OF INCOME MAINTENANCE

Peta Fitzgibbon and Desley Hargreaves

Chapter objectives

- To provide an historical perspective on the role of social work within the bureaucracy
- To value the practice of social work in a national bureaucracy

- To identify the challenges, opportunities, and ethical dilemmas inherent in this field of practice

Introduction

The changing face of Australia's income security system and the broad welfare reform agenda of government, and how this is influencing social work practice in the Commonwealth government's public sector environment, is the context for this chapter. Understanding Australia's social security system, particularly the recent significant changes brought about by the creation of Centrelink and the privatisation of the delivery of employment services, is an integral part of social work knowledge, regardless of the field of practice. The chapter explores the changes, spanning 60 years, which have taken place in the Social Work Service from its origins in the Commonwealth Department of Social Services to its current location within Centrelink, the federal agency that is now in its seventh year. Issues facing social workers in this new environment will be examined within the context of the current direction of social policy and welfare service delivery in Australia: an environment characterised by increasing requirements for active social and economic participation and mutual obligations for citizens receiving income support, and a changing role for government in welfare provision.

The context in which social work is practised is the critical determinant to understanding political and ethical issues that emerge for social workers. Like other fields of practice, social work practice in Centrelink is dramatically changing in the face of the redefinition and redesign of social welfare and service delivery arrangements. The fundamental changes to Australia's social security system that were launched through the McClure report, *Participation Support for a More Equitable Society* (McClure 2000), now constitutes the most significant influence on social work practice within an income support environment. The challenge for social workers is to understand the forces of this change and to create a legitimate place for social work while maintaining its values and purpose in what, at times, can seem to be a hostile environment. The chapter will examine some ethical and practice issues for practitioners, and articulate the role(s) that social workers in Centrelink are playing in shaping a future for themselves and opportunities for their clients and communities. Centrelink currently employs over 560 social work staff in its national network, about 95 per cent of whom are involved in direct service delivery.

Historical overview

Although some Australian states had introduced legislation for age pensions earlier, income security at the federal level began with the introduction of the *Old Age and Invalid Pensions Act* 1908. The years leading up to 1939 were marked by a dearth of national social welfare programmes—although a maternity allowance was introduced and there were some unsuccessful attempts to introduce contributory pension schemes. World War II and the immediate post-war period, however, brought about a significant change in the Australian psyche at the social, economic, and political levels. Great societal changes occurred during the period from 1939 to 1949, heightening the community's awareness of social issues and increasing the Commonwealth's role in social welfare. Uniform taxation was introduced in 1942 and a referendum held in 1946 gave parliament specific power to legislate for a range of social services.

In 1941 the Department of Social Services (DSS) came into operation, independent of the Treasury. In the same year, the Commonwealth Parliamentary Committee on Social Security held an inquiry into aspects of Australia's welfare services, recommending that the department research social problems and the impact of social legislation. It also recommended that the department employ social workers, initially on a temporary basis, to see if they would be a useful addition to its staff. They were to focus on the administration of invalid and old age pensions, maternity allowances, and child endowment. Lyra Taylor, a qualified and experienced social worker with legal qualifications, was appointed in November 1944 as chief research and administrative officer of the Division of Social Work and Research. She had responsibility for the development of the Social Work Service, the development of the social research and policy arm of the department, and for the establishment of the library.

In 1947, in a paper presented at the first Australian Conference of Social Work, Taylor said that social workers in DSS were employed to provide a skilled casework service for the department's beneficiaries, to make the department's administration as humane as possible, and to form a useful instrument for social progress by assembling evidence on social questions (Watkins 1992).

A community liaison and service development role was articulated clearly in 1966, and extended by the Social Work Service in 1973, to enable departmental social workers to assist community organisations in the development and coordination of services at the local level.

Initially, social workers were located in the Division of Social Work and Research at the state level of administration, responsible to the state director. In 1950, eleven staff worked in the central office division, only one of whom was a qualified social worker. Finding trained social workers was difficult in the 1950s, and the department launched a cadetship programme with limited success. It did, however, achieve some success in the 1960s. Records indicate that the department had twenty-one cadets in training by the end of the 1960s.

During the 1960s the Social Work Service was extended to a few regional offices, and staff from state headquarters visited some country offices; however, the service remained highly centralised. The service focused on beneficiaries of some specific payments, as well as the clients of the Commonwealth Rehabilitation Service. Social workers essentially operated independently of other parts of the administration, except for some involvement in the development of policies for subsidy programmes for the aged and disabled. By the end of this decade, sixty-one qualified social workers were employed—not a significant growth in a period of twenty-plus years.

There was further expansion during the years of the Whitlam federal government in the 1970s, which focused on a range of social programmes and the implementation of the Australian Assistance Plan. Much of the responsibility for the new programmes was given to the department, which was renamed the Department of Social Security. As part of an organisational restructure the Social Work Service was placed within a newly created Social Welfare Division. Most senior officers in this new division had social work qualifications. The number of social workers increased from about 100 in 1972–73 to 211 by 1974–75. Ironically, in the late 1970s there was considerable growth in the numbers of social workers employed, despite the so-called era of the Razor Gang and greater austerity in the public service. This growth primarily occurred in regional offices. A Committee of Inquiry into Social Work Activities in 1977 found that there was a need for the Social Work Service in DSS, and that the tasks should be primarily related to income maintenance. From 1977 onwards, the Social Work Service moved from being a centralised generalist service to one that was more integrated with other operational areas of the department, in particular regional offices, and the then Commonwealth Rehabilitation Service. There was also a trend from this time for social workers to move into administrative and social policy positions in the department.

In the 1980s, social workers had an increasing role in management processes in regional offices. A review in 1981 further targeted the income maintenance focus of the social work service. A subsequent review in 1985 examined the structure of the service and its relationships at regional, state, and central office levels. The Social Welfare Division was abolished following the 1981 review and the Social Work Service was transferred to a Benefits Division where it remained for some years. In 1986 the Minister for Social Security established a social security review (Cass 1986) that focused on three major aspects of social security policy: income support for families with children, social security and workforce issues, and income support for the aged. The review resulted in significant social policy changes and further integrated the role of social workers within the income support framework of the department. In 1989, the department engaged in an organisational restructure, with the formation of twenty area administrations and the removal of state offices. This was a significant change as it recognised the need to provide a greater level of professional support to social workers in the management structure. In the 1990s, there was an increased focus on professional practice standards, professional supervision, quality assurance, management information systems, and the use of technology.

The creation of Centrelink in 1997 as the service delivery arm of government brought another significant change in the positioning of social work services. When Centrelink was created, the Department of Social Security still existed as a small social policy department and, though social workers continued to be employed in various policy positions, all the social work positions were moved to the service delivery agency. This coincided with a decision of the Australian Industrial Relations Commission that elevated the national manager of social work services to the senior executive level within the organisation. The Social Work Service used this transition period to develop the Social Work Directions in 1998, which provided the broad framework for social work's repositioning in an agency given a new charter by government to provide integrated human services to the Australian community. The Social Work Directions were a response to the new service and were built around concepts of customer-service partnerships, emerging technologies, and enterprise practice and review, which would see social workers initiate opportunities for service delivery and policy development.

Following the national elections in October 1998 the government reorganised its social policy department. For the first time in more than 50 years, social security lost its departmental status and became part of a much broader social policy agency, the Department of Family and Community Services (FACS). This change, together with the creation of Centrelink, has had a significant influence on social work in the income maintenance field. In the past few years Centrelink has developed a stronger role in providing opportunities for people to find work, assisting in disasters, drought, and industrial crises such as the collapse of the Ansett airline, and administering services and programmes for a diverse range of government agencies that go beyond an income maintenance focus. This is also changing the role of social work as Centrelink shifts its focus from income support alone.

It is clear that the directions taken by governments have shaped and directed the focus of social work practice over the past 50 years. In their analysis of the influence of national social welfare policies on the Social Work Service, Begbie et al. (1986) contend that the official social welfare policies of successive Commonwealth governments have affected the boundaries of the departmental Social Work Service. They further maintain that the Social Work Service has been a sensitive indicator of the types of social welfare policies Commonwealth governments have pursued in the field of income maintenance and associated welfare areas.

Current issues

Challenging the welfare state

Since the mid 1980s, political parties of all persuasions in Australia and in other Western capitalist societies, such as New Zealand, the United States, and the United Kingdom, have progressively distanced themselves from 'welfare' as a sole approach to poverty and social exclusion. There has been a shift of emphasis within government on the nature, role, and delivery of welfare in its broadest sense. It is beyond doubt that Australia is redefining the nature of the welfare state. This move is directing us away from the universal 'safety net' and the underlying culture of rights-based entitlements towards concepts of active participation, limited government intervention, mutual obligation, and reciprocity.

In this environment, it is not surprising to see a realignment of the role of income security. For the first time since 1941, a department of social security—a significant and identifiable feature of Australia's social policy environment—no longer exists. The creation of FACS was seen by government as the opportunity to better integrate and link income support to those services that relate more to prevention, support, and economic and social participation. The new department reflected a desire by government to integrate a fragmented social policy. Furthermore, it consolidated the view that government shares responsibility for social policy with the community and business sector. Prime Minister John Howard repeated this message on a number of occasions during 1998 and 1999:

> Our purpose is to build a new social coalition of government, business, charitable and welfare organisations and other community groups—each contributing their own particular expertise and resources, in order to tackle more effectively the social problems which directly or indirectly affect all members of our society in one way or another (Howard 1999b, p. 6).

The creation of FACS and the demise of DSS, both as conceptual and organisational constructs, represent a significant redevelopment of the income security and social welfare landscape in Australia. It is important not to underestimate the significance of the abolition of DSS in representing this radical shift in social policy. Reflecting his disappointment at the demise of DSS and of the term 'social security', social policy analyst Peter Saunders wrote:

> Firstly, I think that the Australian social security system, though not without its faults, is an important social institution of which we as a nation have every right to be proud. Its basic design and structure is unique among industrial countries and many aspects of it have prompted others to reconsider and reform their own systems in ways that mirror ours (Saunders 1999, p. 3).

He continued:

> It is also important to acknowledge that the term 'social security' refers to both the means of income support policy and to its goal. Although the term has come to be used primarily to describe a system of public transfers to groups in need because of reduced earnings capacity … social security also encapsulates what the system is trying to achieve for the citizens of a country.

In a world in which the perception at least is of increased economic insecurity this emphasis on the provision of social security seems even more appropriate (Saunders 1999, p. 3).

The new social policy direction reflected the government's partnership approach, and reinforced the movement away from a passive welfare system to one that aims to increase economic and social participation through three social policy outcomes as defined by FACS: developing stronger families, stronger communities, and economic and social participation. The latter outcome encompasses the traditional income-support role, now described as 'an engagement of all Australians in society'. The FACS *Strategic Plan* (1999b, p. 8) states that it will:

- encourage economic and social participation by individuals and families by enabling access and promoting opportunities
- foster a culture of self-reliance in the community and provide an effective safety net
- develop partnerships with key stakeholders to improve efficiency and effectiveness of services, to identify emerging problems, and to develop appropriate policy responses.

There is an emerging political consensus that the government needs to create opportunities for new enabling processes and relationships at the community level. This is occurring at a time when the welfare state, which increasingly is being perceived in the political arena as a system that creates dependency, is being questioned. The increasing and enduring nature of entrenched economic and social problems has given new impetus to the concept of 'social capital' (Cox 1995) as a way of recreating, at the community level, social relationships, trust, and cohesion that may offer more long-term solutions to the problems of poverty and dislocation intensified by globalism. This calls for the state to play a supportive rather than a directive role: 'The state needs to turn over its decision-making power, as much as possible, to intermediary associations linking the power of government to the capacity of citizens to engage in mutual trust' (Latham 1998a). This also articulates a new relationship between government, the citizen, and the state, sometimes referred to as 'stakeholder capitalism' (Hutton 1999, p. 114).

The perception that the current income security system is passive is being questioned by voices not from the traditional right. Mark Latham, who led Labor in the 2004 federal election, is the author of several books on globalisation, social capital, and community capacity building. In 1998 he wrote:

Passive systems of welfare and governance are a poor way of creating commonality and trust in a post-industrial society … what is required is a strengthening of the citizen-to-citizen relationship in society, rather than the state-to-citizen relationship (Latham 1998a, p. 26).

Similarly, Noel Pearson, Chairperson of the Cape York Land Council, argues:

It has become patently obvious that the passivity and disempowerment of the welfare condition (where the State controls all resources and hoards within its bureaucracies all rights and responsibilities) is, together with racism, the fundamental cause of social dysfunction in Cape York Aboriginal society (Pearson 1999, p. 20).

He asks all social workers who lament the demise of the current social welfare system without looking for new ways of building government support and reforming our social institutions a fundamentally challenging question: 'We Australians who put our hands up to support the Welfare State need to reconsider what we mean by our social responsibility. We need to ask ourselves: what really is the social and economic destination of welfare?' (Pearson 1999, p. 20).

An alternative view, however, is that social welfare increasingly is being replaced by social control: that government is 'walking away' from its social welfare responsibilities; and that individuals, families, and communities that are structurally and economically disadvantaged are being left to either the charity of non-governmental agencies or to themselves. The response of the Australian Council of Social Services (ACOSS) to the Prime Minister's position on the need for a new social coalition is cautious. Reflecting on the current changes towards greater mutual obligation and the direction of social policy that tends to emphasise individual failings but not the realities of poverty and social exclusion in Australia, former ACOSS president, Michael Raper, commented:

> Around 20 per cent of the working age population of Australia—around two million people—is in receipt of Social Security payments at any given point in time (excluding payments made for children). This proportion has increased steadily over the last twenty-five years; prior to 1974, the level was below 4 per cent (Raper 1999, p. 3).

He further claims that this trend upwards has given rise to the view that the solution is to do away with welfare as we know it, primarily through making it far more difficult to get and by attaching conditions to its retention. This is the 'workfare' model pursued in the United States and comprises some elements of the Work for the Dole scheme. Raper argued that many of the two million people on social security are there intermittently for relatively short periods of time as they find casual work. In fact, 62 per cent of unemployed people and 40 per cent of sole parents stop needing payments within one year. Many combine paid work with their social security payment on an ongoing basis (Raper 1999, p. 3).

The separation of policy from service delivery in the government's social welfare and employment programmes is reflected in the increasing complexity of the purchaser–provider relationships at the Commonwealth level, and emerging issues of accountability in public policy. This has been achieved through creating Centrelink, privatising key elements of employment services through the Job Network, and contracting out the delivery of government services. Even within government, the loops and links that connect policy and service delivery have to be rebuilt as the policy and service delivery arms of governments separate into clearly defined purchaser and provider roles. Saunders identifies the impact of this on social policy and the role that the state should play, with markets and deregulation gaining a greater place, stating:

> Fiscal constraints are still tight and a greater emphasis is being placed on the need to introduce competition into areas of public welfare, or at least to make these increasingly contestable within

a more open competitive framework. Changes in the global economy and the need to improve productivity are also generating their own challenges to social policies (Saunders 1999, p. 5).

Centrelink, the Commonwealth government's 'one stop shop', came into being in an environment influenced by globalisation, privatisation and contestability, corporatisation, increased expectations on consumers, the 'marketisation' of welfare, and a technological revolution. Before Centrelink, the model of service delivery was based on an approach to government service provision that had traditionally delivered entitlements through several largely independent government agencies and slotted customers into income support payment streams. Centrelink now delivers payments and services to its six million customers through a single integrated network that includes 292 customer service centres, twenty-two call centres and over 400 visiting services, and now offers more choice to people in terms of how they do business.

New technologies in service delivery

The key elements in Centrelink's service delivery strategy are to enable choice and to take advantage of the electronic opportunities now available. New technologies are now well developed in Centrelink's call centres. Technological innovation enables the redesign of current labour-intensive, routine processes, replacing them with personal interactions that have a higher value. Centrelink is having to balance the increased interest and demand to have access to these innovations from some customers with other customers' fear that they will be unable to access services through electronic service options (Vardon 1999). There are justifiable reservations about the extent to which technological solutions—such as expert systems, the Internet, and Interactive Voice Response (IVR) and other self-service developments—will, on their own, improve service delivery. However, technology also offers exciting possibilities that give people more control and access to information, and the ability to change their own details. Self-service will be increasingly important in ensuring that people needing assistance to find work and access opportunities are given direct services and support.

Social workers are embracing technology in order to do their work and make decisions that benefit clients. The inclusion of social workers within Centrelink's call centre network in 1998 indicates the extent to which social workers have embraced new technology and are adapting and responding to new ways of providing services to the community.

Welfare reform initiatives—Australians Working Together

The Australian government's 2002 welfare reform initiatives known as 'Australians Working Together' (AWT) (FACS 2004) have had a significant impact on the role of social workers in Centrelink. They brought a more individualised approach to clients with significant workforce barriers and disadvantage, which in itself was something to be applauded. Supporting this approach, a new position of Personal Adviser was created to work specifically with those clients who had been identified as requiring additional assistance to engage with participation opportunities. The focus clearly has been on work outcomes, although there has been recognition of the value of social participation as progress on the pathway to economic participation. The various measures required very few social work specific referrals, but brought to prominence various other specialists. It also saw a significant increase in the number of psychologists in Centrelink.

This created some important challenges for social workers. Limited resource allocations and high expectations required social workers to 'create capacity' to enable them to contribute to the AWT agenda. They experimented with intake models and centralisation of work that did not require face-to-face contact with clients. This also led to some creative and innovative work including group work and collaborative partnerships with other organisations with mutual clients. While client referrals to social workers under AWT have not been high, social workers have taken an active role in supporting the initiatives. Two social workers took prominent roles in the definition of the role of the Personal Adviser and the type of interviewing they needed to engage in with their clients, and also with the development of the national training strategy for the Personal Advisers. Social workers have played an active role in supporting and mentoring PAs and have also provided consultations on more complex cases.

The challenge though has been to work out how social workers work with the psychologists and specialists in this new space. It was very uncomfortable for a time and there was a danger that social workers would see themselves disempowered. Psychologists are very specific about the approach and whom they will work with, whereas the very nature of social work is to widen the focus from the individual to their family and community networks as well. For social workers there has been a continuing need to bring the focus back to the client and in subtle ways to market the contribution social workers have been making. Ironically, many of social work's clients are not covered by the AWT initiative. Part of the tension has been about continuing to service this group of clients while not taking their eye off the contribution to be made to the AWT initiatives.

Since Centrelink's inception, the Social Work Service has made considerable intellectual and conceptual contributions to the business of Centrelink. Under AWT, Centrelink's role was defined as the gateway to participation, involving assessment and referrals as appropriate but particularly to the Job Network or Commonwealth funded programmes. The Social Work Service developed a conceptual model, which has informed the development of a comprehensive whole-of-government approach to assessment for all working-age customers, which is now being trialled and implemented within Centrelink. The success of this model will transform the way Centrelink assesses and refers customers to the services that best meet their needs and assist in providing access to opportunities for work. Similarly, social workers have developed the framework for how Centrelink could partner with the community, including local and state governments, the community, and business sectors, under the theme of 'Community Partnerships and Civic Partnerships'. It is clear that participation outcomes for our clients cannot be achieved without strong engagement with other agencies, levels of government, and the business sector. With both these examples, other parts of the organisation have taken ownership of the concepts. Sometimes they have not been adopted in the way it was intended. Our challenge is to spread the powerful ideas in a way that is more focused on the customer and less focused on the interests of the organisation as a provider of services. Again a fine balance needs to be maintained.

An organisational restructure in January 2004 created an interesting challenge for the Social Work Team at the national level. The portfolio responsibilities were broadened to include a stronger organisational responsibility for marginalised and at risk customers. These include homeless clients, problem gamblers, and customers with mental health issues, and those at risk of domestic and family violence, or at risk of suicide. As an aspirational statement and recognising the value of a strengths-based approach, the team was renamed 'Social Work and Social Inclusion Services'. The challenge is to encourage all parts of the organisation to take responsibility for services to vulnerable customers and to ensure that their needs are considered in the business of Centrelink.

Ethical issues

A number of authors would argue that social workers need to question seriously their place in a bureaucracy. Ife (1997b), for example, suggests that community work is the legitimate place for social work intervention. We contend that social work has a legitimate role in bureaucracy; however, as with any field of practice, social workers need to be able to resolve ethical, value, and practice dilemmas if they are to practise effectively.

Historically, within the Commonwealth income support portfolio, the Social Work Service has contributed significantly to implementing sensitive government policy and programmes: for example, the Australian Assistance Plan, with its community development focus; Supporting Mothers' Benefit; Young Homeless Allowance (YHA); and the Child Support Scheme (CSS). The youth allowance and the child support schemes, in particular, have generated considerable negative publicity, often directed at social workers. Social workers have held personal views about these policies that may have conflicted with the intent of the policies. There are potential conflicts about family responsibility and independence, particularly with young people 18 years and over. Social workers' understanding of family dynamics and poverty make it difficult, at times, to reconcile the intent of policy with the reality of its impact. Knowledge of separation issues, the grief and loss associated with relationship breakdowns, and the impact of domestic violence has to be weighed against the rights of children to know both parents and have the benefit of financial support from the non-carer parent.

Social workers have a very good understanding of the link between private troubles and public issues. One potentially irreconcilable issue for social workers is the responsibility to set aside personal opinions to ensure that the government policy of the day is implemented. This is true, of course, for any public servant. Equally, they have a responsibility to monitor the impact of policy and to give feedback to policy departments, particularly when there are clear, unintended consequences. Through the daily interactions that Centrelink social workers have with customers, they are able to identify and analyse this impact. Social workers, providing case studies supported by well-researched policy submissions, inform policy makers of the impact of policy and programmes on vulnerable customer groups. It also enables the identification of gaps in services. The creation of Centrelink challenged the traditional role of social work in the 'policy loop' as the policy and service delivery arms of income support and other programmes were separated into a purchaser–provider arrangement. Stewart (1996) argues that the interlinking of policy and implementation makes it extremely difficult to separate the two effectively. He contends that policy is adapted and changed through the implementation experience: the purchaser–provider split has highlighted this as an issue for social workers. The ability to influence policy development remains, but there is a sense of disconnectedness and, for some social workers, that with regard to policy social work has been significantly marginalised. New ways of bringing together private troubles and public issues need to be found.

The increased targeting of welfare programmes, and the endorsement by both major political parties of the concept of mutual obligation, has created ethical dilemmas. Concepts of social justice and equitable access have been reframed in market terms and the language used does not always sit comfortably. In addition, the rapid development of technology and its potential use in service delivery has challenged our traditional views of client service. However, social workers in Centrelink have not faced these dilemmas nor worked them through in isolation: the whole human services sector has been faced with such predicaments.

Historically, social workers in DSS did not determine payment entitlements for customers. For a variety of reasons, following the creation of Centrelink, social workers were given this responsibility as an extension of their mandatory involvement in the assessment for entitlements of two customer groups. Some social workers have struggled with this and are not comfortable with the reality of being an administrative decision-maker rather than an advocate for the customer. They have felt very strongly that this could impede the relationship they develop with their client and drive them down an administrative rather than professional path. For others, this function has been seen as an improvement in the service they offer. Some aspects of mutual obligation have challenged social workers: for example, imposing penalties such as breaches that prevent the customer from receiving payment. This is a dilemma because the breach will mean the customer will have a reduced, or perhaps no, means of support. In these cases, the customer will have to seek assistance from community agencies that are under-resourced and struggling to survive. However, often there is a reason for the breach that could have been identified earlier in the process of assessing the customer's entitlement.

Social workers have traditionally worked at the interface between individuals or the community and the bureaucracy. With the creation of Centrelink, social workers were faced with the challenge of accepting that the traditional social work role of advocacy, in theory, was overtaken by an organisation that, in its approach to customers, articulated values consistent with those of social work. Centrelink is a customer-focused organisation and its staff is expected to provide a personalised service to customers. The interpersonal communication skills of staff are being enhanced through training to enable them to provide a more holistic service to customers. Shared behaviours of staff include respecting, listening, exploring, problem-solving, and behaving in an ethical manner. An enormous cultural shift has been required, which takes time. Social workers have had to accept the goal of offering a holistic service, while being aware of the reality that limits such offerings. They have been challenged to share their skills, to extend the boundaries, and contribute to the skills development of staff in a broader way than previously done.

In this customer-focused environment, in which the business of government must be easier for citizens to understand and access, the client–professional relationship has been affected, to some extent, by the new consumerist approach. In some ways, social workers feel comfortable with this in that it challenges the power of large bureaucracies and professionals to determine the needs of service users and methods of service delivery. Some commentators welcome the rise of 'consumerism' and see it as genuinely shifting power to the service user. Yet there is an unease about the extent to which users of social work services can be regarded as consumers in the same way as customers in a shop. Describing service users as customers ignores the control of the social worker, which may have statutory power to impose a course of action on the service user. Also, very often, the public sector offers no choice of services (Banks 1998).

Within the human services field, concepts of social justice and equitable access have been reframed in market terms. The Social Work Service has had to become more entrepreneurial in its approach, carrying out such activities as commissioning market research and actively exploring new business opportunities. For some social workers the new language and the new business approach do not sit comfortably.

As already noted, electronic service delivery is seen as one way of the future for Centrelink. Although it challenges traditional notions of service delivery, the reality is that human services already are being delivered by telephone, video-conferencing, chat rooms, and other media on the Internet. While acknowledging the impersonal nature of these media, their use can enhance access for those who live in rural and remote areas and for those who have difficulty in accessing Centrelink offices: for example, carers, frail aged, and disabled customers, who can conduct their business at a time and in a way of their choosing. The challenge is to ensure that service delivery of this nature considers the needs of those who are not literate, who do not speak English as a first language, who have a disability that impedes the use of technology, or who are not trained in the use of, or do not have access to, the technology. Clearly one of the significant challenges for social justice of the next decade will be how to redress the increasing divide between the 'information-rich' and the 'information-poor'. Centrelink social workers will have a role in ensuring that technologies and service delivery methods designed to extend access do not further marginalise the already disadvantaged.

Ethics in context

A social worker at her local supermarket sees a young woman working as a shelf stacker. The social worker saw the woman that day and knows she is in receipt of the Youth Allowance, but the woman had told the social worker that she was in receipt of no other income. What's the social worker's responsibility in this situation? How does the social worker meet her obligations to:

- her employer?
- her client?

Pushing the boundaries

The events of 12 October 2002 in Bali had a major impact on the role of social workers in Centrelink. Social workers have a clearly mandated role in disaster response within Australia. However, we had never had to think about responding to events that affected Australians offshore. Social workers were involved in four ways. In the immediate aftermath, Centrelink was asked to establish a hotline to answer queries from and provide financial assistance to distressed family members who wanted to travel to Bali or to various hospitals around Australia, and later for assistance with financial costs of funerals and other expenses. Social workers took the more complex or difficult calls. They also supported and debriefed customer service staff who were dealing with the horror and distress shared in those phone calls.

The second aspect was a case management role. The Centrelink Family Liaison Service was established as a centralised contact point for Commonwealth government assistance, and as a safety net for those who chose not to access assistance from other agencies. This role has continued and grown in response to changes in levels of assistance from other agencies, and in the context of stages in the grieving process.

The third area of involvement grew from a request to provide counselling and support to families and individuals travelling to Bali for the trials of the alleged Bali bombers. This developed into a new service model delivered offshore in Bali. Critical to the success of the model was the development of collaborative working relationships with other Commonwealth agencies, particularly the Department of Foreign Affairs and Trade (DFAT) and the Australian Federal Police (AFP). The Social Work Service had not worked with these agencies previously and it was important to quickly grasp the differences in cultures and work on what we shared in common—the need to support the affected families.

Building on this model, the fourth part of the role was the provision of family support services to families travelling to Bali and/or Canberra for services commemorating the first anniversary of the bombings. The national manager of Centrelink's Social Work Service led an interdepartmental team comprising Centrelink social work and administrative staff, consular staff from DFAT, federal agents from AFP who had a liaison role with the families, and four padres from the Australian Defence Forces. The role for Centrelink social workers involved personal support and grief counselling, as well as practical tasks such as meeting families at the airport, and accompanying them to significant sites, such as the Sari Club or the morgue, and to the memorial service.

In late 2003 the Social Work Service was asked to take on an interim case management role for victims of people trafficking and sexual servitude. This request from the Department of Prime Minister and Cabinet, Office of the Status of Women pushed the boundaries of the case management role for a Commonwealth agency. The nature of the work is very different from the normal social work role and has required a significant investment of time and professional skills to establish a new government sponsored service—one that had not been delivered in Australia previously. Nine Commonwealth agencies, as well as state and territory police, are involved with this initiative, which makes relationship management complex and challenging. The response had to be put together in three weeks and was initially planned for three months. The final handover to the successful tenderer occurred at the end of May 2004, requiring creation of the substance of the roles and staff with high levels of experience, strong casework skills, and a willingness to step outside the traditional organisational role.

Both the Bali and people trafficking experience have placed the staff concerned at considerable personal risk—much more than would normally be the case for public servants. This created significant ethical dilemmas for the national manager who was responsible for establishing the services and approaching staff to see if they would be willing to undertake the role. Critical to dealing with these dilemmas was the importance of ensuring that prior to making the decision staff were fully informed of the potential risks and that they were given sufficient time to consider the circumstances. While this did not relieve the enormous sense of responsibility for the personal well-being of the staff, there was some comfort in knowing that the decisions made had been done so from as informed a perspective as possible.

One important outcome of these experiences has been the firm commitment of the organisation to the leadership role of the Social Work Service in the provision of personal support services in disaster, emergency, and crisis situations.

The future for social work

We have outlined the current income maintenance environment in which social workers practice at the beginning of the new millennium. In Centrelink these changes are social workers' reality, and are issues with which social work must engage. These challenges also offer social work great opportunities to take control of its own practice, to see the contradictions as well as the positive opportunities to reconnect to the community, and to focus on outcomes that improve the lives of the most disadvantaged. More than ever, social work not only has to survive in this environment but also has to grow and make itself relevant to this new context and to new values.

One of the defining challenges for Centrelink social workers will be how they contribute to building a future for the organisation and for themselves. Social workers need to contribute to the structure and entity of a strong public sector that works with individuals and families and contributes to local communities. This requires social workers not only to be part of an identifiable professional service but also to work, as they have done historically, in positions throughout the organisation not clearly identified as that of 'social worker'. It requires social workers to deal with complexity, ambiguity, and uncertainty.

The future will hold opportunity for a more entrepreneurial Social Work Service. Innovative ways of working with young people and families are being explored. Social workers will be challenged to develop, in partnership with other organisations, new ways of working with the unemployed and the elderly. Group work will be explored as an alternative to casework where common needs are evident. Social work practice that embraces emerging technologies will also be a feature of this future.

Social workers will continue to have a place in social policy development and research, as they did in the time of Lyra Taylor. For social workers in Centrelink, their environment largely will be characterised by responding to the needs of marginalised and poor people who need the services of government and the community to be brought together in a simple way. For all that has been and is being done to redefine welfare, to articulate concepts of mutual obligation and responsibility, to define core business of government, and increasingly to operate human services as a market, there is no doubt the challenge remains the same: How does a democratic society deal with the ongoing exclusion of individuals and some communities from participating in the mainstream of Australian society and the social problems that stem from this inequality?

The field of income maintenance in the context of changing arrangements for service delivery in the public sector continues to be a very legitimate and relevant field for social work. It reflects the broader trends happening in the human services field. It requires social workers that are prepared to be engaged both at the individual and community level in wrestling with and creating change. It also requires social workers at the senior management and leadership level of organisations to be involved in guiding and influencing the change that can profoundly influence the outcomes for some of our country's most dispossessed. Above all, it requires us to understand that the basis of the welfare state, which so fundamentally influenced the development of modern social work in Australia, is being rewritten. It has implications for all of us and requires urgent attention. To be involved and working in such a field of practice, at this time, is clearly very important for the profession of social work.

Review questions

1   What are the risks and opportunities for social work in becoming more entrepreneurial within such environments?

2   What does it mean for social workers, as government policy moves away from a rights perspective for income support to embrace a greater expectation for people to participate in the labour market?

3   How does social work balance the competing demands of social work practice directly with the poor and disadvantaged, and influence and train other staff to better meet the needs of individuals, families, and communities?

12

EMPLOYMENT, SOCIAL JUSTICE, AND SOCIAL WORK: PRACTICE ISSUES IN A POST-WELFARE STATE

Michael Wearing

Chapter objectives

- To demonstrate how practice issues are formed in the broader societal, historical, and policy context
- To highlight the importance of social and ecological values and ethics in developing an understanding of social work processes

- To lay some foundations for an anti-oppressive practice in social work that recognises diversity and inequality as the basis for social action and change.

Introduction

The labour movement—the organised basis for industrial and political labour—is a key social movement of the twentieth century, which has shaped and changed Australian welfare (Patmore 1991; Roe 1976). The phrase 'wage-earners welfare state' was coined by Francis Castles to describe the industrial citizenship basis of Australian welfare (Richardson 1999, pp. 12–13; Castles 1994; Jamrozik 1994; Castles 1985). The welfare state measures of the post–World War II years came about primarily through the struggles of wage earners and their union representatives for a fair share, a fair go, and a decent standard of living for all working people in Australia. In recent years, the labour movement has also undergone sympathetic revision by social movement theorists to reflect the alliances formed between Labor and feminist, green, and the gay and lesbian movements (Pixley 1998). In a time of rapidly changing identities and cultures the movement has also begun to incorporate issues of social policy and justice for the working and non-working poor, including Indigenous and migrant Australians.

Today, the post-welfare state reflects an almost anti-wage-earner scenario. Highly targeted measures are being put in place to ensure the legitimacy of the state, despite the meaning and measurement of government expenditures being contested (Saunders 1996; Mitchell 1996; Jamrozik 2001). The Goods and Services Tax (GST) was seen as one solution for the increasing costs of social welfare spending in Australia. Some factors that have contributed to the state's inability to pay for welfare over the past 20 years include:

- the social and demographic changes that have led to increased unemployment and dependency of the aged, which have required more social security spending
- the lack of redistribution policies targeted at the income–wealth nexus, such as progressive taxation of the assets of companies, entrepreneurs, and high- and middle-to-high income families and individuals
- the lack of political will on the part of federal and state governments to promote equality and redistribution of wealth.

In this chapter I refer to the institutional context for current social work practice as the post-welfare state or post-welfare. In part, the definition follows Jamrozik (2001, pp. 8–9, 271) who says of these new institutional social welfare arrangements that they support and encourage inequality based on 'the philosophy of competition' and the 'belief in material incentives as stimulus for higher productivity and efficiency'. There is partly 'more of the lean and mean same' in terms of the traditional residualism of Australian welfare in the twentieth century. There is, however, a sharper focus on social exclusion, and coercion and discipline of the poor and marginalised, as well as increasing inequality either by design or neglect on the part of federal and state governments in the last two decades. The constitution of post-welfare also includes a reconfiguring of residual interventions at the level of perceived social and personal risks. These new social programmes focus on 'at-risk' social groups and are commonly wrapped around in the policy rhetoric of conservative communitarian ideology; for example, partnerships, linking up services, capacity, and social capital building. The 'Third Way' politics of such welfare intervention differs markedly from the party rhetoric of Keynesian–Beveridge policy focus in post–World War II Britain and Australia on social need, social democratic ideology, and increased state intervention (Wearing 2001; Smyth & Wearing 2003, 2004).

The changes in the nature of the economy and major political party agendas in Australia can be partly explained by post-Fordism and the shift to flexible specialisation in the nature of work (Grint 1993). Unlike in the immediate post-war Fordist years of mass production and full employment, people no longer have a job for life to maintain their quality of life and well-being; people have to change the types of job and possibly retrain several times in their working life; and there has been relatively high unemployment since the mid 1970s. Since the *Industrial Relations Act* 1997, brought about by Peter Reith, Federal Minister for Workplace Relations, a decentralised industrial environment has operated with enterprise agreement between employers and employees. Decentralised workplaces often exclude union involvement and collective industrial bargaining, and there is, in all the federal policies, an ideological and policy push from neo-liberals and the business elite towards a 'hands-off' state and anti-collectivism (Bell 1997). By 2004, at all tiers of government there was a strong ethos and policy rhetoric of conservative communitarianism or a pursuit of the ideology of community and localism as panacea to social problems (see Smyth & Wearing 2003; Mowbray 2004).

Nonetheless, there are also new developments that resist the privatisation, globalisation, and commercialisation of work and social life, and the manufacture of this conservative and highly moralistic civil society using communitarian rhetoric (see also Hodgson 2004). Social work needs to adopt strong social and ecological values to ensure a commitment to principles that encourage an egalitarian, democratic, and ecologically sustainable society; that is, a 'fair go for all, including nature' social policy. Such values counter the social costs of liberalisation, and challenge and resist the neo-liberal principles of economic efficiency and small government. Social work has a political duty to contribute to local community resistance to global pressures, anti-collectivism, and small-government ideology.

The framework of this chapter links employment policy and social work in three ways:

- The key to new industrial and social citizenship, based on cultural diversity or a civic pluralism, is anti-discriminatory and productive diversity in the workplace (Cope & Kalantzis 1997).
- Anti-oppressive practice must address the rights and needs of those who are socially excluded from paid or well-paid work, such as women, migrants, and the unemployed.
- As described in green movements and theory, the ecological values of preserving nature and sustainable growth should be encouraged (Ife 1995; McNutt 1994).

By using these principles, social work practice can be based on the person-in-context perspective and anti-oppressive values.

This chapter concentrates on direct employment policy as the context for practice, and links criteria for and examples of practice to this policy. As a domain of practice the employment field covers a diverse range of direct and indirect service delivery. For example, a social worker may assist a carer in their transition from the workforce to providing full-time care for an aged relative or person with a disability. There are also many indirect ways in which employment policy affects social work practice in areas such as disability services, aged care, and rural programmes, among others. A welfare approach to practice is taken in this chapter as a guide to social work's interaction with social forces and with government policy, in particular. In the conclusion, some limited ideas for practice are given.

Social work history and the workers' welfare state

The division between the 'deserving' and 'undeserving' has a long history in welfare administration and relief for poor people and the working class. The development of social work in the late nineteenth and early twentieth centuries is connected with various state welfare measures for employment assistance and unemployment relief. These policy arrangements originated in political and economic settlements over the division between capital and labour, and the softening, gradual or otherwise, of social and class conflict by the introduction of such measures.

Social work in the United States, Great Britain, and Australia originated in the scientific charity of the mid to late nineteenth century and the subsequent early twentieth-century professionalisation of almoners and other charity workers (Dominelli 1997b; Garton 1990; Trattner 1974). In the United States, this system of charity, and the professional training that had developed by the beginning of the twentieth century, was given state imprimatur at the end of the Civil War in 1865 through the establishment of the Federal Bureau of Refuges, Freemen, and Abandoned Lands—the first welfare agency in the United States. The bureau administered a programme of temporary relief and enabled many African-Americans to obtain an education and job in their transition from slavery to freedom in the southern states (Trattner 1974). Around this time, outdoor relief and, later, unemployment relief was developed in Australia and, as a result, the casework method was begun to be used by charity organisations.

During the late nineteenth century, colonial liberals countered the laissez-faire doctrine with plans to improve workers' conditions and also as a means to resolving conflict between employers and workers. The liberals wanted to counter the worst excesses of a market economy that, like Great Britain, could degenerate into labour unrest and already showed signs of extensive poverty in rural and urban areas (Garton 1990).

The subsequent depression of the 1890s in Australia demonstrated that radical measures were needed to improve the conditions of workers and those out of work. The labour movement, leading up to and during the 1890s, struggled for change and improvement in working conditions and in wages. In 1904 the Commonwealth arbitration system was established. In 1907 the landmark Harvester judgment under this centralised system established a minimum living wage to support a male worker, his wife, and three children in 'frugal comfort' set at seven shillings per week (Garton 1990, pp. 82–3). Against this backdrop of the emerging workers' welfare state, social work developed from the scientific charity movement and gradually found a base for training in universities during the 1920s to 1940s. Concerned citizens of the time, such as middle-class women and the clergy, saw the need for change and reform based on their observations of the deprivations arising from low wages and poor working and living conditions so evident in the inner-city slums, and elsewhere.

The shift from charity work to social work in this period also indicates the role of the state in gradually assisting the professionalisation of casework and other methods of intervention. Of particular importance in the development of Australian social work in the twentieth century, and its antecedents in the charity movements of the nineteenth century, is the gendering of practice and the dominance of women as role models for practice. Many of these women are well-known historical and political figures in Australia's White history: Caroline Chisholm, who assisted thousands of migrant workers in the 1840s; Catherine Helen Spence, who campaigned for reform in charity organisations during the 1890s; Norma Parker, who made a pivotal contribution to professional social work this century in setting up university courses in Sydney; and Marie Coleman, who placed progressive social strategies on the federal political agenda as Chair of the Social Welfare Commission (1973–76) under the Whitlam and Fraser governments (Garton 1990; Roe 1983). Such compassionate and activist women advocated and lobbied within the system without forgetting progressive social values. Their efforts, and indeed those of many female activists in the Australian welfare state, laid a foundation for anti-oppressive and emancipatory traditions in Australian social work, especially towards low-paid workers, migrants, and the unemployed (Roe 1983).

Safety-net measures such as employment relief established the foundations of the Keynesian period of the national welfare state in the 1940s and the *Social Security Act* 1942 (Battin 1997; Smyth 1994; Watts 1989; Waters 1976). During this period and into the 1950s, the size and scope of state activity in relation to employment and unemployment assistance increased dramatically, in part as a response to the social deprivations of the Great Depression of the 1930s and World War II.

Full employment in the 1950s meant the population was adequately provided for. During the 1960s, however, changes to the labour market meant that hidden poverty and unemployment became more visible. Important structural changes to the labour market and economic production began in the mid 1960s and continue today. These changes have shifted the economy from a manufacturing to a service base. Since the mid 1960s, employment in manufacturing industries levelled off then decreased substantially, and the service industries now employ over a third of all employees in Australia. Graycar and Jamrozik (1993) call this service sector 'the management industries' (using the Australian Bureau of Statistics' classification of public administration; finance, property and business services; and community services). This represents a shift from heavy and labour-intensive industries to a primarily service economy with significantly more capital-intensive industries. A second feature of this change is that women have entered the workforce on a large scale since the 1960s. Both these structural issues have changed the nature and extent of access to paid work.

Table 12.1 summarises Australian labour force trends over 15 years, 1987–2002. The first trend is the continued reliance on, and expansion of, the services sector of industry, and the decline of manufacturing. A second longer-term trend is the increasing participation of women in employment (50 per cent of all work-age women), and the slight decrease in the number of men in employment (about 75 per cent of all work-age males). Finally, there are marked differences in youth unemployment and long-term unemployment when compared with the changes in the unemployment rate over the last 10 years. Both the young unemployed (about 20 per cent or more) and the long-term unemployed (up to 20 per cent) face deep poverty and sustained social and psychological insecurity. Unemployment in general has been in decline in the last five or so years; however, interest rates and inequality have risen in this period. A further point to note from Table 12.1 is the falling union membership over this period and the implied loss of power for collective bargaining, centralised arbitration, and organised industrial action. This decline preceded the decentralised industrial system, and will no doubt be accelerated if left unchecked. Organised labour is making efforts to redress the decline in union membership. Nonetheless, broader social alliances and further education of Australians about the history of the labour struggle are required to keep in check the erosion of union participation.

Table 12.1 Summary of Australian labour force trends: 1987, 1992, 1997, 2002 (%)

Year	1987	1992	1997	2002
Total no. (000s)	(7680)	(8518)	(9186)	(9232)
Participation rates				
Total	56.9	56.2	58.0	63.8
Female	48.7	51.9	53.9	55.3
Male	75.6	74.4	73.7	72.4
Women (as % of total)	39.8	41.9	43.1	44
Paid work				
Female part-time	38.3	41.2	42.9	45.2
Male part-time	6.7	9.7	11.7	14.4
Casual	18.9	22.3	25.7	27.9
Service	67.2	70.9	72.3	74
Manufacturing	16.0	14.2	13.5	11.9
Trade union membership	42.6 (in 1988)	39.6	30.3	23.1
Unemployment				
Unemployment rate	8.3	10.4	8.7	6.6
Youth unemployment rate	20.3	23.8	20.9	19.5

Source: ABS (1998, 1999a, 2003).

The post-Fordist period in the Australian political economy is usually seen as being from the mid 1970s onwards. The seeming contradiction of this period is that though, on the one hand, a restructure of the size, scope, and efficiency of the public sector has occurred, on the other, public spending on the visible social wage—including education, health, social security and welfare, and housing and community amenities—has continued to increase. In a liberal–Keynesian welfare state such as Australia, social provisions such as social security are commonly used to alleviate poverty or provide a social safety net as a welfare measure secondary to that of work (see, for comparison, Jamrozik 1994). It is, however, recognised that the social security system is a central plank in alleviating poverty, combating wages below the minimum wage, and providing a decent standard of living (Gregory et al. 1999).

From 1996 onwards, the conservative Federal Government, under Prime Minister John Howard, accelerated the pace of economic change through liberalisation of the economy by further deregulation and privatisation. This liberalisation followed moves during the Hawke–Keating Labor period in government to open up global markets further and increase market competition in a range of manufacturing and service industries. Today, traditional social policy areas such as health, housing, education, and community services are coming to terms with the contractualism and competitive tendering that such liberalisation brings. In 1999 and 2000, in statements on social policy by the prime minister, the newer framework of self-reliant individualism that requires the poor to meet obligations to society (for a productive economy) was outlined under the banner of welfare dependency. Howard's key phrase 'incentives to avoid poverty' (1999b) is clearly a policy imperative driven by various strategic reforms aimed at getting people to work at any job, even under duress, in order to contribute to economic growth. By 2004, the now more commonplace use of terms such as partnerships, capacity building, and social capital illustrated the incorporation of a 'top-down' conservative communitarian rhetoric and practice into government policies. The 'devil' here is in the policy detail, given the poor injection of life into local social infrastructure under the Howard government. This has commonly translated into reinvigorated social category and identity moralisms on traditional community and family values, further obscuring the divisions of class, race, and gender in a narrow view of building communities. So again there are those who deserve resources and those who pose a risk that deserve discipline within, or exclusion from, society, such as the long-term unemployed. These social categories are often outside market-driven urban or regional economic reform (see Mowbray 2004; Hodgson 2004).

The strengthening of the surveillance net for poor people clearly is a policy objective of the Howard government (see, for comparison, Goodman 1997). Importantly, this sets a policy agenda based on 'deserts' for the unemployed and other vulnerable groups such as people with disabilities. Policy criteria determine who are the genuine or deserving poor, and punish the undeserving poor for not working. The discourses of community, capacity building, welfare dependency, and mutual obligation signals a revitalisation of the strong surveillance and control of the poor of earlier centuries in Great Britain and Australia. In earlier times, as today, welfare recipients were constituted as legal and administrative objects classified, according to eligibility, in laws such as the Elizabethan *Poor Law Act* of 1536, the Speenhamland Law of 1795, and the *Poor Law Amendment Act* of 1834 (Dean 1998; Wearing 1998; Goodman 1997; Berreen & Wearing 1989). There seems little doubt that the policy and rhetoric of the Howard government will increase the classification of poor people and the problematising of them in policy (see MacDonald et al. 2003). This is more so the case as the income safety net continues to tighten (with bigger holes!) under the Howard government's Centrelink and labour market policies, and more disadvantaged people fall through the into deeper poverty.

Employment policy and social work practice

Certain forms of human services in Australia are directly involved in the employment field and are more likely to employ social workers. This field is constituted by specific legal, political, and social arrangements—a few of which are outlined below, such as employment services, social security administration, and community and regional development in disadvantaged or economically depressed communities. Examples of the person-in-context approach that social work offers to the employment field are case management in employment services, and the promotion of job growth in regional development. Both examples hinge on the social value of work, in that growth in jobs, which is sustainable and promotes social development, is a public good for communities. Social workers have a key role to play in voicing and in exercising the social rights and needs of local communities involved in such growth.

Specific modes of individual and collective practice in the employment area borrow some principles from the health sector. Such practices, using the casework method of social work and employment relief at an individual level, are a legacy of the early twentieth century, as mentioned above.

Employment services

Employment services are responsible for job placement of the unemployed and long-term unemployed. Most services fall under the umbrella term 'case management' and exist within a more discretionary and fragmented unemployment-benefit regime. The key legislation is the federal *Employment Services Act* 1994. There are both legal and economic reasons why the current employment service approach is inadequate. Carney and Ramia (1999, p. 139) argue that the transition from a citizenship to contractual state is now evidenced by the major shift from employment benefits to employment services, and that there are serious legal implications in this shift. They contend that under the de-legalised process of contracted employment services, the rights of the unemployed are not adequately protected as they would be in services that have a more solid grounding in contract law.

The Howard government lacks commitment to better social and economic conditions for unemployed people by, for example, lowering the unemployment rate, except via support for economic growth. Despite the difficulties of fully assessing federal spending on job growth, the downward trend in spending on employment services, since the election of the conservative Liberal–National government, is clear. Of the total revenue of the 1999 Federal Budget ($164 billion), less than 1 per cent ($1.2 billion) was spent on decreasing unemployment through the Job Network programme and Work For The Dole programme ($25 million). This compares with $3.8 billion under the Labor government's 1994 *Working Nation* employment services plan (Keating 1994), and thus represents a significant reduction in the size of the employment services budget. These trends have continued to 2004 just prior to the federal election.

Case management can overemphasise administrative and legal compliance at the social cost of not finding unemployed people meaningful jobs. Focusing case-managed services on participation, as an instrumental planning value in policy and in service delivery, may bring greater compliance of clients to service rules and regulation; that is, greater normative control (see Gursansky et al. 2003). However, anti-oppressive social work has an ethical obligation to resist the punitive mentality of such strategies and refocus on participation as a developmental value that includes 'increased knowledge, greater understanding, increased solidarity, trust and sympathy' (Considine 1994, p. 131; see also Gursansky et al. 2003, chap. 6).

Some specific conditions for social work practice in the employment field can be illustrated by using examples of low-paid workers and the unemployed, who, in social justice and social work frameworks, are subject to social exclusion. There is also a need to link policy to practice in social work so that strategies such as cultural and social participation will make a more inclusive society. It is important to ask who speaks for and on behalf of the poor and unemployed people. This question is especially important for the powerless: those who are marginalised, disadvantaged, discriminated against, and excluded from core institutions, and who suffer the stigma of criminality, unemployment, low-paid work, drug or substance abuse, illness and mental illness, disability, and so on.

The question of participation is particularly relevant in considering policy on youth unemployment. Job creation and labour market programmes for youth have a rich history, especially over the last three decades. There are, however, key differences to schemes for the young unemployed today compared with 20 years ago. The period can be characterised by the shift from finding work, as a participatory activity of inclusion in the 1980s, to an employment-policy regime under which unemployed people seeking work are motivated by self-blame and punishment.

Today the approach is much less developmental than the Community Employment Scheme developed in the early to mid 1980s by the Hawke government, under the then Urban and Regional Development Minister, Tom Uren (Orchard 1995). The current conservative government's concept of mutual obligation is based on individualism and self-blame in a policy framework in which it is the individual's responsibility to find work. This denies the structure of the labour market in that there is an oversupply of labour, and a lack of employment demand from industry and the production sector, in general. Further, the Youth Allowance, an example of reform by the Howard government in 1999 to the income safety net for young people, supposedly alleviates the income problems for unemployed youth by assuming that young people are dependent on parents or other guardians until they are aged 25.

Early evaluations were largely unflattering, especially considering the way in which the contractual–competitive approach created an unregulated market environment and overtook the rights approach (Carney & Ramia 1999; Considine 1999; Bacon 1998; King & Maplestone 1998; Wearing & Smyth 1998; Alford & O'Neil 1994). Involvement in one-on-one case management can detract from advocacy and a fuller involvement in activism against the worst excesses of deregulated labour market programmes and growing market-determined inequalities. Further, the diversity and development of service delivery in the community sector—indicated in the 1995 Industry Commission report on the sector (Industry Commission 1995)—needs to be acknowledged before a more detailed evaluation of employment services occurs. An acknowledgment of the organisational and inter-organisational complexities and the contractual and legal basis of community services should yield a more thorough appraisal and evaluation of such programmes (Considine 1999; Wearing 1998). Labour market programmes are an important area of service delivery in the community services sector. The sector is also involved in prevention, advocacy, and self-help programmes, and other forms of case management and brokerage, and has responded to policies not directly related to employment, such as the deinstitutionalisation of the mentally ill, and people with intellectual disabilities.

Regional community development: jobs, nature, and growth?

Much of the explanation today for economic development in regional and low income, outer urban areas is based on liberal principles of the market driving local work participation rates (SMH 1999). Better community development and community economic management can improve local economies, overcome the worst costs of poverty for families, and partly resolve the employment crisis in local communities. Not only do we know that rural workers are not paid as much as their city counterparts, but also that there is economic scarcity, for example, in the supply and types of rural jobs. Examples of the degree of economic and employment crisis in regional areas indicate the extent of rural poverty and disadvantage.

There is a general perception in many rural areas that jobs are being lost because of 'trendy' interest groups involved in 'green' social action. Multinational companies and the business elite have allowed local conflicts to escalate in rural areas, while divesting themselves of any social responsibility for industry closures, job losses, and subsequent remuneration. Two examples in New South Wales were the closures, in 1999, of the Eden tuna cannery and the Camden coal mine. In both cases, the company took flight to find cheaper labour elsewhere, withdrawing the infrastructure from Australia and setting up business in another location.

There is also considerable political mileage—dependent on voter support in a region—for state and federal governments to trade-off economic growth and job creation in regional centres against the loss of jobs, by preserving forests and un-logged areas. This is cloaked in the rhetoric of conservative regional economic development, which invokes tourism and industry as the answer (Ife 1995). A recent example of this was the ability of the Carr government in 1995 conveniently to equate saving the forests with a loss of jobs in the southwest and northeast forests of New South Wales. The truth is more complex. Globalisation, economic rationalism, and drives for economic efficiency over the past 15 years (at least) have contributed significantly to the decline of social infrastructure in 'the bush'. This has included cuts to services, such as rail and banking, and has dried up the productivity of a mixture of public and private services, and jobs in local economies. In this climate, governments have been very effective in playing off interest groups, and avoiding a role in promoting local economies and progressive economic development in communities, such as cooperatives and community banks.

Community development has an important role in social and economic development. The imperative of economic growth versus loss of jobs can be countered with successful regard for ecological values, and use of appropriate technology and local resources to boost the infrastructure of a town and its surrounding regions. Crookwell, a town in New South Wales, has improved its economic and social infrastructure through using windmills to generate town electricity, an ecologically sound power source that also acts as a tourist attraction. Local economies need motivated people and community leadership to make economic and social initiatives happen. Governments at all levels need to refocus on equitable and, where possible, redistributive policies, even through the local tax base, to give regional towns a chance to create sustainable and viable local industries.

A good example of this is the Riverland area of Mildura, Renmark, Red Cliffs, and Swan Hill in southwestern New South Wales, northeastern South Australia, and northwestern Victoria. There are not many economic success stories in rural communities in recent years: this region has, however, undergone remarkable development in recent years, with an expected population growth of 25 per cent by 2020. Free marketeers claim this is to do with divorcing water resources from land ownership, treating water as a commodity or scarce resource that people must respect if only because farmers and others must pay for it. This is a narrow focus on economics (*Australian* 1999). The real social reasons for growth in the area are perhaps more holistic and complex. One interpretation could be that the building of more sustainable and ecologically responsible communities provides common wealth by using civic and commercial leadership to reinvent local industry, with entrepreneurs, experts, and communities making a collective effort. This is not free market ideology and, in fact, fits a political ecology and progressive communitarian approach that aims to preserve scarce natural resources, such as water, to protect against environmental degradation, and offers the immediate to long-term socio-economic benefit of more paid work in local communities.

Elsewhere in the developed world, such as in the Basque region of Spain, the development of large industry cooperatives has had significant redistributive results ('distributism') for their local regions (see, for example, Mathews 1999; Ife 1995). There are also current examples in the domestic tourism industry: local or 'host' communities, such as Indigenous ones, have benefited through ownership and the creation of local employment by adopting explicit environmental and distributive ethics in their tourist marketing and products (Wearing & Wearing 1999). Social work in Australia also could adopt a strong ecological orientation to community development. There are also indirect benefits to community, human, and social rights in arguing for an ecological ethic in that protests to preserve ecosystems can also have human benefit as a flow-on effect.

There are guidelines in Australia and overseas for political and ethical practice in social work from a socio-ecological perspective. The approach to develop an anti-oppressive and critically reflective framework on practice that challenges the processes of exclusion, injustice, and discrimination in Australian society follows.

Social work process and ethical issues

The links between theory, policy, and practice are blurred in the employment field as elsewhere. This occurs when we ask how our ethics or moral theory interact with practice and policy. Social workers need to engage with administrative and policy changes in human services while retaining effective and autonomous practical interventions. Underlying this is a commitment in the profession to a strong ethical orientation, a clearly thought-out knowledge base, skill development, and a dynamic strategic orientation to clients' needs. There have been warnings about making overly ambitious claims in regard to professional social work, not the least of which is the claim that social work is the agent for change (Rein 1976). Nonetheless, from a more modest base, social workers can think of themselves as agents of emancipatory and participatory change—not forgetting the more contemplative benefits of reflection and therapy. Social workers with others can be involved in broad social development, social movements, and action oriented towards meaningful social change. Indeed, social work is a professional network that commonly interacts with new social movements such as the gay and lesbian, green, or feminist movements in Australia. Some criteria for social work processes as well as discussion of the implications for ethics in practice of participating in change follow.

Social work processes

The key social work practice area in the employment field is case management. There are specific legal and ethical practices that relate to case management, not least of which is that the contractual regime de-legitimates the rights of the unemployed person as client. Social work has an important role to play in protecting unemployed people's rights. There are also important community development, group work, and counselling practices in the field. Casework, counselling, group work, community work, management, and research are all carried out in the employment field. There are, in this field and others, the potential inadequacies and dangers in any professional community of trying to 'distil the essentials into an artificially contrived set of unified concepts' (Adams 1998, p. 272).

Nonetheless, the following points provide a starting point for a discussion of practice in the employment field. These points are based on Thompson's (1998, p. 320) five criteria for high-quality practice:

- Systematic practice based on clarity, focus, and partnership—So as to prevent wasted effort and to achieve desired ends, practitioners need to be clear about programme objectives and social goals. In employment services, for example, what are the criteria concerned with obligation towards and rights for the client? Are there ways of working in partnership with clients, experts, entrepreneurs, business people, and others towards the desired socio-economic ends of employment for all who want to work? Can we improve the ecological environment at the same time?
- Assessment should not be narrow and service-oriented—In looking at the circumstances of unemployed people social workers should consider the background of the person, especially in comparison with more affluent groupings and social categories in society such as professionals and the business elite. How is assessment used as part of policy and for whom?
- Interventions should not be routine or unimaginative—Routine in some practice is necessary, but can often be an excuse for not using more imagination to develop innovative

forms of intervention. There are many ways of working with people in communities, and building a more distributive and just social and ecological environment. The example above of developing new local economic communities based on tourism, for example, through more ecologically sensitive criteria and practice is useful here (see, in comparison, Ife 1995; Giddens 1994). Can social workers make values of social justice and ecological sustainability, as well as limits in economic growth, central to their ethics or practice as good social and community development? There are already good examples among Indigenous and rural communities of ecological, community, and economic values and programmes working together.

- In work with service users and providers, social workers need to be culturally sensitive and anti-racist—This criterion cannot be ignored in social work education or practice. Australia is a racist country, and has a history with Indigenous, migrant, and refugee communities over 200 years of White occupation that is racist (Hage 1998). Social workers need to be aware of the cultural hegemony of certain groups—particularly Anglo-Celtic males—in Australia, and the ways in which neocolonial and imperialistic attitudes make other cultures and people inferior. In working with young unemployed people in the western or inner-city suburbs of Sydney, for example, social workers are directly confronted with cultural diversity. Anti-discriminatory and anti-racist practice requires more than just knowledge—it requires good relationships between providers and users of services (Hugman 1998, pp. 78–9). How can the socio-cultural assumptions of social workers be challenged and their skill base broadened to culturally sensitive practice? How can social workers come to know more about the work and life histories of people of diverse socio-cultural backgrounds? In terms of the employment field, social workers can help enable the workplace to become a more culturally sensitive place and, in creating greater cooperation, possibly enhance production (Cope & Kalantzis 1997).
- Good practice must be emancipatory and participatory—Social workers can challenge oppression in action or behaviours that are racist, sexist, ageist, heterosexist, homophobic, and discriminatory to people with disabilities, and so on. If these practices are not challenged in social work, and elsewhere, then they are, by design or default, condoned in the dominant social order. Education and training programmes, in partnership with relevant social groups, can be run to enhance awareness of oppressive practice in social work with disadvantaged and socially excluded people. The teaching and conduct of social work practice must rely on clear principles and objectives, guided by social justice and ecological strategies that are emancipatory and participatory.

Ethical issues

Social workers increasingly are confronted with several difficult and salient ethical issues. Many of these issues can be placed within a framework that considers, in relationships with clients and other workers, questions of gender, trust, power relations, and identity. Some of the issues include: how social work establishes trust (or mistrust) with clients; the gendered nature of delivery (for example, from a female provider to male user, or female provider to female user); the unequal power relationships between provider and user, given professional workers are gaining higher status and credentials; and the devalued social status of unemployed or social security and Centrelink clients. Many clients of employment services are in poverty, and are psychologically and emotionally vulnerable because of their social circumstances and the social forces that have shaped these circumstances. Can social work help to challenge oppressive and institutional forces that place such people in subordinate positions and groups in the social structure?

Over the past 30 years there has been a shift from the participatory state of the Whitlam years (1972–75) to one that emphasises the role of individual responsibility and enterprise. Ethical issues for social work practice in the employment field arise out of the changes in federal government policy since 1996 that emphasise decentralised industrial relations, and competitive labour market policy and programmes that are contracted out. In the employment field, the rise of managerialism or 'doing more with less' staffing and resourcing—particularly in publicly funded health and community services—and the effects of enterprise bargaining in undermining collective wage-bargaining and union activity have had a dramatic effect on the workplace. Managerialism and changes to Australia's industrial system have helped to narrow the professional identity of social work from involvement in social change towards a concern for its own legitimacy and performance accountability. This has led to the not altogether unfounded criticism that some areas of social work are more and more concerned with preserving the status quo of social inequality, with social workers watching their own backs (Adams 1998; Jamrozik & Nocella 1998; Dominelli 1997b). Social work can swim across this conservative tide in a counter-movement that pursues transformative change of self and society by participation in programmes for social justice, social action, and social change.

Effective and competent social work practice in Australia, and in other Anglo-European countries, is moving with the restructuring and reinvention of government policy, and modes of service delivery (Adams 1998; Dominelli 1997b; Payne 1997; AASW 1994). There are, however, cautionary warnings as social work moves into a more privatised and sometimes secretive set of policy arrangements for the socially excluded. For example, in the United States large multinational corporations have an important role in the delivery of service, and continue to win large tenders for service provision in juvenile justice, prisons, housing, health, poverty alleviation assistance, and personal social services. Similar trends toward privatisation are already occurring in Australia, thus raising questions about the public accountability of these services. A further dimension of privatisation that requires investigation is the secretive moral and normative regulation of clients, often carried out by non-state and state service administrations in the name of social work (see, for comparison, Wearing 1998; Berreen & Wearing 1989; Donzelot 1979, pp. 58–95). Social workers need to appreciate the complexities of social issues and problems rather than accept arguments that moralise or impose viewpoints (Jamrozik & Nocella 1998; Schmidt & Goodin 1998).

Ethics in context

1 Professional autonomy—Think carefully about how the autonomous goals, knowledge, and values of the profession conflict with those of the organisation or programme objectives you work with. Develop an independent knowledge and value base if necessary to retain professional autonomy and integrity.

2 Anti-oppressive practice—Think through whether your values align with post-welfare state imperatives of legitimating inequality and oppressive practices across social division of class, gender, race, and the life course. Use your political and social imagination, knowledge of social issues, social justice values, and professional skill to generate healthy criticism of health and welfare organisations, and reorganise and challenge existing arrangements or programmes if they do not align with your professional identity.

3 Continuing education and reflection—Link your professional self to education strategies and endeavours so that via professional development and other avenues you stay engaged with building new thinking and knowledge, reflect on your values, and understand emerging policy and practice issues in your work. Share this learning with your colleagues.

Social work, social policy, and the employment field

Is the end of the workers' paradise nigh? Have Australian working conditions been eroded to the point in current post-welfare arrangements where the balance has tipped against workers? The answer is more complex than we might expect. Under current arrangements, prior entitlements to a good safety net are being eroded, especially for vulnerable groups such as the unemployed and people with disabilities. This is aptly illustrated by the Federal Employment Services' policy of using management and control technologies such as the Job Seekers Classification Instruments (JSCI). Such social and administrative technology problematises and then imposes on the unemployed certain identities that are deficit and in need of remediation (MacDonald et al. 2003, p. 498).

The wage earner–welfare relationship is in turmoil in Australia, given there are more punitive state ideologies to the disadvantaged, which include privatisation of services and a decentralised industrial citizenship. However, the core elements of the safety net constituting income security and a social rights approach remain, at present, intact. Work is a scarce resource for the Australian population, yet access to work and the socio-economic benefits that paid work bring are crucial determinants in our standard of living and quality of life. Perhaps this particularly true of employment policy and practice, especially in labour market programmes that target unemployment. Social work and social policy need to be concerned with unemployment as a social justice issue, given the marked effect being out of work can have on people's lives in terms of poverty and social deprivation. For example, the connection between long-term unemployment and deep poverty is well established. While the Australian unemployment rate, at 7 per cent in July 1999, was the lowest in 10 years, the long-term unemployment rate had risen to 17.8 per cent of all employed persons (ACOSS 1999).

Work is the primary provider of welfare in Australia, and the traditional residualism of the social welfare system is an 'add on' or secondary provider. Inequalities based on access to paid work in a highly privatised economy are burgeoning (Gregory & Hunter 1996; Saunders 1996; Jamrozik 2001). Australia is, in many ways, a post-welfare society based on the new 'brutalism' of work; that is, one that has abandoned any real notion that redistribution or lessening the inequalities, created and perpetuated by markets, can be changed by the state. The brutalism of the new market economy expresses itself among workers and the unemployed as a new and mean individualism, in which there are fewer but much better off winners, and many more who lose in the welfare stakes.

The Australian post-welfare state steers the economy, but can it govern the nature of the market? Australia is part of broader international trends towards a market-oriented and post-welfare statism. The major global winners in this new economic order are large private interest groups, such as multinational companies, and dominant Western powers such as the United States. What are the implications for global inequality, especially for a small marginal Western country such as Australia, and developing countries in our Asia–Pacific region? Australia's shift to a post-welfare state means that, like the company shareholders who benefit from privatisation, only the shareholding insiders of public–private benefits, rather than all Australians, gain advantage from certain social policy and state action (Jamrozik 2001; Ranald 2003).

Where can change come from in dealing with the issues of jobs and social and economic development in this country, and what role can social work play? Beyond the labour movement and state-centred social policy, the activities of new social movements, such as those of ecology and, in particular, feminism, in the twentieth century have made many important gains in terms of resource distribution. There is a need to understand the relationships between movements for change, and professional and policy communities, and build on these relationships. Further, there are creative alliances being built among non-state social policy providers, particularly in the community service sector through churches and other non-profit organisations. Social work has a role to play in forming alliances, and encouraging civic protest and the participation of communities from the bottom up. The middle class, itself, is perhaps protecting its own vested interest in having the state maintain a certain level and form of social wage, and the hidden welfare benefits that go with this wage (Graycar & Jamrozik 1993).

The future of social work

There is little doubt that the Australian state has been reorganised into a more 'lean and mean' set of social arrangements. Governments at all levels need to take more responsibility and indeed have an obligation to redress inequality in a democratic society. Among those who lose out most in the employment field are the working class, the poor, and those who are made inferior or subordinate, such as people with disabilities, Indigenous people, and migrants. Social work needs to practise social criticism seriously in research, report writing, counselling and group programmes, community development, and management. Good poverty alleviation measures are only a part of the answer, and these measures are themselves being eroded in the current government climate. It is no solution to blame poor people for their circumstances, and introduce explicit criteria that define people as deserving or undeserving into programmes based on conditional entitlements to the income safety net and employment services.

Social work can develop broader arguments, strategies, and alliances to challenge and undermine the effects of social inequality, poverty, and oppression. Such strategies and alliances could be, in part, based on socio-ecological development, protest, and advocacy—arguing for social and ecological policies to promote social citizenship and redistribution. In the employment field, social work has an important and potentially innovative role in sustaining people in work as a social right. This can be done by directly assisting people to find meaningful paid work, or helping them to return to the workforce. In indirect ways, social workers can become involved in partnerships and alliances to pursue community development and advocacy for those excluded from paid work.

Review questions

1   What are the characteristics of the post-welfare state?
2   In what ways can social work practice in this field be anti-oppressive?
3   In what ways is unemployment a social justice issue?

13

GERONTOLOGICAL SOCIAL WORK

David Wiles

Chapter objectives

- To appreciate the historical, sociological, and political implications of an ageing Australia
- To elucidate developing academic gerontology and how it explains the processes, problems, and issues of ageing

- To explore key ethical and practice dimensions for social workers in aged care and services

Introduction

The notion that social work theory and practice are at 'something of a crossroads' in Australia is a useful starting point for a consideration of social work with the aged. As a profession, social work is relatively young, and it must respond to the context of an 'ageing' Australia, in a nation settled by Whites only 200 years ago. In many ways, the care of the aged—in terms of broad social policy, various helping programmes, and specific individual interventions—can be regarded as a test of both the 'progress' of the welfare state and the appropriateness of gerontological social work practice. With the rise of the pernicious ideology of economic rationalism around the globe since the turn of the 1980s, and its consequent impact in Australia upon the wider society in general (and social welfare and aged care in particular), this field of practice offers special challenges to a profession dedicated to ideals of helping needy individuals and reforming social conditions. In this chapter, the realities of gerontological social work practice are explored, drawing on history to trace the development of our present patterns of social welfare and professional care, exploring some current practice issues to provide a snapshot of the aged care field, identifying a number of problematic ethical dilemmas that engage those working with and on behalf of seniors, and drawing these elements together to suggest possible strategies for effective gerontological social work practice in the future.

An ageing Australia—history of policy

Social work with the aged needs to be considered in the context of the broad sweep of Australian history and social policy, as well as the more specific story of the development of gerontological helping practice. Since White settlement, early Australian social welfare patterned itself on the 'Old World' model of charity, philanthropy, and voluntarism, grudgingly underwritten in financial terms by the various colonial governments. The first formal attempt at social welfare in Australia was the establishment, in 1813, of the New South Wales Society for Promoting Christian Knowledge and Benevolence in these Territories and the Neighbouring Islands, renamed the Benevolent Society of New South Wales in 1818. The groups targeted by such primitive human services included 'the poor, the distressed, the aged, and the infirm' (Dickey 1987, pp. 22–3). Thus, the aged have always held a prominent place among the identified recipients of welfare, though throughout history and right down to the present day, assessment processes of various types checked whether beneficiaries were 'deserving' or not. From the earliest times in White settlement, a custodial approach to the care of the aged was set in place: in Sydney: 'an asylum for "the aged and impotent poor" under the auspices of a voluntary organisation, the Benevolent Society of New South Wales' was opened, as documented by Berreen (1994, p. 3).

Australian welfare historians often assert that a concern for social control has been as much in evidence as genuine care in relation to the range of target groups. Similarly, commentators suggest that, during the past two centuries, most Australian 'welfare' was provided through the wage packet; thus, formal welfare services were set in place to assist those for whom the 'normal' market mechanisms had failed. In the twentieth century, this social understanding was strengthened by the Harvester Judgment of 1907, which established a 'living wage'. The labour market was seen as the primary source of financial support for individuals and families, with the 'safety net' of public assistance offered as a last resort (Garton 1994). Later in that century, the White Paper on Full Employment of 1945 embodied the social responsibility of federal governments to maintain the level of paid work in the Australian community, with the implication that the foremost and fundamental source of 'welfare' for most citizens would be waged work.

The minor 'greying' of the Australian population a century ago, along with the financial aftermath of the 1890s economic depression, coalesced to create social problems for the aged in regard to income and accommodation. At Federation in 1901, one of the few matters on which general consensus existed was the need for a national old age pension, and payments commenced in mid 1909. According to Davison (1993, p. 20), 'it was the introduction of the Old Age Pension, more than any other factor, that defined old age in early twentieth century Australia. In taking the pension an old person entered an implicit contract to retire from the workforce'. Thus the social institution of retirement was established, and, from this point, the twentieth-century concept of the intergenerational social contract developed, whereby the income, and increasingly the health and accommodation needs, of seniors were financed out of consolidated revenue as a reward for their past lives of working, taxpaying, and contributing to national development. In terms of gerontological social work, care of the aged has long been a primary, though not necessarily popular, field of service. Hospital and medical social work date back to the origins of the profession in Australia, with a major theme being concern for seniors frail in body and mind or suffering other social disadvantages.

Social work with seniors needs to be understood in the context of changing philosophies and patterns of aged care. From the mid 1950s, the Australian federal government made funds available to expand the number of nursing home beds, and subsequently to subsidise the creation of congregate accommodation for the aged. Churches and charities responded readily to such financial incentives. As argued by Healy (1990, p. 129), in the past the care of the aged was mostly conceptualised as a 'medical' problem, and the orthodox response to the problems of the frail aged was usually placement in an 'old folk's home', whether a nursing home, hostel, or perhaps an independent-living unit within a retirement village.

Notions of 'domiciliary' and 'community' care evolved in contrast to the standard residential response to the perceived needs of seniors in Australia. From the 1950s, Meals on Wheels, under a variety of auspices across the states, typified the strategy of assisting the frail elderly to 'age in place'; that is, to continue living in their established homes and neighbourhoods within the general community (Healy 1990).

Sometimes, care in the community was linked with attendance of the aged at a day hospital, where chronic medical conditions could be discreetly monitored and positive socialisation experiences provided. However, the close connection of aged care with the voluntary sector, and the frequent dependence upon volunteerism, can be readily observed. In the 1980s, a number of developments increased governmental, bureaucratic, and professional emphases upon community care for the frail aged and disabled. Most commentators on aged policy identify the McLeay report (McLeay 1982) as a watershed for the care of the aged in Australia. McLeay indicated that many seniors living in residential care facilities were there for reasons connected with accommodation needs rather than health conditions, and argued that community care was both more humane and more economical than the orthodox residential alternatives. These new philosophies and practices were expressed in the 1985 Home and Community Care (HACC) program. Since then, aged care has moved from using residential relocation as the panacea for the problems of the frail aged to the new ideology promoting individual independence in the context of the community for as long as possible, thus preventing 'inappropriate or premature admission to long-term residential care' (Aroni & Minichiello 1992, p. 146). In broad terms, the HACC program and its various offshoots are the backdrop to much contemporary gerontological social work.

In the last two decades a number of social trends have had significant impacts upon work with the aged. On the positive side, the aged and ageing have emerged into the broad social consciousness of the nation: a general awareness of the 'greying' of the Australian population exists, while, in earlier times, issues of ageing and aged care were mostly a minority or specialist interest. This awareness has been expressed in the creation of government offices concerned with policy on age, and in the great variety of federal and state inquiries into ageing, held from the start of the 1990s. Such inquiries always looked ahead to the implied demographic challenges of the twenty-first century.

Associated with this increasing community awareness has been the development of an authentically Australian gerontology, or study of ageing and the aged (Howe 1990). Before the 1980s there was little local research on the aged; however, since that time, specific courses and subjects on ageing have emerged, along with an Australian gerontological literature. For example, Australia's first real multidisciplinary textbook on gerontology, written by Minichiello et al., working at the Lincoln Gerontology Centre based at La Trobe University, was published in 1992.

Unfortunately, the community interest in ageing issues is set within the broader context of the upsurge of the ideology of economic rationalism. The present and future aged population frequently is portrayed in an alarmist way as a 'cost burden' likely to bankrupt the welfare state. Within the aged services as in social welfare generally, our society seems to be moving towards a 'two-tier' system of good private provisions and poor public programmes (Jamrozik 2001). Thus in this hostile environment the former intergenerational contract has been undermined, so that, for instance, in less than two decades retirement incomes have been transformed from a public to a private responsibility, and user-pays principles have been increasingly applied to the health, community, and accommodation services used by seniors. In this antagonistic economic and political environment the gerontological social worker is challenged to find how best to help our senior population.

Issues of practice in gerontological social work

Increasing societal awareness of ageing is reflected in rising professional concern. Although the proportion of seniors within the general population is growing, it is important to recognise that social workers tend to interact with only a section of the senior population; that is, those suffering the particular problems associated with ageing often compounded by other persistent forms of social disadvantage. The ageing experience may be considered according to a range of variables influencing the quality of life of the aged, including socio-economic class, gender, disability, ethnicity, diversity, and living in rural regions. In terms of social class, there is little doubt that the inequalities experienced over the life cycle continue or even intensify into old age, as argued in classic radical critiques of the field (see, for example, Phillipson 1982). In Australia, the aged were identified by the Henderson inquiry into poverty of 1975 as the single largest group prone to poverty and, although over the decades this has shifted towards single parents, old and poor people are still the focus of much social work intervention.

Interestingly, early social gerontology, particularly that emerging from North America, tended to explore the retirement experience of men, ignoring the fact that across the world women usually enjoy greater longevity, making ageing rather more of a women's issue. According to Graycar and Jamrozik (1993, p. 282), 'women are the overwhelming majority of our elderly population. At age 65, for every 100 men there are 107 women; at age 75, for every 100 men there are 134 women; and at age 85 and over, there are 256 women for every 100 men'. Thus, women outliving men as the age range rises, on average, is an increasing trend. The North American-based *Journal of Women and Aging*, which began to be published in the 1980s, is perhaps a relatively recent recognition of these worldwide demographic trends. Although this increased awareness of the demographic realities seems to be good progress, the gender dimensions of ageing as a social issue preclude simplistic generalisations, as further exploration suggests quite distinctive processes and patterns for women (Roberto 1996) and men (Job 1994; Thompson 1994).

The social stereotype of ageing often indicates the inevitable increase of sickness, disability, and problems in living, though descriptive population data are usually more positive. The data suggest, for example, that among the section of the senior population prone to problems—those aged 75 years and over—less than one quarter suffered a disability necessitating outside assistance (McCallum & Geiselhart 1996, p. 90). Although old age increases our vulnerability to a range of health problems, physical difficulties are not necessarily an inevitable consequence of the ageing process. As pointed out by Hammond and Jilek (2003, p. 42), 'ageing and disease should not be equated'.

A significant demographic issue for social work is that, presently, one-fifth of the aged population is from a non-English-speaking background. Fluctuations in the ethnic composition of the population, resulting from migration patterns of long ago, are evidenced in the emergence of ethno-specific social services. Similarly, the variables of diversity and living in rural regions recently have begun to gain more attention in the aged field (Harrison 1999; Williams & McMahon 1998). Overall, differentiation among the aged population suggests that the subjective experience of ageing will be shaped by such objective variables as class, gender, and ethnicity.

Within the aged population there is a common range of human needs to be addressed by gerontological social work. The psychosocial needs of older people, as identified by Yoon (1996), are six-fold: economic, health, social, emotional, cultural, and environmental. Seniors need a sufficient income to meet the requirements of daily living, as well as adequate nutrition, continuing exercise, and management of any diseases or disabilities. Socialising, or perhaps volunteering, is important for the aged to stay connected with wider society, as is maintaining adequate contact with families and friends, and the private challenge of finding meaning in life. Cultural needs include lifelong learning, hobbies, communication, and transportation. Lastly, within this framework, the environmental needs of seniors include housing, safety, and access to community services. Cox and Parsons (1994, p. 121) cite a classification developed by Lowy, the renowned American gerontologist, articulating the 'educational' needs of seniors in relation to coping, contributing, influencing, contemplating, and transcending. While the needs of the aged may be conceptualised in many ways, and while we have seen that determinants such as class, ethnicity, and gender influence the experience of ageing, classifications such as those discussed tend to demonstrate underlying similarities in personal and social needs across the lifespan. This combination of similarities and differences among ageing Australians guarantees the gerontological social worker a rich range of challenges within this field of practice.

Australian gerontological social work practice has also been shaped by the evolution of international gerontology over the years. While such theoretical debates may seem remote, they have filtered through to influence the manner in which aged care and services are provided by our programmes and agencies. From the 1950s, gerontological theory emphasised 'disengagement', yet, more recently, 'activity' approaches to the understanding of ageing and society have been emphasised. In the 1960s and 1970s, disengagement theory was the orthodox framework for social gerontology. As first espoused by Cumming and Henry in 1961, the disengagement theorists argued that the best adaptation to ageing, both for seniors and society, was the gradual detachment of the older person from work and community life, in preparation for death. Consistent with such notions, the practice philosophy suggested that aged care usually could be best provided by segregating those seniors with health or welfare problems into some variant of the 'old folk's home'.

As the weaknesses of the disengagement framework emerged, particularly as longer-lived people continued to participate in community life, intellectual and practice ideologies shifted from the 1970s towards activity theory. As first postulated by Havighurst in 1963, successful adjustment to ageing involves not the withdrawal from the world suggested by disengagement theory, but rather the continuation of activities and connections with the broad community (Aroni & Minichiello 1992). Thus, activity theory meshes with social and political movement towards preventive health education for seniors, positive and productive retirement years, and the provision of necessary assistance through community and domiciliary care.

Of course, neither disengagement nor activity theory is totally satisfactory, as the senior population is quite diverse. Moving from the societal to the individual level, Atchley's (1976) 'continuity' theory, emphasising the psychological commonalities of coping mechanisms across the lifespan, remains a most useful framework for the gerontological social worker. While social work has moved away from the earlier psychological theories, 'continuity' theory is a powerful framework for understanding the older Australian.

The gerontological social worker may encounter the ageing client within a range of settings and situations from traditional hospital-based work through to community care, residential care, and advocacy work. Proactive and preventive work may also take place: for example, retirement planning programmes abound to assist the retiree to make sense of this major life transition (Lowis & Picton 1996). The gerontological social worker may use the full range of practice types through individual casework, group work, and community development, as well as policy and advocacy work.

In casework and counselling the social worker encounters each older person as the cumulative product of their life story. Every senior has traversed an idiosyncratic 'patch', though living among others within the context of community and culture, and so each aged person should be understood and appreciated for their uniqueness.

Intervention with the elderly, as with the wide range of target groups, involves the identification and resolution of the variety of human needs. Gerontological social workers will often assist in regard to personal problems of adjustment, or matters related to income, housing, health care, and domiciliary and community services. It can be readily seen that, leaving aside the particular difficulties often associated with the ageing process, the needs of the aged are much the same as those of younger generations.

What may be qualitatively different in social work with seniors relates to their vantage point in the life cycle: the elderly not only are concerned with meeting the present range of life challenges but also are motivated to interpret and integrate the past with the present. While gerontological social work always deals with the demands of the real world and the satisfaction of the range of human needs, intervention with seniors also involves this more abstract and qualitative aspect requiring subjective appreciation of the past within the present. Robert Butler, an American doctor, revolutionised psychological and professional thinking about the mental life of the elderly. Before Butler, the conventional wisdom in work with seniors had been that maudlin, perhaps self-indulgent, reminiscence should be discouraged. The aged, it was thought, should not be allowed to dwell on or in the past, but rather should be redirected to concentrate their faltering powers upon the present. In his classic article Butler (1963, p. 65) argued for 'life review' reminiscence as a desirable and normative developmental behaviour, portraying such activity as a 'universal occurrence in older people of an inner experience or mental process of reviewing one's life'. This led to the view that such behaviour ought to be encouraged, as it facilitated the happiness and adjustment of the aged.

In working with seniors, then, the tasks of life review should be encouraged. Originally Butler suggested that the threat of impending death puts pressure on seniors to recognise and resolve conflicts from the past, so as to harmonise past experience with present consciousness. Through such 'storytelling' reminiscence, the past is evaluated and reconstructed to help people face the problems and challenges of the latter years. While some have questioned the extent to which Butler's theory has truly universal application (see, for example, Merriam 1995), in broad terms his positive views have been accepted across the aged care field. Subsequent writers have built upon this creative appreciation of reminiscence, offering excellent theoretical overviews (see, for example, Bender et al. 1999; Hendricks 1995; Gillies & James 1994; Bornat 1994). Such a developmental view of the aged—which recognises the intensification of individuality over the life cycle and that seniors confront specific developmental tasks as well as idiosyncratic personal problems of living—dovetails nicely with the broad psychological approaches underpinning social work education. Seniors may be conceptualised as working towards the higher levels of self-actualisation in Maslow's (1970) 'Hierarchy of Needs', or as working through the 'integrity versus despair' dilemma in the developmental stages identified by Erikson. Bright (1997) discusses a range of strategies to promote a sense of 'wholeness' in seniors and adjust to the possible physical, mental, and social losses of old age. Suggested programmes involve various activities and therapies designed to enhance a sense of self-worth and control over destiny.

In counselling older clients, the social worker may engage them in consideration of issues connected with their family of origin, so as to tease out the implicit 'life scripts' that may be at work in counterproductive behaviours, which undermine their sense of life satisfaction. For instance, in some family histories 'toxic' issues or problems not easily solved may take a terrible toll over generations (Davenport 1999; Wiles 1993). Attentive reminiscence work can address such subterranean dynamics across the generations, identifying and resolving such issues. The gerontological social worker needs to have an ear for the spiritual issues implicit in the stories of seniors. The increasing recognition of mortality, as their frailties begin to appear, seems to encourage the elderly to reflect upon the deeper religious and philosophical implications of their past lives. Furthermore, the social worker may assist them to work through the various stages of death and dying (Kubler-Ross 1978). Atchley and Barusch (2004) distinguish between spirituality as a personal, psychological domain and religion as a societal institution, and suggest that seniors negotiate these elements in their inward search for biographical meaning and coherence. The developing practice wisdom seems to be that through conquering the various dilemmas and difficulties of the latter years, seniors may achieve a positive sense of 'gerotranscendence' (Jonson & Magnusson 2001; Lewin 2001). Thus life review may include the specifically spiritual along with the broadly psychological dimension (Teshuva et al. 1997; Magee 1992).

While considering these psychological aspects of working with the older person, it is important to recognise that the integration and harmony commonly associated with life review reminiscence is not always characteristic of the aged. The medical profession may sometimes perceive that psychotherapeutic intervention with older people who are melancholy or 'maladjusted' is not really worth the time or effort, as they may have left only a limited number of years. Tranquillisers may, therefore, be seen as an appropriate form of patient management.

A quarter-century ago, most psychology textbooks barely touched upon the middle to later period of life, though perhaps they closed with a brief treatment of death and bereavement. Nowadays, there are textbooks that focus specifically on midlife to old age, identifying specific developmental tasks appropriate to these stages of the human life cycle (see, for example, Cavanaugh 1993; Rybash et al. 1991). Similarly, the publication of the international journal *Psychology and Aging* in 1986 indicated increasing professional interest in the mental lives of elderly people. Following this trend, Orbach (1996) argues that psychotherapy should not be restricted to just the younger client. The avoidance of intensive therapeutic work with seniors often reflects professional unease with the range of issues that older people may need to process, including bereavement, bodily changes, and fear of death. Orbach suggests that even long-term psychotherapy is appropriate with motivated elderly clients.

Depression among the elderly, though common and often amenable to intervention, often goes unrecognised and untreated (Snowdon 1998). While some depressive states have an organic basis, positive professional intervention focusing on environmental and attitudinal change may well assist the older depressed person. The gerontological social worker also needs to be aware that undiagnosed depression among the elderly, particularly for men, can lead to suicide. As Goldney and Harrison (1998) report, there is a peak in suicide rates for males in late adolescence to early twenties, and another for those aged above 75 years, though Australian statistics show that this self-destructive behaviour had decreased over the twentieth century. As well as facilitating the positive progress of the older client towards psychosocial and personal harmony, the gerontological social worker must also be on the alert for depressive symptoms or suicidal tendencies among aged clients, and be ready to refer them for more intensive psychotherapeutic treatment.

As we have seen, gerontological social work is practised in a range of settings from broad community care through to specific residential care facilities provided for the aged who are frail, or who have diseases or dementia. The scope of social work with older people and the professional challenges involved in such work are explained thoroughly in many texts (see, for example, Beaulieu 2001; Marshall & Dixon 1996; Cox & Parsons 1994). These days, the gerontological social worker in the front line of community care intervenes on behalf of seniors, while the sweeping societal forces of economic rationalism are subverting former certainties in philosophies and programmes for the aged. In Western countries, the withdrawal of the public sector has led to the 'marketisation' of social welfare, as reflected in user-pays practices.

Furthermore, given that prejudices associated with class and age are entrenched in society, social workers confront such inequalities in their daily practice, necessitating anti-discriminatory work practices (Hughes 1995). The modern emphasis on family care, typically recognised as part of the support offered by family, and especially female carers, is also acknowledged as a product of the retreat from state responsibility for aged care. The daily duties of the gerontological social worker may include assessment of seniors who remain in the home in relation to the available family care, and of the needs and stress of carers to work towards an appropriate, effective, and sustainable mix of care (Bland 1996; Nolan et al. 1996; Phillips 1995).

In recent decades, aged residential care has been derided across the world in theory as an inappropriate 'ghettoisation' of older people, yet given the range of frailties to which seniors may fall vulnerable, continuing provision of residential care remains a necessity (Peace et al. 1997). In Australia, for example, a decade of restrictive 'gatekeeping' by Geriatric Assessment Teams and then Aged Care Assessment Teams has reduced the number of seniors in residential care from 7 per cent to 6 per cent. Thus, a significant proportion of gerontological social work still will be in residential care. Interestingly, there are ways that, through involvement of volunteers, or the families of residents within the care programmes, the community can be brought to frail seniors in residential care (La Brake 1996; Jackson 1995). Institutional care is no longer considered to be a panacea for problems associated with ageing, as it was formerly, but it will continue to be the site for much future gerontological social work practice.

Ethical issues in gerontological social work

Since the 1980s, societal and professional interest in ethics has increased in Australia, resulting in attention to codes of ethics across the human services field. However, in an era dominated by economic cutbacks, instability in social services, and increasing levels of need of welfare clients, whether this ostensible concern with ethical practice makes much actual difference is open to question.

It is generally agreed that social work is an essentially moral undertaking, and that a range of ethical concerns informs the profession (Banks 2001; Loewenberg et al. 2004; Hinman 2003; Noble & Briskman 1998). Considering matters of professional conduct, Lawrence (1997) explains that 'ethics is about human agency, both individual and collective, and about the criteria or reasons being used for action and assessment'.

The Code of Ethics of the AASW (2002) is underwritten by nine principles articulating responsibilities of the worker to the client, the profession, and the community. Although the code expounds a commitment to social justice, any impetus towards broad social reform is difficult to generate in these times of welfare cutbacks. Similarly, De Maria (1997) documents the tensions between the shifting professional emphases on social service or social action caused by fluctuating ideologies and philosophies over the years. Thus O'Connor et al. (2000, p. 5) pose the following question: 'How to work within a competitive framework and yet remain wedded to social work's fundamental mission of social justice is a critical area for the future direction of the field.' Perhaps the existence of the code, while intrinsically worthwhile as a statement of general intentions, serves only to initiate an ongoing dialogue about ethical social work practice.

Ethics in Context

You are a medical social worker attached to the geriatric ward of a major teaching hospital. Esme, your client, is a 75-year-old English widow who has recently suffered the amputation of her left leg due to diabetes and heavy smoking. She has lived in Australia for 30 years, and has one married daughter. Naomi, the daughter, is in paid employment, and lives several suburbs away from her mother's state housing unit. Esme tells you that she wants to stay in her seniors flat, living 'independently'. You have interviewed the daughter Naomi, who reports indirectly that her mother is extremely demanding on her time, energy, and emotion. For example, Esme refuses Meals on Wheels because she 'prefers' Naomi's cooking. Similarly Esme declines opportunities for social interaction with her age peers and relatives, wanting only the company and attention of her daughter. Thus Naomi feels obliged to spend weekends sleeping at her mother's place, neglecting her husband and rebellious teenage son. What should you do?

While ethical issues and dilemmas abound in any field of social work, perhaps the key issue in the aged care field is the question of the 'independence' of the frail aged person and support for community care: a natural tension that is intensified in the age of the user-pays approach. Since the release of the McLeay report, various studies have reinforced that most frail seniors wish to continue living independently in their own homes within the general community. Such independence, involving as it does the 'dignity of risk', may not be real if families or volunteers are actually providing daily care. It must also be remembered that this humanitarian approach has also been encouraged due to the financial savings afforded by the rationing of expensive residential care. For each older person in a nursing home in Australia it currently costs around $30,000 every year, while domiciliary care in the community can be provided for merely a tenth of that amount (Bagnall 1999, p. 23). Cost-cutting agendas underpin aged care, confusing and complicating both effective client care and appropriate professional intervention.

The relatively recent problem of elder abuse, first overseas and now in Australia, is an example of how broad societal trends have an impact on gerontological social work practice. The literature has included studies on the incidence and nature of the problem (Craig 1997; Johnson 1995; Schlesinger & Schlesinger 1992), educational kits for workers (Pritchard 1996), protocols and guides (Government of Western Australia 1994), as well as strategies for the amelioration and treatment of this social problem (Baumhover & Beall 1996). Abuse of elders is an area of practice that poses many ethical dilemmas: protecting the vulnerable senior; maintaining, as a goal of practice, delicate systems of support; and enhancing familial connections are important. Furthermore, the emergence of abuse of the aged as a social problem may illustrate a broader underlying ethical dilemma facing contemporary social work practice; that is, how can the profession provide adequately for the care of the aged while economic rationalism keeps the welfare state under prolonged attack?

Ethics in context

1 How can the social worker support the 'independence' of the aged client, when in reality that client is depending on family members?
2 How much client self-determination is possible, if a diagnosis of dementia has been made?
3 How can we advocate for our aged target group to obtain the best intergenerational settlement?

The future for social work

It may be possible to predict, to a certain degree, some of the future trends for gerontological social work. As already argued, the reactionary social trends dating from the 1980s and 1990s had many impacts on aged policy and programmes. Valentine (1999) documents the manner in which the ideology of economic rationalism has undermined our formerly accepted concepts of governmental responsibility, rights of citizenship, sense of community, and motivation to care for those people who are socially disadvantaged; yet these quite fundamental societal and cultural changes have been brought about under the guise of essential economic changes. It is likely that the social effects of these changes will compound in the future, as governments further abandon the public sector and the welfare state, leaving citizens to provide for themselves according to their ability to pay in an increasingly 'two-tier' society (Jamrozik 2001).

In relation to ageing and aged care, such philosophies and strategies are clearly evidenced in a discussion paper released by the former Federal Minister for Aged Care Services, Bronwyn Bishop, in 1999. Bishop soberly notes: 'Australia's population ageing is neither as fast nor as extreme as other developed countries. Other countries have *already* experienced levels of ageing which are *future* scenarios for Australia' [emphases added] (1999, p. 8).

Despite the empirical demographic realities, this dubious blueprint for the future asserts the alarmist rhetoric usually associated with journalists and economists as to the problem of the 'baby-boom time bomb' (Brenchley 1999), threatening to bankrupt the Australian health and welfare system. The four social strategies suggested in the discussion paper include a mix of approaches designed to reconfigure our ageing population according to the requirements of free market capitalism. First, Australians are to be encouraged towards self-funded retirement, with the popular option of early retirement to be discouraged. Second, the ongoing marketisation of aged care according to user-pays principles is to proceed, with cheaper community care being the preferred option. Third, the promotion of preventive strategies for healthy ageing should reduce future health care costs associated with ageing, though there is the potential for 'blaming the victim' when seniors fall ill or become frail. Fourth, the promotion of positive attitudes to ageing, though laudable and plausible, is nothing new, and seems to be connected with commercial awareness of the 'grey dollar': the increased respect for seniors may not be so much due to their acquired wisdom or social contribution, but rather to their perceived worth as consumers.

Such trends are continuing into the twenty-first century. Taking the ongoing privatisation of aged retirement incomes as a specific example of these social directions, Hammond and Jilek (2003, p. 126) argue: 'The Government policy of self-funding retirement has an implicit message that in terms of the tax dollar the elderly are not worth as much as they used to be. The old are basically regarded in economic terms and spending heavily on them is a poor economic and political investment.'

Given these rather gloomy political and ideological trends and the continuing turbulence in community services (McDonald 1999), what are the future prospects for gerontological social work? Caring casework and group work can improve significantly the quality of life for older clients, consistent with the best traditions of social work. Congruent with social justice principles, it is incumbent upon all social workers to acknowledge in their daily practice the societal and structural sources of oppression and disadvantage suffered by our clients and client populations. As Tesoriero (1999, p. 11) indicates, social reform and social development require that social work 'move from managerial and market paradigms and align itself once more with those that are marginalised and disadvantaged'.

Social workers need to be aware of the policy context for the aged—as outlined by Borowski et al. (1997), for example—as well as how advocacy about policy really works in practical and operational terms, as described by Sheen (1999). Linking such policy and pro-gramme concerns, social workers need to focus, in terms of daily work, on 'empowerment-oriented' practice (Cox & Parsons 1994) located within an 'anti-oppressive' ideology (Maidment & Egan 2004). Looking back, the care of seniors was one of the early elements of the Australian welfare state. Looking forward, ethical gerontological social work practice must not restrict itself to the caring casework of which it can be so proud, but should also direct attention to programme reform, policy work, and political action.

Review questions

1 What insights does gerontology provide for working effectively with the aged?
2 How should social workers engage in 'non-ageist' practice?
3 Who is responsible for the income, health, and housing outcomes of seniors? Why?
4 Discuss the development and decline of the Australian aged income system over the twentieth century.
5 What do you see as the challenges for gerontological social workers in the twenty-first century?

14

THE CHALLENGE OF CHILD PROTECTION

Elizabeth Fernandez

Chapter objectives

- To provide an overview of child maltreatment in Australia
- To offer an understanding of how child maltreatment is defined
- To present an analysis of child protection responses in Australia

Introduction

Intervention on behalf of abused and neglected children is an important dimension of child welfare and of enormous importance to social workers. Child maltreatment has been the focus of continuing debate by professionals, politicians, and academics. The definition and scope of the problem, its causes, and how it should be responded to are the subject of wide-ranging opinion. Central to the debate has been the nature of the relationship between the state and family. This relationship entails the right of parents to raise children as they see fit, and the corresponding obligation of the state to intervene when care in the family is inadequate or abusive. The role of the state in monitoring children's well-being is based on assumptions about what is acceptable parenting and what is in the child's 'best interest'. Such judgments are influenced by historical, theoretical, ideological, social, and economic contexts. In this chapter, how child maltreatment is defined, the perceived causes, and the evolving policies and practices that constitute child protection and the debates surrounding them are examined.

The scope of child maltreatment in Australia

The number of notifications of child abuse and neglect over the past decade has increased considerably in most states and territories in Australia. The number of child protection notifications increased by over 60,000 in the last year rising from 137,938 in 2001–02 to 198,355 in 2002–03. There has been a continuing upward trend in the last four years, in that the number of child protection notifications increased from 107,134 in 1999–2000 to 198,355 in 2002–03. From 2001–02 to 2002–03 the number of notifications increased in all jurisdictions except Victoria, Western Australia, and the Northern Territory (AIHW 2004, p. 14).

Following a notification of child maltreatment, the responsible authority in each jurisdiction investigates the allegation. There is variation between jurisdictions in the range of notifications investigated, as the criteria for defining an 'investigation' varies. While the majority of notifications are investigated, the proportion varies from 34 per cent in Victoria to 96 per cent in Western Australia. Rates of children aged 0–16 years who were the subjects of child protection substantiations in 2002–03 ranged from 1.8 per 1000 in Tasmania to 10.1 per 1000 in Queensland, increases during this period being reflected in New South Wales, Queensland, South Australia, Tasmania, and the Australian Capital Territory.

It is difficult to make meaningful comparisons of rates of abuse and neglect because of the differing policies and practices in each state and, consequently, the way in which statistics are compiled in that state. In New South Wales changes to child protection policies, and the proclamation of the new legislation and opening of the helpline, have had a bearing on notifications received and responses required. Police procedures require the police to notify the Department of Community Services in New South Wales (DoCS) about all cases in which they attend an incident of domestic violence and there are children present in the household. An overview of significant changes in policy in other states that affect data trends is available in *Child Protection in Australia 2002–03* (AIHW 2004).

The distribution of types of abuse and neglect substantiated varies across state and territory. Physical abuse is the most common type of maltreatment substantiated in New South Wales (32 per cent), Western Australia and South Australia (28 per cent), and Tasmania and the Northern Territory (42 per cent and 43 per cent respectively). In Victoria and the Australian Capital Territory emotional abuse predominates (44 per cent and 40 per cent respectively), while in Queensland and South Australia it is neglect (38 per cent and 42 per cent respectively), and in Tasmania it is sexual abuse (40 per cent) (AIHW 2004, p. 16).

A higher proportion of females than males is reflected in the substantiated cases. In all jurisdictions except the Australian Capital Territory, the overrepresentation of females is evident in the sexual abuse category: three times as many girls are the subject of substantiations of sexual abuse. Children under one year are most likely to be the subject of substantiation followed by children aged 1–4 years. Many states have procedures for responding to notifications involving young children.

Indigenous children are overrepresented in substantiations of child abuse and neglect in all jurisdictions. Victoria has the highest rate of substantiations for Indigenous children (55.6 per 1000 children aged 0–16 compared with 5.4 for other children). Corresponding rates for Queensland are 15.9 per 1000 compared with 9.7 for other children. The pattern of substantiation of particular types of abuse and neglect for Indigenous children differs from the pattern for other children: for example, in Western Australia 50 per cent of

Indigenous children in substantiations were the subject of a substantiation of neglect compared with 28 per cent of other children; the corresponding percentages in New South Wales are 25 per cent and 17 per cent. However, lower proportions of sexual abuse cases substantiated are consistently found among Indigenous children in all states except the Northern Territory. The underlying causes for the overrepresentation of Indigenous children suggests the intergenerational effects of separation from family, and cultural status and cultural difference in child-rearing practices (AIHW 2004, p. 21).

Child protection services can apply to the court for care and protection orders if risk to the child is serious. This may result in guardianship whereby the state assumes legal responsibility for the child, and may involve removal of the child to out-of-home care. Supervision orders, interim and temporary orders, and voluntary arrangements are among the other options used for child protection purposes. At June 2003 there were 22,130 children aged 0–17 on care and protection orders in Australia (4.6 per 1000 children). Of those children on orders at 30 June 2003, 85 per cent were on guardianship or custody orders, 6 per cent were on supervisory orders, and 6 per cent on interim and temporary orders (AIHW 2004, p. 30). Again, the disproportionate numbers of Indigenous children on care and protection orders (23.1 per 1000 children aged 0–17 years)—which is 6.1 times higher than the rate for other children—is to be noted (AIHW 2004, p. 36).

The child protection system is subject to constant changes, which has an impact on the data. States and territories have their own child protection legislation, policies, and practices, and this influences national data. Therefore, changes in the number of children in the child protection system may reflect changing administrative practices rather than the number of children in need of protection. While data trends may reflect apparent escalation in the incidence of maltreatment, they are likely to indicate increasing professional and community awareness of the rights of children and an increased willingness to act on this awareness to safeguard children's well-being.

Defining child maltreatment

Part of the problem in identifying maltreatment is that there is no agreed and unambiguous definition of abuse. A clear definition is an important prerequisite to improved responses and substantiation. The Australian Institute of Health and Welfare defines child abuse and neglect as occurring:

> When a child has been, is being, or is likely to be subjected to physical, emotional, or sexual actions, or inactions, which result in significant harm or injury to the child. In the main, it refers to situations where there are protective issues for the child because the parent, family member or some other person responsible for the care of the child is unable or unwilling to protect the child from abuse or neglect (AIHW 1999, p. 6).

International child welfare literature is replete with definitions and typologies of specific types of maltreatment; however, the definitions are not without problems. Definitions presented in statutes and in the literature are often descriptive of incidents constituting abuse. *Child Protection: Messages from Research*, which summarised findings from twenty research studies carried out in Britain, paid particular attention to the definition of child abuse (DSRU 1995). The report argues that practitioners invariably assess the context in which incidents of maltreatment occur when defining them as abusive, implying that behaviour becomes abusive when practitioners describe it as such (DSRU 1995). This view is reinforced by Corby who sees child abuse as 'a socially defined construct ... a product of a particular culture and context and not an absolute and unchanging phenomenon' (Corby 1993, p. 39). Definitions are dependent on the context: legislators, courts, medical practitioners, and social workers tend to use definitions most suited to their professional roles and needs (Goddard 1996). The definitions adopted in the legal context influence reporting requirements, decisions about state intervention involving the removal of children to care, or even termination of parental rights.

The question of what is abusive to children is crucial in determining whether and how to intervene. The extreme cases reported in the media are rare. Where professionals are confronted with serious maltreatment in which there are no mitigating circumstances, and which is likely to lead to significant harm if they don't intervene, the duty to protect the child is obvious. In other circumstances, professionals may conclude that abuse has not occurred, and intervention is not warranted. Most notified cases fall into ambiguous categories between these extremes. Deciding whether child maltreatment has occurred in these more common cases presents social workers and other professionals with a major challenge, particularly because of the lack of consensus in defining child maltreatment. Efforts have been made in the past and more recently to clarify definitions and propose policy to assist in defining maltreatment; however, these efforts have been hindered by controversial portrayals of child protection systems as being either under-protective or overly intrusive (Hutchinson 1990).

The initial conceptualisation, in the 1960s, of the problem of maltreatment—the 'battered child syndrome'—was a narrow definition of child maltreatment. This definition has since expanded to include physical neglect, emotional abuse, sexual abuse, and organised abuse by groups such as cults (see Corby 1993). Some writers on the subject endorse the narrowing of the definition to limit the latitude accorded to judges and social workers in their discretionary determinations of the 'best interests of the child' and the bases for coercive intervention (Fernandez 1996). In particular, they argue for more precise standards for legal cases in which neglect is the basis of the claim, based on the notion of specific harms. In light of the limited knowledge, and the alternatives to raising children in their biological families, removing children from their families should occur only if, first, the harm is serious and, second, if it is a type of abuse for which intervention will do more good than harm. Identifying specific harms to be included in definitions of abuse and neglect is important to ensure that state guardianship of children will replace parental custody only when children's lives are threatened, or actual harm is of a magnitude that justifies the costs of intervention (Wald 1982). The focus here is on outcome—for the child and of interventions—rather than on the behaviour of caregivers. However, practitioners are required to make decisions about potential and actual harm. Besharov's (1985) concept of cumulative harm based on duration and intensity of the maltreatment adds a further dimension, focusing concern on the chronicity and severity of maltreatment.

Deficits in parental supervision are likely to have serious consequences for a child in a socio-economically disadvantaged home due to the greater likelihood of inherent safety hazards in the home (Pelton 1978). Determinations of culpability of the perpetrator, and resulting harm to the child in this context, raise further questions. Gil (1975) favours definitions that illuminate abuse at the institutional and structural levels and do not exclusively focus, in the legal sense, on individual culpability. He defines abuse as 'inflicted gaps or deficits between circumstances of living which would facilitate the optimal development of children to which they should be entitled, and their actual circumstances, irrespective of the sources or agents of the deficit' (Gil 1975). This broader definition highlights the structural bases of maltreatment and allows for intervention that enhances the quality of life of all children.

A number of writers introduce the idea of a 'continuum of care' in relation to abuse, with gradations of maltreatment 'ranging from the grossest, most obvious physical injury, to subtle, intangible, emotional deprivation' (Delaney 1976, p. 344). Gil's (1979) observation that physical abuse constitutes 'discipline gone too far' is another illustration of the continuum model. There is also the issue of intentionality on the part of the caregiver, which requires definers to differentiate between accidental and non-accidental injury. Often there is a combination of intentional and accidental elements, and specifying motivations is difficult (Costin et al. 1991).

A number of dynamics influence the definitional and assessment process, including professional and lay attitudes prevalent in the wider community towards parenting behaviours (Giovannoni & Becerra 1979), professional decisions made by social workers and other professionals about using protective services (Costin et al. 1991), and known parenting patterns in ordinary families (DSRU 1995). A well-known North American study by Giovannoni and Becerra (1979), which set out to identify the behavioural threshold of maltreatment espoused by different segments of the community, found that professionals and the wider community varied considerably on the type and severity of the behaviour labelled abusive and neglectful.

It is argued that child abuse is not an absolute concept, and behaviour has to be examined in its context before it is defined as maltreatment; that is, the chronicity and severity of maltreatment prompts intervention. However, some instances of sexual abuse are an exception. Compared with physical abuse or neglect, the thresholds in criminal statutes that define the occurrence of sexual abuse are more explicit. The rules about relativity of context are less easily applied in the case of sexual abuse, and perpetrators outside the family are likely to be implicated in investigations (DSRU 1995).

Determinations of what is abusive are related to decisions made by social workers about how and when to intervene. This involves deciding a threshold, or point at which a behaviour or parenting style constitutes maltreatment when state intervention becomes necessary.

The setting of thresholds is influenced by a range of factors: moral and legal questions, resource considerations, theoretical developments, research evidence, knowledge of the impact of abuse, and concerns of parents and children. Thus, the amount of abuse identified by child protection systems can vary depending on the threshold. Over time, the threshold defining abuse and sanctioning intervention has lowered as a result of the increased emphasis on children's rights, the influence of feminist theories about victimisation, and societal expectation and endorsement of state intervention in family life (DSRU 1995).

Some researchers have argued that the definition of child abuse applied to families is too broad, exposing families to unwarranted intrusion (Gibbons et al. 1995). Others have argued that the state is selective in its concerns, and that the concept of abuse should be widened to include any action or inaction that jeopardises children's well-being. This could include neglect by governments to ensure basic levels of health and development for children (Gil 1979), bullying at school (DSRU 1995), long-term immigration detention of children (HREOC 2004), and men's violence to women, which is often traumatic for children (Mullender & Morley 1994). As Hill and Tisdall have argued, 'the depiction of child abuse and protection as covering certain types of risk and responses has marginalised public attention towards other important threats to children's safety, which have not prompted similar degrees of concerted governmental and professional action' (1997, p. 201).

The issues raised about the dilemmas in defining maltreatment should sensitise social workers and other professionals to the evolving and subjective nature of assessment, and the need to develop criteria that are clear, objective, and defensible. The question of who defines child maltreatment, and the mechanisms for operationalising definitions, has both political and theoretical dimensions. In the next section, the theoretical formulations that inform the aetiology of maltreatment and decision-making about intervention are mentioned.

Theoretical explanations

The theories offered to explain maltreatment of children differ in their assumptions about causation and their analyses at the individual and contextual levels, and have implications for intervention and treatment. Some theories highlight deficits in the abuser or problems in the family's socio-cultural context, while others draw attention to structural factors. Aspects of these different approaches also have been incorporated into multidimensional and interactional models that acknowledge the interplay between individual characteristics and the social context. Overviews of these theoretical frameworks are presented in the international literature on child maltreatment (see, for example, Miller-Perrin & Perrin 1999; Briere et al. 1996; Belsky 1993; Corby 1993; Crosson-Tower 1989). Corby (1993) groups these theoretical frameworks into three major strands: psychological, social psychological, and sociological.

The theories suggest that child maltreatment has many interacting causes, and highlight individual psychological factors, family dynamics, economic, and social factors. Each theory offers a partial explanation, and presents social workers with the option to intervene with

individuals, families, or communities, or with all. Empirical findings substantiating or challenging these theories offer further knowledge to social workers. However, political, moral,
and resource considerations influence the focus of intervention strategies, as current child
protection policies reflect a bias towards intervention at the individual and family levels
(Munro 1998). In general, there has been concern to enhance social workers' knowledge,
and to promote their systematic use of theory and research in daily practice. Importantly
social work education through its emphasis on critical analysis and reflection can encourage
practitioners to challenge bureaucratic dominance, enabling them to operationalise the
knowledge and values that underpin the social work profession (Buckley 2000). Equally
important is the need to refine theory by researching social work practice in child protection.
Social workers' articulation and evaluation of their own practice is important in this regard.

Historical overview—before and after the 'discovery' of child abuse

Developments in child welfare in the United Kingdom and Europe affected the direction of
child welfare provision in Australia. As early as the mid nineteenth century, state involvement in the lives of children and families is evident through the establishment of universal
schooling, industrial schools, and boarding-out systems (Van Krieken 1991). Van Krieken
notes the two major features of the state's treatment of working-class children in the 1800s
were transportation to the colonies and institutional care, replaced later by boarding-out
placements for 'delinquent', neglected, or destitute children. Alternative options to residential care appeared around the 1860s as a result of criticism of the barracks system and the
emergence of the 'family principle' arguments, which led to the boarding out of children to
'respectable' working-class families.

The boarding-out system in Australia exemplified the paternalistic role of the state in its
relationship with children, their biological parents, and the foster families that took the children in. State intervention through this system aimed to promote a certain kind of family
life by removing children from 'unacceptable families', and redistributing them to
'respectable' working-class families (Barbalet 1983). The concerns that triggered state
involvement related to inadequate supervision, often attributed to poverty and destitution.
As Horsburgh points out, 'the general picture appears to be that of single parents unable to
continue to care for their children, plus a large proportion of children without any available
guardian' (1977, p. 21).

A major theme of the intervention by the state to meet the needs of children requiring
protection was the emphasis on providing a fresh start, replacing the child's original unsatisfactory environment with protective care. Physical well-being was stressed, with emotional
needs being given low priority, as were the child's bonds with the biological family.
Judgments about children's need for care in this period reflected the 'reform and rescue' tradition, whereby mothers were supervised and regulated (Wilkinson 1986), and 'the child in
need of welfare assistance was regarded as the victim of an immoral and socially inadequate

family situation, and the implementation of welfare policy usually resulted in the child being segregated from his family' (Picton & Boss 1981, p. 21).

The state became highly interventionist in its approach to Aboriginal families. The removal of Aboriginal children from their families, and placement in White families or White institutions, is well documented (Freedman & Stark 1993; O'Connor 1993; Van Krieken 1991; Chisholm 1985; HREOC 1997; Read 1982). In various states, large numbers of children were separated from parents, who were denied rights to visit them, and agreements to return their children were dishonoured. Great care was taken to ensure parents and children never traced each other. Between 1915 and 1940, 1600 Aboriginal children were the subject of such decisions of the Aboriginal Protection Board in New South Wales alone. The policies with regard to Aboriginal children and families have been described as an exercise in social engineering, backed by legal authority and state power and involving the imposition of alien norms and values in questionable attempts at assimilation. With respect to Aboriginal children 'state intervention did bring about a radical and unwanted change in family relationships' (Van Krieken 1991, p. 109). The Australian Institute of Health and Welfare (2004) report has cited trends that demonstrate the over-representation of Aboriginal children in the child protection system. Data on children in both government and non-governmental care reveal that around 20 per cent are Aboriginal children (Bath 1994). Current national data reinforces this picture.

In the mid 1970s there was a re-emergence of interest by the state and media in the incidence and severity of child maltreatment, and children at risk of abuse became a major focus of state departments. In response to the increased identification of child abuse, and well-publicised cases of maltreatment—such as that of Colwell in Britain (Parton & Martin 1989) and Montcalm in Australia (Lawrence 1983)—a strong interventionist stance re-emerged, directives and safeguards to ensure early detection proliferated, and prompt action to deal with child abuse and neglect was taken. The statistics of reported cases showed a staggering increase over a relatively short period. The number of cases reported increased from 42,468 in 1988–89 to 74,436 in 1993–94, an increase of 75 per cent over a five-year period (Angus & Woodward 1995). This increase is attributed to heightened awareness of the problem arising from the training to recognise abuse, and mandatory notification.

The ascendancy of a child protection focus had a large impact on child welfare services. First, preventive programmes and services for children and their biological parents received lower priority, with increased investment of welfare resources in child protection investigations, and more extensive use of legal powers in the form of 'place of safety' orders and 'wardship' proceedings. Second, the increasing number of notifications and validation of reports of abuse, and remand and wardship decisions, required additional foster care and residential placements. Third, the panic about abuse and the concern to prevent it, and subsequent procedures and practices developed to respond to the increased number of notifications of abuse, had implications for the state's response to families and children generally, not only those who were abused or at risk of abuse. Impoverished families in need of services were likely to be caught in the net of child protection and child removal in order to access services.

Issues in child protection

Emergence of the child abuse movement

The 'discovery' of and growth in concern about child abuse since the 1960s has been the subject of an expanding international literature, analysing its emergence as a social concern and the evolving responses to it. Finklehor (1996) suggests that the nature of responses to the concern about child abuse can be attributed to a social movement and moral transformation triggered by two significant social changes: first, the emergence of a class of professional workers specialising in dealing with children and families; and second, the emancipation of women. Their entry into the workplace and the professions, and access to divorce, catalysed a moral transformation in our view of children, and the social and political initiative to intervene on their behalf. These social changes uncovered the existence of violence and abuse in the family previously obscured. As women's representation in government and higher status professions such as medicine, law, and health increased, they brought with them their interest in children, and sensitivity to child welfare concerns increased.

State intervention and the family

Constantly widening definitions of child abuse have meant that physical battery has been expanded to include neglect, emotional abuse, and sexual abuse (Cooper & Ball 1987; Starr 1982). Consequently, the grounds on which the state may intervene also have expanded. While the existence of child abuse is undisputed, there is dissent on the point at which state intervention is justified because definitions of maltreatment are perceived to be relative. Dingwall et al. (1983) observe that moral judgments of the investigator influence attempts to describe the causes and consequences of child abuse. Their analysis of the state family relationship is informative.

Acknowledging that any form of surveillance of child-rearing poses a threat to the family in a liberal state, Dingwall et al. believe the state cannot opt out given the reality of children's dependence on adults. Research carried out in Britain demonstrated the tendency of social workers to resort to the 'rule of optimism', displaying a preoccupation with parental liberties. The outcome, the authors point out, is a system that neither prevents mistreatment nor respects family privacy, but which lurches unevenly between the two poles (Dingwall et al. 1983). Children are to be differentiated from adults in status: they are entitled to be protected by the state from abuse suffered in the parent–child relationship, given that they are unable 'to initiate their own remedies' (Dingwall et al. 1983, p. 224). The authors characterise parents' rights over children as 'duty rights', which parents discharged as trustees of their children with corresponding restrictions on children's autonomy. Viewing child protection from the perspective of children's rights and parental duties, the authors describe the parent–child relationship as an unequal contract into which children do not enter freely. They recognise, though, that both children and society as a whole have a vital interest in the success of that relationship in cultivating the capacity for responsible moral action (Dingwall et al. 1983, p. 220).

Child protection and welfarism

Parton and Otway (1995) have characterised child abuse, in the context of welfarism in the United Kingdom, as a medico-social problem. Social work was accorded a supportive role premised on the assumption that agents of the state and families would work in partnership to meet children's needs. Social work was perceived as being able to effect desired changes in the circumstances of children and families through its intervention. As social scientific knowledge of child and family functioning was given importance, the professions operating from this knowledge base and associated with welfare were drawn into the state's mechanisms of social regulation.

Donzelot in his pioneering study *The Policing of Families* traces the emergence of counselling, advice, and supervision by government and voluntary agencies, a structure through which experts including doctors and social workers 'policed' the family, with juvenile courts representing the 'state as family' (Donzelot 1979). Critical of the various forms of social regulation of the family, he argues that philanthropy and subsequently social work reflected the compromise between the family and its autonomy in raising children, and the state and its responsibility for children's needs and rights. The law and courts thus provided social work, and other health and welfare structures, with both the threat over and a means of intervention with families who were deemed to have failed, as well as the power to remove children (Parton 1991). The interests of the state, and social workers as state agents, were seen to be synonymous with those of the children and families concerned. However, police, courts, and the legal system were marginally involved, and a less legalistic model prevailed. The welfarist approach was, however, challenged by a number of emerging trends (Parton & Otway 1995).

During the 1980s, concerns about civil liberties were raised about the extent and nature of intervention, which had been occurring unchallenged. Morris et al (1980) and Taylor et al. (1980), adopting minimalist positions on state intervention and writing on behalf of children in protective care, advocated natural justice and parents' and children's rights, proposing restricted grounds for compulsory intervention, rights to legal representation and due process, and greater visibility and accountability in decision-making. This discourse prompted acknowledgment of the prevalence of 'system abuse' caused by the practices of professionals and the child protection system, adding yet another dimension to the political and professional agenda of child protection (Nunno et al. 1997; Cashmore et al. 1994; Crime and Misconduct Commission 2004).

The impact of child abuse inquiries

By the 1980s the concept of child protection was coming under attack. During the 1980s and 1990s a series of highly publicised inquiries into the deaths of children judged to be at risk heightened concern, not only about the fatal consequences of child maltreatment but also the quality and pitfalls of child protection systems. In Australia, state-level inquiries into deaths from child abuse of Paul and Montcalm (Lawrence 1983), Daniel Valerio (Goddard 1996), Jordan Dwyer, and Ben (Community Services Commission 1998–99,

1997–98) triggered professional and political debate about child protection, and focused attention on the organisational, procedural, and individual contributory factors at work.

Literature on child abuse inquiries is predominantly from the United Kingdom. Between 1973 and 1994 in the United Kingdom there were forty-five public inquiries into child protection cases, forty-three of them focusing on deaths from child abuse, and two—Cleveland and Orkney—examining the case of children thought to be victims of sexual abuse (Munro 1998). Subsequent inquiries into the deaths of children resulted in further official regulation of practitioners and agencies. Social workers were criticised for their loss of objectivity, and perceived as optimists who put the most favourable slant on a family's situation. At the first sign of improvement in the family situation, social workers were said to become overly optimistic to the detriment of the child (Dingwall et. al 1983). It was thought that social work needed to be restrained by law.

Whereas social workers were criticised for their under-reaction in the cases in which deaths resulted, in the now famous 1988 Cleveland case they were accused of overreaction. In this case, both paediatricians and social workers, preoccupied with rescue, used medical assessments to bring 120 children into protective care using emergency court orders. It was acknowledged that social workers and paediatricians had intervened too prematurely and decisively, bringing under scrutiny the medical diagnostic tests and disclosure strategies used by the professionals involved, including the social workers. Ironically, while it was medical technology and evidence that drew attention to physical abuse in an earlier era, in the Cleveland case it sparked controversy.

Major themes emerging from these inquiries highlighted the lack of inter-agency and professional cooperation, and social workers' failure to isolate the interests of children from those of the parents. The competency and accountability of practitioners in identifying symptoms of child abuse and gathering and evaluating legal evidence of sexual abuse came under scrutiny. As the family was perceived to be undermined in the Cleveland case, there was increased emphasis on legalities, requiring a dual focus to achieve the right balance between the power and responsibilities of judicial, medical, and social work professionals, as well as the optimum balance between family autonomy and state intervention (Parton et al. 1997). The errors of the Cleveland case and the more recent Victoria Climbie case (Laming 2003) were attributed to both the failings of professionals and the inadequacy of child protection policies and systems. However, the interdisciplinary nature of the issues was recognised and the inter-agency dimensions received focus.

Legalism in child protection

Some commentators, in particular Parton and Martin (1989) and Parton et al. (1997), have drawn attention to the forensically dominated responses to child protection in recent years, in which social work with children and families is increasingly reframed in legal and procedural terms. While in the 1960s child maltreatment was conceptualised as a medico-social problem, and medical professionals dominated the construction of knowledge, increasingly it is being construed as a socio-legal problem with legal expertise assuming predominance. This has meant a shift from an initial emphasis on diagnosis and treatment to emphasis on 'investigating, assessing and weighing the evidence' (Wattam 1997). Monitoring and surveillance have dominated responses, and increasingly cases are framed according to legal criteria in which the gathering of evidence is central. Where cases cannot be substantiated with evidence that will stand up in court, they are filtered out of the system (Parton et al. 1997), with a considerable amount of time and resources going into this filtering process, and children's needs being subordinated to the forensic demands of the system. Yet, children and families in the child protection system are often from the most vulnerable sections of the community.

Gibbons et al. argue, from their research in Britain, that too many cases are drawn into the child protection process. They portray the child protection system as 'a small meshed net', representing the organisational filters operated by local child protection systems (DSRU 1995). They tracked 1888 referrals over a 26-week period. Of these referrals, six out of seven children were filtered out and were not placed on a child protection register. In a large proportion of the cases investigated (44 per cent) no action was taken in terms of protective intervention or family support. Only 4 per cent of the cases involved removal of the child using a care order. Similar patterns of filtering and decision-making are reflected in research conducted in Western Australia (Thorpe 1994). Thus, while the child protection system responds to the needs of a few children in grave danger, large numbers are drawn into a stigmatising investigative process and receive no help at all.

The emphasis on collecting evidence from the initial encounter with children and their families sets the tone for subsequent interactions (Jack 1997), in contrast to the welfare-oriented approaches of the 1950s and 1960s. Sharland (1999) argues for a critical appraisal of the efficacy of forensically driven child protection practices in ensuring justice for children, or promoting their welfare. Challenging the pre-eminence of the criminal justice model, she points to the need for a more operational concept of justice that recognises and validates children and their experiences, and which is in tune with their rights.

Children's rights and child protection

The child-rights movement of the 1980s prompted much critical evaluation of child protection services with reference to children themselves. The rights of children to independence are neglected and their autonomy devalued, as children's interests and needs are defined by adults: that is, parents or agents of the state in child protection systems. The works of Eekalaar (1994), Freeman (1987), Franklin (1986), Cohen (1980), Rogers and Wrightsman (1978), and Holt (1975) have focused professional attention on children's rights, but there is no consensus on what legal and social rights children should have, and how these should be guaranteed.

Rogers and Wrightsman identify two major orientations in extending children's rights: the 'nurturance orientation', which stresses 'giving children what's good for them', and the 'self-determination' orientation, giving children the right 'to decide what's good for themselves' (1978, p. 61). Freeman (1987) believes that children are entitled to have their autonomy and self-determination recognised: taking children's rights seriously requires us to take seriously 'nurturance' and 'self-determination' (Freeman 1987, p. 309). The state is also viewed with caution and perceived as having a poor record in relation to children's rights.

Holt (1975) refers to young people in protective care under wardship as prisoners of the state. Freeman notes:

> Children have not been accorded either dignity or respect. They have been reified, denied the status of participants in a social system, labelled as a problem population, reduced to being seen as property. Too often justice for the young has been trumped by consideration of utility, or even worse, of convenience. Think of our attitudes towards the closure of children's homes, the criminal justice process for children, the custody decision-making process after divorce, the punishment of children, and their abuse, child benefits. The list is endless. In what other area are the victims of crimes 'punished' by being removed to an alien environment, as has happened with the victims of physical abuse for the last twenty years, and is now occurring where sexual abuse has (or may have) happened? (1987, p. 300).

Lavery (1986), writing on the rights of children in protective care, takes a critical view of the role of the state. Lavery cites many aspects of protective care in which rights are denied to children and young people. Their effective participation in decisions affecting their future is hampered by lack of access to information, and exclusion from case conferences and reviews; and their rights to information about personal history crucial to their development of identity and self-image are frequently overlooked. Children in protective care also find themselves in educational limbo, as they are marginalised from mainstream education systems.

Alternatives to the 'disease' model in child protection

The discovery of the 'battered baby syndrome' in the 1950s initiated a research programme strongly influenced by the values of medical research. By the 1960s, child abuse was viewed as a clinical syndrome that lay in the parents' psychologically diseased condition (Howitt 1992). Conceptualising the problem as a medical one focused attention away from the effects of such factors as poverty, social deprivation, and discrimination. This placed the family in opposition to the state, and led to the family being marginalised from decision-making processes. The expertise of paediatricians, radiologists, child psychiatrists, and social workers was regarded as crucial to the treatment of child abuse, a distinct diagnostic category (Parton et al. 1997). Research was directed at identifying the symptoms and characteristics that differentiated abusing families to enhance the knowledge base and predictive abilities of practitioners.

Parton (1990) has argued for an alternative to the disease model, with its emphasis on individual identification and treatment as the dominant response. He argues that deprived families are most at risk of being subject to the biased responses of the state, and that discourse on the nature, causes, and incidence of abuse has ignored the prevalence of abuse at institutional and structural levels.

Pelton (1989, 1978) posits links between inadequate care and impoverished living conditions. He argues that child abuse and neglect do not occur in isolation from each other, but are embedded in the context of poverty-related problems such as unemployment, limited education, health hazards, housing, and other physical, psychological, and social problems. He notes that the 'myth of classlessness' encourages the inclination to label impoverished parents as psychologically defective, and ignores socio-economic factors: 'Too often the assessment of blame has been the basis for social responses towards poor people. The conditions of poverty pose greater dangers to children than does child maltreatment' (Pelton 1989, pp. 144–5). Pelton is critical of the ascendancy of the child rescue response, and the dynamics of the child protection system that removes children as the dominant response. The focus on investigation, blame, and subsequent removal of children is seen by Pelton, as well as Parton (1985), as diverting attention from problems of poverty and its effects on families, and directing attention away from pressures to effect radical changes in social, economic, and welfare systems.

Critical of the dual role of family support and investigative and regulative functions carried out by child welfare departments in the United States, Pelton proposes a structure in which investigative and coercive roles are transferred to law enforcement agencies, while child welfare agencies are freed to offer support and prevention unencumbered by investigatory functions. Through such restructuring, Pelton envisages that the child welfare system can achieve a non-punitive, non-investigatory, advocatory role in relation to prevention and support services, on a voluntary basis (Pelton 1991). By dissociating helping and supporting roles from investigative and coercive roles, social workers and agencies would be in a better position to offer prevention and support services on a broader front to families with potential, as well as existing, child welfare problems. It would also reduce potential for harm to children without having to 'assess' culpability, blame, and adequacy, as a criterion for service (Fernandez 1996).

These views are reinforced by Lindsey (1994), who is critical of the residual focus of child protection interventions. He advocates rethinking our collective responsibility for children, and confronting the issue of child poverty by addressing the wider social and economic problems that families face. Frost and Stein (1989) advocate policies of 'structural prevention', and a child welfare practice that acknowledges and responds to divisions of class, ethnicity, and gender.

The analysis by Parton (1985) and Pelton (1989, 1978) that poverty increases the incidence and severity of abuse fails to recognise the role of gender and power in patriarchal relations in the dynamics of sexual abuse (Carment 1989), nor does it acknowledge that oppression of women crosses class boundaries (Dobash & Dobash 1979), and that children are oppressed by adults (Gordon 1985).

Gender and child protection

The presence of women as clients, carers, and front-line workers in the child protection system has been the subject of a growing body of literature (see, for example, Callahan 1993; Dominelli 1991; Smith 1991; Swift 1991; Parton 1990; Hanmer & Statham 1988). Feminist writers have challenged the dominant ideologies and assumptions underpinning child welfare interventions. Profiles of biological parents of children in protective care reflect that a disproportionate number come from disadvantaged socio-economic backgrounds and single-parent female-headed households (Callahan 1993; Sweeney 1983), a trend evident in research (Fernandez 1996; Farmer & Owen 1995). Swift (1995) argues for a reconceptualisation of child protection as a feminist issue, given the strong presence of women in the system, and the fact that child welfare focuses on women's domain of caring for children.

Feminist analyses of the institution of motherhood highlight its socially determined conditions and oppressive aspects (Phoenix & Woollett 1991; Brook & Davis 1985; Wearing 1984). Mothers shoulder a vast number of visible and invisible responsibilities, and are not permitted to fail in these obligations. The ideal of motherhood is sacred: the ideal mother is expected to get married, become pregnant, give birth, bond with her child, assume full responsibility for the child's physical, emotional, economic, and safety needs, and behave in self-sacrificing ways (Chesler 1987).

The assessment of mothers as being inadequate reflects assumptions that good mothering comes naturally, and that 'normal' mothers cope. These assumptions, based on the gendered division of labour, place the predominant responsibility for parenting with mothers, and childcare becomes a major source of their oppression. The pressures of mothering are rarely acknowledged. Poor housing and inadequate nutrition, coupled with the lack of social and emotional support and violence experienced by some women, contribute to the physical and emotional stress that impacts on women's health. The high incidence of maternal depression (Brown & Harris 1978) adds further weight to feminist analysis of the devaluation of women in traditional female roles. Additionally, social prescriptions for ideal motherhood are reinforced by the claims of experts for 'scientific knowledge' (Fernandez 1998).

Legal and social science literature has portrayed mothers as primarily responsible for the quality of care of their children (King & Trowell 1992; Swift 1991). Bowlby (1969), a major proponent of attachment theory, viewed parenting in terms of rigid sex roles in which the mother has continuous responsibility for childcare in the early years; since then, the blame for the psychopathology of child has been attributed to mothers: 'It is to mothers that the system looks as having primary responsibility for any harm that might have been caused, and to rectify that harm' (King & Trowell 1992, p. 21). Mothers are held responsible for the psychological deficits of their children, and are portrayed as inadequate and incapable of protecting their children. In this process, conceptions of mothers as powerful and influential in their children's development, and culpable and destructive, are constructed within patriarchy.

Culture and child protection

Cross-cultural and anti-racism literature also has had an impact on our understanding of child abuse and child protection. It has also been influential in broadening definitions of child abuse, and has revealed deep-rooted stereotypes. The definition of child abuse has been extended to include the pain experienced by black children forced to 'become white' (Cooper 1993). Intrusive practices in child welfare and policies of acculturation have left the Aboriginal community with a legacy of disintegration and dispossession (O'Shane 1993; Butler 1992; HREOC 1997).

Child welfare policy based on Eurocentric views of non-Western child-rearing practices (Jackson 1989) has resulted in overt cultural oppression, with ramifications for individuals and the community as a whole. Children from Aboriginal families face increased chances of experiencing poverty and deprivation arising from low incomes, poor housing, and ill health, compounded by racism (Choo 1990). This does not imply that Aboriginal families do not have the resources and resilience to confront these constraints, but underlines the need to address issues of structural inequality and racism.

International literature attests to the fact that children and parents of colour are subject to ethnocentric bias and heavy-handed child protection interventions that result in the over-representation of children in care (Jones 1994; Hodges 1991; Channer & Parton 1990). Poverty is a significant factor for many ethnic minority families in determining whether an intervention is made (Lindsey 1994). Additionally, their experience in the child welfare system reflects racial bias (Hodges 1991; Hogan & Siu 1988). Such differential treatment is reflected in a higher incidence of entry to protective care, extended tenure in placements, decreased emphasis on family reunification in service goals, and less access to day care and homemaker services, as parents of colour are portrayed as less able to benefit from support services (Korbin 1994; Hodges 1991; Ahmad 1989; Hogan & Siu 1988; Jenkins & Diamond 1985). Jamrozik (1986), commenting on the socio-cultural context of child protection, observes that problems tend to be assessed from 'the perspective of the dominant cultural and professional monism'. For example, he questions whether the older migrant child being asked to look after younger siblings in the parents' absence is more abused or neglected than the child who spends hours in the pinball parlour.

The potential for cultural conflict is nowhere more clearly evidenced than in child protection work, in which parents from different cultural backgrounds find their childcare practices challenged. There are issues of particular significance in working with families from different cultural backgrounds, not the least of which are power differentials, based on assumptions of White superiority, that race and ethnicity bring into play, and constraints on social workers' knowledge base with respect to non-Western cultures (Fernandez 1990). Cultural factors may bear directly or indirectly on definitions of maltreatment because 'while cultures differ in their definitions of maltreatment, all societies have criteria for behaviours that fall outside the realm of acceptability' (Korbin 1987, p. 26). However, caution must be exercised in classifying behaviours that may be harmful to children as culturally acceptable (Dingwall et al. 1983).

Ethics in context

A school notifies you as a worker in child protection that a 6-year-old girl appears to be suffering abuse. Your inquiries reveal the child's mother is living with a new partner. The mother appears to have a drug problem and the family is under acute financial pressure.

- Who is your client in this situation?
- What issues are raised for you with this case?
- How do you proceed?

Conclusion: future directions

In this chapter, how child maltreatment has been defined, trends in the building of knowledge about its causes, and patterns of response to it have been reviewed. In the past three decades, the scope and magnitude of child abuse and neglect have been recognised. The criminalisation of child maltreatment has been significant in establishing that harm to children is unacceptable and punishable. State intervention against child abuse ensures that children are not subject to adult exploitation.

For the most part, child maltreatment has been attributed to parental inadequacies compounded by pitfalls in child protection systems. The focus of child protection policy has been on the residual, protective, and coercive dimensions of statutory social work at the expense of family support services. The current residual model casts social workers in child protection practice as agents of social control, with intervention being focused at the tertiary level after abuse has occurred. Social workers and other practitioners in this field have been thrust into the public gaze, and simultaneously have become targets of criticism, blame, and hostility.

Discourse on coercive intervention to protect children and family support are conflicting, and further highlight the difficulties social workers confront in reconciling competing expectations of their roles as agents of the state. The growth in the compulsory and involuntary dimensions of intervention has also created conflict in social work in child welfare (Cooper 1993). The challenges and dilemmas for social work to construct a response that is both protective and just for children and supportive and empowering for parents are profound. Based on broader concepts of children's needs, policy and practice needs to be directed to offering integrated services that enhance the protection and welfare of children in their families, thereby effecting a balance between protection and prevention (Fernandez 2003).

A dominant theme in child protection practice is the assessment and management of risk, and central to this is the adoption of a language defining risk. Discourses of risk portray social workers as experts who can assess, predict, and differentiate high risk from low risk. Resources and skills are focused on sifting out high-risk cases. In this process, social workers are drawn into a form of practice characterised by Parton et al. as 'risk insurance', implying that social workers are expected 'to resolve problems which are well beyond their remit' (Parton et al. 1997; Ferguson 1997).

Social work will continue to be a crucial element in the nexus between the state and family. However, social workers may consider alternative discourses focused on needs and strengths in order to understand the social world of vulnerable children and families. There is growing consensus that practice needs to move in the direction of responding to children 'in need' drawing on an ecological approach to assessment and intervention, rather than responding reactively to incidents of harm or catastrophe (Department of Health 2000; Fernandez & Romeo 2003). Social work has a distinctive role to play in undertaking empowering, positive work with children and their families, and facilitating their inclusion in mainstream society. Families who are under pressure from poverty, ill health, isolation, and discrimination are less able to respond to their children's needs than those from more advantaged sections of society.

This does not imply that the protection of children from abuse should not be a priority, but that notions of risk are constructed in particular ways in society.

The child protection system is perceived as failing children. Imposed by professionals on children, the system is regarded as potentially abusive. The ascendancy of mandatory reporting and the forensic response to child protection, along with the impact of child abuse investigations on children and families, has been the subject of debate, given the trend in substantiation rates and the fact that a minority of cases reach prosecution and an even smaller number succeed (Ainsworth 2002; Sharland 1999; Parton et al. 1997; Cooper 1993). The requirements of proof raise questions as to whether the criminal and legal process acknowledges the welfare and worth of children (Sharland 1999; Hill & Tisdall 1997). The potential contribution children and young people can make in refining current responses is beginning to be acknowledged through research and policy directed at learning about the experience of children, respecting their autonomy, and including their voices.

The current system responds to allegations of risk and harm, not to needs. The impact on children and families of being drawn into, and subsequently filtered out of, the child protection net if claims of abuse are dismissed has been noted. Large numbers of children and families notified do not receive any service other than investigation (Cooper 1993; McCrudy & Daro 1993). This investigative focus detracts from the development of policy and practice to prevent initial or further harm. Current efforts are directed at intra-familial abuse, and measures to address abuse at institutional and intra-familial level receive low priority (Hill & Tisdall 1997; Nunno et al. 1997). That child maltreatment occurs across the spectrum of levels of family income and education, or that some forms of child maltreatment are more explicitly linked to socio-economic stress, is acknowledged. However, from the 1990s, commentators have affirmed the need for a more comprehensive strategy that is child-centred, family-focused, and neighbourhood-based (Garbarino & Barry 1997; Thompson 1994), and which involves a range of systems—physical and mental health, education, justice, housing, and income support—to achieve a broader safety net for children.

Review questions

1 Why does child maltreatment appear to be on the rise in Australia?
2 Should the problem of child abuse be defined broadly or narrowly? When definitions conflict which definitions should take precedence?
3 What are important considerations in assessing abuse? Does age of the child make a difference? Does intentionality of the perpetrator make a difference?
4 To what extent and under what circumstances should we consider cultural variations in definitions of abuse?

15

HOUSING AND CONTEMPORARY SOCIAL WORK PRACTICE

Michael Darcy and Judith Stubbs

Chapter objectives

- To provide an overview of contemporary housing and urban issues relevant to practice
- To demonstrate the range of opportunities for, and importance of, social work practice in areas related to housing and urban development
- To illustrate the types of ethical issues and complexities related to such a practice

Introduction

The housing field of practice is not just about houses: it is a complex and ongoing social process in which we all participate throughout our lives. It is generally seen as the first call on household income—an address and adequate shelter are minimum requirements for participation in the most basic aspects of social life, including employment and education. The price paid for housing has a direct impact on purchasing power of households, even affecting the quality and quantity of food and clothing that people can afford to buy. Housing exists in particular locations and varies in quality and appropriateness in ways that affect every aspect of individual and family life, from where and whether a person works or goes to school, to whether and how often they see relatives and friends, and even the way they see themselves and express their social identity and status. The very necessity of adequate housing makes the housing consumer vulnerable to exploitation. They cannot choose not to consume some form of housing.

Housing is also an industry that holds a unique economic importance. Families moving into and occupying houses create demand across the economy, not just in the building industry. Everything from the manufacture of building materials and household appliances to the demand for water and electricity is affected by the level of demand for housing. This in turn is related to housing affordability.

Capitalist society is characterised by commodity production; that is, things are mostly produced for their exchange value rather than their use value, and this determines in large measure the allocation of resources. Housing is no exception. Around 95 per cent of housing in Australia is privately produced and owned. This does not mean, however, that government does not play a role in determining affordability and consumption patterns, but it is true that many poorer people, even if employed, have great difficulty gaining access to secure affordable and appropriate housing. Other people, who may experience disability, health problems, and language or cultural difference, can be subjected to discrimination in the private rental market, which compounds their existing disadvantage. Policies that affect either the supply or the demand for housing affect housing affordability and always have a social justice impact.

History of intervention in housing

The complex area of housing made its way onto the public policy agenda for the first time in Australia around the turn of the century; however, not so much as a policy in its own right but as a subset of concerns about public health, crime, and morality. Several decades of rapid urban expansion, following the gold rushes of the 1850s, resulted, in the 1870s, in at least two colonial administrations (South Australia and New South Wales) enacting public health legislation that included powers to deal with unfit dwellings. The public health debate intersected with concerns about the effects on the moral welfare and behaviour of people living in overcrowded and unhygienic conditions. According to Pugh (1976, p. 9), the responses to poor housing conditions of the late nineteenth and early twentieth centuries, 'enable us to discern a number of attitudes ... to Australia's urban slums'. These are, firstly, that unsatisfactory housing conditions were seen as related to 'vice, ... low standards of human behaviour, and ... social ills' leading to concern for the 'moral welfare of immigrant women' and also 'over the morals, behaviour and social development of children'. Policy responses 'featured voluntary charity as a social ideal with government fulfilling a facilitating role and providing some funds'. Examples of philanthropy include the Church of England's housing estate at Glebe, Sydney, and the Melbourne Family Care Organisation's estate at Emerald Hill, Melbourne.

So, while poor housing conditions were seen as warranting the concern of the state, this was primarily because of the perceived consequences in terms of the behaviour of tenants, and the potential dangers this posed for the wider society. Public concern did not extend to direct action by governments to improve housing conditions for poorer people, although government was prepared to support the efforts of charitable and benevolent organisations. This was in accord with the dominant belief that direct subsidisation of housing for poorer people would be interpreted as inhibiting the free operation of market forces and even perhaps of destroying the incentive of poorer people to work to better themselves, and the opportunities for the better off to provide charity.

Despite the evident and persistent housing crises in the major Australian cities between the time of Federation and the Great Depression, especially for low income groups, no government, state or federal, was able to maintain sustained involvement in housing provision, except by providing loans to individuals to buy their own houses (Darcy 2001, p. 78). The worldwide depression of the 1930s provided the necessary moment of crisis for the emergence of new and different elements in housing policy. The former approach of subsidising private purchase of houses was exposed as inadequate when, 'the depression starkly revealed that home purchase was beyond the means of both the chronically poor and the newly unemployed' (Marsden 1986, p.14).

However, the series of institutional responses made by state governments, and in particular those in Victoria and New South Wales, resulted in those states establishing housing authorities that acted as developer and landlord. This continued to be justified and motivated by slum clearance objectives based on the physical determinist arguments of, among others, the town planning and social work professions, and were intended as limited social services aimed at reducing the perceived costs to the wider community of people living in substandard housing (Pugh 1976). The New South Wales Housing Conditions Investigation Report, published in 1936, illustrates the nature of the housing policy discourse of the day:

> We are strongly in favour of treating housing as a national undertaking (because) the work is of a character which private enterprise cannot undertake even in normal times ... the provision of decent housing accommodation for those at present living in overcrowded slum conditions probably produces a greater social amelioration than any other form of expenditure of like amount (quoted in Marsden 1986).

The establishment of the Commonwealth Housing Commission in 1943 represented the first deliberate and sustained attempt by the Commonwealth to explore a range of policy options that were clearly and unambiguously concerned with housing (Commonwealth Housing Commission 1944). Clearly the shortages created by World War II, and the anticipated demand for housing when service personnel returned and began to start families, was a major consideration and provided a further challenge to the liberal faith in the market's ability to meet housing demand. Just as in South Australia in the decade before the war, the decision of government, at this particular time, to canvass a more interventionist role in the market economy was strongly informed by the economic ideas of Keynes (see, for example, Skidelsky 1986).

Grieg (1995) reports that there was broad acceptance of the idea of greater state intervention in housing at the time because the combination of depression and war meant that what had been seen simply as a problem affecting poor people in the inner cities now extended to the 'submerged middle class', who were the victims of rapid social change and dislocation. State intervention, as proposed in the Commonwealth Housing Commission report, and as understood by this group, would not be primarily a welfare programme for poor slum dwellers but a strategy to restore the aspirations of middle Australia, which had been interrupted by the disastrous international events of the thirties and forties (Grieg 1995, pp. 34–5).

Australia's federal system of government, and in particular the concentration of the major income tax and other revenue collection powers at the Commonwealth level, means that social housing policy has been, to a large extent, determined by means of formal negotiations between Commonwealth and state governments. The outcome of these formal negotiations is a series of written agreements known as the Commonwealth–State Housing Agreement (CSHA). The first CSHA was negotiated in 1945, and, in this and subsequent agreements, the Commonwealth government and the state governments collectively have set out their expectations of each other and the responsibilities they accept in respect of the provision of social housing. This policy framework has varied and developed from one agreement to the next, but has covered policy areas such as housing management, eligibility, rent, and sale of public housing stock (Quadroy 1989; Murphy 1995; Hayward 1996). However, the potential of the original CSHA to become a unifying framework for all policies relating to housing has never been realised. Indeed, even during the post-war years, known as the 'long-boom', the history of intervention in housing is far from one of unequivocal support for and expansion of public housing. As Paris et al. (1985, p. 105) argue that there have always been at least two competing discourses of social housing in Australia, which they characterise as 'public housing' and 'welfare housing', with the latter clearly dominant in public policy for at least the last 30 years. Thus the social housing system at its height in the 1970s and 1980s represented only around 7 per cent of all housing in Australia, and, for the most part, provides only for those in the most desperate need. Meanwhile housing for the vast majority, whether rich or poor, has been left in the domain of the market.

Contemporary housing and urban issues relevant to practice—the political, legislative, and social context

Housing affordability has emerged as one of the most serious issues facing Australia and particularly cities such as Sydney and Melbourne in the past few years (NSW Ministerial Task Force on Affordable Housing 1998; Powall & Withers 2004). What has previously been viewed as a cyclical problem is increasingly acknowledged as an issue that is a more permanent feature of Australia's urban environment. As such, it requires a range of more active policy responses (Hall & Berry 2002, 2004). These include strategies aimed at retaining existing affordable housing stock, as well as a substantial increase in affordable housing opportunities across all communities within and outside of larger urban centres.

After World War II, Australia, like many other countries, faced a housing shortage. Many countries put housing provision at the centre of their national policy objectives, but different countries took different paths. Australia chose to place owner-occupation at the centre of its efforts to support wide participation in the housing market. Housing, however, is very different from other products mediated by markets because it is very durable, immovable, and grows in value while it is being consumed.

Two generations on we see the consequences of policy directions set in the 1940s. Most private wealth is held as housing, and almost all housing wealth is in private hands. This wealth is almost untouched by taxation, and most political parties see this as unchangeable.

Australia has effectively naturalised the culture of home ownership. Those without housing wealth have had virtually no political voice and are doubly disadvantaged by tenancy laws that generally favour property owners over tenants, discrimination by landlords and their agents, and the stigma associated with living in public housing. At the same time the net effect of housing subsidies and tax expenditures (for example, first home owners' schemes and Capital Gains Tax exemption) has been to benefit those with the most wealth.

We should be wary of naturalising the home ownership culture. In countries where home ownership is less common and more housing wealth is in social control, affordability is greater in all tenures. By privileging one form of tenure we have also made it less accessible, and home ownership is now falling dramatically in Sydney and Melbourne, meaning that for the first time there is emerging a class of educated and relatively affluent tenants. Although this is sometimes a choice related to housing flexibility in the early housing 'career' (for example, the propensity for younger people and those without children to rent closer to their place of work), increasingly it is due to significant decrease in the real value of wages relative to housing costs (Department of Prime Minister and Cabinet 1992; Productivity Commission 2003).

The worsening affordable housing crisis is occurring within a political context that has seen the progressive disengagement of the state from concerns with housing and urban equity (Dalton 1996) Though this has intensified since the mid 1990s, (Stubbs 2003)[1] the influences of neo-liberal ideology on government policy can be traced to at least the early 1980s (Dalton 1999). This is in contrast to the post-World War II period where a an acute housing shortage combined with a Keynesian approach to state activity (Heilbroner 1991, pp. 249–87) saw a commitment to improved home ownership opportunities as a cornerstone of social policy. Under the Commonwealth–State Housing Agreements, outlined above, large-scale public housing construction programmes were undertaken from the late 1940s and 1950s. These were accelerated during the 1970s and early 1980s, with the construction of large public housing estates predominantly on the urban fringe (Stubbs 2003). Their construction was also linked to labour market policy. It was envisaged that such housing would accommodate the growing number of manufacturing and related workers close to industry, and that services and related employment opportunities would follow. Economic and labour market restructuring and changes to government policy meant that such employment opportunities often did not eventuate, or that employment was severely curtailed with cycles of economic downturn in the early 1970s, 1980s, and 1990s. Subsequent cuts to federal funding have left the social housing sector highly residualised (Hall & Berry 2004)[2], and largely able to accommodate only those in most serious housing need.

In 2004, home ownership has declined significantly compared with a decade ago (Powall & Withers 2004). Further, subsidies in the form of exemptions available through the federal and state taxation systems generally benefit higher income households and more established home owners and investors, rather than those starting out in the housing market (Yates 2004). For those at the bottom end of the housing market, for the first time in decades the amount of public housing stock is decreasing in absolute terms, though it has been declining relatively for the past 10 years (Powall & Withers 2004). It currently stands at less than 5 per cent of total housing stock, down from more than 7 per cent in 1986. However, the most vulnerable in the housing market are arguably low income private renters, many of whom are still in 'housing stress' (Yates et al. 2004) even after receiving Commonwealth Rental Assistance.

A pervasive discourse underpins the state's withdrawal from direct involvement in affordable (including public) housing. This is about the extent to which government can intervene in an urban system that is increasingly dominated by global economic influences[3], and a housing market that is said to be driven by the choice of individual consumers and therefore largely outside of government influence (Stillwell 1997, 1998a, 1998b) Such free-market proponents argue correctly that the vast majority of Australia's housing is built by the private sector, as noted earlier. Compared with other OECD countries, Australia has always had a relatively small social (public and community) housing sector. Some maintain that Australia has entered a post-welfare state where the key aspects of the social wage have been severely constrained and now serve a remedial function only (Jamrozik 2003). Housing has become perhaps the most residualised social provision compared, for example, with health and education that have maintained a more universal entitlement despite an increased shift to private provision.

However, other commentators argue that rather than a weak state that is limiting its involvement in urban affairs, a strong state, albeit with a particular ideology, continues to impact upon the housing and urban system in important ways and with increasingly regressive outcomes (Zukin 1982; Dalton 1999). Policies related to taxation, direct or effective subsidies, and delegation of formerly state housing responsibilities to the private market are underpinned by a range of policies and regulatory provisions. Decisions about zoning, building codes, and the timing and funding of infrastructure, including human services, also impact upon the housing market. Operating at the federal, state, and local government levels, these policies and regulatory provisions influence to a greater or lesser extent where, when, and how housing is constructed, what social and physical infrastructure is provided, the cost of housing, access to services, and wider investment decisions of individual purchasers and the housing and development industry (Stubbs et al. 2004).

In this way, others argue that redistributive effects of government involvement are still experienced. However, the benefits of such government intervention are increasingly distributed to better off home owners and investors, and away from those who most need them—poorer first home buyers and public and private renters (Yates et al. 2004).

The Australian affordable housing context

Some features of the current affordable housing crisis in Australia include the following:

- The price of Australian housing grew by 70 per cent in the decade to 2003 in real terms, placing it well above the OECD average (Powall & Withers 2004).
- Unlike earlier housing booms, rapid housing price inflation has spread from more expensive areas of major capital cities, across most subregions, and to areas outside the major capital cities (Yates et al. 2004).
- Median house prices are now nine times the average per capita income compared with only six times the average income before the most recent upswing in housing process in 2001 (Yates et al. 2004).
- Despite low interest rates, the number of first home buyers has halved since 2001 (Yates et al. 2004). For an increasing number of Australians, home ownership is a dream that will never become a reality. As such, private rental is no longer a transitional phase for a growing housing market segment (Brotherhood of St Lawrence 2003), but a permanent and increasingly unaffordable option for many households. Younger people, and lower income and particularly single income households, are most severely affected (Brotherhood of St Lawrence 2003). Despite Australians' preference for home ownership, rental housing must be regarded as a permanent solution for an increasing number of people.
- There are currently no local government areas in Sydney where a household on a median income can afford to buy, and very few where it can afford to rent without falling into housing stress (Randolph & Holloway 2004).
- For private renters on low incomes in all parts of Sydney, and substantial parts of other major capital cities, the situation is particularly bleak. All Sydney postcodes are generally unaffordable for lower income families, even those on Commonwealth Rent Assistance. Even the cheapest rental options are not generally cheap enough to keep Rental Assistance recipients out of rental stress. For example, in the areas with the largest supply of low cost rental accommodation in Sydney, 56 per cent of very low income families on Rent Assistance were paying more than 30 per cent of their income on their rental costs (Powall & Withers 2004).
- Older renters, and single person and single income families are most vulnerable in the private rental housing market.
- Changing labour market conditions have contributed to the current housing crisis, with a marked growth in casual and part-time low-end service sector employment, and a substantial decrease in the number of full-time male jobs (Stubbs 2003). Housing affordability problems increasingly affect people who could be defined as 'key workers', or those involved in work that is essential to or of high benefit to the community whose wages do not allow them to live affordably, close to their place of work.
- Public housing waiting lists are at an all-time high and unlikely to decrease in the future. There are currently almost 100,000 households on the public housing waiting list in New South Wales alone, with a 10-year waiting list in most subregions of Sydney (NSW Department of Housing 2004). Those housed are increasingly priority or high-

need families. Although still the most cost-effective option for the lowest income earners in housing markets like Sydney and Melbourne,[4] recent research indicates that the sector may not survive beyond the next 10 to 15 years at current rates of loss (Hall & Berry 2004).

- There is particular pressure on the existing supply of housing at the most affordable end of the housing market, and particularly in caravan parks and manufactured housing estates in areas accessible to the metropolitan labour markets[5]. Recent data indicates the actual or imminent loss of 3000 permanent sites in New South Wales caravan parks and manufactured housing estates alone since November 2001[6]. This is due to conversion of long-term sites to more lucrative short-term or tourist sites, and the redevelopment of manufactured housing estates or caravan parks for conventional residential subdivision in urban fringe areas, and the redevelopment of central coast parks for flat or unit developments. This removes the last housing option for many of Australia's most vulnerable families as they are generally there due to their inability to access the conventional rental housing market in the first instance (Stubbs 2003).

- The social problems created by rapid development of new residential areas on the metropolitan fringes have been a fact of life in Australia for at least 20 years. Relatively cheap outer urban land provides an attractive alternative to state public housing providers faced with ever growing waiting lists, and to developers seeking to satisfy the enormous demand at the lower-priced end of the home purchase market. However, such rapid population increases, where a disproportionate number of new residents are low income purchasers or public housing tenants, and often without due consideration of factors such as the prospects of developing local employment opportunities, have a massive impact on the social and economic infrastructure of the affected areas. The result has been that already disadvantaged groups have been further disadvantaged in terms of their access to basic social services and other forms of assistance.

All of these factors must be considered not just as questions of social justice, but also in relation to urban sustainability. A city or region that cannot offer housing opportunities to lower paid workers, young families, and older citizens faces serious social consequences and labour market imbalances in the future. Ultimately, the current affordable housing crisis brings to the forefront issues about the type of society in which Australians want to live.

Current areas of social work practice in housing

For all the reasons outlined above social workers have a vital professional interest in housing, whether at the level of broad social policy, or the building of local communities, or in securing housing or related assistance for individual clients. Each of these areas of practice impinges on and intersects with the others and, in an important sense, all social work professionals work on housing or housing-related matters much of the time.

Today, practitioners working on housing and urban issues may be found in a range of community-based, voluntary, government, and private practice settings. Some of these roles might be characterised as direct housing practice, in that the workers deal explicitly with the provision and management of housing and related services, while others are indirect insofar as the worker may be employed to work in fields such as mental health, disability, youth work, or social planning, but is regularly required to understand and assist with housing issues and problems.

Direct housing workers

The first group of direct housing workers are involved in the provision and management of housing and do work with applicants for housing including intake, assessment, and allocation or referral to other providers. In smaller organisations, or at the management level of larger ones, they are also involved in development and application of intake, assessment, and allocation policies, protocols, and procedures, and in the development and implementation of wider organisational management and administrative policies and procedures, including those related to funding accountability and financial management.

Once applicants become tenants, housing managers find themselves in the role of landlord, although ethical and professional considerations mean that this role is very different to that of a private landlord. It includes tenant support, mediation, and conflict resolution, and tenant consultation and participation regarding policies and organisational practices. As housing managers, practitioners also manage maintenance and other responsibilities related to property ownership, develop ideas for new capital or service programmes or projects, negotiate with development partners and planning authorities, and prepare submissions.

Housing managers might be employed by: state public housing authorities; community-based or voluntary sector housing associations; specialist housing programmes such as emergency, crisis or supported accommodation; or programmes for Indigenous or other cultural groups.

The second group of direct housing workers do not manage housing and tenants, but work with or advocate for clients specifically in relation to their housing situation. Their work includes community development, outreach support, advocacy, and referral in specific settings including caravan parks and public housing estates, or among other disadvantaged groups such as homeless people. It also includes tenancy advice and advocacy, and casework or policy work with tenants' organisations.

Indirect housing workers

Practitioners involved in social planning, community development, or other less direct service practices are often engaged at the intersection of housing, services, and wider urban issues. They provide an interface between local communities and institutions, including the one for which they work. The skills and knowledge required are diverse and comprehensive. A practitioner is likely to be involved in community profiling and community needs assessment; consultation and participation strategies; social and economic impact assessment of developments or proposals; facilitation, negotiation, and advocacy; knowledge and application of relevant legislation and policies; development of programmes or projects in consultation with particular needs groups or local communities; development of community services plans; and work as part of multidisciplinary teams to develop housing strategies or social or strategic plans. Settings may include local councils or state government departments; community-based or voluntary agencies such as community centres, youth or aged services; statutory bodies such as relevant courts or tribunals; or private practice.

Policy development, research, and evaluation are all areas in which housing and urban practitioners are also likely to be engaged. As well as skills related to research, critical analysis, and evaluation, practitioners in these areas will have a broad knowledge base across a range of relevant legislative, policy, and institutional contexts. Practice settings include peak bodies related to housing or service advocacy; local, state, and federal departments related to housing, planning, and urban development; and universities and other tertiary institutions.

Practice issues

Most social workers involved in casework, in a wide range of practice settings, at some time are required to assist clients with housing issues—whether that be a matter of finding affordable housing, dealing with tenancy issues, or with the consequences of housing location such as finding required support services. This is particularly true in the post-deinstitutionalisation era when specialised institutional housing for people suffering from disabilities or physical or mental health problems is considered inappropriate, yet no additional resources have been provided to the social housing system to accommodate their needs.

All of the issues described above impact upon a social work practice that is engaged with housing. Practitioners working at the direct service level, including those doing referrals and advocacy, are likely to be confronted on a daily basis with the human impacts of a serious decline in affordable housing options for their clients, and a diminishing social housing system. Those working in social planning and community development are operating within a policy and institutional environment where it can be difficult to gain recognition for the importance of affordable housing and related issues. This can make it difficult to secure resources necessary to deal with housing concerns where other matters are viewed as a priority. Those practitioners engaged with policy and research may find that their work and their proposals join the ever-increasing body of work that indicates the social and economic validity of direct engagement with housing policy and provision, yet cannot find support at the institutional level for an increase in socially just urban engagement.

Problems in the housing system also impact on the work of other practitioners; for example, those in physical or mental health, emergency support, education, and training and employment services. An underlying problem faced by clients presenting to these service areas is frequently a basic lack of access to affordable or appropriate housing, which has flow on effects to other aspects of an individual or family's well-being, or ability to participate in other aspects of community life.

When engaged in the direct provision and management of housing, social work practitioners will often need to decide between the relative needs of families in severely substandard accommodation. Many are increasingly concerned that they might be giving false hope to the applicants they interview each week, most of whom join long and increasing waiting lists. Although interviewing families in desperate need on a daily basis, workers are aware that the majority of these families will not receive a priority allocation, and are likely to wait years for a home. The concern is that such applicants rely upon a placement and do not seek other options, or remain in their current often highly unsuitable or even dangerous housing situation while waiting for a subsidised property to become available. Housing workers debate the ethical dilemma of closing the general waiting list to new applicants—thus removing any hope of being housed for new applicants—versus allowing new families to continue to join the list in the knowledge that they may remain in their current situation for many years.

When social housing allocations are restricted to only those in the most desperate need, and in an environment where resources have not been allocated to replace institutional care with appropriate housing in the community, housing managers frequently need to mediate the competing needs of existing tenants. For example, tenants who display challenging or anti-social behaviours might seriously impinge on the well-being of their neighbours, yet have no other housing options. These are the ethical dilemmas and complexities that face direct service workers and housing managers on a daily basis in a housing sector where resources are severely inadequate, and need is growing. They require the development and application of comprehensive assessment and management systems, and objective allocations criteria, to decide between what appear to be equally serious cases. Inherently, they also require professional judgment and more subjective decisions about the degree of relative need and appropriate service responses and priorities. Such debates are occurring at allocations meetings of public, community, and emergency housing providers throughout Australia at the present time. The ethical dilemmas produced by the shortage of secure affordable housing highlight the need for professionals in the field to advocate strongly for increases in social housing provision.

Practitioners involved in social planning, policy, and research also face significant ethical dilemmas that have the potential to have far-reaching impacts on the lives of some of the most vulnerable in society. These dilemmas also occur within resource constraints that make a choice between alternative service needs necessary, though not always desirable. Tensions between satisfying individual and community needs and maximising the utility of decisions underpin many of these dilemmas. The impact of the more highly residualised nature of public housing on the tenant profile has also meant that certain estates house a very high proportion of families with complex needs, which can have a significant impact upon other tenants in the neighbourhood.

Housing authorities need to make decisions about how to manage the future of such public housing estates (Randolph & Wood 2003), and whether segments of estates or estates in their entirety should be demolished and redeveloped in partnership with private sector developers. A much lower proportion of social housing would then be provided in these areas, but greater social mix might result in a more manageable estate and less stigma for tenants—although at the cost of dislocation for existing tenants and fewer allocations for those waiting. Behind these social objectives sit the more pressing need to shed stock that is a financial liability (Hall & Berry 2002) and sell assets to fund the development of new housing, which cannot be built due to the progressive federal funding cuts under recent Commonwealth–State Housing Agreements (Randolph & Wood 2003).

Social work practice in housing and urban social justice at all levels is likely to be one of the most challenging endeavours in which a practitioner can be involved. However, the fundamental importance of adequate, secure, and affordable housing to all other aspects of a person's life make it one of the most important and rewarding areas of social practice. It is one that requires a wide range of skills, knowledge, and commitment in whatever arena it is practiced. Whatever the practice area, social practitioners who are multi-skilled—with a broad base of knowledge across issues such as housing and urban policy, human services, and labour market and economic development—will find themselves in demand.

Ethics in context

1   How do practitioners decide between the needs of competing applicants?
2   How can the need to provide 'housing of last resort' be reconciled with the need to protect other tenants from anti-social or challenging behaviours?
3   Can demolishing and redeveloping some public tenants' homes be the way to make estates more liveable and manageable for those who remain?

Review questions

1   What are some common ethical dilemmas faced by housing managers in relation to tenants? Can you think of examples and outline the key considerations in each situation? How would you resolve each of these issues, and what justification would you give? To what extent do your decisions comply with the AASW (2002) Code of Ethics?
2   Consider the problem of residualisation of housing estates and the proposed solution of increased social mix. How might you decide upon the preferable course of action, and whose views should be taken into account? What weight should be given to the competing needs of current tenants, those on the waiting list, and the future of public housing generally?

Notes

1   The election in 1996 of the conservative Federal Coalition Government has resulted in an intensification of free-market and competition policies put in place by the previous Labor Government.
2   Around 90 per cent of those currently housed in NSW public tenancies are on some form of Centrelink payment, and 'priority allocations' have increased from 20 per cent to 40 per cent of new allocations in the past decade (Hall & Berry 2004).
3   See, for example, Latham (1998, pp. 11–28) for one aspect of contemporary Labor thinking on the role of the state in a globalised world economy.

4   Hall & Berry (2002) note that building public housing stock is seventeen to twenty times more cost-effective than the provision of Commonwealth rent Assistance subsidies to low income private tenants.
5   Interview: Park and Village Tenants Service, June 2004.
6   NSW Park and Village Tenants Service, July 2004.

16

CRIMINAL JUSTICE—EXTENDING THE SOCIAL WORK FOCUS

Elizabeth Moore

Chapter objectives

- To introduce elements of crime and criminal justice institutions in Australia
- To outline key shifts in criminal justice ideology and approaches that influence social work practice in this context

- To provide an overview of practice opportunities and approaches to social work in criminal justice contexts
- To identify key dimensions of practice, issues, and dilemmas

Crime and crime control institutions in Australia

> Crimes, then, are wrongs which the judges have held, or Parliament has from time to time laid down, are sufficiently injurious to the public to warrant the application of criminal procedure to deal with them (Smith & Hogan quoted in Bates et al. 1996, p. 73).

While definitions of crime are debated, common to criminal justice systems of western industrialised democracies is the aim of preserving the social order and protecting citizens from offensive or injurious behaviour. The foundations of criminal justice systems are the legal statutes and common law, or 'judge made' case law, which establish certain acts as criminal, and therefore able to be singled out for the attention of the institutions of crime control.

The particular acts and behaviours that are outlawed are both socially and politically constructed, varying through time and between societies. Societal change can reduce opportunities for a particular crime to be committed and create new opportunities for the commission of socially harmful conduct and the introduction of criminal laws. Graycar and Grabosky (2002) observe that demographic change, economic reform, globalisation, and technological advancement create new opportunities for crime. They describe the incidence of motor vehicle theft as 'inconsequential' a hundred years ago, but now significant, and the previously 'private matters' of child abuse and domestic violence as now firmly within the criminal justice sphere. The political construction of crime arises from the ability of more powerful social interests to influence both the definition of certain acts and behaviours as criminal, and the allocation of state resources to their enforcement. The most stark Australian example originated with colonial settlement by the British. The application of the principle of *terra nullius* denied the fact of prior occupation by Indigenous people. The imposition of British systems of governance and law forcibly removed the original occupants from their lands. The colonial agricultural economy rendered activities central to the Indigenous subsistence economy liable to prosecution for offences such as land trespass and animal theft. The British denial of citizenship rights to Indigenous people resulted in their outlawing inter-racial marriage and the right of an Indigenous parent to care for a child believed to be of mixed race (HREOC 1997). While social change has seen these laws repealed, their impacts reverberate in many domains of Australian social life, including criminal justice.

Others (for example, Shannon & Young 2004) observe that criminologists frequently discuss crime in terms of the categories of 'white collar crime' committed against society by powerful elites and corporations; 'street crimes' involving harm to victims' property or safety; and 'moral, victimless crimes' where offenders undermine social values, such as through illicit drug use or illicit sex between consenting adults. In Western capitalist democracies, the resources of the institutions of criminal justice, both the law making and law enforcement arms, are predominantly focused on street and victimless crime, the focus of this paper.

Crime in Australia

Public perceptions of crime are typically inaccurate, based on the visible activities of police and media reports of police activity and judicial decisions. It is therefore essential to any understanding of crime that a more accurate picture is obtained. The Australian Bureau of Statistics' (ABS) indicators of crime are based on victim surveys and police reports. Use of both measures redresses the biased picture of crime portrayed by official statistics that exclude unreported crimes and reported crimes that do not eventuate in police action.

Crime victimisation rates derived from the ABS *Crime and Safety Survey* of 1998 focus on the more serious offence categories that affect the largest number of households (cited in ABS 2002). In the 12 months preceding the survey 8 per cent of Australian households had experienced a break-in or attempted break-in. Among over 15 year olds, 0.5 per cent had experienced a robbery and 4 per cent an assault. Of females over 18 years, less than 0.5 per cent had experienced a sexual assault (ABS 2002). Below are some official statistics on recorded crime in 1999–2000.

For offences against the person:

- males were more likely than females to be victims
- assault was the most common offence
- females were four times more likely than males to be victims of sexual assault.

For property crime:

- unlawful entry with intent (UEWI) and other theft were the most frequent of the more serious offences
- there was an increase since 1995 of victimisation rates by 13 per cent for UEWI, 9 per cent for motor vehicle theft, and 38 per cent for other theft.

Victims' ages:

- the highest level of crime victimisation was for 15–24 year olds, followed by 25–34 year olds

Defendants' sex and ages:

- 87 per cent of finalised matters involved male defendants
- 52 per cent were 17–29 years, and 22 per cent 20–24 years
- median age for males was 29, and females 28.

ABS (2002, pp. 31–45)

Graycar and Grabosky (2002) observe that in Australia consistent factors in criminal activity through the last 100 years have been alcohol (though now also substance abuse), high representations of people with impaired mental functioning, and of males, among offenders sentenced to imprisonment. While the denial of citizenship rights to Indigenous people resulted in their exclusion until 1967 from voting and official data collections, they were and still are more likely to come into contact with law enforcement officials. Today Indigenous people are overrepresented both as crime victims and offenders, and at the end of the twentieth century were fifteen times more likely to be imprisoned than the non-Indigenous population (Graycar & Grabosky 2002). This reflects the high rate of economic and social disadvantage among both the general prison and total Indigenous populations of Australia.

Institutions of crime control

The foregoing portrayal of crime obscures the complexity of criminal justice administration in Australia. Each state and territory is responsible for criminal legislation and the administration of criminal justice, with the federal government role being strongest in matters of national significance. What constitutes a crime is defined in some states and territories by a criminal code passed by their parliament, with others relying on 'judge made' common law[1]. There is added complexity in the administration of the institutions of criminal justice, with each state and territory's police, court, and corrections institutions being governed by their own legislation that sets out their powers, functions, and structures. Each state and territory also has a separate system for responding to adult and juvenile crime.

The criminal justice process involves the identification of a criminal act, a decision to prosecute by law enforcement personnel, judicial adjudication of the case, and determination of offender sanctions. Crime control has, until the last 40 years, been almost exclusively the preserve of law enforcers, including the police, judiciary, lawyers, and corrections personnel. Police exercise their discretion to arrest and charge. Lawyers, who represent either the prosecution or defence, tender evidence to respectively support or oppose the criminal charge in an adversarial legal contest that is adjudicated by a member of the judiciary—a magistrate or judge. The judiciary determines guilt and dispenses criminal sanctions. Practitioners with juvenile and adult corrections agencies advise the judiciary on the availability and appropriateness of punishments that involve offender surveillance, imprisonment, or rehabilitation, and administer these.

Contemporary adult and juvenile criminal justice systems have a more extensive reach than their precursors, beyond the traditional law enforcement approach of prosecuting and punishing adjudicated offenders. This paper describes recent innovations in crime control that have extended opportunities for contributions from broader community interests, as well as social work practitioners who support and advocate for these interests. A brief journey through key ideological shifts in criminal justice provides a foundation for understanding the origins and rationale for contemporary systems.

Ideological foundations of criminal justice

As a penal colony Australia's criminal justice system was inherited from Britain. White and Haines's (2004) account of the origins of the British criminal justice system explains how the role of the state, which comprises the institutions and systems of governance, changed with the emergence of capitalism. The state served the interests of the monarchy and hereditary classes, and the emergent classes of merchants and mass producers. A justice system evolved that was based on individual rights and the rule of law, and enshrined the principles of access to, and equality before, the law.

The ideology of eighteenth century classical liberalism underpinned the development of the criminal justice system. Classical theory regarded individuals as self-interested in nature and capable of freely choosing their actions. Their relationship with the state was regarded as a social contract in which individuals have rights and obligations in exchange for state protection of the rights of all citizens. Criminal acts were thus seen as violations of both the law and the social contract; the result of wrong choices by offenders who must be held responsible. The function of the criminal justice system was to uphold the social contract by punishing offenders. The goal of punishment was deterrence, which was intended to make an impact on the individual offender and society in general. The pleasure–pain principle applied to sentencing decisions held that the punishment should be sufficiently harsh to outweigh any pleasure derived from the criminal act, and no more.

In the early nineteenth century, England's overcrowded prisons had visibly high incidences of vagrancy, drunkenness, and mental illness among inmates. The growth and poor condition of the prison population provided the environment in which philanthropists and social scientists could positively contribute to criminal justice ideology and processes. Philanthropists who observed the high incidence of poverty and vulnerability among the prison population provided support to individual prisoners and advocated for the protection of prisoner rights and prison reform. Reformers questioned the humanity of the system and challenged the notion that all citizens were equally served by the rule of law. The combined influence of these moral agents and those engaged in positivist social science paved the way for the behavioural science and social work contributions to criminal justice.

Positivist theories of crime

In their account of the history of the British criminal justice system White and Haines (2004) observe that classical 'just deserts' arguments still feature in contemporary discourse about crime and punishment. They explain how nineteenth century positivist social science, the foundation of both criminology and the behavioural science professions, provided alternative perspectives that are also evident in contemporary discourse and practice.

Positivists focused on the relationship of crime to individuals, society, and the institutions of criminal justice. They applied methods developed in the natural sciences in the belief that: '… society ("civilisation") is progressing ever forward, and that the social scientist can study society, provide a more accurate understanding of how society works, and ultimately provide a rational means of overcoming existing social problems and ills by using scientific method' (White & Haines 2004, p. 38).

Positivist explanations of crime are usefully categorised by White and Haines (2004) into three groups of theories, which are evident in contemporary discourse. The first to emerge were individual pathology theories. Subsequent explanations located the causes of crime in strains between individuals and society and, later, in the interactions between individuals and the institutions of criminal justice. Each theoretical development influenced changes in the principles applied in criminal law, or criminal jurisprudence, and the emergence and contribution of the professions to criminal justice process.

Individual pathology

Individual pathology explanations, which emerged in the 1870s, focus on 'criminal attributes' of convicted offenders, and offer biological, psychological, and bio-social explanations of individual difference. The focus on individual difference challenges the assumption of classical criminology—that all citizens are equally able to exercise rational choice. Clearly children and people with a mental illness are less capable of purposively planning to commit a crime. This notion of diminished responsibility is recognised in law, with a requirement for the prosecution to prove not only that an alleged offender committed the criminal act (*actus reus*), but also that they had a guilty mind at the time (*mens rea*). The focus on individual difference also contributed to the establishment in the mid nineteenth century of separate children's reformatories and, at the turn of the twentieth century, children's courts. These reforms acknowledged the vulnerability of children and their potential to be provided with a pathway out of crime, initially through harsh discipline and moral training, and later through rehabilitation. Contemporary psychological theories of human development and personality provide the foundation for offender assessment and rehabilitation (for example, Farrington 1996, cited in White & Haines 2004). Critics of individual pathology theories of crime focus on their potential to apply discriminatory and erroneous labels to individual offenders that fail to take account of social factors.

Social strain theories

These theories of crime emerged and flourished in the United States between the 1920s and 1960s (for example, Shaw & Mackay 1946; Merton 1957; Cohen 1955; all cited in White & Haines 2004), offering social explanations based on evidence of a coincidence of poor living conditions, unemployment, and criminal offending. Here, criminal behaviour is attributed to strains between individuals and society, arising from conflicts between individual aspirations and opportunities; mainstream societal and other cultural values; and socially accepted and learned behaviours. In contrast to individual pathology theories, they regard offenders as 'normal' people responding to 'abnormal' situations (Gibbons, cited in White & Haines 2000, p. 76). This group of theories justifies the extension of crime control efforts beyond the individual into communities through the identification of 'high risk' communities and crime prevention programmes. They also justify the extension into the social environment of efforts to reform or rehabilitate individual offenders.

Social interactionist theories

These theories of the 1960s and 1970s (for example, Becker 1963; Lemert 1969; Matza 1964; all cited in White & Haines 2004) shifted the focus of criminologists to the interactions of individuals with the institutions of criminal justice. Of particular interest was the criminalisation process through which the state creates crime by outlawing certain acts and investing criminal justice institutions and personnel with legal authority to intervene. The labelling of certain acts as 'crimes' and individuals as 'criminal' is regarded by these theorists as outcomes of the exercise of state power. The application of these theories to criminology drew attention to the bias inherent in the law enforcement process and its potential to further entrench some offenders into criminal careers. An unintended consequence of offender involvement with police and courts is negative social stigma and exclusion from positive aspects of social life. The attachment of the negative label to a person can result in a self-fulfilling prophecy, in which the offender comes to identify with and behave in accordance with this negative label. Their exclusion from positive social involvements such as school, employment, and formal recreation can also increase their risk of further offending. Stigma and social exclusion can lead to stronger identification by the offender with the negative label and commission of further criminal acts. Interactionist theories thus provided a rationale for diversionary and graduated interventions and sanctions that aim to use the least intrusive measures and limit offender contact with formal court proceedings and imprisonment (for example, Schur 1973, cited in White & Haines 2004).

Positivist theories that explain crime on the basis of individual pathology, social strains, and social interactions continue to feature in criminological discourse, as have other theories in criminology that are not discussed here, such as critical and feminist criminology. These three groups of theories are discussed here because their influence is apparent in contemporary developments in criminal justice administration, and they mirror the focus of social work on individual functioning, social conditions, and the social ecology of individuals.

Contemporary developments in crime control

Cunneen and White (2002) see the expansion of crime control measures, beyond mere law enforcement and its traditional agents, as evidence of criminal justice interventions operating at the primary, secondary, and tertiary levels. Primary level crime prevention initiatives target communities in efforts to change the physical or social conditions conducive to crime. At the secondary level are measures that aim to divert identified offenders from court adjudication and deter them from continued offending. There have also been changes to tertiary level interventions, both in the focus of corrections programmes and the role of the court.

The expansion of crime control measures, beyond mere law enforcement and its agents, is evident in five recent developments. Crime prevention, diversionary and restorative justice measures, victim participation, offender treatment programmes, and problem solving courts are all features of the contemporary criminal justice landscape. Social work professionals could contribute toward practice in any of these fields. Indirect social work practice involves policy, planning, and community development work. Direct practice involves work with individuals and groups who come into contact with the criminal justice system as offenders or crime victims.

Crime prevention—planning and community development

Crime prevention initiatives first emerged with social strain theories, and in the 1960s aimed to ameliorate the negative impacts of poverty, and break the pathway from poverty to delinquency and crime through social enhancement initiatives such as early childhood enrichment programmes. With the 1990s rediscovery of crime prevention internationally, there emerged a wider range of initiatives that target either the physical or social conditions conducive to crime. They variously aim to reduce opportunities for crime, address risk factors among vulnerable populations, or increase opportunities for positive participation and empowerment of marginalised sectors of the community at the local level (Cunneen & White 2002).

Many local government instrumentalities now incorporate primary and secondary level crime prevention measures. For instance, a building code might incorporate a requirement for plans seeking development consent to demonstrate how natural surveillance has been taken into account in reducing the chances of criminal activity going unobserved. Social plans often identify fears and risks of crime in the community and incorporate measures to address these. For example, a cultural programme within a social plan might include a mural project that targets youth identified as at 'high risk' of offending, with the aim of legitimating their art and reducing levels of unwanted graffiti. Commercial interests, such as car manufacturers, retailers, and insurance companies, are also involved in crime prevention activity, often in partnership with police and/or local government. The increased role of local government in social planning provides opportunities for social work contributions in designing and implementing the planning processes and participating in community consultations.

Informal justice—diversion and restorative conferences

The introduction of graduated interventions has led to the formalisation of police discretionary powers to respond to criminal incidents by way of warnings and cautions. Diversion from formal justice administered through court adjudication aims to hold offenders accountable for their conduct and minimise the negative consequences of official intervention.

Restorative justice conferences that have, since the 1990s, been introduced to an increasing number of jurisdictions are often positioned as diversionary informal justice measures. A rationale for their introduction is Braithwaite and Pettit's (1990) republican theory of crime, which views crime as violating key civic freedoms of victims, offenders, and the wider community. Braithwaite (1989) argues that the response to crime should aim to restore social harmony through a process of reintegrative shaming. Critics debate the appropriateness of the notion of 'shame'; however, the intention is to create a social audience to the misdeed that can engage in a process of reconciliation, through offender remorse and apology and victim acknowledgment or acceptance, and pave the way for the offender's positive social reintegration. In contrast to classical 'just deserts' thinking that focuses on offender responsibility for deeds, the focus here is on offender accountability to those harmed by their misdeed. The aim is to attach the negative label to the offence and not the offender. These theoretical developments coincided with the introduction of indigenous principles of justice in adult and juvenile jurisdictions in Canada and New Zealand, thus providing practice models in the forms of sentencing circles and family group conferences, respectively (La Prairie 1995).

In contrast to the adjudicative process of formal court proceedings, restorative conferences provide a less formal mechanism for offender accountability. Offenders meet their victims, each with the support of family or friends, hear about the nature, extent, and level of harm caused by their offence, and strive toward a remedy that can be the basis for reparation, in the widest societal sense. Participants include offenders, victims, and people drawn from their respective communities of care, as well as other affected citizens. Depending on the particular model and circumstances of each case, practitioners within key community educational, recreational, and social service organisations might well contribute to both the process and the implementation of the agreed outcome.

Formal justice and crime victims

In the 1970s critics of the justice system that emerged under classic liberal ideology observed that in criminal justice proceedings the state assumes ownership and control of criminal conflicts to the exclusion of those most affected—victims and the wider community—to the economic advantage of law enforcement officials and lawyers (Christie 1977). Parallel developments in alternative dispute resolution, victim–offender mediation, and victims' rights movements all served to promote victim advocacy, support, and participation in criminal justice. Strang (2001) identifies two strands in victims' movements—one pursuing rights and the other support of victims—which have in common a sense of injustice at: '[victims being] … the forgotten third parties in a justice system which conceives of criminal behaviour as a matter between the offender and the state, with no formal role for the individuals who suffer the crime' (Strang (2001, p. 71).

The rights-focused agenda pursues victims' desires for information about the progress and decisions made in the case against the offender, participation in the court disposition, and ability to influence the sentencing outcome (Strang 2001). The support agenda is primarily focused on the alleviation of suffering by victims, and secondarily on their treatment and rights within the criminal justice process.

Contemporary Australian criminal jurisdictions have attempted to accommodate victims' rights and needs in various ways. Charters of victims' rights acknowledge their unique experience and serve as a reminder to all participants in criminal justice proceedings of victims' rights to be informed, to participate, and to have their needs taken into account in decisions affecting their safety and well-being. Support services to crime victims and witnesses aim to assist them through the process. Victim impact statements provide a mechanism through which the sentencing judge or magistrate can take account of the nature and extent of harm caused by the offence and any need for future protection. Administrative bodies such as victim compensation tribunals provide mechanisms through which victims can seek access to rehabilitative services and compensation.

The influence of 1970s feminism, which resulted in legal recognition of child abuse and domestic violence as appropriately dealt with by the criminal justice system, also expanded the legal protections and support services available to women and children experiencing violence. Australian jurisdictions now recognise the unacceptably high incidence of male violence against women and children in both the public and private spheres, and have introduced laws that aim to protect victims and prosecute offenders. Crisis services for sexual assault and other forms of violence against women provide them with a place to seek help and safe alternative accommodation for women and children experiencing domestic violence. Practitioners in court support services validate women's decisions to seek help and meet their needs for information and emotional support in seeking legal protection. These services are typically managed and delivered by social work and welfare practitioners.

Tertiary intervention—corrections surveillance and rehabilitation

Adult and juvenile corrections departments of state and territory governments are responsible for providing tertiary level correctional intervention. They provide the judiciary with pre-sentence reports on individual offenders, community corrections, and prison services. While few corrections departments require employees to be qualified in the behavioural science professions, many psychologists and social workers have pursued careers in this field. Recent developments in theory and practice of corrections intervention have a person-in-environment and community corrections focus. Community corrections programmes have been described as a 'ragbag collection of programs aimed at reducing the prison population' (Leivesley, quoted in Dawes & Grant 2002, p. 103). They are a virtual museum of the impact of ideological shifts in responding to crime. Recent developments relevant to correctional social work practice are the shift from surveillance to rehabilitation of offenders, and the introduction of risk assessment tools and case management approaches. These developments have been led by innovative practice with young offenders.

Surveillance

Surveillance of offenders was favoured in the 1980s due to the combined influences of the less interventionist ideas of interactionist theories and disenchantment with the outcomes of educational and psychotherapeutic programmes. The goal of rehabilitation was displaced by those of justice, offender responsibility, and punishment as retribution, restitution, and reparation. To the community corrections mix were added attendance and community service orders programmes. These interventions emphasise offender surveillance and are highly prescriptive of the activities of offenders and practitioners. They specify the duration of the offender's order and the number of hours of attendance or service, with the role of practitioners being to monitor offender compliance by monitoring registers and conducting surprise visits.

Rehabilitation

Rehabilitation, or treatment, has recently again found favour, with a vast number of effective treatment programmes featuring in the literature. Revisiting the 'nothing works' pessimism of the 1970s (Martinson 1974), McGuire and Priestley's (1995) review of 'what works' isolates psychotherapy, medical treatment, and punishment as ineffective in reducing crime, and elicits six key principles that underpin the design and assembly of the many effective treatment programmes. These principles are:

1 risk classification that matches high risk offenders with high levels of intervention
2 a focus on criminogenic needs, identifying and addressing client problems and behaviour that support offending
3 responsivity that involves matching practitioner and offender learning styles
4 community-based intervention in proximity to the offenders' home environment that promotes life-long learning
5 treatment modality that spans statutory and other agency contexts, is multi-modal, and is skills oriented using cognitive, behavioural, or cognitive-behavioural approaches
6 programme integrity evidenced by stated aims, related methods of intervention, adequate resources, appropriately trained staff, and systematically recorded monitoring and evaluation (McGuire & Priestley 1995).

Risk assessment

Risk assessment tools are increasingly being used to determine the type, level, and duration of offender surveillance needed to ensure that an offender complies with their court order. As punishment alone has been found to be ineffective in reducing recidivism, surveillance is increasingly being paired with an appropriately targeted rehabilitative intervention. The most promising targets for individualised treatment of juvenile offenders have been identified as personal and social adjustment (Andrews & Bonton, cited in Rutter et. al. 1998). Criminogenic needs instruments are increasingly being used to determine the personal and social factors that contribute to an individual's offending, and thus the focus of intervention. Hoge and Andrews's (1995, 1996) 'youth level of service/case management inventory' aims to assist practitioner decision-making about the level of intervention and rehabilitative goals. Practitioners using this model adopt a person-in-society focus that takes account of factors such as offending history, family and living circumstances, education and employment, peer relations, substance abuse, leisure, behaviours, and attitudes.

Problem-solving courts

Therapeutic justice is the most recent development in Australian criminal justice administration. In the United States, this approach has been developed through the experience of problem-solving courts that respond to offences involving drugs, domestic violence, or mentally ill offenders. As a result of their perceived success, the following general principles of 'therapeutic jurisprudence' have been adopted by Chief Justices in the United States: '… integration of treatment services with judicial case processing, ongoing judicial intervention, close monitoring of and immediate response to behaviour, multidisciplinary involvement, and collaboration with community based and government organisations' (Wexler 2002, p. 27).

The model is based on partnerships between justice, health, and social service personnel. It combines law enforcement, surveillance, individual treatment, and social integration measures that aim to have offenders take responsibility for their conduct by dealing with the criminogenic factors assessed as contributing to their criminal conduct. Australian examples are the New South Wales adult and youth drug courts, introduced following recommendations of the 1999 Parliamentary Drug Summit. Central to this model is a case management approach based on multidisciplinary assessment and the combination of treatment, social support, and surveillance that is monitored through the court during a long period of remand.

Framing social work practice in criminal justice contexts

Despite the few identified social work positions within the institutions of criminal justice, many social workers practice in this field. The foregoing discussion indicates the increased opportunities for social work professionals to contribute their expertise within contemporary Australian criminal jurisdictions. The relevance of social work to criminal justice contexts is grounded in its professional purpose and focus: 'The focus of social work and welfare practice is the interaction between individuals and the social arrangements. The purpose of practice is to promote the development of equitable relationships and the development of individuals' power and control over their own lives, and hence to improve the interaction between individuals and social arrangements' (O'Connor et al. 2003, p. 11).

The disadvantage and vulnerability among offenders, crime victims, and crime-prone communities makes them an appropriate target for social work practice and its person-in-society concern. The values of individual worth, empowerment, and self-determination apply to practice with those affected by crime. They underpin victim advocacy and support where criminal incidents have resulted in individual loss of personal freedom and well-being, and where communities are marked by high levels of fear of crime. They are also appropriate in practice with offenders whose personal or social vulnerability might have contributed to their propensity to offend. Notions of empowerment and anti-discriminatory practice are also relevant to practice with crime victims and offenders whose negative experiences of formal criminal justice institutions can be disempowering and, at worst, marked by institutional or individual discrimination.

Social work methods that intervene at the level of the individual, group, community, and policy all have application in crime control, and crime victim and corrections services. Indirect practice involving community development, planning, and policy functions might focus on primary crime prevention measures, secondary prevention, and diversionary measures or tertiary victim and offender interventions.

More typically, social workers are engaged in direct practice with crime victims and offenders. This can involve crisis support, court support and advocacy, assessments for court, case management, rehabilitation, and corrections. Social workers in government and non-governmental agencies that are not part of the criminal justice system, but whose functions and client groups bring them into contact with it, might well become involved at any stage of the criminal justice process. They can be called upon by police, prosecuting authorities, defence lawyers, the judiciary, and corrections agencies. At the time of the criminal incident and initial police response, a social worker might provide crisis support to a victim or offender.

Direct social work practice with crime victims can take place during the crisis immediately following a criminal incident, or throughout the legal process. Practice activities can involve linking crime victims with mainstream and specialist services, counselling during the crisis and with the longer-term impacts of trauma, and assistance with the legal process. Assistance during the legal process can involve meeting victims' needs for information, accessing services relevant to their situation, and assisting them to prepare for court, particularly when giving evidence as a witness or providing a victim impact statement. Witness assistance services are usually delivered through government departments such as police, public prosecutors, legal aid, or attorneys-general. Other support services are delivered by practitioners in government-funded non-governmental agencies. Social workers employed in statutory child protection have a unique mandate to initiate and pursue legal action to protect child victims of violence, and are thus involved in all stages of criminal justice process. Social workers in other agency contexts may well be called upon to provide their expert account or opinion of victim harm.

Direct social work practice with offenders can occur at any point from the time of police apprehension to the supervision of court orders. A social worker might conduct the role of independent observer at a police interview, with a view to protecting the interviewee's rights and providing support. They might assist a person arrested by police to demonstrate their ability to meet and comply with bail conditions imposed by police or the court. During the prosecution process a social worker might well be called upon by the prosecutor, defence solicitor, or the judiciary to provide expert evidence or opinion. Perhaps the most frequent social work role involves assisting judicial sentencing decisions by providing pre-sentence reports that offer psychosocial assessments of offenders, advise on risks of repeat offending, and make recommendations regarding the appropriateness and suitability of corrections pro-grammes. Corrections practitioners also develop and deliver programmes that target particu-lar offenders or offence types and conduct case planning or management functions within community or custodial settings (Owen & Richards 2000). Non-correctional social workers also can be involved in providing assessments to court and implementing court decisions.

The person-in-society framework of social work practice draws on its knowledge base in sociology and psychology. The foregoing discussion of criminology is grounded in sociologi-cal thinking. Despite the criticisms of individual pathology explanations of crime, the disci-pline of psychology has much relevance to social work practice in criminal justice contexts. For example, social ecological theories that explain individual development and difference within the context of relationships of family, peers, and social institutions are relevant to assessment. Humanistic theories that explain the dynamics and methods of the helping rela-tionship in bringing about change in individuals and groups provide a theoretical basis and a framework for skill identification in counselling crime victims and offenders. While social work practice draws on a wide knowledge base, it also has a unique body of knowledge, theory, and skills. It is differentiated by problem solving and task-centred models of practice, which involve collaborative and contracted client intervention marked by goal setting and transfer of practitioner skills to clients. Trotter (1999) provides an Australian example of the distinct contribution that social work theory can make to practice with involuntary clients generally, and offenders. Based on research into probation practice, Trotter identified ele-ments of effective practice and combined these in a model that can be applied to practice with involuntary clients. The model incorporates role clarification, pro-social modelling, and collaborative problem solving.

Ethical considerations

The social work curriculum of Australian universities has largely ignored criminal justice as a field of practice. The contributions of social work academics with criminal justice expertise to the Australian social work literature are few in number, but address significant dilemmas that arise in this field. Trotter (1999) and Borowski (1997) have focused on practice with involuntary clients in helping roles that incorporate social control. Owen and Richards (2002) focus on the legal mandate, social control, balancing victim and offender rights, challenges to confidentiality and privacy, and the privatisation of prison services.

Legal obligations, authority, and accountability

A full appreciation of the legal dimension of the role is essential to social work practice in criminal justice contexts. Legal obligations such as mandatory reporting of child abuse can affect all social work practitioners, and limit client privacy and confidentiality. Legal author-ity to intervene creates additional dilemmas of balancing the social control mandate with the social care ethos of social work and introducing a compulsory element to relationships with clients. For example, practitioners in child protection have the dual role of initiating legal action in response to an incident of abuse, and forming a helping relationship with the child and their carers that can protect their long-term care. Corrections practitioners have the multiple roles of protecting offender rights, providing social support, and conducting surveillance and rehabilitation. They are also legally authorised to report to court, implement sanctions, and initiate breach action when an offender has not complied with a court order. Legal authority also implies accountability to the law, through the court. The focus on role clarification in Trotter's (1999) approach to practice with involuntary clients addresses dilemmas that arise from involuntary aspects of the relationship and accountability to the court.

Autonomy versus competing accountabilities

In criminal justice contexts, practitioner autonomy is influenced not only by the legal authority conferred by statutory law but also by the legal order imposed by the judiciary in individual cases, as well as by administrative decisions within the agency. Court orders can specify the nature, duration, location, and conditions of intervention. Practitioners must also account to their employers. In statutory practice, where the amount and nature of agency work is determined by legal statute and court order, workflow and workload systems are key management tools. Managers concerned with the efficient and effective use of practitioner hours sometimes introduce policies and guidelines that reduce practitioner discretion. This can be with a view to eliminating potential risks to the agency, clients, victims, or the community, or even political risks to the government of the day. This is experienced by practitioners in prison environments, who constantly balance issues of ensuring security while delivering effective inmate programmes.

Balancing victim and offender interests and rights

The contemporary accommodation of victim participation in formal and informal justice processes brings into sharp focus the issue of potential conflicts between victim and offender rights. Victim participation can involve contact with offenders when confronting them with the harmful impacts of their conduct or pursuing reparation. Such practices raise issues about the relative benefits and costs to both parties and the community. Perhaps more actual or potential harm might be done to victims in the pursuit of the interests of the offender or broader community. Conversely, tilting the balance toward victims' rights, where the desire is for revenge through 'just deserts' sentencing, might also tilt the balance too far toward damage to offenders and the community.

Ethics in context

Think of a recent example highlighted in the media where these dilemmas are present, and consider your reaction to the rights and interests of both the victim and the (alleged) offender.

Conclusion

As in other fields of practice, social workers practising in criminal justice must seek out the contextual and specialised knowledge and skills needed to practise effectively. This requires grounding in criminology and criminal justice process. They will also need a clear understanding of the legal obligations, authority, and limitations that shape agency policy and programmes and their own practice. Ultimately they must be confident about the unique contribution that social work can make, and identify and manage the boundaries between their profession and others in this multi-agency and multidisciplinary context.

Review questions

1 What contribution can social workers make to crime prevention? Consider both rural and urban communities.
2 Summarise the developments in the ideological foundations of the criminal justice system.
3 What is the relationship between Indigenous Australians and the criminal justice system?

Notes

1 Queensland, Western Australia, Tasmania, and the Northern Territory have enacted Criminal Codes: 'New South Wales, Victoria and South Australia by and large retain the common law as their source of criminal law, so that in these States the prevailing law is that originally introduced from England but significantly modified by legislation and case law' (Bates et. al. 1996, pp. 73–4).

Part 3

*Emerging Trends and Issues
in Social Work*

17

SOCIAL WORK, SUSTAINABILITY, AND THE ENVIRONMENT

Jennifer McKinnon

Chapter objectives

- To show that social work practice is positioned within a larger environmental context
- To introduce the concept of sustainability as it applies to social work practice

- To outline the ways in which social workers might gear their practice toward sustainability

Background

The environmental movement has grown to the point where the language of 'sustainability' has infiltrated the daily lexicon of recent life in both Western and non-Western nations, and is the focus for debate and research in many academic disciplines. Indeed, green parties, often aligned with the issue of sustainability, have become a force in politics in many countries around the world, and in 2004 Latvia became the first country to appoint a president from a green party (BBC 2004). Many professional associations have also recognised that, even though their profession might not ostensibly be related to environmental issues, they cannot ignore their responsibility as an educated and mindful group to contribute in whatever way they can to developing an attitude of ecological responsibility within their profession. Hence we have seen growth in the initiation of groups with names such as 'International Association of Doctors for the Environment', 'Canadian Association of Physicians for the Environment', 'Argentine Association of Doctors for the Environment', 'The Professional Association for China's Environment' (a non-government organisation), 'The New England Ecological Economics Group', 'Environmental Law Alliance Worldwide', 'Lawyers for the Environment', 'Psychologists for the Environment', and 'Scientists for the

Environment'. This growing professional interest in issues of the environment and sustainability has resulted in a vibrant discourse within these professions, and in many cases professional journals have emerged as an outlet for discussion and theory building.

Incorporation of green issues seems to be finding little purchase, though, in the arena of social work discourse, and it is possible that social workers will be left behind as this debate develops into policy and into actions that will affect the daily lives of social worker's clients, client-groups, and themselves. Coates (2004, p. 8) maintains that 'social workers commonly view social problems as quite distinct from environmental ones', and, like most people in Western cultures, focus on human nature and social interaction as being quite separate from nature, which in turn is viewed as nothing but a 'benign background for human concern and activity' (Coates 2004, p. 10).

A search of the indexes of the major social work journals of Australia, the United States, and the United Kingdom for the period 1987 to 1997 (that is, the decade following the release of the United Nations World Commission on the Environment and Development report) revealed only seven articles that included the terms 'sustainability' or 'environment' in their titles (McKinnon 1998). This result appears to indicate that there has been little social work interest in the links between our professional focus on social systems and the broader economic and environmental systems. However, sustainability issues will become more and more entrenched in social policy and social work practice considerations (Coates 2004; Besthorn 2003), just as environmental issues have slowly but surely infiltrated the everyday thinking of the social mainstream and are no longer restricted to the margins of social awareness. It is imperative that social workers recognise the ecological impacts of their own work and then contribute to the enhancement of socially just outcomes by articulating the economic and environmental benefits that can be gained through sustainable social development.[1]

The social justice imperatives upon which social work is based also provide a compelling rationale for the profession's interest in and action on environmental issues. The need to ensure the viability of natural systems on Earth has become more urgent over the past three decades: social work as a profession can no longer ignore the intertwined nature of social, environmental, and economic systems. While the social environment has been a focus for social work since the dawn of the profession, the physical environment has taken a back seat: we have been more concerned with relationships between people and with the resources they need. Together with social policy that has a broad social justice interest, the past focus of social work practice, and of theory development broadly, has been the social environment. This position largely ignores the physical environment, and views agriculture, horticulture, farming, and forests and parkland as irrelevant to the social work domain: housing, for example, is considered important only in terms of its role as domicile or shelter for individuals and families. In developing countries such as India, indigenous social work has taken a broader approach to social and welfare considerations—the everyday physical world of individuals and the community is considered important.

Pollution and degradation generally occur in areas in which populations are vulnerable. Petrochemical plants, for example, are built in areas where the land is cheapest. There are many examples of this in the United States: industrial-chemical plants are built in neigh-bourhoods that are predominantly African-American, or where the land around is the only land cheap enough for poorer families to live (Hoff & Polack 1993). Similarly, the Union Carbide Bhopal disaster, which resulted in poisonous gases leaking into surrounding parts of the central Indian city in 1984, is another example of the environmental vulnerability of society's poorest. Corporate Watch (2000), an environmental watchdog on the Internet, found it ironic that, 15 years after the disaster, justice still evaded the victims of Union Carbide's negligence in Bhopal. They remind us that '[the] victims' continuing search for justice is a reminder that the odds are stacked against the poor, against the victims, in favor of the rich, powerful corporations' (Corporate Watch 2000).

Why, then, is it important or useful for social workers to have an interest in environmen-tal issues, and to be active in considering the environment in all aspects of their work? First, environmental degradation is one of the single biggest social justice issues affecting the world, yet it has been largely ignored, and relegated to the 'too hard' basket. Social justice is at the heart of all social work codes of ethics, which oblige social workers to be socially aware—part of this awareness includes environmental awareness. Second, the drive towards consumption and materialism in the Western world is indicative of changing societal values, and it is important for the social worker to understand this. These values can be expected to flow on to developing nations due to the current worldwide preference for economic values over social ones. Through the International Federation of Social Workers (IFSW), social workers are connected with the global community and have direct access to the United Nations. Social workers have the resources to affect attitudes toward consumption and materialism by 'thinking globally and acting locally'. Third, in order to grow, develop, and survive, humans need clean air, drinking water, shelter, and good soil to produce food. Biological well-being is an obvious prerequisite to positive social functioning, as Maslow's (1970) Hierarchy of Needs makes clear. Likewise, the AASW (2000) Code of Ethics states that the satisfaction of basic human needs is encompassed in the concept of social justice, and environmental manage-ment is also incorporated as an aspect of social justice in the code.

This chapter begins with the assumption that, overall, the current Western way of organ-ising our society is unsustainable (Hunt 1992), that current natural resource management practices are unsustainable (Australian Conservation Foundation 2000), and that the cur-rent economic orthodoxy, if it continues, will lead us down a very unsustainable path (Trainer 1995). I make these assumptions because we are faced daily with the realities of environmental crisis and with the growing divisions between the 'haves' and the 'have-nots'—mainly aligned along the political north–south divide.

Current issues

The environment

The environment, in its broader sense, refers to the combination of physical features, geo-graphical sites, social interaction, flora, and fauna that contribute to the delicate balance of

Earth's atmosphere and ecosystems. The social environment cannot exist if the ecological balance becomes so degraded that life cannot be sustained, and this understanding is at the heart of the imperative for attention by social work to this issue. Literature addressing questions about environmental sustainability is dominated by discussion of the interdependence of social, economic, and environmental systems. The field of social ecology has gained greater recognition and popularity in the past decade, providing even greater impetus for interest by social workers in this field.

The United Nations Conference on Environment and Development (UNCED), held in Rio de Janeiro in 1992, made important links between the demands of social and environmental sustainability. One of only five documents agreed upon at the conference, *Agenda 21* (United Nations 2003), is a guide for individuals, businesses, and governments on the actions they can take to aid the development of sustainable processes. *Agenda 21* has two features: it argues that there is clear interdependence between social, economic, and environmental development, and it foresees as essential the intensification of global democratisation processes.

However, the United Nations World Commission on the Environment and Development (WCED)(1987) identified that sustainability is only achievable through recognition of the inextricable links between social, economic, and environmental factors and systems, and action that reflects such a recognition. It is not seen as possible, by the WCED and many others (Hartmann 1998; Yencken & Porter 2001), to achieve sustainability in any one of these fields without a concomitant effort in the other two. Indeed, the best that could be hoped for in such a situation would be amelioration only. Although social work has a demonstrated understanding and expertise in social issues, factors, and systems, and a strong professional interest in relevant economic issues (Boulet 2003), it will only be when social workers manage to combine a working knowledge of important environmental and economic factors into their field of specialty—that is, the social—that social workers will be able to contribute to enactment of a sustainable social environment and to sustainability more generally.

The identification of an environmental crisis (Vanclay & Lawrence 1995) over recent decades, and the understanding that our present situation is unsustainable (Dovers 2001) has resulted in an emphasis on the importance of sustainability, which acknowledges a growing understanding of the interdependence of social, economic, and environmental systems, and their ability to affect the ecology of the Earth (Dovers 2001). Given that social workers have a particular understanding of and expertise in social issues, it seems that social workers have a starting place for making a contribution, should they choose to do so, to overall sustainability; that is, via the field of social sustainability. One might argue that this is exactly what social work has always been doing; that is, ensuring the manifestation and maintainability of desired social conditions through attention to need and outcomes for individuals, families, groups, and communities. Indeed, social work has demonstrated considerable interest in the economic factors that affect social conditions—bodies of theory such as structural social work (Mullaly 1997) and critical theory as it is applied to social work (Allan 2003) have emerged from this tradition.

Social sustainability

The term 'social sustainability' is itself a contested one (Dovers 2001; Howden 2002). Much of the literature that purports to discuss social sustainability is actually written from an economic or an environmental perspective, and addresses neither the issue of what is meant by 'social sustainability' nor the strategies that might be needed to ensure that desired social systems are sustainable. The Economic and Social Committee of the European Union (2000) maintains that structural changes are needed in our societies if we are to achieve genuine sustainable development worldwide.

Dovers (2001, p. 3) refers to sustainability as a 'profound social challenge', due to the requirement that a society that is ecologically sustainable and humanly desirable will require a 'new order of things'. Dovers refers here to the change of intrinsic values that is needed to, first, halt and then reverse the effects of: natural resource depletion; air, social, and water pollution; and climate change. Trainer (1995, 1998) expands on this notion by looking at the implications for social welfare. He comes to the conclusion that a sustainable society is only attainable through achievement of much simpler lifestyles, higher levels of self-sufficiency, development of cooperatives, and a steady-state (or no-growth) economy.

With the advent of modern technology, human activity has altered the biosphere in ways that are harmful to living systems and, as a result, human populations face a series of difficult challenges such as economic and geographic displacement and adverse changes to health (Berger & Kelly 1993). From its earliest days, social work has worked toward bettering and preserving human welfare, so it is appropriate for social workers to play a role in humanity's adaptation to ecological changes. The ecological crisis is integrally related to current social and political concerns. Hoff and Polack (1993) predict that the environment will be a factor in future solutions for other issues such as hunger, employment, health, international development, and debt reduction. The environmental crisis is not regarded as a challenge to basic social work values and practice; rather, the ecological model of social work practice, as viewed by Hoff and Polack, is similar to the ecological model of science, both of which emphasise circular exchanges in an ongoing reciprocal process.

The path of social workers who want to take part in the development of a sustainable society is not an easy one: the lack of interest thus far by the profession means that social workers are working outside the mainstream of their profession. The level of personal commitment needed is very high as resistance from the community to these goals will be even stronger than that shown by other social workers. There is a general sense in the media that the environmentalism of the 1970s and 1980s has had its day, and environmentally responsible goals are often presented as being at odds with the aspirations of the majority (Tindale 1995).

What part can social workers play in ecologically sustainable development? If we accept as our goal 'development that meets the needs of current generations without compromising the ability of future generations to meet their needs' (WCED 1997), it is obvious that some of the current structures of society will need to be reviewed. Many see community-based structures as the likely future successor to the family, church, market, and state, and as the primary focus for the meeting of human need (Ife 1997a). Social work has an important role to play in the transition to a sustainable society. This role, depending as it does upon social work skills in community-building and establishing community-based services, requires that the community development aspect of social work practice becomes a more significant feature of the social work profession and the training that social workers receive.

Ethical issues

The Australian Association of Social Workers (AASW) website describes social work as:

> ... the profession committed to the pursuit of social justice, to the enhancement of the quality of life, and to the development of the full potential of each individual, group and community in society.
>
> Social workers pursue these goals by working to address the barriers, inequities and injustices that exist in society, and by active involvement in situations of personal distress and crisis. They do this by working with individuals, groups and communities in the pursuit and achievement of equitable access to social, economic and political resources, and by working with individuals towards the realisation of their intellectual, physical and emotional potentials.
>
> Social workers are committed to working within a stated value position and in accordance with a code of ethics.
>
> Social work practice is informed by professional education based on an analysis and understanding of human development and behaviour, and of complex social structures and processes.

AASW (2004)

The AASW (2002) Code of Ethics (the Code) is the document devised by the Association to express the values and principles that are integral to, and which characterise, the social work profession. The Code, in describing the values and principles of the profession, lists 'social justice' as a key value, along with 'human dignity and worth', 'service to humanity', 'integrity', and 'competence' (AASW 2002, pp. 4–7). The 'social justice' list includes six items that express the social work profession's understanding of social justice. Included in these six, along with items such as 'the satisfaction of basic human needs' and 'equal treatment and protection under the law', is 'social development and environmental management in the interests of human welfare'. It seems that the AASW has a desire for the profession to be seen as valuing the environment, at least insofar as it can be 'managed' in the interests of human welfare.

While the term 'environmental management in the interests of human welfare' reflects the innate anthropocentrism (Goldman & Schurman 2000) of the aims of the profession, it does firmly link the interests of social work with achievement of good environmental outcomes. Further, this incorporation goes some way toward addressing the criticism that some in the social work profession have made about moves to attend to environmental matters more seriously within social work's professional boundaries. The criticism has been that 'the environment' is a middle-class issue, irrelevant to those in situations of poverty or domestic violence who need immediate and practical assistance from social workers (Cannan 2000).

In fact, attempting to address environmental problems is an attempt to deal with issues affecting the very survival of the planet. Unless the Earth retains its ability to support human life, there will be no point having a profession with the expertise to deal with social issues. Survival is not a middle-class issue (Cannan 2000), and the issues of environmental and social sustainability come very much within the purview of the social justice arena.

Ethics in context

Imagine you are a social worker leading a relatively typical Western lifestyle, with an 'ecological footprint' far in excess of that made by most people who live in less developed nations. You have become aware of the plight of the small Pacific Island nation of Tuvalu, which, as a result of global climate change, is threatened with being completely submerged in the not-too-distant future as sea levels rise. In fact, you heard one commentator say: 'Isn't it ironic that one of the least industrially developed nations is likely to be the first casualty of industrial development'.

- Does the AASW code of ethics compel you to take any action in regard to this situation?
- Do you know the size of your own 'ecological footprint'?
- What steps can you take to reduce your own ecological footprint, as well as that of the organisation for which you work?

The future for social work

For social workers, there are numerous implications for practice. Once we are aware of the inextricable links between social, economic, and environmental systems, it is obvious that the primary social systems focus of social workers has ramifications beyond the social aspects of human existence on this planet. This awareness demands that we and our representative associations explore the issue and investigate ways that social workers can carry out their professional roles and duties while having a positive, rather than a deleterious, impact on future sustainability.

Social work literature has used the ecological model in a limited way (Hoff & Polack 1993), applying it only to an understanding of social and cultural exchanges when it could, in fact, extend to examining exchanges with the physical environment. In the Hoff and Polack conception, social workers are encouraged to draw on environmental discourse—using the concept of reciprocal exchange between humans and their physical environment—to develop appropriate interventions. Just as the Landcare movement evolved in response to the realisation by the farming sector in Australia that its future is dependent upon the adoption of sustainable land management practices (Lockie 1994), there is a growing general realisation that social and cultural practices also need to adapt to ensure that society itself is sustainable (Gamble & Weil 1997; Berger 1995; Hoff & Polack 1993). In the language of contemporary environmental researchers and activists, what is needed is sustainable development: that is, ecological science, economic patterns, and policy changes that provide for human needs while maintaining or even improving the physical environment from which resources are drawn (WCED 1987).

Social work applications for the principles of sustainable development are numerous. Penton (1993) suggests that ecological social work practice should aim to resolve problems creatively and with minimum intervention, fit in with the beliefs and lifestyles of clients and their social systems, and remove linear (cause and effect) analyses of client problems, developing instead circular definitions of problems. Social workers can and should be involved in a range of environmental issues because of their skills and values. Scientists and environmentalists are warning that our natural environment is deteriorating at an alarming rate. Social workers have the theoretical base and the practice skills to respond to the social dimensions of environmental issues at the local, national, and international levels. As has been demonstrated, social work cannot aspire to help people resolve social problems without considering the wider picture related to the health of the Earth as a whole. This expands the person-in-environment concept (Hepworth & Larsen 1997) that is central to social work practice. Social work practice potentially could include an ecological and environmental perspective in a number of ways.

Research

The traditional concern of social work for disadvantaged populations gives social workers a natural interest in research on the discriminatory effects of environmental pollution. Social work researchers in health care, for example, could appraise potential environmental links to developmental disabilities, cancer, and other diseases.

Environmental issues also are germane to research in community organisation and advocacy (Hoff & Polack 1993). An example of this is the environmental movement itself, which arguably has been one of the most visible social movements in recent decades, and is a rich source of research data on organising methods. An important trend in the environmental movement has been that of citizens organising to resist the pollution of their local communities. Hoff and Polack suggest that social work research can bring a unique transactional viewpoint to evaluating these efforts, demonstrating the deleterious relationship between environmental exploitation and the threats to human life and community.

Social movements generally are a rich source of knowledge for social work. The role of social movements in developing new knowledge (Ekins 1992), and in transporting new knowledge from the margins of society to the mainstream (Touraine 1985), can provide a unique link for social work researchers to the environmental issues affecting community members at the vulnerable margins of society.

Community organising

Social work skills in networking can be creatively applied to link environmental groups with relevant issues such as racism or high Aboriginal infant mortality rates (Gamble & Weil

1997). Reciprocally, social work skills in organising could aid newly aroused community groups to fight the dangers caused by toxic products and other environmental threats. In addition, social workers' understanding of the intrinsic relationship between person and environment gives them the potential to be mediators between environmental advocates and those concerned with jobs and economic viability.

Social workers in rural areas may also have a place in exposing the servitude of farmers to chemical companies, and in assessing anecdotal evidence that chemicals are developed that create the need for use of further chemicals, thus increasing dependency (Vanclay & Lawrence 1995). Farming families have real concerns regarding their health, in a climate that encourages, and even advocates, chemical overuse (Alston 1995). Nevertheless, rural poverty historically has restricted the ability of those affected to challenge such paradigms (McClinton & Pawar 1997).

Direct practice

Social work's humanistic foundations and social workers' skills in fostering human relationships offer them the opportunity to play a vital role in helping individuals and families to discover values and lifestyles that emphasise 'being' (that is, creative expression, cultivation of personal relationships, altruistic involvement in one's community) over 'having' (acquisitive or addictive behaviours of people to seek satisfaction through acquiring things). The relationship between lifestyle and personal satisfaction can be explored creatively not only in individual and family therapy (Penton 1993) but also through workshops, groups, and public education methods (Hoff & Polack 1993).

Social policy

Environmental change will involve political, economic, and social change. Policy practitioners have the difficult task of connecting these elements to seek specific legislative changes that protect both people and their sustaining environments (Berger & Kelly 1993). This could involve social workers in advocacy (for example, for funding for development of sustainable models), interpreting the concept of well-being in a way that is different from the interpretations of those who see environmental protection as a utilitarian trade-off between economic growth and well-being, and resisting political efforts to reduce social spending in order to address environmental needs. Social workers could, for example, have had a voice on the issues raised at the 1998 World Summit on Greenhouse Gases in Japan (which resulted in the Kyoto protocol).

International issues

Environmental issues will play an increasing role in future responses to socio-political issues such as population growth, poverty in developing nations, resolution of wars, international debt, and the development of international governance mechanisms (Global 2000 Revisited 1997). The reality of the new international political economy requires that social action to relieve domestic concerns occurs in the light of this global context. Isolationist strategies and attitudes increasingly will become less acceptable. The Global 2000 Revisited report (1997) asserts that a healthy Earth is an essential prerequisite for a healthy human population. Attaining this goal involves work at the global level to create the social and economic conditions necessary to stop unsustainable growth of the human population and to reduce consumption by the wealthiest. We will need to ensure that services such as civil order, education, and health care are offered, and that soils and species are preserved everywhere. Additionally, society will need to find ways to increase agricultural yields while reducing dependence on energy sources that damage the environment: achievement of a sustainable environment will involve conversion from energy sources that emit carbon dioxide to renewable non-polluting sources that are available even to the poor, and will require sharp cuts in the emissions of other greenhouse gases. In order to do this, social workers can be part of the global voice calling for an immediate end to emission of chemicals destroying the ozone layer, and can fight for equity between nations and peoples of developed and underdeveloped countries.

Sustainable development requires a strengthened and democratised local and regional planning system, as well as a broader national and economic industrial plan. Private enterprise can flourish within this framework that lays down the overall objectives for society, and sets the ecological limits beyond which development cannot be allowed to go. This approach opens up possibilities for different kinds of development and approaches to economic growth. Social workers, for example, could be involved in the development of small community economic systems, such as Local Energy Transfer Systems and local currency groups (Trainer 1998).

There are also a number of established frameworks that may be helpful more broadly to social workers who wish to make a commitment to social sustainability through their work. *Agenda 21* is a United Nations (1992) document that outlines the social issues that need to be addressed in order to achieve ecologically sustainable development. Probably more relevant to social workers is the *Earth Charter* that has been developed as part of a five-year, worldwide consultation process. The *Earth Charter* (Earth Charter Initiative 2000) relates more specifically to the interaction between social systems and the other systems that will need to be integrated if we are to achieve social sustainability. This charter necessitates a four-fold approach to achieving sustainability: respect for nature, universal human rights, economic justice, and a culture of peace. Both *Agenda 21* and the *Earth Charter* can be used by social workers to inform their practice and to raise their level of awareness of the everyday decisions that are made that can have a bearing on ecological outcomes.

The Australian Collaboration (2001), an affiliation of national community organisations, calls for Australia to change its focus on economic growth as an indicator of prosperity, and to focus instead on genuine progress indicators. They report five different kinds of damaging growth: that which does not translate into jobs; that which is not matched by the spread of democracy; that which destroys cultural identity; that which despoils the environment and squanders the resources needed by future generations; and growth where most of the benefits are claimed by the rich. Social workers need to be aware of the ways in which economic imperatives can supplant important socio-cultural and environmental objectives. The Australian Collaboration (2001) calls for a new approach to overall government policy-making—one that incorporates issues of equity, transparency, reconciliation, democracy, freedom of speech, and media diversity, to name a few. To leave many of the Australian conditions and trends as they currently are is 'a recipe for long-term social and environmental disaster with equally serious economic consequences' (The Australian Collaboration 2001, p. 90).

Conclusion

Although, in the past, social work has not focused on the broader environment, social justice principles demand that we inform our work with an understanding of environmental issues, and that we use our skills and knowledge to bring about fundamental social change aimed at achieving ecologically sustainable development.

Politically and personally, acceptance of such responsibility will not be easy: resistance is to be expected among the profession and in the community generally. The principles of participatory democracy are extremely important. Change is difficult, and communities are in the best position to make decisions about their future when they are fully informed about options. Community development is bound to become a more intrinsic part of social work practice in the future, and social workers prepared to assist communities to tackle environmental, social, and economic aspects of their development will be best placed to facilitate ecologically sustainable development.

'Think global; act local' is a slogan from the environmental movement that may also prove useful to social workers as they engage with the community and incorporate environmental and economic considerations into their work. This slogan might be useful to social workers on a number of levels. 'Thinking global' requires of us that we be aware of what is going on around the world, and that we consider the broader consequences of our everyday actions. 'Acting local', though, is the element of the slogan that reassures us that, even though the problems of the world may be enormous, that we should nevertheless direct our actions at the local level. Such exhortation asks for action, rather than just a purely cognitive understanding of the global issues, which may otherwise lead to inactivity as the overall issues seem overwhelming.

Social workers can think of making a contribution to sustainability at many different levels: through clinical casework, professional supervision, line management roles, group work, family work, community work, as well as the various other roles social workers pursue in a 'non-social work' capacity.

Review questions

1 How can social workers, in their professional capacity, make a contribution toward sustainability?

2 In what ways are the concepts of social justice and environmental justice linked?

3 In tandem with economic and environmental management changes, what kind of social change is needed if overall sustainability is to be achieved?

Note

1 In using the term 'development', linked here as it is with social sustainability, I refer to development in its broadest sense; that is, to do with the progression toward the highest aspirations of the members of the society, rather than assuming any kind of link with the term development in its economic sense.

18

SOCIAL WORK IN RURAL AND REMOTE AUSTRALIA

Brian Cheers and Judy Taylor

Chapter objectives

- To present social work in rural and remote areas as a distinct field of practice with unique issues
- To introduce rural social care as a new, contextualised, grounded approach to practice

- To present concepts and approaches to address the issues facing Indigenous peoples in rural and remote Australia

Introduction

Social work and social welfare in Australia have been shaped by the global and national economic, cultural, and ideological environment of the past 200 years (Cheers 1996). During this period, Australia developed as a highly urbanised nation, with the overriding priority being economic growth through capitalism and industrialisation, supported by an ideology emphasising individualism, competition, and materialism. In essence, social welfare and social work are primarily urban responses to the urban problems accompanying this modernist agenda. Because people living in rural and remote areas served this agenda well (Sher & Sher 1994), and were distant from the urban centres where most Australians live, their social problems remained largely invisible and unacknowledged until fairly recently. However, global and national economic, political, social, and technological changes over the past few decades have unveiled rural needs and created new ones that, by the early 1990s, could no longer be ignored by Australian society (Cheers 1996; Cheers & Clarke 2003). In response, mainstream welfare policies, structures, and methods were extended to rural areas where many of their inadequacies were exposed. Not to be deterred, rural social workers and other social care practitioners have been developing alternative frameworks that are more appropriate to rural contexts.

Rural Australia

In 1996, 14.1 per cent of the total Australian population were living in settlements with fewer than 1000 residents, and 27.3 per cent in places with fewer than 100,000 people (ABS 1997a). For the most part, rural Australians are scattered throughout the continent in numerous diverse settlements in a variety of ecological contexts, with no particular type dominating the landscape (Sorensen 1993). The people, too, are diverse, coming from a range of cultural, social, and economic backgrounds. Contrary to popular belief, only one in four rural workers is employed directly in primary industries (Castles 1995) and, depending on definitions, between 4 and 17 per cent of rural people are farmers (Sher & Sher 1994).

Australia is one of the most urbanised countries in the world, and the least densely populated overall (ABS 1997a). In 1994, almost three quarters of Australians were living in fourteen major cities of 100,000 people or more (McLennan 1996, p. 78), and there were only seventeen places with between 25,000 and 100,000 people. Australia lacks a scattering of smaller provincial cities that can serve as major regional service centres for their rural hinterlands. This poses formidable service problems, especially with respect to the more remote settlements. It has also resulted in political and economic power being focused in the major urban areas; unusually high dependence on centralised Commonwealth, state, and territory governments rather than regionally based local governments; and inequitable distribution of resources and infrastructure (Cheers 1998).

Aboriginal and Torres Strait Islander people are far more likely than other Australians to live in rural areas. In 1996, 69.7 per cent of the Indigenous population were living in places with fewer than 100,000 people, compared with 27.3 per cent of all Australians (ABS 1997b). They are also more widely dispersed than the general population and far more likely to live in more remote areas (ABS 1997b).

That Australia's welfare system has failed rural people is evidenced by the many disadvantages they experience relative to urban residents. They are generally disadvantaged with respect to virtually all social and economic indicators, including life chances, income levels, poverty, unemployment, living costs, housing quality, health status, education, and a range of social problems, and in gaining access to health, welfare, community, personal support, and essential services (Cheers 1998). For instance, thirty-three of the thirty-seven poorest federal electorates in Australia are in rural areas (Lawrence 1995), and rural people suffer higher rates of premature mortality, morbidity, hypertension, and psychiatric disorders (Aoun et al. 1994; Rolley & Humphreys 1993). With respect to social issues, the suicide rate for young rural men is more than 50 per cent higher than the urban rate (Department of Human Services and Health 1995). Furthermore, disadvantage on most indicators increases as we move from urban areas to smaller and more remote communities (Cheers 1998). Generally speaking, Indigenous people are the most disadvantaged of all Australians on virtually all social and economic indicators (Cheers 1998). However, it is less well known that, overall, those living in rural areas are disadvantaged compared with urban Indigenous people on some indicators such as housing, unemployment, various health measures, and the provision of health, welfare, and essential services (Madden 1994). For example, in 1988 the Indigenous infant mortality rate was four times higher in rural South Australia than in Adelaide (South Australia Health Commission 1988). Similarly, in 1993 one in four Indigenous communities in northern Australia had neither a water supply that satisfied national health standards nor an adequate garbage disposal service (Madden 1994).

Over the past few decades, global and national economic, industrial, and technological changes have exacerbated the problems of rural Australians (Cheers 1996; Cheers & Clarke 2003; Lawrence & Hungerford 1994). Rural-based industries such as agriculture have declined in importance to the Australian economy, resulting in governments and private businesses such as banks withdrawing support. For instance, from the 1950s to the early 1990s the contribution of agriculture to Australian export earnings declined from 80 per cent to 20.6 per cent (Epps & Sorensen 1993). Primary producers have faced increasing competition as a result of market globalisation and national economic and industry restructuring policies. This, combined with rising production costs, falling commodity prices, recessions and droughts, has brought financial hardship to farmers, with many being forced to leave the land. Sixteen per cent of all Australian farmers left the industry between 1991 and 1996 (Garnaut & Lim-Applegate 1998). To survive financially, more farm families have increased their working hours and been forced into 'pluriactivity' (Le Heron et al. 1991). This has been particularly hard on farm women, many of whom are working triple shifts combining farm, off-farm, and domestic work. Compared with 1968, for instance, in the mid 1990s 54 per cent more women were working full time on the farm, while those engaged in off-farm part-time work had increased by 148 per cent (Ferguson & Simpson 1995).

The declining fortunes of primary producers have had an impact on other local businesses, workers, and residents, reducing incomes, employment opportunities, and job security. Unemployment has increased markedly in rural areas since the 1960s as full-time permanent positions have been lost or replaced by part-time, casual, and contract employment. Since 1968, for instance, by the mid 1990s 101,700 jobs had been lost from agriculture alone (Ferguson & Simpson 1995).

Along the way, many rural communities and residents have increasingly lost their capacity to determine their own futures. Smaller towns have been deserted as residents have left properties and homes in search of employment, education, and services (Cheers 1995). Those who have left, and many that have remained, have suffered financial losses, emotional difficulties, and social problems (Cribb 1994). Of particular concern has been the departure of long-term residents, such as farmers and the aged, who carry the community narratives from the past, and the young people who carry them into the future (Cheers 1998; Rolley & Humphreys 1993). As rural populations have declined, community solidarity and support networks have weakened, governments have decreased funding levels, services, and infrastructure support, and private companies such as banks have closed offices. These responses have intensified the cycle of decline, resulting in further community disintegration and personal impoverishment.

On the other hand, some communities, such as retirement and tourist destinations, have grown rapidly. In many places, this has exacerbated the problems of the poor, the aged, young people, and the unemployed, who have been forced to pay higher accommodation, transportation, and other living costs, and face reduced service levels due to increased demand (Bone et al. 1993).

The policy context

Because these changes have had an impact on whole communities they have required community-level strategies, in addition to responses targeted at individuals and families. Each community has been affected differently requiring context-specific responses. As many of the social impacts have been connected to economic factors, they have demanded responses relating to local economic planning. However, our welfare system has not been up to the task of responding effectively to these changes and, in attempting to do so, its inadequacies in relation to rural issues have been exposed.

This is not surprising given that the structure of Australian social welfare has always disadvantaged rural people in comparison to those living in urban areas. There are many reasons for this. For instance, our welfare system is overwhelmingly focused on individuals and families, rather than whole communities; consequently, the relationship between individual and community well-being, and the importance of building, supporting, and resourcing the capacity of rural communities to identify and respond to local needs, have tended to be undervalued. Similarly, because our welfare system tends to view social issues in isolation from their economic and cultural contexts, welfare policy, planning, and education have become isolated from other sectors such as economic planning, industry development, and ecological sustainability (Cheers 1996, p. 188).

Furthermore, the domination of social welfare by urban-based central Commonwealth and state governments, rather than local government and community-based organisations, has helped to separate social policy formulation and service development from the communities in which people live. Central government domination, concerns about consistency of service standards, and the urban foundations of Australian welfare have also contributed to the adoption of uniform service approaches that tend to be unresponsive to particular geographic, social, and cultural contexts. For instance, the emphasis on 'in-reach' models, where users of a service go to a service, has resulted in many people in remote areas missing out on resources.

Australia also has a 'categorical' system of welfare provision in which a fragmented array of services and resources are provided in response to tightly defined needs by separate organisations according to highly targeted funding programmes. This has created difficulties in responding holistically to the interconnected nature of many rural issues, whether at the level of the individual, family, or community. It has also resulted in funding formulas based on the number of people in a locality with a highly specific need that have left smaller communities without services (Cheers 1998).

The essential character of Australian social policy, social welfare, and social work has been further entrenched by the 'market welfare' approach to the administration of social welfare services adopted since the 1980s (Taylor 1999b). These policies have resulted in withdrawals of rural services and diminution of the capacity of community-based organisations to contribute to service development and community-building (Boss 1998). Government control over service models, structures, and methods has intensified, while the quantity and quality of consultation with non-governmental organisations has decreased, thereby reducing the opportunity and resources for consumer and community participation.

The advent of 'market welfare', particularly competition policy, has been such a profound development that it is clearly the most identifiable and powerful influence on Australian social welfare today (Rogan 1996). Two major inquiries—the Coalition of Australian Governments' *Report of the Task Force on Health and Community Services* (1995) and the Industry Commission's report into *Charitable Organisations in Australia* (1995)—have influenced the application of competition policy to the welfare sector. These reports have been used to support policy reforms in social welfare administration, such as the purchaser–provider framework, competitive tendering, output-based funding using quantitative performance measures, more tightly targeted funding, various contractual arrangements, and an accounting approach to accountability. However, there has been insufficient analysis of the implications of these reforms for rural welfare (Taylor 1999b) and no proper evaluation of their implications for health and welfare service provision by community-managed organisations to Indigenous people. Clearly, the principles developed by the Coalition of Australian Governments (COAG) supporting self-management of services by and for Indigenous people conflict with those of competition policy because self-managed Indigenous organisations cannot be competitive against mainstream providers.

Reports indicate that competition policy is having adverse consequences for rural communities (Boss 1998; Raysmith 1998; Taylor 1999b; Whitelum & Cheers 2002). The viability of many rural community-based organisations is being threatened: some services are being withdrawn unnecessarily, reducing the choice that service users have over provider and service model, which is the opposite of the stated intention of the reforms. Furthermore, the tendering process is placing unfunded costs and extra burdens on small rural organisations and creating friction, distrust, secrecy, and division among them, making cooperation and service coordination difficult. Reports also indicate that management committee members of community-based organisations are spending more time trying to position themselves so that they can continue to provide services at a sustainable level in the new policy environment (Burdekin Community Development Association 1997).

Of great concern is the transfer of ownership and control over service development and delivery from local organisations and their communities to external structures and administrators who are poorly positioned to understand and relate to local needs, priorities, and perspectives. Increasingly exclusive emphasis is being placed on 'vertical accountability' of services to government funding bodies outside the community at the expense of 'horizontal accountability' to local people and organisations. At the same time, government control over service models, structures, and methods has intensified, and consultation of government funding bodies with non-governmental and community-based organisations has decreased. These trends have significantly reduced service-user and community participation in service development, management, and delivery, and the capacity of community-based groups and organisations to advocate in the interests of their members and to oppose these reforms (Whitelum & Cheers 2002). They no longer have resources to take on issues alone, funding to peak bodies has been reduced, and the functions and roles of ministerial and departmental advisory structures are being undermined. Most disturbing has been the disbanding of the Aboriginal and Torres Strait Islander Commission and the taking over of its functions by the Australian Government. This represents yet another attack on self-control and ownership of Indigenous issues by Indigenous Australians, which has further reduced their opportunities to influence planning for their own welfare.

In the non-government sector, competition policy is increasingly aggregating service providers through amalgamation and the formation of strategic alliances, leading to small local agencies being squeezed out by large organisations based in capital cities and major regional centres (Raysmith 1998; ACOSS 1997).

Many simply cannot compete with larger statewide organisations with more established administrative and financial infrastructures that use cheaper, more efficient, but far less effective 'fly-in, fly-out' models in remote areas.

This transfer of ownership and control is making it increasingly difficult for local people to plan and develop services in response to pressing locally identified needs, and continues the colonial attitude of the 'government knows best' towards Indigenous people and their communities. In most instances it is essential—morally and in the interests of service relevance and effectiveness—that local Indigenous community-based organisations manage services to Indigenous people.

Under competition policy, the setting of outcome-based benchmarks and output-based funding also disadvantages rural communities. While uniform benchmarking reduces the responsiveness of services to local conditions, output-based funding means that rural communities do not have resources to initiate or contribute to community-building through, for example, community development, social advocacy, social-needs analysis, social planning, and coordinating with broader regional planning activities (Raysmith 1998).

In relation to rural people, the essential weakness of Australian social welfare is that it revolves around centralised policy formulation, funding, and service structures, which increasingly have become removed from the immediate contexts of rural people's daily lives, natural caring processes, and other community services that have such profound impacts on individual and community well-being. However, in response to the needs and demands of their communities and clients, rural practitioners have been developing innovative responses that are being organised into the idea of rural social care. The concept of rural social care is based on a deeper meaning of social welfare in rural contexts (Cheers 1998; Cheers in press). Rural social care comprises all the arrangements and processes, including both formal structures and informal (or 'natural') interaction, through which people meet each other's social, emotional, and material needs (Cheers 1998). These include:

- 'natural' or informal support
- formal provision of social care: managing, funding, providing, and evaluating services
- direct social care practice

- social care development: social planning, participative community development, advocacy, and community services development
- contextualised rural social policy formulation
- developmental research, including participatory action research methods.

The concept of rural social care embeds services, organisations, and practitioners in the totality of caring interaction in particular rural contexts. Mainstream Australian social welfare, on the other hand, tends to view them as the focal point of human caring and as extensions of standardised urban-based services.

Policy frameworks

Australian rural social policies vary according to their relative emphasis on different frameworks: 'urbo-centricity', economic reductionism, economic modelling, reactive residualism, mainstreaming, rural targeting, and development (Cheers 1998). Urbo-centricity, economic reductionism, economic modelling, and mainstreaming are poorly suited to rural contexts. Urbo-centric policies are developed primarily to solve urban not rural problems. For instance, from time to time state governments have attempted to solve public-housing crises in cities by relocating people on low incomes to low-cost rental accommodation in country towns, frequently resulting in their isolation from social and support networks and alienation from new communities. Economic reductionism redefines social and personal problems as economic issues, then attempts to solve them through economic strategies. For example, the Commonwealth government's *Working Nation* statement (Keating 1994) assumed that social problems such as poverty could be solved by increasing regional employment opportunities, despite substantial evidence to the contrary (see, for example, Lichter & McLaughlin 1995; Lichter et al. 1994). Similarly, economic modelling constructs social policies and welfare-services funding according to free-market economic principles. National competition policy, for instance, is based on the assumption that competition between service providers is the most efficient and effective way to distribute scarce resources, and incorporates a number of market-style 'technologies'.

Reactive residualist policies are developed, usually hastily, to respond to the problems caused by economic change after they have occurred. For instance, before 1991 farmers were ineligible for mainstream income security provisions because of their assets. In response to declining incomes, special provisions were introduced to make it possible for some farmers to access benefits. That these provisions failed is demonstrated by the fact that a year later only sixty-three farmers had taken advantage of them (Cheers 1998). Since then, income security policy has undergone several changes as inequities continue to be exposed. Still, however, in contrast with unemployed wage earners, farmers are only given benefits for a year, and must sell their businesses to obtain maximum benefits.

The mainstreaming of rural needs—that is, viewing them as identical to urban needs and responding with the same kinds of services and resources—dominated the policy landscape until recently. Examples include 'in-reach' rather than 'outreach services' (Cheers 1998), and funding services according to how many people in a geographic location have a highly specific need (Cheers 1998).

In contrast, rural targeting and developmental frameworks are more suited to rural communities. Rural targeting policies direct services and provisions to particular places. Examples include multipurpose services in smaller towns, outreach services such as mobile counselling for remote communities, and funding arrangements in which resources from a number of targeted programmes are 'pooled' and distributed according to needs, priorities, and service approaches identified by local people (Cheers 1998; Taylor 1999b). Finally, development policies aim at building the capacity of communities to manage local issues and problems. These typically involve planning, establishing, facilitating, and developing social care arrangements in response to current and projected social issues. Strategies include participative community development, social planning, and community services development involving partnerships between governments, community-based organisations, and local communities.

From a developmental point of view, social care is one of a number of strategies that rural communities use to manage change in the interests of community, individual, and family well-being; others include integrated local-area planning by local government, economic development, infrastructure development, and land management (Cheers 1998).

Community

To understand how social care contributes to the management of change, we need to understand rural communities. According to social interaction theory, geographically localised communities have four core facets: locality, local society, a community field, and interaction with the wider society (Cheers & Luloff 2001; Luloff 1998; Wilkinson 1991). Locality is simply the physical space or geographic territory in which people live. Local society is the organisation of social institutions, associations, interactions, and relationships in the social life of a locality, arranged, for example, into organisations and various social groupings based on culture, occupation, and ethnicity.

All local societies have several social fields through which people and groups pursue their various interests through social interaction and organisational structures. Fields most relevant to managing regional change and some typical organisations in each include:

- the economy—regional economic development organisations
- infrastructure—local government
- education—parents and citizens associations
- health care—hospital boards
- social care—councils for social development
- ecology—Landcare groups
- religion—churches
- recreation—sports clubs.

However, a local society is not a community unless it also has a community field through which people express their shared commitment to the well-being of the community as a whole (Wilkinson 1991). They do this through acts of 'community agency' (Luloff 1998) that interrelate and coordinate the various social fields in the community, harnessing their knowledge, expertise, resources, and energy for the common good. Such acts characterise the community field, although they also occur in other social fields. Typical organisational structures in the community field include local government and community councils in Indigenous communities. Research has shown that a strong community field is positively associated with: economic growth (Luloff 1998); social–emotional aspects of community well-being such as community attachment, cohesion, and solidarity (Flora 1998; Flora et al. 1997; Wilkinson 1991); and successful resolution of local social problems (see, for example, Bourke et al. 1996; Claude et al. 1999; Luloff 1996). The fourth facet of rural communities—interaction with the wider society—comprises the vertical links that a community and its organisations have with external structures, such as government departments, in contrast with the horizontal links among local people and organisations (Cheers 1998, pp. 73–5; Warren 1963).

Although the community field is central to a community's efforts to manage change, other social fields also develop structures, resources, and processes that contribute to the well-being of the whole community and a strong community field. Rural social care does this primarily through five methods. Social planning involves identifying and anticipating future social needs and planning services and resources, ideally in relation to more comprehensive local area planning coordinated through local government (Cheers 1998). Community services development involves developing services that are responsive to local contexts, needs, and priorities, and attracting resources to support them, usually in partnership with Commonwealth, state, and local governments (Taylor 1999a). Community development involves contributing to community-building by facilitating participation in social planning, community services development, and change-management strategies in other social fields and the community field (Cheers 1998; Cheers & Luloff 2001). Social care can also be linked with other social fields; for example, through practitioners contributing information to planning in these fields and, conversely, using information from them in social care development (Cheers 1998). Finally, the field of social care also provides opportunities for local people to express their commitment to their community and each other by facilitating 'natural' or informal helping, and through involvement in service development, management, and delivery (Boss 1998; Cheers 1999).

Practice issues: rural social care in practice

Future social work practice in rural and remote areas inevitably will build upon the past efforts of practitioners to respond to the needs of their communities within the policy and organisational constraints under which they have been operating. It is now possible to integrate their experiences across a variety of activities with an understanding of rural communities into a knowledge base to inform policy and practice. In brief, rural social care:

- 'expresses' community and is a function and responsibility of government
- is contextualised in local society
- contributes to whole-community, individual, and family well-being

- interrelates with the community field and other social fields
- focuses on whole communities, individuals, and families
- is participative and preventive
- is positioned at the intersection of horizontal and vertical ties
- advocates local needs and those of rural people more generally.

There are many examples of rural social care programmes and practice (Cheers 1998). For instance, the Remote Area Aboriginal and Torres Strait Islander Child Care Program (RAATS-ICCP), originating in Far North Queensland, is a vivid example of a programme that has contributed to a number of remote Indigenous communities (Department of Family Services and Aboriginal and Islander Affairs 1994). This programme demonstrates the benefits of community involvement and control, and a holistic and preventive approach to social care, enabling communities to develop childcare services as an expression of community, out of concern for the well-being of children and families. The RAATSICCP represented a genuine working partnership of Aboriginal and Torres Strait Islander people with the Department of Families, Youth and Community Care, which evolved on the basis of mutual trust and respect. Probably for this reason, the programme proved to be one of the most innovative and significant social care initiatives undertaken in rural areas of Queensland. It developed in 1991 to address the issues of social justice and equity of access to services for families with children in remote Aboriginal and Torres Strait Islander communities in North Queensland. Before its introduction, per capita funding for childcare meant that these children missed out on childcare services. In response to community members' expressed desire for the opportunity to provide a safe and nurturing environment in which their children could develop, the department helped them come together to form an advisory structure to support each other, and generate ideas, advise government, and assist in allocating funds. Government officers helped to facilitate, but did not control, this process. Consequently, community members were involved in, and owned, the process of service development and, with support, they developed the entire programme and all its elements. The balancing act that was required to meet needs across cultures and service models was facilitated through the advisory-group process, which was not always easy.

Through the programme, these communities established forty-eight extremely diverse childcare services throughout Far North Queensland and the Torres Strait, ranging from, for example, safe, stimulating outdoor play areas to mobile playgroups, and from family centres to licensed long-day-care facilities. In addition, various seminars were sponsored and training events conducted. Community advocacy on a range of issues occurred on an ongoing basis. The programme depended on the participation and decision-making of local representatives within their communities. Elements drawn from the idea of social care included building networks, formulating social policy in response to needs identified by communities themselves, developing enduring community structures that could pursue other local initiatives as they emerged, and enabling people to regain their ability to express a sense of community. Much of the work in the programme was done voluntarily by women out of concern for their children. These processes and activities and the benefits of the programme for children, families, and whole communities can be identified in ways that fit mainstream categories, but this is not possible within mainstream policy contexts.

The RAATSICCP is just one example of the rich body of knowledge being generated from the field of social care practice in rural and remote contexts. These contexts provide a different angle on social work that has the potential to make a significant impact on urban practice and policy because they require practitioners to work creatively within policy constraints while maximising scarce resources and involving the community.

Many new approaches have emerged from the field. For instance, through integrated service-delivery strategies, innovative services are now being provided to meet the needs of individuals and families who fall beyond programme boundaries, typically when working with people experiencing homelessness, disability, violence, and abuse. These strategies have also been used to meet needs not yet identified through, for example, neighbourhood centres and accommodation-based services. They can be especially useful in Indigenous communities that work with the holistic idea that all issues in a person's life are interconnected.

Innovative, more flexible funding models have also been developed to support rural social care practice: cross-programme funding, for instance, entails pooling funds from a variety of targeted programmes to meet the most pressing locally identified needs in small rural and remote communities. These funds can be used in relation to a range of needs and activities, including community development, which are negotiated with the community.

Ethics in context

Sometimes we assume that information is private when, in fact, it is shared by a number of people in the community. Although this does not, in itself, give practitioners permission to disclose confidential information, it does remind us that we are working in a public arena. This is especially clear when public information about a client is incorrect and potentially damaging. For example, during their temporary absence from town the rumour was circulating that a local man and woman had become lovers and that they were, in the local parlance, 'druggies'. Because of this, they and their respective children had been labelled as deviant. The rumours had particularly serious repercussions for the woman and her children because her ex-husband (who lived elsewhere) was seeking custody and he was being supported in this action by the town's police sergeant. I was aware from information they had given me in confidence that the rumours were false. I also knew that I had sufficient standing with local people to quash the rumours. However, I could not contact the people concerned because they were on his remote property, which did not have a telephone. Should I adhere to the ethic or allow the gossip to continue? I chose to set the record straight and, for this, the couple later thanked me.

The future for social work

We can take heart from the evidence that there is a growing pool of social workers who prefer rural work and life, and are committed to developing rural practice (Lonne & Cheers 2000a, 2000b; Lonne 2002). Nevertheless, while contributing to rural social care in their communities, they practise in a state of tension between the vision and ideals of the framework and the constraints of government policy. On the one hand, as community members, they are compelled to practise in ways that respond to their particular contexts, and which contribute to the community field. Positively, there are signs that their efforts to do so may be supported in the future by more adequate preparation through professional education; the AASW national rural and remote special interest group; guidance from the literature; and, most importantly, a profession that appears to be rediscovering its ideological foundations.

On the other hand, rural social care practice will continue to face a number of challenges. For instance, their location in statutory positions with fairly specialised functions and mandated responsibilities makes it difficult for rural social workers to focus on community well-being and whole human lives, and be involved in community agency activities. Similarly, vertical structures continue to dominate the rural social care landscape, pressuring many practitioners to focus exclusively on highly targeted services, and to withdraw from community agency activities. Finally, although rural communities will continue to encourage practitioners to contribute to community-building structures and processes, the viability of these is being threatened by lack of support from genuine rural and regional development policy frameworks at Commonwealth and state levels. For this reason, it falls to every rural practitioner to advocate for policies that will help rejuvenate their communities and rural Australia generally.

Review questions

1 What would you say are the special characteristics of social work practice in rural and remote areas?

2 How might you adapt your practice to suit this environment?

19

SOCIAL WORK WITH REFUGEE SURVIVORS OF TORTURE AND TRAUMA

Robin Bowles

Chapter objectives

- To introduce relevant information about refugee survivors of torture and trauma necessary for understanding this field of practice

- To describe the development of the social work field of practice in New South Wales and the current issues
- To introduce some ethical issues for working as a social worker in this field

Introduction

The field of practice with refugee survivors of torture and trauma has been established relatively recently, both internationally and within Australia. However, the problem of human rights abuses and forced exile caused by oppressive regimes has existed since the early days of human history. In this chapter, social work with traumatised refugees—people who have suffered from state-sanctioned violence or war, and have been forced to flee their homelands—is examined. In fear of persecution if they return to their own country, refugees have sought asylum in many countries including Australia.

Related areas of practice include working with tortured or traumatised Australian-born people such as the Indigenous population and Australian war veterans. These significant topics merit attention, as they involve large populations within Australian society whose situations arise from specific historical events that shaped our nation. Social work with people of non-English-speaking backgrounds is also a broad area of practice that intersects with work with refugees. To work in this field of practice is to be confronted both with the vulnerability of people to tragedy and painful events, and with the depth of cruelty in human nature (Herman 1992). Central to the social work code of ethics is a commitment to social justice and valuing the rights of all people. Working with refugee survivors of human rights abuses is, therefore, an important field for social workers, and relates to the core values of social work.

The worldwide situation for refugees

The United Nations defines refugees as people who are outside their own country and who cannot, or do not want to, return because of a well-founded fear of being persecuted for reasons of race, religion, nationality, political opinion, or membership of a particular social group. The 1951 Convention was initially applied to refugees from Europe following World War II, and the Protocol of 1967 extended protection to people fleeing persecution from situations all around the world (Silove 2002). Most Western nations including Australia signed these conventions and prior to this last decade there was an international acceptance of these principles.

Over the last 50 years, the numbers of people in refugee-like situations have increased significantly. Silove et al. (2000) writes that during the last two decades of the twentieth century there were more than thirty-five civil wars and a larger number of lower-intensity conflicts. These included 'ethnic cleansing' and violent attacks on civilians, including women and children, by local militias and warlords or non-government paramilitary forces. These conflicts have led to large population movements, and many displaced people with 'refugee-like' experiences who do not fit the United Nations definition, and who have not been able to gain refugee status either from the United Nations or regional agreements on the status of refugees. These include the 'internally displaced persons' (IDPs)—people who have fled and are still living in a dangerous situation in their own country.

There are at least seventeen million (UNHCR 2004) 'Persons of Concern' who are within the UNHCR mandate. 'Persons of Concern' include refugees (9.7 million, January 2004), asylum seekers, internally displaced persons, returnees, and stateless people. The majority of people fleeing their country seek refuge in neighbouring areas, usually in countries in the developing world. Only a minority of these people will lodge applications to be resettled in other countries. Some will travel directly to countries in which they hope to settle and lodge applications once they have arrived. These people are 'asylum seekers'.

Pittaway (2002) writes that examining the answers to the complex problems of refugees includes analysing the root causes of refugee flow. This includes acknowledging the (at least partial) responsibility of the developed world in supporting and generating many of the circumstances that contribute to this flow of refugees. While this critical issue is beyond the scope of this chapter, it is significant that 80 per cent of the world's refugees and displaced people are women and children.

Recent international developments in response to the growing refugee crisis

During the period 1980 to 1999, the majority of the five million people seeking asylum in the developed world were allowed to live in the community while awaiting the outcome of their refugee applications (Silove et al. 2001). However, in response to the threat of larger

numbers of asylum seekers and refugees, governments of developed nations have implemented policies to deter people from seeking asylum. The last 10 years have seen an erosion
in the previously humane international commitment towards helping refugees. Some of
these policies of deterrence include more stringent visa restrictions, rigorous border checks
and document validation, and the interruption of voyages of vessels suspected of containing
smuggled asylum seekers (Silove et al. 2000). The most disturbing aspect of this trend is the
tendency to confine asylum seekers, including children, in detention centres, often for
lengthy periods, while their cases are being assessed. For example, in 2000 the United States
detained five thousand asylum seekers at any one time. However, Australia stands alone in
placing in detention all individuals without valid visas irrespective of whether or not they
were seeking asylum (Silove et al. 2001).

Isolated centres, such as Woomera in Australia, are surrounded by barbed-wire fences,
with their remoteness making access to health, social, and legal services difficult. Detainees
may be denied access to study and work, and live in continuous anxiety about the future.
The length of time they must spend in detention is often unknown to them. Escapes, riots,
hunger strikes, protests, and violent outbreaks have occurred in detention centres in different countries, pointing to the psychological effects of imprisoning traumatised people who
have not committed any crime (Silove 2002). Independent inquiries in several countries
have raised serious concerns about human rights violations in detention centres for asylum
seekers. In Australia there have been numerous reports by the Human Rights and Equal
Opportunity Commission (HREOC) into mandatory detention, and also by the
Commonwealth Ombudsmen's Office. The National Inquiry into Children in Immigration
Detention, announced in November 2001, was another significant inquiry in Australia.

Alternative systems are now in place in some countries, where rather than being detained
asylum seekers live in the community but are monitored by the government. Family or
friends or agencies may pay financial bonds to ensure that a person complies with the
requirements of the immigration system. These systems are imperfect but do allow a degree
of freedom and dignity for asylum seekers (Silove et al. 2001).

Australia's humanitarian programme and recent developments in policy concerning asylum seekers

Since World War II, of the 5.5 million people who have migrated to Australia more than
560,000 people have arrived under humanitarian programmes, initially as displaced persons and more recently as refugees (Crock 1998). World events have influenced Australia's
pattern of refugee intake. For instance, after World War II, large numbers of displaced
people from Europe settled in Australia. Since that time, people have fled from totalitarian
governments, and/or from ethnic or religious persecution. Countries from which refugees
have fled include: Hungary (1950s); Czechoslovakia (1960s); Chile, Argentina, Uruguay,
Colombia, Brazil, El Salvador, Peru, and other Latin and Central American countries (1970s
and 1980s); Afghanistan, Iran, Iraq, Palestine, Vietnam, Cambodia, Laos, Burma
(Myanmar), China, Sri Lanka, Fiji, and countries of the former Soviet Union (1970s,

1980s, and 1990s); Somalia, Eritrea, Ethiopia, Sudan, Sierra Leone, other African nations, and countries of former Yugoslavia (1990s to the present). The most recent arrivals have been from situations and/or conflicts in Kosovo, East Timor, Iraq, and Afghanistan; from other Middle Eastern countries; and from African nations such as Sierra Leone, Liberia, and Sudan. Currently Australia accepts approximately 12,000 humanitarian entrants each year.

Crock (1998) describes the historical ambivalence in the Australian community towards accepting asylum seekers. On the one hand, Australia has been seen to be a generous country, accepting refugees since the end of World War II. Australians have been proud of their harmonious multicultural society, which stands in contrast to the hatred and violence of many ethnic groups living side by side in other countries. Australia's refugee resettlement programme is outstanding.

Crock describes how, on the other hand, racism and discrimination have always been part of the nation's development, too. There is a fear of invasion by 'boat people' (which is interesting given that the White civilisation in Australia began with an 'invasion' by boat people, many of whom were people who had been abused and discriminated against). This is accompanied by ignorance of the realities of the torture and trauma experiences and losses suffered by refugees, and a low level of recognition of Australia's international responsibilities towards refugees. These attitudes were born out in the 'near hysteria' in some sections of the community regarding the arrival of the Vietnamese boat people, and in 1993 opinion polls that showed that popular acceptance of Asian migration was tenuous. During the 1990s the One Nation Party advocated an end to the immigration programme.

By 2001, Australia's treatment of asylum seekers had caused much controversy and dismay both within Australia and across the world. With the world watching, Australian authorities turned away asylum seekers who had been rescued by a Norwegian ship, the MV *Tampa*, and used the navy to relocate them to the island of Nauru in the Pacific Ocean, and other destinations (the so-called 'Pacific solution'). Later, 350 boat people drowned off Indonesian shores and another boat was engulfed in flames (Silove 2002). Australia's treatment of asylum seekers became a major agenda item at various international meetings; for example, the UN World Conference Against Racism (Durban, August 2001), a meeting of the Society for International Development (Den Haag, September 2001), and at the Executive Committee Meeting of the UNHCR (Geneva, September 2001) (Pittaway 2002). Then early in 2002 over 200 detainees at the Woomera Detention Centre embarked on hunger strikes and acts of self-harm. Australia had previously been regarded as a leader in humane treatment of refugees, and now was seen as a renegade state (Silove 2002).

Sidoti described the current refugee policy as lacking any clear formulation in law or ethics, and being based on public fear and government manipulation (Sidoti 2002). He has proposed a set of basic principles and practices that are more in accordance with fundamental principles of being Australian and being human beings. While Australians may be warned that they are facing a huge influx of refugees, in fact our country is relatively inaccessible to asylum seekers. In contrast, many poor countries of Africa, Asia, and the Middle East host millions of displaced people, and even among developed nations Australia ranked 17 out of

21 industrialised countries in the number of asylum seekers received in 1999. Recent studies have shown that asylum seekers have suffered the same types and intensity of trauma as people who have been approved as refugees, and the main difference between the two groups is that asylum seekers have used alternative measures to reach safety (Silove 2002).

The impact of torture and trauma on refugees

McGorry (1995) cites several studies that show that the majority of refugees have suffered significant levels of trauma and have also experienced many losses (Westermeyer 1991; Krupinski & Burrows 1986; Krupinski et al. 1973). A significant number of refugees also have suffered torture. In the most significant finding of her research about refugee women, Pittaway (1991, pp. 68–9) notes that the extent and degree of torture and trauma experienced by refugee women before arriving in Australia has been grossly underestimated: almost three-quarters of the sample of 204 women had suffered medium to high levels of trauma. Australian torture and trauma services indicated to the New South Wales Refugee Health Policy Advisory Committee in 1997 that 80 per cent of refugees from particular countries had suffered significant levels of torture and trauma. Silove (2002) documents studies that show high levels of exposure to trauma among asylum seekers, but with some variation according to ethnicity and background. For example, exposure to murder varied between 27 and 92 per cent, to personal life threat between 44 and 88 per cent, and to torture between 26 and 72 per cent.

Torture and ill treatment of prisoners has been reported in over 100 countries (Evatt 1996). The many forms of physical and psychological maltreatment are summarised by Cunningham et al. (1990). Physical torture commonly reported includes beatings, forced standing (often while naked), bondage, suffocation, burnings, electric shocks, sexual abuse, mutilation, and submersion in or irrigation with cold water. Psychological torture can include sleep disruption causing disorientation; sensory deprivation, hallucinations, and paralysis caused by drugs; solitary confinement; denigration and insults; sham executions; false accusations; prolonged interrogations; and being forced to watch loved ones being raped, tortured, or killed (Cunningham et al. 1990). Hosking (1990) points out that torture is not limited to any one geographical region, race, or political regime; yet, there appears to be a higher rate of torture in countries with military dictatorships or regimes that do not allow individuals or groups to participate in the political decision-making process.

The purpose of torture is not only to punish individuals or to extract information but also to destroy the integrity of the individual's personality (Reid & Strong 1988). Political opponents are then broken—a useful tactic in spreading terror and forcing compliance with those in power. Writing in 1989 just before his murder in El Salvador, the Jesuit priest Martin-Baro suggested that the psychological effects of state violence on the general population included people's thinking and behaviour becoming stereotyped, polarised, and rigid; people becoming isolated and losing their confidence in themselves and each other; and a general devaluing of human life (1989). Martin-Baro outlines the societal dimensions of state terrorism clearly:

I would like to emphasise the social dimensions of torture, disappearances, abductions, and terrorism. It is important because for every tortured Salvadoran, there are at least a thousand Salvadorans paralysed by terror. For every Salvadoran killed, there are at least 10,000 who are violently forced to abdicate from their personal options and values. For every disappeared person, there are at least 100,000 Salvadorans who are systematically denied their right to conduct their own lives and to determine their life projects. And that is why we think that even when we are speaking of very deep psychological problems, we are talking about political problems (1989, p. 5).

Most refugees come from countries in which there have been years of political, social, and economic instability. Many flee international or civil wars, and situations of military dictatorship, oppression, and violence. People suffer from ill health as a result of famine, disease, and poor medical facilities. Their economic circumstances are affected by political corruption and deprived living conditions. They fear persecution from the authorities or certain groups within society. Many lose their livelihood. Some see their close family members 'disappear' or arrested, tortured, imprisoned, or killed (Hosking 1990).

The situation in Afghanistan is one example of far-reaching destruction that has occurred over three decades, and which has continued to create enormous numbers of refugees and displaced people. These circumstances were brought about through war, and the activities of oppressive regimes, warlords, and militias, backed by powerful nations. This situation has led to the deaths of more than two million people, the disabling of hundreds of thousands of people, and has resulted in more than six million refugees. People were attacked by air and artillery bombardments, millions of landmines were placed, and there were mass killings, torture, and imprisonment. People died from poisoned water, were burnt, or were thrown from planes and there was a particularly large number of civilian casualties, mainly women and children. The result of the Soviet occupation was a group of warring factions and a people who had been divided by the occupying force as a way of controlling resistance (Bowles & Haidary 1994; Dadfar 1994). In addition, Pilger (2003) describes how US and British governments colluded with the warlords and mujahideen, helping to fund and train over 100,000 Islamic militants in Pakistan to overthrow the Soviet Union in Afghanistan thus contributing to the development of the Taliban, and other militant groups.

During the period 1992–93, millions of Afghans returned from Pakistan to Afghanistan, only to suffer from the fighting between the mujahideen warlords, and then from the severe oppression under the Taliban regime (Maley 2003). Zia-Zarifi (2004) describes how currently warlords, militias, and brigands dominate Afghanistan, with the Taliban forces also becoming more powerful again. Attacks on US troops, on the government of President Hamid Karzai, and the foreign community supporting him continue. Many women and girls have again been forced out of schools and jobs due to the insecure situation and power of local fundamentalist warlords and militias. Villagers have been kidnapped and held for ransom; there has been widespread rape of women, girls, and boys; there has been robbery and murder; girls' schools have been burnt down; and the death rate of mothers giving birth is the highest in the world. There is very little safety or rule of law outside the main cities.

Poppy cultivation and the heroin trade have blossomed again, reinstating Afghanistan again as the world's leading producer of heroin. Foreign states—for example, Pakistan, Iran, Saudi Arabia, India, Uzbekistan, and Russia—are again becoming involved in the country's affairs for their own reasons (Zia-Zarifi 2004; Pilger 2003).

Refugees escaping from their country can be exposed to danger and violence: for example, Krupinski and Burrows (in Hosking 1990) estimate that 30 per cent of Vietnamese 'boat people' were robbed by pirates, and over 10 per cent were raped or abducted. Nearly one hundred thousand Indochinese boat people died on the seas, by starvation when engines failed, or by pirate attack. Refugees who escaped from their countries by sea often are not allowed to land when they reach a new destination. For example, as described above, in 2001 Australian authorities turned away asylum seekers who had been saved by the MV *Tampa*, relocating them to Nauru. There have been more recent examples of refugees dying at sea; for example, as described above, the drowning in 2001 of 350 boat people near the Indonesian shores (Silove 2002).

Those who escape by land—for example, from Cambodia or Laos—often have been forced to hide from soldiers, cross minefields, swim across wide rivers under artillery fire, and try to avoid capture by border police. Refugees escaping the massacres of the civil war in Somalia describe having to walk for several months to the refugee camps in Kenya, experiencing attacks by militias, starvation, and exhaustion. People who manage to reach refugee camps generally live in appalling situations: the camps are overcrowded and unsanitary, and there is often insufficient food and water. There is a lack of effective law enforcement and internal security. Violence is common. Soldiers and gangs may rape, blackmail, or rob other refugees in the camp. Pittaway (2002) describes how domestic violence and sexual assault are frequent, and how women and children are the most vulnerable to violations of their fundamental rights.

People may survive in refugee camps for years with little hope of resettlement. A Khmer colleague described how, suddenly, waves of panic and terror can sweep through a refugee camp; people live in constant fear and feel helpless and angry. Mehraby describes the situation in one camp for Afghan refugees:

> The houses were very small with two to three rooms and small windows with plastic coverings rather than glass. A house this size would be shared by three families … there was one school for the 15,000 children, and it went to primary school level only. Girls were not allowed to attend … There was one public health clinic. The main health problems were infectious diseases. Most deaths among children at the camp could have been prevented by immunisation (1999, pp. 14–15).

The issues facing refugees in Australia

Aroche and Coello (1994) suggest that there are three main challenges faced by refugees in their country of resettlement: torture and trauma issues; migration and resettlement issues, including grieving and the losses associated with living in exile; and normal life cycle stages, including personality and family issues. They point out that these challenges not only affect individuals but also families, social networks, and communities, and influence how these people and groups interact with the social and political systems in the country of resettlement. In addition, these challenges must be dealt with in the context of the cultural, psychological, educational, and religious dimensions of the individual, family, or community.

Coping with experiences of torture, trauma, loss, and migration

Many survivors of torture and trauma experience chronic symptoms that continue for many years, including hyper-arousal (causing, for example, sleep problems, irritability, poor memory, and concentration); re-experiencing the traumatic events (traumatic nightmares, intrusive memories, and flashbacks); and numbing and dissociation (avoiding thinking about the past, avoiding people or places that are a reminder of the past, being unable to remember aspects of the traumas, general social withdrawal, inability to feel certain emotions, and restricted sense of the future). Herman (1992) describes this condition as the 'dialectic of trauma' in which the survivor vacillates between a constant re-experiencing of the trauma, and trying to block out the unbearable memories. It appears that in the early period following the trauma hyper-arousal and re-experiencing the trauma predominate, whereas later numbness and dissociation seem stronger.

Herman (1992, p. 33) writes that traumatic events such as torture confront human beings with the extreme experiences of helplessness and terror, and people come face to face with violence or death. During torture a person's sense of identity, trust in others, and life-sustaining personal beliefs are deeply attacked, casting them into a state of existential crisis. Hence, the primary effects of torture are on the psychological structures of the self, and also on the systems of attachment and meaning that link individual and community (Herman 1992, p. 51).

The developmental stage of life in which the trauma started is important in understanding the effects upon a person and family. The issues faced by survivors who have been traumatised from an early age are deeply embedded in themselves and in their relationships. The severity and length of the trauma is also relevant to understanding different reactions and recoveries: some people may have survived years of imprisonment and torture; others, one night of detention and assault. While not meaning to minimise the effect in the latter example, severity of experience is an important dimension for understanding the effect of trauma upon survivors.

There is an important emphasis in this field of practice on not 'pathologising' people who have normal responses to abnormal experiences: psychiatric labels, such as chronic or complicated post-traumatic stress disorder, can deflect attention from the political situations of abuse in which the symptoms started. At the same time, these categories of symptoms can be a helpful framework for people to understand their confusing and debilitating condition.

Trauma can be 'carried' by an entire family and by groups and refugee communities. The loss, disappearance, or torture of a parent or sibling traumatises all family members, and living with a person with a severe post-traumatic and/or grieving condition continues to be distressing. Domestic violence may be experienced in a family in which one member has been arrested and tortured, then acts out aggressively or in response to internal triggers from imprisonment. Many refugee families live in an ongoing state of crisis, re-enacting traumas and instability from the past. The psychological and social effects on the general population of living under state terrorism, as previously described by Martin-Baro, can be seen in the distrust and division that is rife in many refugee communities (Aroche & Coello 1994).

The view that refugees are traumatised people with multiple problems is only one side of the story. It is important to affirm the survival skills and strengths that these people have developed through their experiences. While avoiding stereotyping refugees as 'victims' or 'heroes', it must be recognised that these are determined people who have come through overwhelming life events to finally reach a country of resettlement. Many are, in fact, out-standing individuals who have suffered for their convictions. The challenge is to recognise the depth of suffering of refugees, together with affirming the courage needed to endure such horrible experiences and their aftermath.

In addition to suffering from reactions associated with traumatic experiences, refugees have to endure many major losses; for example, deaths and disappearances of family members, friends, and comrades. Refugee colleagues have pointed out that these losses are for many more disturbing and painful than the aftermath of trauma. In addition to the normal grieving and adjustment of moving to a new country, other issues faced by refugees in the migration process include being forced to flee (rather than choosing to leave) their homes, not being able to return home, and not having chosen to come to Australia but rather escaping here as a last resort.

Many refugees in Australia feel guilty and can agonise over relatives 'lost' in a war zone back home, or starving and sick in hopeless situations in refugee camps. Many refugees cannot properly begin their new lives in Australia as they may still be emotionally and finan-cially focused on the situation of close relatives overseas. Some refugees may come from cul-tures in which the extended family lives together; therefore, the definition of 'close' relative can include a large number of people. The grieving following separation from these relatives is deep. Many refugees spend a considerable proportion of their lives trying to care for family members overseas: for example, saving money to send to relatives in camps, and enduring protracted processes to sponsor relatives to come to Australia.

Hence, in addition to suffering from severe trauma symptoms, refugee survivors of tor-ture and trauma also have to cope with painful losses and separations. Most refugees present with a combination of symptoms of trauma and grief, and these can be expressed at the level of the individual, family, or community (Savage 1999; Bowles et al. 1995).

Physical health issues

Physical health issues may be directly or indirectly related to traumatic refugee experiences, or be an outcome of living in a situation of poverty and political instability. Physical health problems of refugees can include infectious diseases such as intestinal parasites and tubercu-losis; poor dental health; torture- and war-related injuries and disabilities; low levels of immunisation; somatisation of psychological problems; delayed development of children;

and urinary tract infections, incontinence, and obstetric problems as a result of female genital mutilation (FGM). Forms of FGM are practised in the Horn of Africa, the Middle East, and in parts of South-East Asia, and these practices appear to be culturally related (NSW Refugee Health & STARTTS 2004).

Resettlement issues: practical issues; visas

Working with Refugees: A guide for Social Workers (NSW Refugee Health & STARTTS 2004) summarises some significant practical factors that have an impact on the process of resettlement for refugees, including unemployment, income support, accommodation, English-language ability, and education for children and living in rural or isolated areas. Although refugees may be suffering from a combination of trauma and grief-related psychological issues and physical health issues, pressing practicalities for survival generally are what concern them upon arrival in Australia. These factors tend to exacerbate each other.

Major factors affecting resettlement have been the recent changes in Australian immigration policy, which particularly affect asylum seekers, as described above. People arriving in an 'unauthorised manner' (by plane or boat) without a visa are placed in detention centres while their applications are processed. Asylum seekers who arrive with visitor visas are permitted to remain in the community, but may spend years waiting for the processing of their applications, and approximately one third of them are not permitted to work nor have access to Medicare. Since 2001, people with a Temporary Protection Visa (TPV) have been granted a three-year protection period in Australia, and then must apply again for protection, and they may be granted another temporary or a permanent visa. These TPV holders have no right to sponsor their spouse or children, and have limited access to Centrelink and other services. They are permitted to work and have access to Medicare (NSW Refugee Health Service & STARTTS 2004).

Silove and Steel (2000) describe the growing evidence that the stress facing asylum seekers adds to effects of the previous trauma in creating the risk of ongoing symptoms. Clients on TPVs face constant anxiety about the future; one client said to me that she felt as if she was on 'death row'. Currently there are 8000 people in Australia on TPVs according to Amnesty International (May 2004). Many of these people include young men who escaped life-threatening situations, leaving behind family members in danger, and who now live in fear for the fate of their relatives. Of 9160 'unauthorised boat arrivals' between July 1999 and June 2002, 8260 had successful asylum claims—evidence that the majority of those people arriving by boat had strong reasons to board (Refugee Council of Australia 2004). Silove (2002) describes these people with a TPV, or who have been placed in detention, as the 'new underclass' in Australia, as they are living without any rights of citizenship, family reunion, or permanent resettlement.

Allegations of abuse, untreated medical and psychiatric illnesses, suicidal behaviour, hunger strikes, and outbreaks of violence among asylum seekers in detention centres have been reported. Amnesty International is currently conducting a campaign to have the 150 children in detention centres (as at May 2004) and their families released, following the

HREOC (Human Rights and Equal Opportunity Commission) National Inquiry into Children in Immigration Detention.

Resettlement issues: children and adolescents

In addition to visa and detention problems, there are specific issues for groups of refugees, such as children, adolescents, women, men, and the aged. For refugee children, problems include high vulnerability to disease in refugee camps, poor physical development due to lack of nutrition, arrested psychological development due to early trauma, deprivation and family breakdown, separation anxiety and low self-esteem, disrupted education, and lack of care for unaccompanied (without parents) minors.

Refugee adolescents also suffer these problems, which complicate the development of their adult identity and may lead to acting out using drugs or sexual behaviour. In addition, they may find that they are confronted with two value systems (from their home country and from Australia) when they are trying to develop their own identity. This can create family tension. In addition, teenagers and children may be used as family interpreters as they tend to learn English more quickly than their parents, and this changes the roles in the family (NSW Refugee Health & STARTTS 2004).

Resettlement issues: women

For refugee women, a major problem is the high rate of sexual abuse suffered as part of the refugee and war trauma. The Service for the Treatment and Rehabilitation of Torture and Trauma Survivors (STARTTS) estimates that at least one third of refugee women have experienced sexual assault, and for some nationalities this proportion is much higher (Refugee Health Policy Advisory Committee 1997). Swiss et al. (1998) reported that 49 per cent of Liberian women surveyed had experienced physical or sexual violence from soldiers during the war. Refugee women suffer from many health problems—for example, cervical cancer and sexually transmitted diseases—due to lack of facilities and screening in refugee camps over long periods, and due to cultural practices such as female genital mutilation as mentioned above. Childbirth can be especially traumatic for refugee women as it may trigger memories of sexual abuse. Domestic violence is another common problem for refugee women whose partners may have been tortured and act out the abuse on their wives. The isolation and loss of extended family network of refugee women also makes them more vulnerable. They may find that their family role in Australia becomes different from their role in their home country, and this may be liberating and at the same time put pressure on their marriage.

Women with a 'women at risk' visa have permanent residence, and are likely to have recently suffered experiences of danger, as they were granted the visa because they were at special risk of sexual or physical violence. They are single women or single mothers, and have special support needs; for example, counselling and social support.

The Australian Law Commission Report of 1994 (Crock 1998) found that female refugees were greatly disadvantaged in a number of respects. First, in 1994, there were three men admitted into the country for every one woman. As a response to this finding, the gender balance of the overseas programme has been corrected and, by 1997, the ratio was almost even. Second, female applicants were less likely than men to be able to demonstrate 'good settlement prospects', having received fewer educational and career opportunities in their homeland. Women found it harder to prove that they would be in danger of persecution at home: they often had support roles and did not have the public profile that was more common for men and that was the objective basis for their fear of attack.

A major issue is whether rape and sexual harassment is persecution: in many countries a major form of oppression is systematic or random acts of rape by military groups, yet it is often seen as a by-product of war rather than as persecution. In general, it can be argued that the definition of a refugee fits more comfortably with male experience than female experience, even though over two thirds of the world's refugees are women (Crock 1998).

Resettlement issues: men
Refugee men are more likely to have experienced longer terms of imprisonment and lengthier, extreme forms of torture. Many have been soldiers. They are more likely to have bullets or shrapnel embedded in their bodies, and to have poorly set broken bones and other injuries. Many TPV holders are young men who have left their families overseas; approximately half the men in the Refugee and Humanitarian Program in 2002–03 were under the age of 20. Often they spend long periods of isolation in Australia. If they have a permanent visa they may wait for lengthy periods for applications to sponsor their families to Australia to be processed. Some suffer from drug-, alcohol- and smoking-related problems, and from sexually transmitted diseases (other than HIV/AIDS for which there is offshore screening). Other problems include unemployment and poor self-confidence due to their loss of status in the family as the breadwinner and traditional head of the family. Men are less likely to seek support from groups or from counsellors, or to attend general health services. However, at some torture and trauma services they form a majority of clients (Refugee Health Policy Advisory Committee 1997; NSW Refugee Health & STARTTS 2004).

Resettlement issues: ageing refugees
Older refugees include those who arrived in Australia soon after World War II or who have aged in Australia, and those who have recently arrived as elderly migrants to join their refugee adult children. Their particular problems include a lack of English, particularly as memory declines; isolation, including lack of family and close friends in Australia; and loss of status and the respect paid to elderly people in their society of origin. Elderly refugees may suffer from trauma symptoms, which may develop long after the trauma occurred: experiences in old age can trigger trauma reactions; for example, situations in nursing homes with staff. Memory problems—for example, due to dementia—can trigger suppressed traumatic memories also (Refugee Health Policy Advisory Committee 1997; NSW Refugee Health & STARTTS 2004).

Refugee resettlement: provision of services

The Refugee Resettlement Working Group (1990) outlined the extensive role played by the non-government sector in refugee resettlement, complemented by limited government funding programmes largely provided by the Department of Immigration and Multicultural Affairs. The broad policy is that non-governmental organisations offer the best service for resettlement of refugees as they understand the needs of refugees, are accessible, and can provide the most appropriate support. In general, these non-governmental organisations are run by small, newly arrived refugee groups that can themselves be stressed and fragile. Devolving responsibility for service provision to them places a greater responsibility, including a financial one, upon them.

The establishment of specialised services for refugee survivors of torture and trauma is a relatively new development. Following World War II, Jewish welfare societies worldwide pioneered services offering assistance for Jewish survivors of the holocaust (Cunningham 1996). The first service specifically for refugee survivors of torture (the Rehabilitation and Research Centre for Torture Victims in Denmark) began in the mid 1970s, and others began to be set up in Europe and North America in the late 1970s and early 1980s. Corresponding services were established in countries in which human rights violations were being carried out, especially in Latin America (McGorry 1995). By 1997, it was estimated that there were at least 265 centres worldwide (Cunningham 1996). They include services within repressive countries, in which health professionals and volunteers may work at considerable risk to the safety of themselves and their families; services in countries of first asylum (for example, health workers in refugee camps), who usually work long hours with few resources; and services in countries of resettlement (Cunningham & Silove 1993). A central issue for most services is the combining of community development and individual clinical approaches in order to meet the broad needs of the client group (McGorry 1995).

In Australia, the first clinic for assisting tortured refugees was established in Brisbane in 1985 at the Mater Misericordiae Hospital Child and Family Psychiatric Service. The report by Reid and Strong (1987) to the New South Wales Government Department of Health led to the establishment of the first torture and trauma service, STARTTS, in Sydney in August 1988, and assisted the development of other services in other states, such as the Victorian Foundation for Survivors of Torture.

Related services in New South Wales include the New South Wales Refugee Health Service (established in 1999) and the New South Wales Transcultural Mental Health Service (established in 1993). The former focuses more on physical and general health issues for refugees rather than specifically torture and trauma issues, and has a broad role in provision of information and training, healthcare assessment and advice. The latter has a specialist role in promoting access to mental health services for people of non-English speaking background. Mainstream health services are also becoming more accessible for refugees, through the bilingual counsellor programme and through training programmes run by STARTTS and New South Wales Refugee Health Service.

Recent developments in social work in this field include a community development project managed by social workers and others from New South Wales Refugee Health and STARTTS to produce a resource for social workers to use when working with refugee clients, primarily in the health field. This resource was written by a steering committee of senior social workers and others from various agencies, following a research project by a social work student who had surveyed many social workers to ask them what kind of information they would like in such a resource. This resource *Working with Refugees: A Guide for Social Workers* was launched at the International Social Work Conference in Adelaide in October 2004, and is the first of its kind for social workers in Australia.

Social work practice in torture and trauma services: practice issues

Torture and trauma services in Australia operate on a diverse range of models; some following a more traditional medical model, and others combining a range of interventions within a broad community development framework. In the more traditional services, the roles of social workers tend to be more family- and welfare-oriented. In services combining community development approaches with psychological and other interventions, the roles of the social worker tend to be more flexible and diverse. Generalist social work training, which examines both the individual and society, is a good introduction to understanding this field. Training about the welfare system gives a good background for advocacy and resettlement work, which is an important aspect of most social work with refugees. The overt emphasis of practice on human rights abuses is congruent with the social work code of ethics that demands commitment to the principles of social justice.

Case Study

Social work in the Service for the Treatment and Rehabilitation of Torture and Trauma Survivors (STARTTS)

STARTTS has gradually developed within a broad framework of community development, within which are many levels of intervention for refugee survivors of torture and trauma. These include work with individuals and families; group work; community work, networking with refugee communities; influencing the mainstream health system; social policy development; and other work at a socio-political level (Aroche & Coello 1994). STARTTS provides a psychiatric service, body-work service, youth programme, and employment programme, and, more recently, has received funding to coordinate an early intervention programme for refugees. In 1999, STARTTS was responsible for the mental-health needs of refugees from Kosovo and East Timor brought to temporary 'safe havens' in New South Wales.

A feature of STARTTS is the high proportion of workers who have a refugee and/or non-English-speaking background. The development of the service and referral of clients has relied greatly upon the understanding and commitment of these workers who have formed a bridge between STARTTS and the refugee communities. In the period from 1988 to 2004, STARTTS developed from having a handful of workers to having seventy-nine staff in 2004. STARTTS's policy from the beginning was that staff should not follow defined professional roles within the medical model—that is, the social worker looks after families, the doctor manages the team and performs medical assessments, and the psychologist does testing and psychotherapy. Instead, the philosophy was to use all the skills, both professional and personal, of each worker (Cunningham & Silove 1993). Staff from a variety of professional backgrounds—social work, psychology, art therapy, community nursing, and welfare training—were employed to fill generalist counsellor and project officer or bicultural counsellor positions.

Initially there were two social workers at STARTTS: one became the first permanent manager of the service, and the other (the author) was the first counsellor and project officer. At first the team was small and tried to respond to the needs of the client group rather than fitting rigid role definitions. In the early days, both social workers were involved in a broad range of tasks; gradually, as more staff were employed, they were able to specialise in a particular area. STARTTS was set up to develop into a specialist service, providing expertise and research to the mainstream health sector about working with refugee survivors of torture and trauma.

Currently social workers are employed as managers, community development workers, clinical trainers and supervisors, and counsellors and project officers specialising in psychotherapy and clinical supervision or family therapy, or working as generalists providing both counselling and community development work. A number of social workers are also working in a newly established early intervention programme as case managers. Some social workers have refugee backgrounds and work as bicultural counsellors with a particular refugee community.

McGorry (1995) argues that there are many reasons that a community development perspective is an appropriate global framework for establishing a torture and trauma service. Torture and organised violence are outcomes of systematic power abuses. Community development helps a community of people address their own needs, confronting the use of power, and examining issues such as access, justice, and participation. It challenges processes that prevent access and equity in society. The social work literature and training has much to offer this field of community development. Important elements of community work in this field include influencing state and national policy concerning refugees, and becoming involved in international processes, such as the work of Amnesty International, which aim to prevent human rights abuses. Other activities include development of self-help groups, consultation with refugee communities, and organising youth camps for refugee children and adolescents.

Another aspect of practice with traumatised refugees is helping them to deal with their deep psychological and physical wounds. STARTTS uses a range of helpful interventions, including various forms of psychotherapy, medical and psychiatric interventions, physiotherapy, body work, traditional medicine, and group therapy. Social workers are mainly working as clinical supervisors, psychotherapists, family therapists, and case managers. The clinical work is challenging on a number of levels. First, the professional has to consider the broader political issues and recognise the injustices inflicted upon their clients. Social workers need to understand the political conflicts that their clients have experienced. At a more immediate level, political dimensions of race, gender, and power differences in the therapeutic relationship are also important.

Second, there is no single therapeutic paradigm suitable for all clients, and research on clinical work is still at the exploratory stage. Therefore, professionals, including social workers, specialising in various approaches and orientations (for instance, cognitive, behavioural, and supportive psychoanalytic psychotherapy; Rogerian counselling; brief family-therapy interventions; and others) have to work in creative tension. Flexibility, open-mindedness, lack of dogmatism, and appreciation of the different contributions that each intervention makes are all necessary for a team to function effectively.

Third, professionals cannot only focus on individual or family dynamics, but have to recognise the broader socio-cultural and religious dimensions of the psychotherapy: a perspective that is congruent with the broad emphases in social work training. It is stimulating to examine the philosophical and cultural roots of our Western therapeutic theories and practice: Are they applicable to people from other cultures and classes? Are they connected with the healing practices of other cultures? What is the role of religious faith and political belief in psychotherapy, particularly in the context of working with people from different religions and political ideologies? While none of these are new questions, they are only beginning to be examined in refugee torture and trauma work. In the modern context of the shifting and mixing of the world's population, questions of cross-cultural psychology and understanding are becoming highly relevant. Working with interpreters in a psychotherapeutic relationship, for instance, is a complex aspect of clinical practice with this client group that is being explored.

Fourth, the practical issues facing refugees upon resettlement cannot be ignored. Most counsellors and therapists also are working as advocates for their clients in the broader society: for instance, helping them gain permanent residence, and assisting them with housing, social security, recognition of qualifications, and referral to medical, dental, and other treatments, and English classes. Becker (1991) makes the point that the inner and outer turmoil experienced by refugees is linked—both aspects must be addressed. Talking with clients about their feelings when they have nowhere to live does not address the most salient issue. At the same time, only addressing practical concerns is unlikely to be successful as the internal chaos of refugees may continue to destabilise their life (see, for example, Nguyen & Bowles 1998; Silove et al. 1991a, 1991b). McGorry (1995) notes the complex nature of this combination of counsellor and advocate roles, and the need for skilled supervision of workers in order for it to be successful.

There is a danger of social workers becoming submerged in this field of practice as it is so complex and engrossing. It is important to maintain links with social workers in other health areas and with professionals of similar values and ideologies in other fields. This networking will also prevent workers in torture and trauma becoming too precious about their work, and can facilitate the cross-fertilisation of ideas.

Ethical issues and conflicts in refugee torture and trauma work

Current Australian policies of deterrence—for example, mandatory detention of people without visas, 'the Pacific Solution', and the issuing of three-year TPVs urgently require reviewing. A number of alternative models have been placed in the public view by expert bodies. For example, the model proposed by the Refugee Council of Australia provides for three levels of security—closed detention, open detention, and community release—with the idea that closed detention is only for identity and security checking and is time-limited. The recommendations of the STARTTS and FOS Submission (2002) to the HREOC Inquiry into Children in Immigration Detention also include early release from detention provisions for torture and trauma survivors, and major changes to the temporary protection visa system, if not complete abolishment. This submission describes in detail the damaging effects of detaining children who are asylum seekers, and strongly argues against this policy (STARTTS & FOS 2002).

It is stressful working within such a system, and, as with all social work, there is a tension between being a social change worker and a social control agent. It is important to discuss ethical issues with colleagues and supervisors in order to help clients and, as far as possible, to work for a more humane immigration system in the network with others. Racism and the lack of public understanding about, or denial of, the torture and trauma backgrounds of refugees and asylum seekers are further problems in the Australian context—as in other countries that receive refugees. These attitudes provide support for harsh policies and laws towards refugees and asylum seekers. Manipulation of public opinion has been cleverly carried out. For example, asylum seekers lately have been branded as 'queue jumpers', are suspected of being terrorists, and have been wrongly accused of 'throwing their children overboard'. Social workers in this field are in a position to stay aware of the facts about asylum seekers, and to play an educative role as far as possible.

The ethical issues specific to this work demand that we face the broader political conflicts and inequalities that create the refugee problem, and try to determine what response is moral and reasonable. The massive dimensions of the international refugee crisis make the work of a small refugee service in Australia seem insignificant. Vast numbers of people live in danger and poverty, and workers can feel overwhelmed. The narrow definitions of eligibility for refugee status need to be revised at both the United Nations and national levels. The problems facing refugee women and children, who make up 80 per cent of the world's refugees, need to be taken further into account within both international and Australian law and social policy.

Workers may wish to take a stand on these issues and support lobbying and direct-action groups, yet, in their spare time, often need to restore themselves rather than stay 'at work'.

They may also experience a conflict of professional interest working in public health and, at the same time, being critical of government policies. Workers may be engulfed by horror hearing the feelings and stories of the clients. The vicarious traumatisation of workers who deal with survivors of abuse is well documented (Pearlman 1996; Pearlman & Saakvitne 1995; Herman 1992; Bustos 1990). All people who work with trauma inevitably are affected by it and have continually to process the issues in order to prevent burnout. Without regular supervision, psychotherapy, and support it is easy for workers to start acting out dynamics of trauma with each other.

A key to surviving torture and trauma is being able to reconnect with others, and to keep replenishing a core of hope inside oneself. This is true for clients, workers, and anyone else confronted with these terrible experiences of abuse and loss. These issues are overwhelming if workers try to face them on their own. Paradoxically, torture and trauma experiences can lead to people joining together to build new lives for refugee survivors.

Ethics in context

You are a social worker working as a counsellor at a torture and trauma service. You have been requested to visit an asylum seeker in a detention centre. This person is suffering from nightmares and panic attacks. You have been told that this person is a survivor of torture and that his family is in danger in his country of origin. What should you do?

Issues to consider: What is your opinion of detention centres? Are you supporting this system by going? Is it possible to provide counselling at a detention centre? Is an alternative location possible? What is your agency's view of visiting the detention centre? What will happen to this person if you don't go? Is it possible for any other health worker to go? Are you the most appropriate person? What other services does his person and his family need? What country is he from and what is happening there?

The future for social work

Social workers can make a valuable contribution to this field of practice. The social work code of ethics, valuing social justice and dignity of all people, is highly relevant for working with survivors of torture and trauma, many of whom have suffered for their beliefs. The broad psycho-social-political emphasis in the social work perspective is ideally suited to work with this client population. The emphasis in social work training on community development is also relevant for work not only as community workers and managers but also as clinical workers who advocate extensively for their clients. Social workers have had a strong influence on the broad directions of this field of practice to date, and their contributions are respected and valued.

It must be said that this area of social work practice is rewarding. The capacity of people to rebuild a life of meaning, to hope, and to trust others again after suffering such shattering experiences is constantly surprising. The enduring sense of support and commitment between colleagues of varying cultural backgrounds overrides professional barriers. This work is personally challenging, and offers much scope for social work theory, practice, and research development.

Review questions

1 What are your thoughts about asylum seekers coming in boats to Australian shores?
2 What contribution can social work make to working with refugee survivors of torture and trauma?
3 What do you think about Australia's refugee programme since World War II?

Acknowledgments

Appreciation is extended to all members of the STARTTS team and colleagues in other services and practices for their support and advice over the years. In particular, I wish to thank my colleagues Rise Becker (my clinical supervisor), David Findlay (STARTTS librarian), and Jorge Aroche, Miriana Askovic, Melinda Austen, Helen Basili, Jasmina Bayraktarevic-Hayward, Franka Bosnjak, Jackie (Xhevrje) Binakaj, Gary Cachia, Cecilia Carranza, Nicola Carter, Marc Chaussivert, Rahat Chowdhury, Mariano Coello, Sharni Cohen, Vera Crvenkovic, Peter Davis, Mary Dimech, Vladimir Dubossarsky, Michael Dudley, Johnathon Duignan, Patricia Dunn, Gul Evren, Pearl Fernandez, Ramiz Gasanov, Pedro Gomez, Deborah Gould, Prabha Gulati, Zalmai Haidary, Indira Haracic-Novic, Pam Hartgerink, Gordana Hol-Radicic, Amal Hormiz, Mohammed Amir Hossain, Janet Irvine, Rowena Isaac, Vandy Kang, Sevinj Kanik, Denise Kerry, Cherie Lamb, Monica Lamelas, Borka Licanin, Andrew MacPherson, Lucy Marin, Nooria Mehraby, Esber Melham, Shakeh Momartin, Carmela Morano, Patrick Morris, Lachlan Murdoch, Yasmina Nasstasia, Ian Nicol, Tiep Nguyen, Lisa Osborn, Chris Paulin, Viliam Phraxayavong, Cathy Preston-Thomas, Andrea Pritchard, Fatana Rahimi, Sevdail Ramadani, Naren Ramanathan, Graciela Ramirez, Arna Rathgen, Paula Raymond, Elizabeth Rowe, Susan Roxon, Pratima Roy, Robert Sainz, Daud Saeed, Marisa Salem, Julie Savage, Derrick Silove, Holly Smith, Chris Sochan, Victor Storm, Kerry Stuart, Ruth Tarn, Meng Eng Thai, Thuy Tran, Selja Tukelija, Rosa Vanovac, Norma Weaver, Adnan Zagic, and Frank Zivkovic. Their suggestions, ideas, and resources have been included in this paper, and they have all taught me about this work. I wish to particularly acknowledge Mrs Margaret Cunningham, a pioneer in the torture and trauma field of social work.

20

INTERNATIONAL SOCIAL WORK: NATURE, SCOPE, AND PRACTICE ISSUES

Jeanette Conway and Manohar Pawar

Chapter objectives

To increase social workers' knowledge of the place of international social work practice within the profession and to encourage contributions to and participation in its future development. Social workers are introduced to:

- the historical, international base of the profession
- pathways for developing specific definitions of international social work practice

- models of international practice
- examples of regional and international social work practice and education
- the international bodies of the profession and key global organisations
- issues social workers face in international social work practice
- signposts towards the future of international social work practice.

Introduction

The internationalisation of Australian social work

Australian social work has been characterised by international exchanges of knowledge, skills, and resources since its earliest days in the 1920s. Social workers from other Western countries introduced to Australia the fields and methods of practice and the models of education with which they themselves were familiar. Hospital casework methodology supported the earliest social workers who worked in hospital and health settings. By the 1930s models of group work, community work, and social research were introduced for use in the more general service and policy fields. These early forms of specifically targeted social work developed to deal with issues faced by those who were vulnerable and marginalised in rapidly industrialising Australian cities.

In the immediate post–World War II period, Australian social workers were invited to collaborate with the Australian Red Cross in international reconstruction work. Although few in number, female Australian social workers contributed to the efforts of the Australia Red Cross Field Forces in New Guinea, the work of the United Nations Relief and Rehabilitation Administration in post-war Germany, and the rehabilitation of former prisoners of war in reception centres in Britain and Singapore. The Australian Association of Social Workers (AASW) was founded in 1946. From its inception it dealt with matters that went beyond national boundaries, making decisions and developing policies that were intended to benefit social workers in many countries.

The first 'general international social welfare forum' took place in Paris in 1928 (Lawrence 1965, p. 87) and became known as the International Conference of Social Work. The first international event in which the AASW participated was the fourth meeting of this international body, which was held in Atlantic City (1948). Australia was represented over the next 14 years at biannual conferences in Paris, Madrid, Toronto, Munich, Tokyo, Rome, and Rio de Janeiro (Lawrence 1965). In 1968, an evolved International Federation of Social Workers (IFSW) organisation began conference collaboration, in its own right, with the International Association of Schools of Social Work (IASSW). Since then, the AASW has remained involved to varying degrees with both of these separate bodies. They will later be discussed in some detail.

At the first AASW National Conference in 1947, inaugural president, Norma Parker[1], from Western Australia, spoke of the 'international and national lives' of Australian social workers, emphasising the post-war international bonds that were developing with overseas colleagues. She encouraged association members to go abroad, as she had done, and, in time, enough people took up the suggestion for her to talk of 'the migration overseas' of Australian social workers.

It is estimated that in the early 1950s about forty Australian social workers were either working or studying abroad. Britain was the favoured destination at that time, with others choosing to go to the United States or Canada (Lawrence 1965). In the heyday of the British Empire, the rapid post-war industrialisation of Australian cities provided fertile ground for the consolidation of the dominant Western models of practice (O'Connor et al. 1991) and the growth of university-based schools of social work. These passed on the theories and knowledge underpinning the foundational models of practice that were unquestioned as global benchmarks. Though formally committed to the development of international social work, the AASW's involvement remained spasmodic and 'relatively neglected' (Lawrence 1965, p. 32) until the late 1960s.

Those social workers who maintained overseas professional contacts were often people who had or were seeking international experience. Typically, they were social work academics on sabbatical, higher-degree students, and practitioners committed to a particular field of practice. It has been this relatively small and often geographically scattered group that has provided representative Australian voices in cross-national and international forums over a number of years, and maintained links with fields of practice in other parts of the world.

Although Australians and others had been involved in international meetings and activities over many years, first as committed individuals and then as formal association members, they did not have a universally accepted definition of their profession. Instead, it was implicitly encompassed in the guidelines for social work education used in many parts of the world. The earliest definition of international social work was adopted in 1982 at the International Federation of Social Workers (IFSW) general meeting in Brighton, England. Tabled as a document called 'Definition and classification of social workers', it was prepared for a revised edition of the International Labor Organisation's (ILO) world directory defining and classifying occupations and professions. AASW members contributed to the drafting of the document, as did social workers from eight other nations (IFSW 1982).

Increasing numbers of Australian social workers now participate in international and regional social work activities organised by their international professional bodies, IFSW, the International Association of Schools of Social Work (IASSW), and by other relevant global bodies. For example, through recent biannual IFSW global meetings in Hong Kong (in 1996), Jerusalem (1998), and Montreal (2000) Australians have contributed to the development of the profession's own international definition. This now affirms social work as one profession, not several, and is based on a set of universal human values, which are manifested in different ways in many nations and cultures: IFSW and IASSW jointly accepted this definition at executive meetings in Montreal 2000. In so doing both organisations understand it to be a work-in-progress, open to multiple national, cultural and local interpretations:

> Social work in its various forms addresses the multiple, complex transactions between people and their environments [and] is an interrelated system of values, theory and practice … Its values are based on respect for the equality, worth and dignity of all peoples … [and it] draws on theories of human development and behaviour and social systems to analyse complex situations and to facilitate individual, organisational, social and cultural changes, [while] the priorities of [its] practice will vary from country to country and from time to time depending on cultural, historical and socio-economic conditions … (AASW 2000b, p. 7).

What is international social work practice?

Australian-driven social work scholarship and practice is not sufficiently developed for international social work practice to be either a mainstream emphasis in professional education or a widely understood professional employment field. Australian social workers are yet to develop robust debate about what does or does not belong to this specific field. Beyond Australia, international social work practice has been described as a 'problematic concept … a weakly framed activity' (Harris 1990, p. 204), and as being 'imprecise in meaning' (Midgley 1990).

In Midgley's view (2001), there are three core clusters in current discourse that need to be included in conceptualising international social work practice. These are: skills and knowledge (Midgley 2001; Friedlander 1955); contacts and exchanges (Midgley 1990; Healy 1995); and global awareness (Asamoah et al. 1997). His recommendation is that the final product would need to incorporate a number of 'different approaches'. The following three areas may be helpful in focusing a continuing discussion.

Practice development skills

In reviewing recent international social work practice literature, Pawar (2000) identifies five practice development areas. Within these areas, globally oriented workers apply and strengthen their international practice skills wherever in the world they are located. The five areas cover:

- choosing people-centred work in macro and micro social development processes within the full range of available organisations and agencies
- promoting the well-being of local populations by a meticulous, mutual development, dovetailing, sharing, and transfer of knowledge, practice methods, curricula, and human resources in response to ever-changing sets of social arrangements
- promoting values, knowledge base, and practice and skills, including those of indigenous peoples
- learning from the similarities and differences in social worker's roles
- advancing appropriate professionalisation and collaborative social work structures.

Four conceptual dimensions

Healy (2001) conceptualises international social work practice across four dimensions, linking practice, education, and policy. Within her overall concept, international social work is widened to include international social work practice within one's own country.

Her four dimensions are: internationally related domestic practice and advocacy; professional exchange; international practice; and international policy development and advocacy.

Issued-based global practice

Cox and Pawar (in press) argue that an international social work practice definition must promote and underpin action. In today's world this action needs to address 'the various global challenges that have a significant impact on the well-being of large sections of the world's population'. They stress that implementing this approach could contribute to the further enhancement and global integration of the professional body (see further discussion below).

Models for international social work practice

An Australian discourse about developing frameworks for international social work practice is still in its infancy. In this section we consider four models:

- bureaucratic outreach
- targeted multi-level intervention
- holistic social development action
- an integrated perspectives approach.

Bureaucratic outreach

Kammerman (1995) attempted to organisationally locate an international social welfare field of practice. Her scholarship focused on locating pathways for a range of welfare service deliveries in the bureaucracies of advanced nations. Within this framework she suggested that an international social welfare field of service could be identified as an outward-reaching extension of the personal service sector within human service bureaucracies. This analysis assumed the existence of government-based organisational structures supporting predetermined outreach services.

The first substantial international social service to set up in Australia was an enlightened example of a bureaucratic outreach service. International Social Service (ISS), a small and specific casework agency in which social workers collaborated with social workers from other countries, opened an Australian office in Sydney in 1954. At that time, it offered inter-country professional casework for newcomers to Australia who were separated from families in Europe. Before ISS (Australia) was established, migrant workers employed on the Snowy Mountains Hydro-electric Scheme were travelling back and forth to Europe dealing with matters of family concern. The ISS was part of an international organisation that had a centrally based administrative centre in Europe and field operations based in strategic parts of the world. The overseas agencies in such organisations usually modelled themselves on the administrative guidelines of the parent country and serviced specific target populations according to approved organisation and legislative guidelines, using established service-delivery, staff-recruiting, and evaluation methods. Today, ISS is undergoing thoughtful discussion relating to enhancement and evolution of its original vision.

Targeted multi-level intervention

Studt (1965) describes social work quite differently from Kammerman. From Studt's perspective, practice occurs within social environments that are defined spaces, with unambiguous boundaries, of social work action. Therefore they are professionally identifiable. Within these environments, social workers go about their core tasks of dealing with the many complex transactions—remedial and developmental—that occur at the constantly moving interface of individuals, families, peoples, and their environments.

Within this framework she raises three sets of questions for each field of practice:

1 What is the social problem? How are the boundaries of the population expressing concern about it defined? What are the norms by which the problem is identified? What concerns are evoked for people and what do they want to do about them?
2 What is the social task? How can it be addressed according to both community norms, and the requirements of those consequently identified as dysfunctional in some way?
3 What is the service system? What are the relevant organisations, and what human and material resources are available? What is the perceived role of those raising the problem? (Studt 1965, pp. 4–18).

Holistic social development action

Elliott (1993) has developed a descriptive social development framework for holistic, international social work practice. It bases practice on social development principles that inextricably link economic and social well-being, and encourages these principles to be applied across levels of human activity that are of concern to social workers. An important aspect of Elliott's work is that she links the values of social development to a version of systems theory in which the complex contexts of economic, political, socio-cultural, scientific, and religious systems can be analysed, interpreted, and acted upon from an overarching and unifying perspective (Elliott 1993, p. 30). This activist social development framework encourages the integration of international dimensions into all levels of social work planning and action (Elliott 1993). Elliott has shaped this framework from a global model that has long been familiar to international economists and policy makers working in 'institution building, empowerment and conscientization' (Elliott 1993, p. 26).

Her framework allows for identification of social work methods, processes, and skills that are appropriate to a social development approach and which are applicable to a multitude of practice situations. It therefore provides workers, whatever their field of practice, with the means to explore issues more thoroughly and act on them more insightfully. Elliott's work furthers that of Studt's by demonstrating how social workers can more accurately identify the complex, interactive, and fluid points at which professional social work intervention is appropriate.

An integrated perspectives approach

Cox and Pawar (in press) suggest an integrated perspectives approach for international social work practice. Briefly, their perspective uniquely integrates human rights and ecological, global, and social development perspectives. Each perspective reinforces the other and all four together synthesise values and ethics, human life in the natural environment, inclusiveness of all people and nation states, and people-centred development. They can connect and integrate perspectives around human rights, and ecological, global, and social development that not only shape effective responses to critical issues at any intervention level but also assist in the development of a critical understanding of them. This model aims to better facilitate responses to the multiplicity of cross-national and global issues social workers face today.

Regional fields of practice

Although few funding resources are made available to them, Australian social workers have collaborated in significant educational and social work activities in the Asia–Pacific region since the 1980s. The achievements of social workers in programmes such as those described serve as signposts to the emerging shape of international and regional fields of social work practice.

Work towards the elimination of child prostitution

In 1992, Australian social worker Bernadette McMenamin[2] went to Thailand to help launch a campaign called ECPAT (End Child Prostitution, Pornography and Trafficking). Little did she know that her work in a tiny Bangkok office would help launch a global movement committed to the prevention, protection, and reduction of sexual abuse and exploitation of children in Australia and overseas. This organisation, now called Child Wise, is strategically engaged around the world through national, regional, and international coalitions in providing community awareness, education, and training programmes, as well as collaborating in development of appropriate policy and law reforms.

'Choose with Care' is one significant project of this organisation. Supported by Australia's Department of Family and Community Services, this specialised staff educational programme aims to build child-safe organisations and is now being requested worldwide (Child Wise 2004). The success of this agency's work is an example of how a social work understanding of knowledge and skill transferability from developing to developed world can contribute to increased well-being at both local and international levels.

An inter-country HIV/AIDS research project

This project has assisted in understanding transmission of HIV/AIDS in northern Thailand. The research project was carried out by a social worker from Sydney University in collaboration with colleagues from Thammassat University, Bangkok, and the Thai Provincial Public Health Development. This project demonstrated the principle of mutual transfer of knowledge and skills across national and cultural boundaries—that is, key aspects of a successful Australian education and care project, coupled with the grass-roots skills and knowledge of local people (Hart 1997, p. 249).

A women's community development research project in Sri Lanka and Indonesia

Called Asian Women Migrant Workers Practice project and auspiced by a consortium of regional organisations, this activity linked together Australian social work academics from La Trobe University's Regional Social Development Centre (RSDC) and key personnel from international bodies such as the International Labor Organisation (ILO) and International Social Service (ISS), as well as local non-governmental agency staff in participating countries (Cox et al. 1993; Cox & Britto 1986). This programme focused on researching models for pre-employment and pre-departure programmes in Indonesia, and the establishment of a Repatriates Counselling Service in Sri Lanka at the end of the Gulf War in 1990.

A regional educational project on trends in social work curriculum development

Auspiced by Australian and Pacific Association for Social Work Education (APASWE), a regional study of social work curriculum development trends was completed in 1986. Eighteen schools, including five Australian schools, participated (Cox & Britto 1986). Building on this work, the La Trobe centre conducted another major project. This involved a survey of 100 schools of social work from thirteen Asia–Pacific countries and an international workshop to facilitate the incorporation of a social development perspective into social work education (Cox et al. 1997a, 1997b; also see Singh 1995; Pawar 1999).

A curriculum development project for China

A seminar, jointly organised by APASWE and the sociology department of Peking University of China, was held in Beijing in 1988, marking the opening up of China to the West and signalling both a readiness of the region to collaborate, if required, in the assessment of China's social needs, and the rebuilding of social work schools and curricula (Chamberlain 1991). It also signalled a new professional sensitivity to the cultural, social, political, and economic traditions of this vast nation. A number of Australian social workers attended (Asia–Pacific Region Social Work Education Association 1992).

An Asia–Pacific training manual for informal care and welfare systems

This manual is the result of a research project of The Centre for Rural Social Research, Charles Sturt University (Pawar & Cox 2004), and can be broadly employed both in developed and developing countries for training relevant social work and welfare personnel from government and non-governmental organisations (NGOs) and communities. The project involved participants from ten Asia–Pacific countries (see www.csu.edu.au/faculty/arts/humss/community/html/index.html).

International knowledge building

International social work education

In Australia, there are no centralised structures or funding sources for international social work educational initiatives, as have existed in Europe through the Erasmus and Socrates programmes (Lorenz 1997). Nevertheless, many Australian schools of social work are developing their own programmes, particularly in international fieldwork placements. Sometimes resources are combined with those of other departments in their universities and most websites provide specific information. Individual universities also continue to expand their links with social workers and other human service personnel in the main social education centres of Europe, Canada, the United States, and key Asia–Pacific locations. One long-standing international student fieldwork programme is organised by Dr. Frank Tesoriero (University of South Australia). He regularly organises placements with the Rural Unit for Health and Social Affairs in Vellore District in Tamilnadu, India (www.unisanet.unisa.edu.au/learn/FieldEd-Overseas/?PATH=/Resources/FieldEd/).

International social work conference development, facilitation, and management

In the last decade, Australia has hosted two full-scale international events. The first full-scale international social work conference held in Australia—the 2nd International Conference on Social Work in Health and Mental Health—occurred as recently as 1998. This was the culmination of a grass-roots movement of health and mental health social workers. This movement has taken on a life of its own, while at the same time maintaining strong links with the profession's international peak bodies. Four conferences have taken place: Jerusalem (1995), Melbourne (1998), Finland (2001), and Quebec (2004) with a fifth planned for Hong Kong (2007). For many Australian social workers, the experience of the Melbourne event was their first introduction to the collegiality of an international profession. The second such event, Global 2004, occurred in Adelaide in 2004. This was the first IFSW and IASSW full-scale, biennial Congress to be hosted in Australia. It attracted the largest contingent of overseas social workers ever to visit this country and brought with it a focus on the global concerns of civil society with special emphasis on poverty, human rights, and indigenisation.

Practice-based international exchanges in the health field

Two international practice-based exchange programmes have been operating since 1989: one at Mount Sinai Medical Centre, New York (three months—leadership enhancement) and the other at Beth Israel Hospital, Boston (one month—specific interest focus). Returning social workers share their new expertise with colleagues and, in turn, provide hospitality when programme exchange scholars visit Australia. These exchanges were developed by a small group of Australian health sector social workers from the field and academia who sought to redress the lack of opportunities social workers had for professional international experience.

International organisations and professional bodies

At the international level, the work of social work is supported and represented by three complementary peak bodies: the International Association of Schools of Social Work (IASSW), the International Federation of Social Workers (IFSW), and a third body, the International Council on Social Welfare (ICSW), which, while closely linked to the profession, has an operative mandate wider than social work. Renewed efforts are now re-linking ICSW activities more strongly to the international social work enterprise. These three bodies evolved from the Paris conference of 1928 (Lyons 1999). While the IFSW and IASSW have been committed to jointly hosting global conferences whenever feasible, a formal agreement now exists guaranteeing biennial joint conferences from 2010 onwards. Also, over the past four years, joint task forces of experts have produced three important international documents that build on the *Definition of Social Work* document (Montreal 2000): *Global Standards for Social Work Education and Training, Globalisation and the Environment*, plus a reviewed ethics document, *The Ethics of Social Work—Principles and Standards*. All three were jointly approved by IFSW and IASSW General Meetings in Adelaide (2004).

The International Association of Schools of Social Work (IASSW)

The IASSW, founded in 1928 in Paris, was the original international social work organisation representing schools of social work at tertiary level worldwide (Kendall 2000). IASSW's administrative site is dependent on the location of the incumbent International President. Its major aims are the development and promotion of excellence in social work education research and scholarship; and the creation and maintenance of a community of social work educators. There are five regions: Africa, Latin America, Europe, North America and the Caribbean, and Asia and the Pacific. Australia belongs to this last region. Created in 1970, it is structured as the Association of Social Work Education (APASWE). A major IASSW project at the time this paper is being written is the 'International Exchange and Research Collaboration'. Its questioning discourse is focused on how international social work education deals with the legacies of the West's cultural, academic, and economic imperialism. IASSW international connections include: the United Nations (UN), UN Economic and Social Council, UN Children's Fund (UNICEF), UN Division for Social Policy and Development, UN Women's Watch, UN High Commission for Human Rights, and Inter-University Consortium for International Social Development.

The International Federation of Social Workers (IFSW)

The IFSW began in 1956, six years after an International Conference on Social Work (Paris, 1950) agreed to its creation. The IFSW is the successor of the International Permanent Secretariat of Social Workers whose original role was the support of IASSW's early development. AASW has been involved in the development of IFSW since 1952.

Major aims are the multi-level promotion of social work as an international profession, underpinning this work with universal practice standards, guidelines, and policies; and the promotion and advancement of the development of national associations or professional unions of social workers.

It has five regions: Africa, Asia and the Pacific, Europe, Latin America and the Caribbean, and North America. IFSW has a full-time Secretary General and Assistant located in Berne, Switzerland. It holds special consultative status with the UN Economic and Social Council. It holds accredited status with International Labour Organisation, UNICEF, the Council of Europe, the European Union, and most recently UN Habitat (Nairobi).

International Council on Social Welfare (ICSW)

The International Council of Social Welfare (ICSW) is the third of the international bodies with its origins in the Paris Conference of 1928. ICSW advocates and represents the needs of tens of thousands of grass-roots organisations through a broad international network in more than 50 countries. It contributes to policy development, design, and delivery of services. It provides social workers with valuable links to a wide range of welfare and community workers, as well as to key representatives of a wide range of international human service agencies.

The Secretary General is based in London and there are other key administrative centres in Bangkok and Kampala. ICSW has special representatives at the UN (New York and Geneva). Other international peak body collaborations include Highest Consultative status with UN Economic and Social Council, and links with UN Agriculture and Food Organisation, ILO, UNICEF, United Nations Educational, Scientific, and Cultural Organization (UNESCO), and World Health Organization (WHO).

Commonwealth Organisation for Social Work

The Commonwealth Organisation for Social Work (COSW) had its beginnings at the IFSW Conference in Sri Lanka (1994). It is open to social workers and those who support the principles of social work. It has a representative base in London with the Honorary Secretary General residing in Australia.

COSW's major goals are to provide a Commonwealth network of information about social work and social development and to facilitate support and sharing of technical knowledge and expertise between and among Commonwealth countries and their social worker organisations (McIntyre 2001). It is committed to the development of civil society and the well-being of Commonwealth citizens with a special emphasis on the needs of the people of sub-Saharan Africa (Knight et al. 2002).

There is an agreement between IFSW and COSW to work together on matters of mutual concern. These matters include social policy, project development and implementation, and indigenous professional education and representation at Commonwealth Heads of Government Meetings (CHOGMs). COSW's evolution has been due to the vision and determination of a small core of volunteer social workers from a number of Commonwealth countries including Australia.

AASW's International Social Work Committee (ISW)

AASW's International Social Work Committee (ISW) is sited wherever the Convenor resides. It commenced in the early 1990s as International Relations Committee (IRC) with the aim of establishing substantial international networks for the AASW. By the mid 1990s, as part of an AASW restructuring, it became the AASW's International Social Work Committee.

It's long-term goals are: to promote an understanding of Australian social work within an international context; to initiate project development at regional and international levels; to support regional and international social policy development; and encourage appropriate development of social work associations in neighbouring countries.

Social work and international advocacy

As detailed above, social work's international bodies are formally linked to and regularly collaborating with resource people within a range of key global agencies. All are in pursuit of mutually shared goals of social development, human rights, and well-being. With the twin advances of social work's international organisational consolidation and the advent of speedy international electronic communication, professional social workers can now claim professional advocacy and lobbying opportunities that were unthinkable only a decade ago. Social workers now have international and national systems in place that provide opportunities for collaboration across national boundaries on matters of mutual concern. National organisations are only as strong as their members. New opportunities bring new dilemmas. While new technology brings benefits to social workers in a number of countries, its absence creates new gulfs of deprivation in others. Creative international solutions to dilemmas such as these, for the benefit of all, are among the profession's most pressing challenges.

International aid agencies and Australia

A brief outline of Australian government and non-governmental international agencies follows. Australian social workers are yet to develop widespread working relations with them. Governments' international aid programmes are often influenced by political and economic motivations, though part of the aid has implications for social work and welfare activities. A major bilateral aid programme in Australia is the Australian Agency for International Development (AusAID). Non-governmental international organisations are very active in relief, welfare, and social development. A peak Australian body in this sector is the independent Australian Council for International Development (ACFID) with about 80 members. It oversees the distribution of Australian NGO support to about 130 countries. Well-known Australian-based international NGOs are Australian Volunteers International, Action Aid Australia, CARE Australia, Child Wise (ECPAT), and World Vision Australia. For further details on Australian NGO international activities visit ACFID's website (www.acfid.asn.au).

Ethics in context

1   Is it possible to practise social work cross-culturally in a non–imperialistic manner? How do you react to this question and what are the reasons for your answer?

2   Globalisation is considered to be a positive phenomenon for some countries, but has a negative effect for other countries. Where the interests of two different countries intersect, how does one decide whose interests are primary?

Future issues in international social work

More examples of international social work practice are required

Much international social work literature addresses only broad principles and generalised ideals, and is filled with recommendations about the functions of international social work: 'International social work should focus on the profession and practice in different parts of the world ... [it should] emphasise a cross-national or global examination of what social workers do' (Hokenstad et al. 1992, p. 4), etc. However, there are still few examples in the literature of the actual practice of international social work.

Successful translation of universal principles into local social work practice

As the establishment of national social work associations in the developing world continues, new social work voices are raising new priority issues. A major issue is the translation of universal principles into local practice. Historically, the promotion and growth of international social work has occurred in a linear direction from west to east (or north to south).

Although quite subtle, this continues to occur as a remnant of an imperialist perspective, insufficiently sensitive to local and indigenous strengths and practices. In international practice, more than any other, the ideological dichotomy between social workers from the dominant Western schools of social work and those who come from developing non-Western countries is well recognised (Elliott 1993, p. 21). In the West, the dominant emphasis has been that of individualism and clinical specialisation, while in non-Western countries it is been communal consensus, community action, and social development (Mazibuko 1996, p. 10). There is no doubt this dichotomy continues to exist and is increasingly a focus of attention within the international social work community. However, the effects of economic, trade, and social advances within developing countries and the return home to these countries of internationally educated social work graduates is now gradually creating a third and blended ideological phenomenon, which is beginning to develop creative bridging dialogues between West and East.

For example, efforts to address east–west disparity issues at international conferences and seminars are resulting in a growing interest in the transferability of social work methods. Those that have proven successful in one sphere can be adapted to the other (Healy 1998; Tesoriero 1996). There is a growing awareness, for instance, that the needs of those who are marginalised in major cities of the West may be successfully addressed with methods similar to those used to address the needs of the poor in developing countries (Tesoriero 1999).

The requisite breadth and depth of social work knowledge and skills

Drucker (2003), a social work consultant to a wide range of UN agencies, USAID, and NGOs, wonders whether social work can 'genuinely claim to be an international profession with an international perspective and knowledge base' when the profession is largely absent from the site of today's major development or disaster management locations around the globe. He asks: 'What is our record on the global scene in the cause of promoting attention to social issues and demonstrating action in the main stream of development? Do we actually possess the requisite education skills and vision to work and teach others in the international arena?' Emphasising the profession's bleak record in moving issues such as these to mainstream agendas, he recalls Martinez-Brawley's 'back to basics' observation that the survival of social work as an international profession depends on its 'knowledge and educational base' moving 'beyond the confines of western countries' (Drucker 2003, pp. 55–65).

Adequate skill levels in cross-cultural practice

Even though current Australian human service delivery policies are shifting towards mainstream and away from multiculturalism, social workers engaged with people who are recent arrivals from other countries know that their practice and its outcomes are weakened when inadequate attention is given to the removal of language barriers and the improvement of communication sensitivity and competency.

Difficulty in maintaining professional social work values and principles in the workplace

Social work values and principles such as human dignity and worth, human rights, confidentiality, self-determination, and people-centred development may be challenged and sometimes violated in workplaces today. Social work graduates who work under job descriptions that are not explicitly social work designated and who are working with new arrivals to a country may be particularly vulnerable. In some agencies where team-leadership responsibilities are shared with a variety of non-social workers, a managerial work culture of task efficiency and budget constraint may create cultural and professional dilemmas. Social workers may find themselves sandwiched between an ethical compulsion to act and a legal or administrative regulation to curtail, and even avoid, action. Professional social workers in such situations are required by their national Code of Ethics to develop appropriate strategies to meet their own standards alongside the administrative and legal service requirements of the workplace.

Signposts towards the future of international social work

The broad overview sketched out in this chapter provides readers with a framework for international social work. Many signposts towards the future are imbedded within it. The following issues are seen as capable of influencing the future scope and viability of social work practice in the international field:

- development of a robust international social work practice definition underpinned by the international definition of the profession and the more recent, additional companion documents
- development of knowledge and skills that are appropriate, suitable, and effective for collaborative activities locally and globally
- increased understanding, usage, and development of international social work networks and structures leading to development and implementation of worldwide networks and action strategies addressing major concerns
- access to social work education and practice where it is least available and most needed
- facilitation of the transfer and sharing of social work knowledge on an egalitarian basis with appropriate acknowledgement
- increased political, structural, educational, and practice recognition of the similarities between social workers and welfare workers in the international field, in order to advance collaborative action.

Review questions

1 Discuss your understanding of international social work.

2 Compare and contrast the three definitional views of international social work practice.

3   Which model of practice would you prefer to employ when you begin to work professionally? Discuss reasons for your choice.
4   What have you learnt about professional bodies and international organisations in
this chapter?
5   What are the three most critical issues in international social work?
6   As a social worker reflect on what you want to do to address these issues.

Notes

1   Professor Norma Parker died early in 2004 and has been hailed as 'a legendary figure for Australian social
workers ... widely regarded as the founder of Australian social work' (Dodds 2004).
2   Bernadette McMenamin, a social worker, is Child Wise (ECPAT) National Director in Australia. In acknowledgment of her long-term commitment to the elimination of child sex exploitation through national and
regional agency coalitions, she is the recipient of two prestigious Australian awards: The Australian of the Year
(Victoria) in 2003 and Order of Australia (AO) in the Queen's Birthday Honours List in 2004.

Bibliography

AASW, *see* Australian Association of Social Workers.

Abelove, H., Barale, M. & Halperin, D. (eds) 1993, *The Lesbian and Gay Studies Reader*, Routledge, New York.

Aboriginal and Torres Strait Islander Commission 2004, *New arrangements in Indigenous Affairs*, <www.atsic.gov.au/ATSIC_ATSIS_Closure/Default.asp> (accessed 13 August 2004).

ABS, *see* Australian Bureau of Statistics.

ACOSS, *see* Australian Council of Social Service.

Adams, M. 1971, 'The compassion trap', in V. Gornick & B. K. Moran (eds), *Women in Sexist Society: Studies in Power and Powerlessness*, Basic Books, New York.

Adams, R. 1998, 'Social work processes', in R. Adams, L. Dominelli & M. Payne (eds), *Social Work: Themes, Issues and Critical Debates*, Macmillan, London, pp. 253–72.

Adams, R. 1997, 'Preventing verbal harassment and violence toward gay and lesbian students', *Journal of School Nursing*, vol. 13, no. 3, pp. 24–8.

Age 2002, 'Battle for boy ends in double tragedy', 3 August.

AHMAC, *see* Australian Health Ministers Advisory Council.

Ahmad, B. 1989, 'Child care and ethnic minorities', in B. Kahan (ed.), *Child Care Research, Policy and Practice*, Hodder & Stoughton, London, pp. 214–30.

AIHW *see* Australian Institute of Health and Welfare.

Ainsworth, F. 2002, 'Mandatory reporting of child abuse and neglect: does it really make a difference', *Child and Family Social Work*, vol. 7, no. 1, pp. 57–63.

Alford, J. & O'Neil, D. (eds) 1994, *The Contract State: Public Management and the Kennett Government*, Deakin University Press, Melbourne.

Allan, J. 2004, 'Mother-blaming: a covert practice in therapeutic intervention', *Australian Social Work*, vol. 57, no. 1, pp. 57–70.

Allan, J. 2003, 'Theorising Critical Social Work', in J. Allan, B. Pease & L. Briskman (eds), *Critical Social Work: an Introduction to Theories and Practices*, Allen & Unwin, Sydney.

Alston, M. 2000, *Breaking through the Grass Ceiling: Women, Power and Leadership in Rural Organisations*, Harwood Academic Publishers, Amsterdam.

Alston, M. 1997, 'Violence against women in a rural context', *Australian Social Work*, March, pp. 15–22.

Alston, M. 1995, *Women on the Land: The Hidden Heart of Rural Australia*, UNSW Press, Kensington.

Altman, D. 1992a, 'AIDS and the discourses of sexuality', in R. Connell & G. Dowsett (eds), *Rethinking Sex: Social Theory and Sexuality Research*, Melbourne University Press, Carlton.

Altman, D. 1992b, 'The most political of diseases', in E. Timewell, V. Minichiello & D. Plummer (eds), *AIDS in Australia*, Prentice Hall Australia, Sydney.

Amnesty International 2004, *Defending Refugees Human Rights—Issues and Campaigns*, <www.amnesty.org.au/whats_happening/refugees?MySourceSession=414d45df9> (accessed January 2004).

Anderson, A. 1998, 'Strengths of gay male youth: an untold story', *Journal of Child and Adolescent Social Work*, vol. 15, no. 1, pp. 55–71.

Anderson, J. 1999, Speech to the National Press Club, <www.dotrs.gov.au> (accessed March 2004).

Anderson, M. 1997, 'Aboriginal employment issues', in J. Tomlinson, W. Patton, P. Creed & R. Hicks (eds), *Unemployment Policy and Practice*, Australian Academic Press, Brisbane, pp. 103–6.

Angus, G. & Woodward, S. 1995, *Children Abuse and Neglect, Australia 1993–94*, Australian Institute of Health and Welfare, Child Welfare Series, No. 13, AGPS, Canberra.

Aoun, S., Underwood, R. & Rouse, I. 1994, 'A pilot study of psycho-social morbidity in rural general practice', in D. McSwan & M. McShane (eds), *Issues Affecting Rural Communities, Rural Education Research and Development Centre*, James Cook University of North Queensland, Townsville, pp. 110–16.

Appleby, G. & Anastas, J. 1998, *Not Just A Passing Phase: Social Work with Gay, Lesbian and Bisexual People*, Columbia University Press, New York.

Aroche, J. & Coello, M. 1994, 'Toward a systemic approach for the treatment and rehabilitation of torture and trauma survivors in exile: the experience of STARTTS in Australia', paper presented at the 4th International Conference of Centres, Institutions and Individuals Concerned with Victims of Organised Violence, 5–9 December, DAP, Philippines.

Aroni, R. & Minichiello, V. 1992, 'Sociological aspects of ageing', in V. Minichiello, L. Alexander & D. Jones (eds), *Gerontology: A Multidisciplinary Approach*, Prentice Hall, Sydney.

Asamoah, Y., Healy, L. M. & Mayadas, N. 1997, 'Ending the international-domestic dichotomy: new approaches to a global curriculum for the Millennium', *Journal of Social Work Education*, vol. 33, no. 2, pp. 389–401.

Asia–Pacific Region Social Work Education Association and Sociology Department of Peking University of China (eds) 1992, *Status Quo, Challenge and Prospect: Collected Works of the Seminar of the Asia Pacific Regional Conference of Social Work Education*, Peking University Press, People's Republic of China.

Atchley, R. C. 1976, *The Sociology of Retirement*, John Wiley & Sons, New York.

Atchley, R. C. & Barusch, A. S. 2004, *Social Forces and Aging: An Introduction to Social Gerontology*, 10th edn, Wadsworth/Thomson Learning, Belmont, California.

Atkins, D. (ed.) 1998, *Looking Queer: Body Image and Identity in Lesbian, Bisexual, Gay and Transgender communities*, Haworth Press, New York.

ATSIC, *see* Aboriginal and Torres Strait Islander Commission.

Austin, D. M. 1997, 'The profession of social work: in the second century', in M. Reisch & E. Gambrill (eds), *Social Work in the 21st Century*, Pine Forge Press, California.

Australian 1999, 'Riverland renaissance', 28–29 August.

Australian Association of Social Workers 2004, *About Social Work*, <www.aasw.asn> (accessed 25 May 2004).

Australian Association of Social Workers 2002, *Australian Association of Social Workers Code of Ethics*, (2nd edn), AASW, Barton.

Australian Association of Social Workers 2000a, *Australian Association of Social Workers Code of Ethics*, AASW, Canberra.

Australian Association of Social Workers 2000b, 'Definition of social work', *AASW National Bulletin*, vol. 10, no. 5, October, p. 7.

Australian Association of Social Workers 1998, *Policy and Procedures for Establishing Eligibility for Membership of AASW*, AASW, Canberra.

Australian Association of Social Workers 1997a, 'Definition of social work', *AASW National Bulletin*, vol. 7, no. 3, June, p. 3.

Australian Association of Social Workers 1997b, 'Norma Parker Address', *AASW National Bulletin*, vol. 7, no. 5, October, pp. 4–6.

Australian Association of Social Workers 1997c, 'Social policy: proposed amendments to the Native Title Act 1993', *AASW National Bulletin*, vol. 7, no. 5, October, pp. 15–16.

Australian Association of Social Workers 1994, *Australian Social Work Competency Standards for Entry Level Social Work*, AGPS, Canberra.

Australian Bureau of Statistics 2004, '2004 Year Book Australia', Commonwealth of Australia, Canberra.

Australian Bureau of Statistics 2002, 'ABS crime and justice data', in A. Graycar & P. Grabosky (eds), *The Cambridge Handbook of Australian Criminology*, Cambridge University Press, Cambridge.

Australian Bureau of Statistics 2003, *Australian Social Trends*, AGPS, Canberra.

Australian Bureau of Statistics 1999a, *Australian Social Trends*, AGPS, Canberra.

Australian Bureau of Statistics 1999b, *Disability, Ageing and Carers: A Summary of Findings, (4430.0)*, AGPS, Canberra.

Australian Bureau of Statistics 1998, *Australian Social Trends*, AGPS, Canberra.

Australian Bureau of Statistics 1997a, *Australian Demographic Statistics, June Quarter 1997 (3101)*, AGPS, Canberra.

Australian Bureau of Statistics 1997b, *Population Distribution, Indigenous Australians (4705.0)*, AGPS, Canberra.

Australian Bureau of Statistics, Australian Institute of Health and Welfare, and Department of Health and Family Services 1998, *Indigenous Disability Data—Current Status and Future Prospects; Report on Proceedings of the Canberra Workshop, April 1998*, Commonwealth of Australia.

Australian Conservation Foundation 2000, 'Natural Advantage: a blueprint for a sustainable Australia' *Habitat*, vol. 28, no. 5, pp. 13–20.

Australian Council of Social Service 1999, *Government Policies Fail to Stem Rise in Long-term Unemployment*, ACOSS media release, <http//www.acoss.org.au> (accessed July 2004).

Australian Council of Social Service 1998, *Take Care in Tough Times*, <www.acoss.org.au/media/1998/takecare2.htm> (accessed 30 November 2004).

Australian Council of Social Service 1988, *Australians Living on the Edge*, <www.acoss.org.au/media/1998/edge3.pdf> (accessed January 1998).

Australian Council of Social Service 1997, 'Contracts, tenders and competition', *Impact*, 1 & 12 September.

Australian Health Ministers 2003, *National Mental Health Plan 2003–2008*, Mental Health Branch, Commonwealth Department of Health and Ageing. Canberra.

Australian Health Ministers 1998, *Second National Mental Health Plan*, Commonwealth Department of Health and Family Services, Mental Health Branch, July.

Australian Health Ministers 1992, *National Mental Health Policy*, AGPS, Canberra.

Australian Health Ministers 1991, *Mental Health Statement of Rights and Responsibilities, Report of the Mental Health Consumer Outcomes Task Force*, AGPS, Canberra.

Australian Health Ministers Advisory Council 2003, *National Practice Standards for the Mental Health Workforce*, Mental Health Branch, Commonwealth Department of Health and Ageing, Canberra.

Australian Health Ministers Advisory Council 1996, *National Standards for Mental Health Services*, AHMAC National Mental Health Working Group, AGPS, Canberra.

Australian Institute of Health and Welfare 2004, *Child Protection in Australia 2002–03*, AIHW Cat. No. CWS 22, AIHW (Child Welfare Services No. 34), Canberra.

Australian Institute of Health and Welfare 2003a, *Australia's Welfare 2003*, AIHW, Canberra, pp. 330–88.

Australian Institute of Health and Welfare 2003b, *Australia's Young People: Their Health and Well-being*, AIHW, Canberra.

Australian Institute of Health and Welfare 1999, *Child Protection Australia 1997–98*, AIHW Cat. No. CWS8, Canberra.

Australian Law Reform Commission 1993, *Equality before the Law*, Canberra.

Australian Parliament 1986, *Disability Services Act*, AGPS, Canberra.

Aviram, U. 1997, 'Social work in mental health: trends and issues', *Social Work in Health Care*, vol. 25, no. 3, pp. 1–9.

Bacon, W. 1998, *Dumping on Centrelink. Jobs Crises: Special Report*, Centre for Independent Journalism, Sydney.

Bagnall, D. 1999, 'The old and the dutiful', *Bulletin*, May 18, vol. 117, no. 6174, pp. 22–7.

Baines, C., Evans, P. & Neysmith, S. (eds) 1991, *Women's Caring: Feminist Perspective on Social Welfare*, McClelland & Stewart, Toronto.

Baldock, C. V. 1994, 'The family and the Australian welfare state', *Australian Journal of Social Issues*, vol. 29, no. 2, pp. 105–19.

Baldock, C. V. & Cass, B. (eds) 1988, *Women, Social Welfare and the State in Australia*, Allen & Unwin, Sydney.

Ballard, J. 1992, 'Sexuality and the State in the time of epidemic', in R. Connell & G. Dowsett (eds), *Rethinking Sex: Social Theory and Sexuality Research*, Melbourne University Press, Carlton.

Banks, S. 2001, *Ethics and Values in Social Work*, 2nd edn, Palgrave, Hampshire, England.

Banks, S. 1998, 'Professional ethics in social work', *British Journal of Social Work*, vol. 28.

Barbalet, M. 1983, *Far from a Low Gutter Girl: The Forgotten World of State Wards, South Australia 1887–1940*, Oxford University Press, Melbourne.

Barker, M. 1991 'Intercultural communication in health care', in B. Ferguson & E. Browne (eds), *Health Care and Immigrants: A Guide for the Helping Professions*, MacLennan & Petty, Australia.

Barnes, C., Mercer, G. & Shakespeare, T. 1999, *Exploring Disability: A Sociological Introduction*, Polity Press, Cambridge.

Barrett, M. & Mackintosh, M. 1982, *The Anti-Social Family*, Verso, London.

Bates, E. & Linder-Pelz, S. 1990, *Health Care Issues*, 2nd edn, Allen & Unwin, Australia.

Bates, F., Blackwood, J. B., Boersig, J., Mackie, K. & McPhee, J. 1996, *The Australian Social Worker and the Law*, Law Book Company, Sydney.

Bath, H. 1994, 'Out of home care in Australia: a state by state comparison', *Children Australia*, vol. 19, no. 4.

Batten, R., Weeks, W. & Wilson J. (eds) 1991, *Issues Facing Australian Families: Human Services Respond*, Longman Cheshire, Melbourne.

Battin, T. 1997, *Abandon Keynes: Australia's Capital Mistake*, Macmillan, London.

Baume, P. & Kay, K. 1995, *Working Solution. Report of the Strategic Review of the Commonwealth Disability Services Program*, AGPS, Canberra.

Baumhover, L. A. & Beall, S. C. (eds) 1996, *Abuse, Neglect, and Exploitation of Older Persons: Strategies for Assessment and Intervention*, Health Professions Press, Baltimore.

Baxterwatch 2004, *Children in Detention*, <www.baxterwatch.net> (accessed 29 October 2004).

BBC 2004, 'Latvia Appoints World's First Green President', *BBC online*, <www.bbc.co.uk/worldnews_Latvia> (accessed 15 May 2004).

Beaulieu, E. M. 2001, *A Guide for Nursing Home Social Workers*, Springer, New York.

Becker, R. 1991, 'Refugees in search of a home', paper presented at the 'Trauma and its Wake' Conference, Sydney.

Beecher, S. 1986, 'A gender critique of family therapy', in H. Marchant & B. Wearing (eds), *Gender Reclaimed: Women in Social Work*, Hale & Iremonger, Sydney.

Beels, C. & McFarlane, W. 1982, 'Family treatment of schizophrenia: background and state of the art', *Hospital and Community Psychiatry*, vol. 33, pp. 541–9.

Begbie, R., Brennan, A., Cunliffe, M., Healy, M. & McAuliffe, J. 1986, *A Review of the Role and Structure of the Department's Social Work Service*, Department of Social Security, Canberra.

Bell, S. 1997, *Ungoverning the Economy*, Oxford University Press, Melbourne.

Belsky, J. 1993, 'Etiology of maltreatment: a developmental–ecological analysis', *Psychological Bulletin*, no. 114, pp. 413–34.

Bender, M., Bauckham, P. & Norris, A. 1999, *The Therapeutic Purposes of Reminiscence*, Sage, London.

Berger, R. 1995, 'Habitat destruction syndrome', *Social Work*, vol. 40, no. 4, pp. 441–7.

Berger, R. & Kelly, J. 1993, 'Social work in the ecological crisis', *Social Work*, vol. 38, no. 5, pp. 521–5.

Berk, L. 2002, *Human Development and Social Work*, 2nd edition, Pearson Custom Publishing, French's Forest.

Berkman, C. & Zinberg, G. 1997, 'Homophobia and heterosexism in social workers', *Social Work*, vol. 42, no. 4, pp. 319–32.

Berreen, R. 1994, '"And thereby to discountenance mendacity": practices of charity in early nineteenth century Australia', in M. Wearing & R. Berreen (eds), *Welfare and Social Policy in Australia: The Distribution of Advantage*, Harcourt Brace, Marrickville.

Berreen, R. & Wearing, M. 1989, 'The network of surveillance', in R. Kennedy (ed.), *Australian Welfare: Historical Sociology*, Macmillan, Melbourne, pp. 74–101.

Besharov, D. J. 1985, 'Abuse: the need to narrow the grounds for state intervention', *Harvard Journal of Law and Public Policy*, vol. 8, no. 3, pp. 539–88.

Besthorn, F. 2003, 'Radical ecologisms: insights for educating social workers in ecological activism and social justice', *Critical Social Work*, vol. 3, no. 1, pp. 66–107.

Bhabha, H. 1994, *The Location of Culture*, Routledge, London.

Bickenbach, J. E. 1993, *Physical Disability and Social Policy*, University of Toronto Press, Toronto.

Birchall, A. 1999, 'The experience of women with mental illness as mothers', BSW (Hons) thesis, School of Sociology & Social Work, University of Tasmania.

Bird, C. (ed.) 1998, *The Stolen Children: Their Stories*, Random House, Sydney.

Bishop, B. 1999, *The National Strategy for an Ageing Australia: Background Paper*, April, Commonwealth of Australia, Canberra.

Bittman, M. 1991, *Juggling Time: How Australian Families Use Time*, Office of the Status of Women, Department of Prime Minister and Cabinet, Commonwealth of Australia, Canberra.

Bittman, M. & Rice, J. 1999, 'Are working hours becoming more unsociable?', *Social Policy Research Centre Newsletter*, no. 74, August.

Black, B. 1984, 'Social work role in community mental health', unpublished paper delivered at conference of Senior Social Workers in Health, New York.

Blanch, M. 1979, 'Imperialism, nationalism and organised youth', in J. Clarke, C. Critcher & R. Johnson (eds), *Working Class Culture*, Hutchinson, Birmingham, p. 103.

Bland, R. (ed.) 1996, *Developing Services for Older People and Their Families*, Jessica Kingsley, London.

Bland, R. 1995, 'Beyond positivist paradigms', *THEMHS Conference Proceedings 1995*, pp. 134–40.

Bland, R. & Darlington, Y. 2002, 'The nature and sources of hope: Perspectives of family carers of people with serious mental illness', *Perspectives in Psychiatric Care*, vol. 38, no. 2, pp. 61–9.

Bland, R., Joughin, G. & Oliver, I. 1999, *Social Work and Mental Health Competencies Project*, produced by AASW for the Mental Health Branch, Commonwealth Department of Health & Human Services, Canberra.

Bland, R. & O'Neill, M. 1990, 'Rediscovering welfare concepts in social work practice in community mental health', *Australian Social Work*, vol. 43, no. 4, pp. 3–8.

Blumenfeld, W. (ed.) 1992, *Homophobia: How we all Pay the Price*, Beacon Press, Boston.

Bone, R., Cheers, B. & Hil, R. 1993, *The Needs of Young People in the Whitsunday Shire*, Welfare Research and Studies Centre, James Cook University, Townsville.

Bornat, J. (ed.) 1994, *Reminiscence Reviewed: Perspectives, Evaluations, Achievement*, Open University Press, Buckingham, England.

Borowski, A. 1997, 'Working with juvenile offenders in correctional settings: practice with the involuntary client', in A. Borowski & I. O'Connor (eds), *Juvenile Crime, Justice and Corrections*, Longman, Melbourne.

Borowski, A., Encel, S. & Ozanne, E. (eds) 1997, *Ageing and Social Policy in Australia*, Cambridge University Press, Australia.

Boss, P. 1998, 'Victims of ideology: the looming crisis for child and family welfare services', unpublished paper.

Boulet, J. 2003, 'Globalising Practice in the International Context', in J. Allan, B. Pease, L. Briskman (eds), *Critical Social Work: An Introduction to theories and practices*, Allen & Unwin, Sydney.

Bourke, L., Jacob, S. & Luloff, A. 1996, 'Response to Pennsylvania's agricultural preservation program', *Rural Sociology*, vol. 61, pp. 606–29.

Bowlby, J. 1969, *Attachment and Loss*, vol. 1, Hogarth Press, London.

Bowles, R. & Haidary, Z. 1994, 'Narrative family therapy with survivors of torture and trauma: an Afghan case study', paper presented at the 4th International Conference of Centres, Institutions and Individuals Concerned with Victims of Organised Violence, DAP, Philippines, 5–9 December.

Bowles, R., Haidary, Z. & Becker, R. 1995, 'Family therapy with survivors of torture and trauma: issues for women in an Afghan case study', paper presented at the 3rd National Women's Health Conference, Changing Society for Women's Health, Manning Clark Centre, Australian National University, Canberra.

Bradshaw, J. 1981, 'A taxonomy of social need', in P. Henderson & D. Thomas, *Readings in Community Work*, Allen & Unwin, London.

Braithwaite, J. & Pettit, P. 1990, *Not Just Deserts: A Republican Theory of Criminal Justice*, Clarendon Press, Oxford.

Braithwaite, J. 1989, *Crime, Shame and Reintegration*, Cambridge University Press, Sydney.

Brake, M. 1980, *The Sociology of Youth Culture and Youth Subculture*, Routledge and Kegan Paul, London.

Brenchley, F. 1999, 'The baby boom time bomb', *Bulletin*, July 27, vol. 117, no. 6184, pp. 40–1.

Brennan, D. 1999, 'Children and social policy', in J. Bowes & A. Hayes (eds), *Children, Families, and Communities: Contexts and Consequences*, Oxford University Press, Melbourne.

Briere, J., Berliner, L., Bulkley, J. A., Jenny, C. & Reid, T. (eds) 1996, *The APSAC Handbook on Child Maltreatment*, Sage, California.

Bright, R. 1997, *Wholeness in Later Life*, Jessica Kingsley, London.

Briskman, L. 2003, 'Indigenous Australians: towards postcolonial social work', in J. Allan, B. Pease & L. Briskman (eds.), *Critical Social Work: An Introduction to Theories and Practices*, Allen & Unwin, Crows Nest, pp. 92–106.

Briskman, L. 2001, 'Beyond apologies: the Stolen Generations and the churches', *Children Australia*, vol. 26, no. 3, pp. 4–8.

Brock, P. 1993, *Outback Ghettos: A History of Aboriginal Institutionalisation and Survival*, Cambridge University Press, Melbourne.

Brook, E. & Davies, A. 1985, *Women, The Family and Social Work*, Tavistock, London.

Brotherhood of St Lawrence 2003, *Changing Pressures*, Brotherhood of St Lawrence, Melbourne.

Brown, C. 1995, 'Foreword', in C. Cloke & M. Davies (eds), *Participation and Empowerment in Child Protection*, John Wiley & Sons, Chichester, England.

Brown, G. W. & Harris, T. 1978, *The Social Origins of Depression*, Tavistock, London.

Browne, E. 1996, *Tradition and Change: Hospital Social Work in NSW*, Australian Association of Social Workers, NSW branch.

Browne, E. & Davidson, J. (2004), 'Who's Afraid of the Big Bad Wolf? Corporatism, Managerialism and Professional Ethics', *ISAA Review*, vol. 3, no. 1.

Bryson, L. 1992, *Welfare and the State: Who Benefits?*, Macmillan, London.

Buckley, H. 2000, 'Child protection: an unreflective practice', *Social Work Education*, vol. 19, no. 3, pp. 253–63.

Burbidge, A. 1998, 'Changing patterns of social exchanges', *Family Matters*, vol. 50, Winter.

Burdekin, B. 1989, *Our Homeless Children*, Report of the National Inquiry into Homeless Children, Human Rights and Equal Opportunities Commission, AGPS, Canberra.

Burdekin Community Development Association 1997, *Submission to the Inquiry into the Tendering of Welfare Service Delivery*, submission to the House of Representatives Standing Committee on Family and Community Affairs, Ayr.

Burns, A. & Goodnow, J. 1985, *Children and Families in Australia*, Allen & Unwin, Sydney.

Bursian, O. 1995, 'Economic liberalism and the community services industry: a case study', *Just Policy*, no. 3, June, pp. 3–10.

Bustos, E. 1990, 'Dealing with the unbearable: reactions of therapists and therapeutic institutions to survivors of torture', in P. Suedfeld (ed.), *Torture and Psychology*, Hemisphere, Washington DC.

Butler, B. 1992, 'Aboriginal child protection', in G. Calvert, A. Ford & P. Parkinson (eds), *The Practice of Child Protection: Australian Approaches*, Hale & Iremonger, Sydney, pp. 14–22.

Butler, R. N. 1963, 'The life review: an interpretation of reminiscence in the aged', *Psychiatry*, vol. 26, pp. 65–76.

Butow, H. 1994, 'Concepts of impairments, disability and handicap', *Interaction*, vol. 7, no. 5, pp. 12–14.

Buxton, A. 1999, 'The best interests of children of gay and lesbian parents', in R. Galatzer-Levy & L. Kraus (eds), *The scientific basis of child custody decisions*, Wiley, New York.

Callahan, M. 1993, 'Feminist approaches: women recreate child welfare', in B. Wharf (ed.), *Rethinking Child Welfare in Canada*, McLelland & Stewart, Toronto, pp. 172–209.

Cannan, C. 2000, 'The environmental crisis, greens and community development', *Community Development Journal*, vol. 35, no. 4, pp. 365–76.

Carbery, G. 1995, *A History of the Sydney Gay and Lesbian Mardi Gras*, Australian Lesbian and Gay Archives, Parkville.

Carment, A. 1989, 'Does poverty increase the incidence of child abuse?', *Impact*, vol. 19, no. 6, October–November, pp. 12–15.

Carney, T. & Ramia, G. 1999, 'From citizenship to contractualism: the transition from unemployment benefits to employment services in Australia', *Australian Journal of Administrative Law*, vol. 6, no. 3, pp. 117–39.

Carter, J. 1990, 'Foreword', in T. Gilley, *Empowering Poor People*, Brotherhood of St Laurence, Victoria.

Cashmore, J., Dolby, R. & Brennan, D. 1994, *Systems Abuse: Problems and Solutions*, A Report of the NSW Child Protection Council, Sydney.

Casper, L. M., McLanahan, S. S. & Garfinkel, I. 1993, 'The gender poverty gap: what can we learn from other countries?', Office of Population Research working paper, Princeton University, New Jersey.

Cass, B. 1986, *Income Support for Families with Children*, Social Security Review Issues Paper No. 1, AGPS, Canberra

Castles, F. 1994, 'The wage earners welfare state revisited', *Australian Journal of Social Issues*, vol. 29, no. 2, pp. 120–45.

Castles, F. G. 1985, *The Working Class and Welfare: Reflections on the Political Development of the Welfare State in Australia and New Zealand 1890–1980*, Allen & Unwin, New Zealand.

Castles, I. 1995, *Yearbook Australia*, ABS, Canberra.

Cavanaugh, J. C. 1993, *Adult Development and Aging*, 2nd edn, Brooks/Cole, Pacific Grove, California.

Chadwick, A. 1994, 'For disabled people the body is the principal site of oppression, both in form and what is done to it', *Australian Disability Review*, vol. 94, no. 4, pp. 36–44.

Chamberlain, E. 1991, 'The Beijing seminar: social work education in Asia and the Pacific', *International Social Work*, vol. 34.

Channer, Y. & Parton, N. 1990, 'Racism, cultural relativism and child protection', in The Violence Against Children Study Group (ed.), *Taking Child Abuse Seriously: Contemporary Issues in Child Protection Theory and Practice*, Unwin Hyman, London, pp. 105–20.

Chapman, A. 1997, 'The messages of subordination contained in Australian anti-discrimination statutes', in G. Mason & S. Tomsen (eds), *Homophobic Violence*, Hawkins Press, Sydney.

Cheers, B. (in press), *The Place of Care—Rural Human Services on the Fringe in Rural Social Work: Special Issue of papers from the International Conference on Rural Human Services*, Centre for Rural and Regional Development, University of South Australia, Whyalla.

Cheers, B. 1999, 'Rejuvenating community in rural Australia', in P. Munn & A. Handley (eds), *Healthy Communities for the Bush: Proceedings of the 3rd National Conference for Regional Australia and the First Broken Hill Human Services Conference*, University of South Australia Library, Adelaide, pp. 2–24.

Cheers, B. 1998, *Welfare Bushed: Social Care in Rural Australia*, Ashgate, Aldershot.

Cheers, B. 1996, *Global Change and Rural People*, Monograph Series No. 2, Centre for Development Studies, Edith Cowan University, Perth.

Cheers, B. 1995, *Integrating social and economic development in regional Australia*, Critical Social Justice Paper No. 2, Centre for Social and Welfare Research, James Cook University, Townsville.

Cheers, B. & Clarke, R. 2003, 'Impacts of globalisation in rural Australia', in M. Shanahan & G. Trueren (eds.), *Globalisation: Australian Regional Perspectives*, Wakefield Press, Kent Town.

Cheers, B. & Luloff, A. 2001, 'Rural community development', in S. Lockie & L. Bourke (eds), *Rurality Bites: The Social and Environmental Transformation of Rural Australia*, Pluto Press, Annandale.

Cheers, B. & Taylor, J. 2001, 'Social work in rural and remote Australia', in M. Alston & J. McKinnon (eds) *Social Work: Fields of Practice*, Oxford University Press, Sth Melbourne.

Chesler, P. 1987, *Mothers on Trial: The Battle for Children and Custody*, McGraw-Hill, New York.

Chesterman, C. 1988, *Homes Away From Home—Final Report of the National Review of the Supported Accommodation Assistance Program prepared for the Commonwealth, State and Territory Welfare Ministers*, AGPS, Canberra.

Chesterman, J. & Galligan, B. 1997, *Citizens without Rights: Aborigines and Australian Citizenship*, Cambridge University Press, Melbourne.

Chevannes, M. 2002, 'Social construction of the managerialism of needs assessment by health and social care professionals', *Health and Social Care in the Community*, vol. 10, no. 3, pp. 168–78.

Child Wise 2004, *Annual Report July 2002–June 2003*, Child Wise, South Melbourne.

Chisholm, R. 1985, *Black Children: White Welfare? Aboriginal Child Welfare Law and Policy in New South Wales*, Social Welfare Research Centre Report and Proceedings No. 52, University of New South Wales, Sydney.

Choo, C. 1990, *Aboriginal Child Poverty*, Longman Cheshire, Melbourne.

Christie, N. 1977, 'Conflicts as property', *British Journal of Criminology*, vol. 17, no. 1, pp. 1–15.

Clark, D. 1993, 'Commodity lesbianism', in H. Abelove, M. Barale & D. Halperin (eds), *The Lesbian and Gay Studies Reader*, Routledge, New York.

Clarke, J. 1988, 'The feminisation of poverty: in search of theory', *Family Research Bulletin*, no. 16, October, pp. 7–10.

Claude, L., Bridger, J. C. & Luloff, A. E. 1999, 'Community well-being and local activeness', in P. Schaeffer & S. Loveridge (eds), *Small Town and Rural Economic Development: A Case Studies Approach*, Greenwood Press, Westport.

Cleak, H. 1995, 'Health care in the 1990s: practice implications for social work', *Australian Social Work*, vol. 48, no. 1, pp. 13–20.

Coalition of Australian Governments 1995, *Report of the Task Force on Health and Community Services*, COAG, Canberra.

Coates, J. 2004, 'From ecology to spirituality and social justice', *Currents: New Scholarship in the Human Services*, <fsw.ucalgary.ca/currents/articles/articles/coates/main.htm> (accessed 31 May 2004).

Cocks, E. 1998, *An Introduction to Intellectual Disability in Australia*, 3rd edn, Australian Institute on Intellectual Disability, Western Australia.

Cohen, H. 1980, *Equal Rights for Children*, Littlefield, Adams, Ottawa, NJ.

Commonwealth Housing Commission (Australia) 1944, *Final report of the Commonwealth Housing Commission,* Ministry of Post-War Reconstruction.

Community Services Commission 1993–94, 1995–96, 1997–98, 1998–99, *Annual Reports*.

Compton, B. & Galaway, B. 1989, 'Nature of social work', in *Social Work Processes*, 4th edn, Wadsworth, Belmont.

Considine, M. 1999, 'Markets, networks and the new welfare state: employment assistance reforms in Australia', *Journal of Social Policy*, vol. 28, no. 2, pp. 181–203.

Considine, M. 1994, *Public Policy: A Critical Introduction*, Macmillan, Melbourne.

Cooper, D. 1993, *Child Abuse Revisited: Children, Society and Social Work*, Open University Press, Buckingham.

Cooper, D. & Ball, D. 1987, *Social Work and Child Abuse*, Macmillan Education, Houndmills, Basingstoke.

Cope, B & Kalantzis, M. 1997, *Productive Diversity*, Pluto Press, Sydney.

Cope, B., Pauwels, A., Slade, D., Brosnan, D. & Neil, D. 1994a, *Local Diversity, Global Connections: Vol. 1: Six Approaches to Cross-cultural Training*, Office of Multicultural Affairs, AGPS, Canberra.

Cope, B., Pauwels, A., Slade, D., Brosnan, D. & Kalantzis, M. 1994b, *Local Diversity, Global Connections, Vol. 2: Core Principles for Effective Cross-cultural Training, A Training Manual*, Office of Multicultural Affairs, AGPS, Canberra.

Corby, B. 1993, *Child Abuse: Towards a Knowledge Base*, Open University Press, Philadelphia.

Corporate Watch 2000, <www.corpwatch.org/trac/bhopal/index.html> (accessed March 2001).

Costin, L., Bell, J. & Downs, S. 1991, *Child Welfare Policies and Practice*, Longman, New York.

Council for Aboriginal Reconciliation 1997, *Finding Common Ground: Towards a Document for Reconciliation*, July Council for Aboriginal Reconciliation, Australian Capital Territory.

Covington, C. 1979, *Justice for Children: The British Juvenile Justice System—A Historical Perspective*, Justice for Children, London.

Cox, D. & Pawar, M. (in press), *International Social Work*, Sage, California.

Cox, D., Pawar, M. & Picton, C. 1997a, *Social Development Content in Social Work Education*, Regional Social Development Centre, La Trobe University, Melbourne.

Cox, D., Pawar, M. & Picton, C. 1997b, *Introducing a Social Development Perspective into Social Work Curricula at All Levels*, Regional Social Development Centre, La Trobe University, Melbourne.

Cox, D. R. & Britto, G. A. 1986, *Social Work Curriculum Development in Asia and the Pacific: A Research Report*, Department of Social Work, University of Melbourne, Victoria.

Cox, D. R., Owen, L., Patrick, I. & Picton, C. 1993, *Counselling Returning Migrant Workers: Evaluation of Migrant Workers Repatriates Counselling Services Program in Sri Lanka Following the 1990 Gulf War*, Regional Social Development Centre, Graduate School of Social Work, La Trobe University, Victoria.

Cox, E. 1995, *A Truly Civil Society*, ABC Books, Sydney.

Cox, E. 1993, 'The economics of mutual support: a feminist approach', in S. Rees, G. Rodley & F. Stilwell (eds), *Beyond the Market: Alternatives to Economic Rationalism*, Pluto Press, Leichhardt, pp. 270–6.

Cox, E. O. & Parsons, R. J. 1994, *Empowerment-Oriented Social Work Practice with the Elderly*, Brooks/Cole, Pacific Grove.

Cox, G. 1994, *The Count and Counter Report; A Study into Hate Related Violence Against Lesbians and Gay Men*, Gay and Lesbian Rights Lobby of NSW, Sydney.

Cox, G. 1990, *The Streetwatch Report: A Study into Violence Against Lesbians and Gay Men*, Gay and Lesbian Rights Lobby of NSW, Sydney.

Craig, Y. J. 1997, *Elder Abuse and Mediation: Exploratory Studies in America, Britain and Europe*, Avebury, Aldershot, England.

Crawford, J., Kippax, S., Rodden, P., Donohoe, S. & van de Ven 1998, *Male Call 96*, National Centre in HIV Social Research, Macquarie University, Sydney.

Crewe, N. & Zola, I. (eds) 1983, *Independent Living for Physically Disabled People*, Jossey-Bass, San Francisco.

Cribb, J. 1994, 'Farewell to the heartland', *Australian Magazine*, 12–13 February, pp. 10–16.

Crime and Misconduct Commission 2004, *Protecting Children: An Inquiry into Abuse of Children in Foster Care*, Crime and Misconduct Commission. Queensland, Australia.

Crock, M. 1998, *Immigration and Refugee Law in Australia*, Federation Press, Sydney.

Crosson-Tower, C. 1989, *Understanding Child Abuse and Neglect*, Allyn & Bacon, Massachusetts.

Crow, L. 1996, 'Including all of our lives: renewing the social model of disability', in C. Barnes & G. Mercer (eds), *Exploring the Divide: Illness and Disability*, Disability Press, Leeds, pp. 55–73.

CSC, *see* Community Services Commission.

CSTDA, *see* Commonwealth of Australia and the States and Territories of Australia.

Commonwealth of Australia and the States and Territories of Australia 2003, *Commonwealth State/Territory Disability Agreement, in Relation to Disability Services 2002–2007*, FACS, Canberra.

Cunneen, C. & White, R. 2002, *Juvenile Justice: Youth and Crime in Australia*, Oxford University Press, Melbourne.

Cunningham, M. 1996, 'International trends in torture and trauma services', in *First National Conference of Services for Torture and Trauma Survivors*, STARTTS, Sydney.

Cunningham, M. & Silove, D. 1993, 'Principles of treatment and service development for torture and trauma survivors', in J. P. Wilson & B. Raphael (eds), *The International Handbook of Traumatic Stress Syndromes*, Plenum Press, New York.

Cunningham, M., Silove, D. & Storm, V. 1990, 'Counselling survivors of torture and refugee trauma', *Australian Family Physician*, vol. 19, no. 4.

Curra, J. 1994, *Understanding Social Deviance From the Near Side to the Outer Limits*, HarperCollins, New York.

Dadfar, A. 1994, 'The Afghans: bearing the scars of a forgotten war', in A. Marsella, T. Bornemann, S. Ekblad & J. Orley (eds), *Amidst Peril and Pain: The Mental Health and Well Being of the World's Refugees*, American Psychological Association, Washington DC.

Dalley, G. 1988, *Ideologies of Caring*, Macmillan, London.

Dalton, T. 1999, 'Making Housing Policy in Australia: Home Ownership and the Disengagement of the State', unpublished PhD thesis, RMIT, Melbourne.

Dalton, T. 1996, 'Participation', in A. Farrar & J. Inglis (eds), *Keeping it Together: State and Civil Society in Australia*, Pluto Press, Sydney.

Daniels, K. & Murnane, M. 1989, *Australia's Women*, University of Queensland Press, St Lucia.

Darcy, M. 2001, 'From Public Housing to Social Housing: Discourses of the State and Community After Fordism', unpublished PhD thesis, University of Sydney.

Dartington Social Research Unit 1995, *Child Protection: Messages from Research, Studies in Child Protection*, Her Majesty's Stationery Office, London.

Davenport, G. M. 1999, *Working with Toxic Older Adults: A Guide to Coping with Difficult Elders*, Springer, New York.

Davies, B. D. & Gibson, A. 1967, *The Social Education of the Adolescent*, University of London Press, London.

Davis, A. 1995, 'Managerialised health care', in S. Rees & G. Rodley (eds), *The Human Costs of Managerialism*, Pluto Press, Australia.

Davison, G. 1993, *Old People in a Young Society: Towards a History of Ageing in Australia*, Lincoln Papers in Gerontology, No. 22, Lincoln Gerontology Centre, La Trobe University, Melbourne.

Dawes, J. & Grant, A. 2002, 'Corrections', in A. Graycar & P. Grabosky (eds), *The Cambridge Handbook of Australian Criminology*, Cambridge University Press, Cambridge.

De Jong, G. 1983, 'Defining and implementing the independent living concept', in N. M. Crewe & I. K. Zola (eds), *Independent Living for Physically Disabled People*, Jossey-Bass Australia.

De Maria, W. 1997, 'Flapping on clipped wings: social work ethics in the age of activism', *Australian Social Work*, vol. 50, no. 4, pp. 3–19.

De Maria, W. 1992, 'Social work and mediation: hemlock is the flavour of the month?', *Australian Social Work*, vol. 45, no. 1.

Deakin Human Services 1999, *Education and Training Partnerships in Mental Health*, Commonwealth Department of Health and Aged Care, Canberra.

Dean, M. 1998, 'Administering asceticism: reworking the ethical life of the unemployed citizen', in M. Dean & B. Hindess, *Governing Australia*, Cambridge University Press, Sydney, pp. 87–107.

Delaney, J. J. 1976, 'New concepts of the family court', in R. E. Helfer & C. H. Kempe (eds), *Child Abuse and Neglect, the Family and Community*, Ballinger, Cambridge, MA.

Department of Community Services 1985, *New Directions: Report of the Handicapped Programs Review*, AGPS, Canberra.

Department of Families and Community Services 2004, *Australians Working Together*, <www.facs.gov.au/internet/facsinternet.nsf/whatsnew/29_9_99speech.htm> (accessed 13th June 2004).

Department of Families and Community Services 2002, *Building a Simpler System to Help Jobless Families*, <www.facs.gov.au/internet/facsinternet.nsf/aboutfacs/respubs/nav.htm> (accessed 13 June 2004).

Department of Families and Community Services 2000, *Participation Support for a More Equitable Society*, Final Report of the Reference Group on Welfare Reform, <www.facs.gov.au/welfare_reform_final/home.htm> (accessed 13 June 2004).

Department of Family and Community Services 1999a, 'ABS survey shows one in five Australians has a disability', *Disability News*, Issue 21, July, p. 8.

Department of Family and Community Services 1999b, *Strategic Plan*, July, Canberra.

Department of Family Services and Aboriginal and Islander Affairs 1994, *Remote Area Aboriginal and Torres Strait Islander Child Care Program: Services Progress Summary*, DFSAAIA, Brisbane.

Department of Foreign Affairs and Trade 2004a, *Australia Now: Australia, a Culturally Diverse Society*, DFAT, Canberra, <www.dfat.gov.au/facts/culturally_diverse.html> (accessed 30 September 2004).

Department of Foreign Affairs and Trade 2004b, *Republic of Nauru Country Brief*, DFAT, Canberra, <www.dfat.gov.au/geo/nauru/nauru_brief.html> (accessed 29 October 2004).

Department of Health 2000, *Framework for the Assessment of Children in Need and Their Families*, The Stationery Office, Norwich.

Department of Health and Family Services 1997, *Contact Tracing Manual*, AGPS, Canberra.

Department of Human Services and Health 1995, *Youth Suicide in Australia: A Background Monograph*, AGPS, Canberra.

Department of Immigration and Multicultural and Indigenous Affairs 2004a, *Australian Multicultural Policy*, DIMIA, Canberra, <www.immi.gov.au/multicultural/australian> (accessed 16 September 2004).

Department of Immigration and Multicultural and Indigenous Affairs 2004b, *Fact Sheet 7: Productive Diversity: Australia's Competitive Advantage*, DIMIA, Canberra, <www.immi.gov.au/facts/07productive.htm> (accessed 22 September 2004).

Department of Immigration and Multicultural and Indigenous Affairs 2004c, *Immigration Detention Facilities*, DIMIA, Canberra, <www.immi.gov.au /detention/facilities.htm> (accessed 29 October 2004).

Department of Immigration and Multicultural and Indigenous Affairs 2003, *Multicultural Australia: United in diversity: Updating the 1999 New Agenda for Multicultural Australia: Strategic directions for 2003–2006*, Canberra, <www.immi.gov.au/multicultural/_inc/pdf_doc/united_diversity/united_diversity.pdf> (accessed 16 September 2004).

Department of Prime Minister and Cabinet 1992, *The Findings of the Housing and Locational Choice Survey*, AGPS, Canberra.

Deutsch, L. 1995, 'Out of the closet and on to the couch: a psychoanalytic exploration of lesbian development', in J. Glassgold & S. Iasceza (eds), *Lesbians and Psychoanalysis*, Free Press, New York.

Devore, W. & Schlesinger, E. G. 1981, *Ethnic-sensitive Social Work Practice*, Mosby, St Louis.

DFAT, *see* Department of Foreign Affairs and Trade.

DFCS, *see* Department of Family and Community Services.

DFSAAIA, *see* Department of Family Services and Aboriginal and Islander Affairs.

Dickey, B. 1987, *No Charity There: A Short History of Social Welfare in Australia*, Allen & Unwin, North Sydney.

DIMIA, *see* Department of Immigration and Multicultural and Indigenous Affairs.

Dingwall, R., Eekelaar, J. & Murray, T. 1983, *The Protection of Children: State Intervention and Family Life*, Basil Blackwell, Oxford.

Dobash, R. & Dobash, R. 1979, *Violence Against Wives: A Case Against Patriarchy*, Open Books, London.

Dodds, I. 2004, 'Condolences on the passing of Prof Norma Parker', email, April 16.

Dodds, I. 1997, 'Social work: the year 2000 and beyond', in *Social Work Influencing Outcomes*, Proceedings of the 25th AASW National Conference, AASW, Canberra.

Dominelli, L. 2002. *Feminist Social Work Theory and Practice*, Palgrave, Basingstoke, Hampshire.

Dominelli, L. 1997a, *Anti-Racist Social Work*, 2nd edn, Macmillan, London.

Dominelli, L. 1997b, *Sociology for Social Work*, Macmillan, London.

Dominelli, L. 1991, 'Race, gender and social work', in M. Davies (ed.), *The Sociology of Social Work*, Routledge, London, pp. 82–201.

Donzelot, J. 1979, *The Policing of Families: Welfare Versus the State*, Hutchinson, London.

Dovers, S. 2001, 'Institutions for Sustainability', *TELA—environment, economy and society issue*, Centre for Resource and Environmental Studies. Australian National University, Canberra.

Doyle, R. 2001, 'Social work practice in an ethnically and racially diverse Australia', in M. Alston & J. McKinnon (eds), *Social work: Fields of Practice*, Oxford University Press, Melbourne, pp. 58–68.

Draper, M. 1995, 'In sickness and health', in W. Weeks & J. Wilson (eds), *Issues Facing Australian Families*, (2nd edn), Longman Cheshire, Melbourne, pp. 343–61.

Driggs, J. & Finn, S. 1991, *Intimacy Between Men*, Plume, Penguin, New York.

Drucker, D. 2003, 'Whither International Social Work? A Reflection', *International Social Work*, vol. 46, no. 1, pp. 43–81.

DSRU, *see* Dartington Social Research Unit.

Du Rant, R., Krowcbuk, D. & Sinal, S. 1998, 'Victimization, use of violence, and drug use at school among male adolescents who engage in same-sex sexual behavior', *Journal of Pediatrics*, vol. 133, no. 1, pp. 113–18.

Dudgeon, P. 2000, 'Counselling with indigenous people', in P. Dudgeon, D. Garvey & H. Pickett (eds), *Working with Indigenous Australians: A Handbook For Psychologists*, Gunada Press, Curtin Indigenous Research Centre Curtin University Of Technology, Perth, pp. 249–70.

Durby, D. 1994, 'Gay, lesbian and bisexual youth', in T. DeCrescenzo (ed.), *Helping Gay and Lesbian Youth*, Harrington Park Press, Binghamton.

Duthu, K. 1996, 'Why doesn't anyone talk about gay and lesbian domestic violence?', *Thomas Jefferson Law Review*, vol. 18, no. 1, pp. 23–40.

Earth Charter Initiative 2000, *The Earth Charter*, The Earth Council, San Jose, Costa Rica.

Economic and Social Committee of the European Union 2000, *Opinion of the Economic and Social Committee on the Communication from the Commission—Europe's Environment: What Directions for the Future*, European Union, Brussels.

Eekelaar, J. 1994, 'The interest of the child and the child's wishes: the role of dynamic self determinism', in P. Alston, S. Parker & J. Seymour (eds), *The Best Interest of the Child: Reconciling Culture and Human Rights*, UNICEF, Clarendon Press, Oxford, pp. 42–61.

Egan, J. 2000, 'Lonely gay teen seeking same', *New York Times Magazine*, December 10, pp. 110–17, 128, 130–3.

Eisen, P. & Wolfenden, K. 1988, *A National Mental Health Services Policy*, report to Australian Health Ministers Advisory Council, (limited circulation).

Ekins, P. 1992, *A New World Order: Grassroots Movements for Social Change*, Routledge, London.

Elliott, D. 1993, 'Social work and social development: towards an integrative model for social work practice', *International Social Work*, vol. 36.

Engel, G. 1980, 'The clinical application of the biopsychosocial Model', *American Journal of Psychiatry*, vol. 137, no. 5, pp. 25–34.

Epps, R. & Sorensen, T. (eds) 1993, *Prospects and Policies for Rural Australia*, Longman Cheshire, Melbourne.

Epps, W. 1918, *The Story of an Australian Hospital*, S. D. Townsend, Sydney.

Epstein, M. & Shaw, J. 1997, *Developing Effective Consumer Participation in Mental Health Services: The Lemon Tree Project*, Victorian Mental Illness Advisory Council, Melbourne.

Evatt, E. 1996, 'Coping in the age of torture', in *First National Conference of Services for Torture and Trauma Survivors*, STARTTS, Sydney.

FACS, *see* Department of Family and Community Services.

Falloon, I., Boyd, J. & McGill, C. 1984, *Family Care of Schizophrenia*, Guilford Press, New York.

FamCA 2002, Family Court of Australia at Melbourne *Re. Patrick* (An Application concerning contact) ML 10036 of 1999, Melbourne.

Faria, G. 1997, 'The challenge of health care social work with gay men and lesbians', *Social Work in Health Care*, vol. 25, no. 1, pp. 65–72.

Farmer, E. & Owen, M. 1995, *Child Protection Practice: Private Risks and Public Remedies—Decision Making Intervention and Outcome in Child Protection Work*, Her Majesty's Stationery Office, London.

Ferguson, B. 1991, 'Concepts models and theories for immigrant health care', in B. Ferguson & E. Browne (eds), *Health Care and Immigrants: A Guide for the Helping Professions*, MacLennan & Petty, Australia.

Ferguson, H. 1997, 'Protecting children in new times: child protection and the risk society', *Child and Family Social Work*, no. 24, pp. 221–34.

Ferguson, J. & Simpson, R. 1995, *The Australian Rural Labour Market*, Discussion Paper, National Farmers' Federation, Barton, ACT.

Fernandez, E. 2003, *Protecting Children By Strengthening Families: A Study of Outcomes of Intervention Through Children's Family Centres*, University of New South Wales, Sydney.

Fernandez, E. 1998, 'Realities of women's caring: rethinking child welfare interventions', in E. Fernandez, K. Heycox, L. Hughes & M. Wilkinson (eds), *Women Participating in Global Change*, International Association of Schools of Social Work, Women's Symposium.

Fernandez, E. 1996, *Significant Harm: Unravelling Child Protection Decisions and Substitute Care Careers of Children*, Ashgate, England.

Fernandez, E. 1990, 'The cultural basis of child rearing', in B. Ferguson & E. Browne (eds), *Health Care and Immigrants: A Guide for the Helping Professions*, McLennan & Petty, NSW, pp. 97–121.

Fernandez, E. & Romeo, R. 2003, *Implementation of the Framework for the Assessment of Children in Need and their Families: The Experience of Barnardos Australia*, University of New South Wales, Sydney, Australia.

Fincher, R. & Nieuwenhuysen, J. 1998, *Australian Poverty: Then and Now*, Melbourne University Press, Melbourne.

Finger, A. 1990, *Past Due: A Story of Disability, Pregnancy and Birth*, Seal Press, USA.

Finklehor, D. 1996, 'Introduction', in J. Briere, L. Berliner, J. A. Bulkey, C. Jenny & T. Reid (eds), *The APSAC Handbook on Child Maltreatment*, Sage, California.

Flora, J. L. 1998, 'Social capital and communities of place', *Rural Sociology*, vol. 63, no. 1, pp. 481–506.

Flora, J. L., Sharp, J., Flora, C. & Newlon, B. 1997, 'Entrepreneurial social infrastructure and locally initiated economic development in the nonmetropolitan United States', *The Sociological Quarterly*, vol. 38, no. 4, pp. 623–45.

Fook, J. 1993, *Radical Casework: A Theory of Practice*, Allen & Unwin, Sydney.

Fook, J. 1986, 'Feminist contributions to casework practice', in H. Marchant & B. Wearing (eds), *Gender Reclaimed: Women in Social Work*, Hale & Iremonger, Sydney.

Fotheringham, M. J. & Sawyer, M. G. 1995, 'Do adolescents know where to find help for mental health problems? A brief report', *Journal of Paediatric and Child Health*, vol. 31, pp. 41–3.

Foucault, M. 1986, 'Disciplinary power and subjection', in S. Lukes (ed.), *Power*, Basil Blackwell, Oxford.

Foucault, M. 1980, *Power/Knowledge: Selected Interviews and Other Writings, 1972–1977*, C. Gordon (ed.), Pantheon, New York.

Franklin, B. (ed.) 1986, *The Rights of Children*, Blackwell, London.

Frederico, M., Cooper, C. & Picton, C. 1997, *The Experience of Homelessness Among Young People From Cambodia, Laos and Vietnam*, Department of Immigration and Multicultural Affairs, Canberra.

Freedman, L. & Stark, L. 1993, 'When the white system doesn't fit', *Australian Social Work*, vol. 46, no. 1, March, pp. 29–36.

Freeman, M. D. A. 1987, 'Taking children's rights seriously', *Children and Society*, vol. 1, no. 4, Winter, pp. 299–319.

Freire, P. 1970, *Pedagogy of the Oppressed*, Seabury, New York.

French, S. 1993, 'Disability, impairment or something in between?', in J. Swain, V. Finkelstein, S. French & M. Oliver (eds), *Disabling Barriers—Enabling Environments*, Sage, London, pp. 17–25.

Friedlander, W. 1955, *Introduction to Social Welfare*, Prentice Hall, New York.

Frost, N. & Stein, M. 1989, *The Politics of Child Welfare: Inequality, Power and Change*, Harvester/Wheatsheaf, London.

Gaha, J. 1999, 'Promoting inclusion—redressing exclusion—the social work challenge', 1999 Norma Parker Address (unpub.), Brisbane.

Gamble, D. & Weil, M. 1997, 'Sustainable development: the challenge for community development', *Community Development Journal*, vol. 32, no. 3, pp. 210–22.

Garbarino, J. & Barry, F. 1997, 'The community context of child abuse and neglect', in J. Garbarino & J. Eckenrode (eds), *Understanding Abusive Families: An Ecological Approach to the Theory and Practice*, Jossey Bass, California.

Garnaut, J. & Lim-Applegate, H. 1998, *People in Farming*, ABARE Research Report 98.6, Commonwealth of Australia, Canberra.

Garnets, L., Herek, G. & Levy, B. 1993, 'Violence and victimisation of lesbians and gay men: mental health consequences', in L. Garnets & D. Kimmel (eds), *Psychological Perspectives on Lesbian and Gay Male Experiences*, Columbia University Press, New York City.

Garnets, L. & Kimmel, D. 1993, 'Lesbian and gay male dimensions in the psychological study of human diversity', in L. Garnets & D. Kimmel (eds), *Psychological Perspectives on Lesbian and Gay Male Experiences*, Columbia University Press, New York.

Garofalo, R., Wolf, R., Kessel, S., Palfrey, J. & Du Rant, R. 1998, 'The association between health risk behaviors and sexual orientation among a school-based sample of adolescents', *Pediatrics*, vol. 101, pp. 895–902.

Garton, S. 1994, 'Rights and duties: arguing charity and welfare 1880–1920', in M. Wearing & R. Berreen (eds), *Welfare and Social Policy in Australia: The Distribution of Advantage*, Harcourt Brace, Marrickville.

Garton, S. 1990, *Out of Luck: Poor Australians and Social Welfare 1788–1988*, Allen & Unwin, Sydney.

Gay & Lesbian Rights Lobby 2004a, <www.glrl.org.au/publications/major_reports.htm> (accessed October 2004).

Gay & Lesbian Rights Lobby 2004b, <www.glrl.org.au/> (accessed October 2004).

Gay and Lesbian Rights Lobby of NSW 1994, *The Bride Wore Pink: Legal Recognition of Our Relationships Discussion Paper*, Gay and Lesbian Rights Lobby, Sydney.

Gay & Lesbian Rights Lobby, Victoria 2004, http://home.vicnet.net.au/> (accessed October 2004)

Gay Men and Lesbians Against Discrimination 1994, *Not a Day Goes By: Report on the GLAD Survey into Discrimination and Violence Against Lesbians and Gay Men in Victoria*, GLAD Melbourne.

George, J. & Davis, A. 1998, *States of Health: Health and Illness in Australia*, (3rd edn), Addison Wesley Longman, Australia.

Germain, C. & Gitterman, A. 1996, *The Life Model of Social Work Practice: Advances in Theory and Practice*, New York, Columbia University Press.

Gibbons, J., Conroy, S. & Bell, C. 1995, *Operating The Child Protection System*, HMSO, London.

Giddens, A. 1994, *Beyond Left and Right Politics*, Polity Press, Cambridge.

Gil, D. G. 1998, *Confronting injustice and oppression: Concepts and strategies for social workers*, Columbia University Press, New York.

Gil, D. G. 1979, *Child Abuse and Violence*, AMS Press, New York.

Gil, D. G. 1975, 'Unravelling child abuse', *American Journal of Orthopsychiatry*, vol. 45, pp. 346–56.

Gilding, M. 1991, *The Making and the Breaking of the Australian Family*, Allen & Unwin, Sydney.

Gillies, C. & James, A. 1994, *Reminiscence Work With Old People*, Chapman & Hall, London.

Gimenez, M. 1999, 'The Feminization of Poverty: Myth or Reality?', *Critical Sociology*, vol. 45, no. 2, July, pp. 333–5.

Giovannoni, J. M. & Becerra, R. M. 1979, *Defining Child Abuse*, Free Press, New York.

GLAD, *see* Gay Men and Lesbians Against Discrimination.

Global 2000 Revisited 1997, *An Overview*, <www.igc.apc.org/millenium/g2000r/overview.html#choice> (accessed March 2000).

GLRL, *see* Gay & Lesbian Rights Lobby.

Goddard, C. R. 1996, *Child Abuse and Child Protection*, Pearson, Australia.

Goddard, C. & Briskman, L. 2004, 'By any measure, it's official child abuse', *Children out of Detention*, <www.chilout.org/news/by_any_measure.html) (accessed 30 October 2004), (this article first appeared in the Melbourne *Herald Sun*, 18 February 2004).

Goldman, M. & Schurman, R. 2001, 'Closing the "Great Divide": new social theory on society and nature', *Annual Review of Sociology 2000*, pp. 563–84.

Goldney, R. C. & Harrison, J. 1998, 'Suicide in the elderly: some good news', *Australasian Journal on Ageing*, vol. 17, no. 2, pp. 54–5.

Goodman, J. 1997, 'Scapegoating and surveillance: unemployment policy in Australia', *Arena*, February–March, pp. 20–4.

Gordon, L. 1985, 'Child abuse, gender and the myth of family independence: a historical critique', *Child Welfare*, vol. 64, no. 3, pp. 213–24.

Government of Western Australia 1994, *Guardianship and Administration: A Guide for Service Providers who Work in the Fields of Medical and Health Care, Aged Care, Disability Services, Social Work, Welfare and Community Services*, Public Guardian's Office, Perth.

Gramick J. 1983, 'Homophobia: a new challenge', *Social Work*, vol. 28, pp. 137–41.

Graycar, A. & Grabosky, P. (eds) 2002, *The Cambridge Handbook of Australian Criminology*, Cambridge University Press, Cambridge.

Graycar, A. & Jamrozik, A. 1993, *How Australians Live: Social Policy in Theory and Practice*, 2nd edn, Macmillan, Melbourne.

Gregory, B. & Hunter, B. 1996, 'Increasing regional inequality and the decline of manufacturing', in P. Sheehan, B. Grewal & M. Kumnick (eds), *Dialogues on Australia's Future*, Centre for Strategic Economic Studies, Victoria University, pp. 307–24.

Gregory, B., King, E. & Martin, Y. M. 1999, 'Labour market deregulation, relative wages and the social security system', in S. Richardson (ed.), *Reshaping the Labour Market*, Cambridge University Press, Sydney, pp. 200–22.

Greig, A. W. 1995, *The Stuff Dreams Are Made Of: Housing Provision in Australia 1945–1960*, University of Melbourne Press, Melbourne.

Griffin, J. 1997, 'Anti-lesbian/gay violence in schools', in G. Mason & S. Tomsen, *Homophobic Violence*, Hawkins Press, Sydney.

Griffin, J. 1994, *The Schoolwatch Report: A Study into Anti-Lesbian and Gay Harassment and Violence in Australian Schools*, Gay and Lesbian Family Association, Sydney.

Grint, K. 1993, *The Sociology of Work*, Polity Press, Cambridge.

Grossman, A., D'Augelli, A. & O'Connell, T. 2001, 'Being lesbian, gay, bisexual, and 60 or older in North America', *Journal of Gay & Lesbian Social Services*, vol. 13, no. 4, pp. 23–40.

Gursansky, D., Harvey, J. & Kennedy, R. 2003, *Case Management: Policy, Practice and Professional Business*, Allen & Unwin, Sydney.

Hage, G. 1998, *White Nation: Fantasies of White Supremacy in a Multicultural Society*, Pluto Press, Sydney.

Hall, J. & Berry, M. 2004, *Operating deficits and Public Housing: Policy Options for Reversing the Trend*, AHURI (RMIT–NATSEM Research Centre).

Hall, J. & Berry, M. 2002, *Risk Management and Efficient Housing Assistance Provision*, AHURI (RMIT & Sydney University Research Centres).

Hamilton, Clive 2003, *Growth Fetish*, Allen & Unwin, Crows Nest.

Hammond, G. & Jilek, R. 2003, 'Caring for the Aged', *The Australian Women's Weekly*.

Hanmer, J. & Statham, D. 1999, *Women and Social Work: Towards a Woman Centred Practice* (2nd edn). Macmillan, London.

Hanmer, J. & Statham, D. 1988, *Women and Social Work: Towards a Woman Centred Practice*, Macmillan, London.

Hanson, P. 1996, *Maiden speech*, September, <www.gwb.com.au /gwb/news/onenation/phsm/maiden.htm> (accessed January 2000).

Harding, A., Lloyd, R. & Greenwell, H. 2001, *Financial Disadvantage in Australia—1990 to 2000*, The Smith Family, <www.natsem.canberra.edu.au/pubs/poverty01.html> (accessed January 2002).

Harris, R. 1997, 'Social work and society', in M. Davies (ed.), *The Blackwell Companion to Social Work*, Blackwell, Oxford, pp. 8–24.

Harris, R. 1990, 'Beyond rhetoric: a challenge for international social work', *International Social Work*, vol. 33.

Harrison, J. 1999, 'A lavender pink grey power: gay and lesbian gerontology in Australia', *Australasian Journal on Ageing*, vol. 18, no. 1, February, pp. 32–7.

Hart, J. 1997, 'Care issues of people living with HIV/Aids in a province in north-east Thailand', in *Proceedings of Asia & Pacific Regional Conference of APASWE & IFSW Asia Pacific: Enhancing Social Integration: Structure, Process and Intervention for Social Development*, Bangkok.

Hartley, R. (ed.) 1995, *Families and cultural diversity in Australia*, Allen & Unwin, Sydney.

Hartley, R. & Woolcott, I. 1994, *The Position of Young People in Relation to the Family*, National Clearinghouse for Youth Studies, Australian Institute of Family Studies, Tasmania.

Hartmann, F. 1998, 'Towards a social ecological politics of sustainability', in R. Keil, D. Bell, P. Penz & L. Fawcett (eds), *Political Ecology: Global and Local*, Routledge, New York.

Hatfield, A. 1987, 'Families as caregivers: a historical perspective', in A. Hatfield & H. Lefley (eds), *Families of the Mentally Ill—Coping and Adaptation*, Guilford Press, New York.

Hawkins, J. D. & Catalano, R. F. 1992, *Communities that Care: Action for Drug Abuse Prevention*, Jossey-Bass, San Francisco.

Hayward, D. 1996, 'The reluctant landlords? A history of public housing in Australia', *Urban Policy and Research*, vol. 14, no. 1, pp. 5–35.

Healy, B. 1998, 'Social development: a key idea for mental heath policy and practice', in *Abstracts of Joint World Congress of IFSW/IASSW Peace and Social Justice—The Challenges Facing Social Work*, Jerusalem.

Healy, J. 1990, 'Community services: long-term care at home', in H. Kendig & J. McCallum (eds), *Grey Policy: Australian Policies for an Ageing Society*, Allen & Unwin, Sydney.

Healy, L. M. 2001, *International Social Work: Professional Action in an Interdependent World*, Oxford University Press, New York.

Healy, L. M. 1995, 'Comparative and international overview', in T. D. Watts, D. Elliott & N. Mayadas (eds), *International Handbook on Social Work Education*, Greenwood Press, Connecticut.

Heilbroner, R. 1991, *The Worldly Philosophers,* Penguin, London.

Heller, B. W., Flohr, L. M. & Zegans, L. S. (eds) 1989, 'Psychosocial interventions with physically disabled persons', *Mind and Medicine*, vol. 16, no. 259.

Hendricks, J. (ed.) 1995, *The Meaning of Reminiscence and Life Review*, Baywood, Amityville, New York.

Hepworth, D. & Larsen, J. 1997, *Direct Social Work Practice*, Wadsworth, Belmont.

Herek, G. 1993, 'The context of antigay violence: notes on cultural and psychological heterosexism', in L. Garnets & D. Kimmel (eds), *Psychological Perspectives on Lesbian and Gay Male Experiences*, Columbia University Press, New York.

Herman, J. 1992, *Trauma and Recovery*, HarperCollins, New York.

Hershberger, S., Pilkington, N. & D'Augelli, A. 1997, 'Predictors of suicide attempts among gay, lesbian and bisexual youth', *Journal of Adolescent Research*, vol. 12, no. 4, pp. 477–97.

Hill, M. & Tisdall, K. 1997, *Children and Society*, Addison Wesley Longman, UK.

Hinman, L. M. 2003, *Ethics: A Pluralist Approach to Moral Theory*, 3rd edn, Harcourt Brace

Hodges, V. G. 1991, 'Providing culturally sensitive intensive family preservation services to ethnic minority families', in E. M. Tracy, D. A. Haapala, J. Kinney & P. J. Pecora (eds), *Intensive Family Preservation Services: An Instructional Sourcebook*, Mandel School of Applied Social Sciences, Case Western Reserve University, Cleveland, pp. 95–116.

Hodgson, L. 2004, 'Manufactured civil society: counting the cost', *Critical Social Policy*, vol. 24, no. 2, pp. 139–64.

Hoff, M. & Polack, R. 1993, 'Social dimensions of the environmental crisis: challenges for social work', *Social Work*, vol. 38, no. 2, pp. 204–9.

Hogan, P. T. & Siu, S. F. 1988, 'Minority children and the child welfare system: an historical perspective', *Social Work*, vol. 33, pp. 493–8.

Hoge, R. D. & Andrews, D. A. 1995, Australian Adaptation of Youth Level of Service/Case Management Inventory: Multi-Health Systems Inc.: New York.

Hoge, R. D. & Andrews, D. A. 1996, *Assessing the Youthful Offender: Issues and Techniques*, Plenum, New York.

Hokenstad, M. C., Khinduka, S. K. & Midgley, J. 1992, *Profiles in International Social Work*, National Association of Social Workers, Washington DC.

Holt, J. 1975, *Escape from Childhood: The Needs and Rights of Children*, Penguin, Harmondsworth.

Horne, M. 1997, *Values in Social Work*, Wildwood House, Aldershot, England.

Horsburgh, M. 1977, 'Child care in New South Wales in 1870', *Australian Social Work*, vol. 29, no. 1, pp. 3–24.

Hosking, P. (ed.) 1990, *Hope After Horror: Helping Survivors of Torture and Trauma*, UNIYA, Sydney.

Hough, G. 1995, 'Dismantling child welfare', in S. Rees & G. Rodley (eds), *The Human Costs of Managerialism: Advocating the Recovery of Humanity*, Pluto Press, Leichhardt, pp. 173–82.

Howard, J. 1999a, 'Transcript of the Prime Minister, The Hon. John Howard, MP, Motion of Reconciliation', press release.

Howard, J. 1999b, 'Building a stronger and fairer Australia: liberalisation in economic policy and modern conservatism in social policy', paper presented to the Australian Unlimited Roundtable, <www.pm.gov.au/news/speeches/99/australiaunlimitedroundtable.htm> (accessed May 2000).

Howden, P. 2002, 'Indicators of Social Sustainability', *Natural Resources Management Strategy*, Murray-Darling Basin Commission, Canberra.

Howe, A. L. 1990, 'Gerontology in Australia: the development of the discipline', *Educational Gerontology*, vol. 16, no. 2, pp. 125–49.

Howitt, D. 1992, *Child Abuse Errors: When Good Intentions Go Wrong*, Harvester Wheatsheaf, England.

HREOC, *see* Human Rights and Equal Opportunities Commission.

Hughes, B. 1995, *Older people and Community Care: Critical Theory and Practice*, Open University Press, Buckingham, England.

Hugman, R. 1998, *Social Welfare and Social Value*, Macmillan, Houndsmill.

Human Rights and Equal Opportunity Commission 2004, *National Inquiry into Children in Immigration Detention*, <www.humanrights.gov.au/human_rights/children_detention_report/report/> (accessed October 2004).

Human Rights and Equal Opportunities Commission 1997, *Bringing Them Home: National Inquiry into the Separation of Aboriginal and Torres Strait Islander Children from their Families*, Commonwealth of Australia, Canberra.

Hunt, J. 1992, 'Defining a sustainable society', in J. Anderson (ed.), *Education for a Sustainable Society; Papers Presented at the 31st National Conference of the Australian College of Education*, Canberra.

Hutchinson, E. D. 1990, 'Child maltreatment: can it be defined', *Social Service Review*, March, pp. 60–78.

Hutton, W. 1999, in C. Macintyre, 'From entitlement to obligation in the Australian welfare state', *Australian Journal of Social Issues*, vol. 34, no. 2.

IASSW, *see* International Association of Schools of Social Work.

Ife, J. 1988, 'Social work education for an uncertain future', in E. Chamberlain (ed.), *Change and Continuity in Australian Social Work*, Longman Cheshire, Melbourne.

Ife, J. 1997a, 'Realising the purpose of social work for stakeholders—maintaining the vision and making a difference in a world of change', *Conference Proceedings—25th AASW National Conference*, 1997, Australian National University, Canberra.

Ife, J. 1997b, *Rethinking Social Work: Towards Critical Practice*, Longman Cheshire, South Melbourne.

Ife, J. 1995, *Community Development*, Longman, Melbourne.

IFSW, *see* International Federation of Social Workers.

International Federation of Social Workers 1982, in IFSW 1996, 'Definition of the Social Work Profession', paper for IFSW General Meeting, Hong Kong.

Industry Commission, Commonwealth of Australia 1995, *Charitable Organisations in Australia*, AGPS, Melbourne.

Irwin, H. 1996, *Communicating with Asia: Understanding People & Customs*, Allen & Unwin, Sydney.

Irwin, I., Winter, B., Gregoric, M. & Watts, S. 1995, *As Long As I've Got My Doona: A Report on Lesbian and Gay Youth Homelessness*, Twenty-Ten Association Inc. and Australian Centre for Lesbian and Gay Research, University of Sydney, New South Wales.

Island, D. & Letellier, P. 1991, *The Men Who Beat the Men Who Love Them*, Haworth Press, New York.

Jack, G. 1997, 'Discourses of child protection and child welfare', *British Journal of Social Work*, no. 27, pp. 659–78.

Jackson, S. 1989, 'Child protection: the current debate', *Family Research Bulletin*, vol. 17, March, pp. 11–13.

Jackson, V. R. (ed.) 1995, *Volunteerism in Geriatric Settings*, Haworth Press, New York.

Jamrozik, A. 2003, *Social Policy in the Post-Welfare State*, Pearson Education, Melbourne.

Jamrozik, A. 2001, *Social Policy in the Post-Welfare State*, Pearson Education, Melbourne.

Jamrozik, A. 1994, 'From Harvester to deregulation', *Australian Journal of Social Issues*, vol. 29, no. 2, pp. 162–70.

Jamrozik, A. 1986, 'Cross cultural issues in child abuse and neglect: implications for methods of intervention', paper given at the 6th International Congress on Child Abuse and Neglect, Sydney.

Jamrozik, A. & Boland, C. 1989, 'Social welfare policy for a multicultural society', in J. Jupp (ed.), *The Challenge of Diversity: Policy Options for a Multicultural Australia*, AGPS, Canberra, pp. 218–29.

Jamrozik, A. & Nocella, L. 1998, *The Sociology of Social Problems*, Cambridge University Press, Sydney.

Jamrozik, A., Boland, C. & Urquhart, R. 1995, *Social change and cultural transformation in Australia*, Cambridge University Press, Melbourne.

Janeway, E. 1971, *Man's World, Women's Place: A Study in Social Mythology*, Dell, New York.

Jenkins, S. & Diamond, B. 1985, 'Ethnicity and foster care: census data as predictors of placement variables', *American Journal of Orthopsychiatry*, vol. 55, pp. 267–76.

Job, E. 1994, *The Experience of Ageing: Men Grow Old Too*, University of New England Press, Armidale.

Johannesen, T. 1997, 'Social work as an international profession', in M. C. Hokenstad & J. Midgley (eds), *Issues in International Social Work: Global Challenges for a New Century*, NASW Press, Washington DC.

Johnson, D. 1996, 'The developmental experience of gay/lesbian youth', *Journal of College Admission*, Summer/Fall edition, pp. 38–41.

Johnson, T. F. (ed.) 1995, *Elder Mistreatment: Ethical Issues, Dilemmas, and Decisions*, Haworth Press, New York.

Jones, A. 1994, 'Anti-racist child protection', in T. David (ed.), *Protecting Children from Abuse: Multi-Professionalism and the Children Act 1989*, Trentham Books, England, pp. 25–38.

Jones, M. 1996, *The Australian Welfare State: Evaluating Social Policy*, 4th edn, Allen & Unwin, St Leonards.

Jonson, H. & Magnusson, J. 2001, 'A new age of old age?: Gerotranscendence and the re-enchantment of aging', *Journal of Aging Studies*, vol. 15, no. 4, pp. 317–32.

Jordan, W. 1997, 'Social work and society', in M. Dawes (ed.), *The Blackwell Companion to Social Work*, Blackwell, Oxford.

Jupp, J. 1989, 'Introduction', in J. Jupp (ed.), *The Challenge of Diversity: Policy Options for a Multicultural Australia*, AGPS, Canberra, pp. 1–3.

Kalantzis, M. 2001, *Recognising diversity*, Barton Lecture No. 3, NSW Centenary of Federation Committee, <www.zulenet.com/see/MaryKalantzis.html> (accessed 30 September 2004).

Kammerman, S. 1995, 'Fields of practice', in C. H. Meyer & M. Mattaini (eds), *The Foundations of Social Work Practice*, NASW Press, USA.

Kanter, A. S. 2003, 'The globalization of disability rights law', *Syracuse Journal of International Law and Commerce*, vol. 30, no. 2, Summer, pp. 241–69.

Karger, H. J. & Midgley, J. (eds) 1994, *Controversial Issues in Social Work*, Allyn & Bacon, Sydney.

Kayess, R. 1993, 'Independence: doing or deciding?', *Quad Wrangle*, Spring, pp. 2–4.

Keating, P. 1994, *Working Nation: The White Paper on Employment and Growth*, AGPS, Canberra.

Kendall, K. A. 2000, *Social Work Education. Its Origins in Europe*, Council on Social Work Education, Alexandria.

Khadra, M. H. 1998, 'What price, compassion?', *Medical Journal of Australia*, vol. 169, pp. 42–3.

Kiddle, M. 1950, *Caroline Chisholm*, Melbourne University Press, Melbourne.

King, A. 1998, 'Income poverty since the early 1970s', in R. Fincher & J. Nieuwenhuysen (eds), *Australian Poverty: Then and Now*, Melbourne University Press, Melbourne.

King, B. & Maplestone, P. 1998, 'Payment for a radical social experiment? A report on the employment assistance market', unpublished School of Social Work placement report, University of New South Wales, Sydney, p. 14.

King, M. & Trowell, J. 1992, *Children's Welfare and the Law: The Limits of Legal Intervention*, Sage, London.

Kirk, S. & Einbinder, S. 1994, *Controversial Issues in Mental Health*, Allyn & Bacon, Needham Hts, MA.

Kisker, G. 1964, *The Disorganized Personality*, McGraw-Hill, New York.

Knight, B., Chigudu, H. & Tandon, R. 2002, *Rewriting Democracy: Citizens at the Heart of Governance*, Earthscan Publications Ltd, London.

Knight, J. 1998, 'Models of health', in J. Germov (ed.), *Second Opinion*, Oxford University Press, Melbourne.

Koht, H. 1931, *Nineteen-Thirty-One Peace Prize Presentation Speech*, <http://nobel.sdsc.edu/laureates/peace-1931.html> (accessed October 2004).

Korbin, J. E. 1994, 'Sociocultural factors in child maltreatment', in G. B. Melton & J. D. Barry (eds), *Protecting Children from Abuse and Neglect: Foundations for a New National Strategy*, Guilford Press, New York.

Korbin, J. E. 1987, 'Child Abuse and neglect: the cultural context', in R. E. Helper & R. S. Kempe (eds), *The Battered Child*, University of Chicago Press, Chicago, pp. 23–41.

Krupinski, J. & Burrows, G. 1986, *The Price of Freedom: Young Indochinese Refugees in Australia*, Pergamon, New York.

Krupinski, J., Stoller, A. & Wallace, L. 1973, 'Psychiatric disorders in East European refugees now in Australia', *Social Science and Medicine*, vol. 7, pp. 31–49.

Kubler-Ross, E. 1978, *On Death and Dying*, Tavistock, London.

La Brake, T. 1996, *How to Get Families More Involved in the Nursing Home: Four Programs that Work and Why*, Haworth Press, New York.

La Prairie, C. 1995, 'Altering course, new directions in criminal justice, sentencing circles and family group conferences', *Australian and New Zealand Journal of Criminology*, vol. 28, pp. 78–99.

Laming, L. 2003, *The Victoria Climbie Inquiry*, HMSO, St Clements House, UK.

Langan, M. & Day, L. 1999, *Women, Oppression and Social Work: Issues in Anti-Discrimination Practice*, Routledge, New York.

Langmore, J. 1998, 'Globalisation and social policy', address to the 2nd International Conference on Social Work in Health and Mental Health, University of Melbourne, January.

Larbalestier, J. 1996, 'Symbolic violence: reflections on the violence or representation in social and welfare work', in R. Thorpe & J. Irwin (eds), *Women and Violence: Working for Change*, Hale & Iremonger, Sydney.

Latham, M. 1992, 'An unreliable witness? Legal views of the sexual assault complainant', in J. Breckenridge & M. Carmody (eds), *Crimes of Violence: Australian Responses to Rape and Child Sexual Assault*, Allen & Unwin, Sydney.

Latham, M. 1998a, 'Social capital and the need for devolution', *Family Matters*, Australian Institute of Family Studies, no. 50, Winter.

Latham, M. 1998b, *Civilising Global Capital: New Thinking for Australian Labor*, Allen & Unwin, Sydney.

Lavery, G. 1986, 'The rights of children in care', in R. Franklin (ed.), *The Rights of Children*, Basil Blackwell, Oxford, pp. 73–96.

Lawrence, G. 1995, *Futures for Rural Australia: From Agricultural Productivism to Community Sustainability*, Rural Social and Economic Research Centre, Central Queensland University, Rockhampton.

Lawrence, G. & Hungerford, L. 1994, 'Rural restructuring: sociological meaning, social impacts and policy implications', in D. McSwan & M. McShane (eds), *Issues Affecting Rural Communities*, Rural Education Research and Development Centre, James Cook University of North Queensland, Townsville, pp. 280–6.

Lawrence, J. 1999, *Argument for Action: Ethics and Professional Conduct*, Ashgate, England.

Lawrence, J. 1997, 'Editorial: ethics an apt focus for the journal's 50th anniversary', *Australian Social Work*, vol. 50, no. 4, p. 2.

Lawrence, R. J. 1983, *Responsibility for Service in Child Abuse and Child Protection*, Report and Recommendations of the Enquiry into the Statutory and Moral Responsibility of the Department of Youth and Community Services in New South Wales in the Light of an Analysis of the Case of Paul Montcalm, 27 October 1982, NSW Government Printer, Sydney.

Lawrence, R. J. 1965, *Professional Social Work in Australia*, Australian National University, Canberra.

Le Heron, R., Roche, M., Johnston, T. & Bowler, S. 1991, 'Pluriactivity in New Zealand's agro-commodity chains', *Proceedings of Rural Economy NA and Society Section, Sociological Association of Aotearoa (NZ) Conference*, Agribusiness and Economics Research Unit, Lincoln University, Discussion Paper No. 129, pp. 41–55.

Lechte, J. & Bottomley, G. 1993, 'Difference, postmodernity and imagery in multicultural Australia', in K. L. Clark, D. Forbes & R. Francis (eds), *Multiculturalism, Difference and Postmodernism*, Longman Cheshire, Melbourne, pp. 22–37.

Leeder, S. 1999, 'Dark side to the future of Medicare', *Sydney Morning Herald*, 23 July.

Lefley, H. 1993, 'Involuntary treatment: concerns of consumers, families, and society', *Innovations and Research*, vol. 2, no. 1, pp. 7–9.

Leonard, P. 1997, *Postmodern Welfare: Reconstructing an Emancipatory Project*, Sage, London.

Lesbian and Gay Community Action of South Australia 1994, *The Police and You*, LGCASA, Adelaide.

Lewin, F. A. 2001, 'Gerotranscendence and different cultural settings', *Ageing and Society*, vol. 21, no. 4, pp. 395–415.

Lichter, D., Johnston, G. & McLaughlin, D. 1994, 'Changing linkages between work and poverty in rural America', *Rural Sociology*, vol. 59, pp. 395–415.

Lichter, D. & McLaughlin, D. 1995, 'Changing economic opportunities, family structure and poverty in rural areas', *Rural Sociology*, vol. 60, pp. 688–706.

Lindsay, R. 2002, *Recognizing spirituality: The interface between faith and social work*, University of Western Australia Press, Perth.

Lindsey, D. 1994, *The Welfare of Children*, Oxford University Press, New York.

Lockie, S. 1994, 'Landcare in the balance', *Rural Society*, vol. 4, no. 3/4, Centre for Rural Social Research, Wagga Wagga.

Loewenberg, F. M., Dolgoff, R. & Harrington, D. 2004, *Ethical Decisions for Social Work Practice*, F. E. Peacock, Itasca, Illinois.

Lonne, B. & Cheers, B. 2000a, 'Recruitment, relocation and retention of rural social workers', *Rural Social Work*, no. 5, December, pp. 13–23.

Lonne, B. & Cheers, B. 2000b, 'Rural social workers and their jobs: an empirical study', *Australian Social Work*, vol. 53, no. 1, pp. 21–8.

Lonne, R. E. 2002, 'Retention and Adjustment of Social Workers to Rural Positions in Australia: Implications for Recruitment, Supports and Professional Education', unpublished PhD Thesis, University of South Australia.

Lorenz, W. 1997, 'ECSPRESS—The thematic network for the social professions', *Irish Social Worker*, vol. 15, no. 1.

Lowis, M. & Picton, C. 1996, 'Retirement preparation and enrichment: a practical program', *Australian Social Work*, vol. 49, no. 2, pp. 19–26.

Luke, C. & Luke, A. 1998, 'Interracial families: Difference within difference', *Ethnic and Racial Studies*, vol. 21, no. 4, pp. 21, 728–54.

Lukes, S. 1974, *Power: A Radical View*, Macmillan, London.

Luloff, A. 1998, *What Makes a Place a Community?*, The Fifth Sir John Quick Bendigo Lecture, La Trobe University, Bendigo.

Luloff, A. 1996, 'The doing of rural development research', in H. Echelberger (ed.), *Rural America: A Living Tapestry*, proceedings of the Research Fit Module, 3rd Annual US Forest Service Rural Communities Assistance Conference, USDA Forest Service, Randor, PA, pp. 25–30.

Lum, D. 1996, *Social Work Practice and People of Color*, 3rd edn, Brooks/Cole Publishing Company, Pacific Grove.

Lyons, K. 1999, *International Social Work: Themes and Perspectives*, Ashgate Arena, Aldershot, England.

McCallum, J. & Geiselhart, K. 1996, *Australia's New Aged: Issues for Young and Old*, Allen & Unwin, St Leonards.

McClinton, J. & Pawar, M. 1997, 'A feasibility study for poverty alleviation in rural Australia', *Rural Society*, Centre for Rural Social Research, Wagga Wagga.

McCrudy & Daro 1993, 'Child maltreatment: a national survey of reports and facilities', *Journal of Interpersonal Violence*, no. 9, pp. 75–94.

McDonald, C. 1999, 'Human service professionals in the community services industry', *Australian Social Work*, vol. 52, no. 1, pp. 17–25.

MacDonald, C., Marston, G. & Buckley, A. 2003, 'Risk Technology in Australia: the role of the Job Seeker Classification Instrument in employment services', *Critical Social Policy*, vol. 23, no. 4, pp. 498–525.

McGorry, P. 1995, 'Working with survivors of torture and trauma: the Victorian Foundation for Survivors of Torture in perspective', *ANZ Journal of Psychiatry*, vol. 29, no. 3, pp. 463–72.

McGuire, J. &. Priestley. P. 1995, 'Reviewing "what works": past, present and future', in J. McGuire (ed.), *What Works: Reducing Offending: Guidelines from Research and Practice*, Wiley, Chichester.

McIntyre, D. 2001, *A Guide to the Contemporary Commonwealth*, Palgrave London.

McKinnon, J. 1998, 'Social Workers and the Community: The Possibilities of Permaculture', unpublished Masters dissertation, Charles Sturt University, Wagga Wagga.

MacKinnon, L. 1998, *Trust and Betrayal in the Treatment of Child Abuse*, Guilford Press, New York.

McLeay, L. (chair) 1982, *In a Home or at Home: Accommodation and Home Care for the Aged*, Report of the House of Representatives Standing Committee on Expenditure, AGPS, Canberra.

McLennan, W. 1996, *Year Book Australia*, ABS, Canberra.

McMahon, A. 2003, 'Redefining the beginnings of social work in Australia', *Advances in Social Work and Welfare Education*, vol. 5, no. 1, pp. 83–94.

McMahon, A. 2002, 'Writing diversity: ethnicity and race in Australian social work, 1947–1997', *Australian Social Work*, vol. 55, no. 3, pp. 172–83.

McNutt, J. 1994, 'Social welfare and the environmental crisis', in M. D. Hoff & J. McNutt (eds), *The Global Environmental Crises: Implications for Social Welfare and Social Work*, Avebury, Aldershot, pp. 36–52.

Madden, R. 1998, 'Disability definitions and concepts: working towards national consistency', in Australian Bureau of Statistics, Australian Institute of Health and Welfare & Department of Health and Family Services, *Indigenous Disability Data—Current Status and Future Prospects*; Report on Proceedings of the Canberra Workshop April 1998, Commonwealth of Australia.

Madden, R. 1994, *National Aboriginal and Torres Strait Islander Survey 1994 Detailed Findings*, Australian Bureau of Statistics, Canberra.

Madden, R., Black, K. & Shirlow, M. 1993, 'Disability services', *Australia's Welfare Services and Assistance*, AGPS, Canberra.

Magee, J. J. 1992, 'Empowering themselves: a spiritual path for shame bound older adults', *Journal of Religious Gerontology*, vol. 8, no. 4, pp. 17–25.

Maidment, J. & Egan, R. (eds) 2004, *Practice skills in Social Work and Welfare: More Than Just Common Sense*, Allen & Unwin, Crows Nest.

Makrinotti, D. 1994, 'Conceptualisation of childhood in a welfare state: a critical reappraisal', in J. Qvortrup, M. Bardy, G. Sgritta & H. Wintersberger (eds), *Childhood Matters: Social Theory, Practice and Politics*, Ashgate, Aldershot, England.

Maley, W. 2003, 'Comments on Events in the Islamic Transitional Government of Afghanistan', <www.nauruwire.org/WilliamMaley.htm> (accessed October 2004).

Mallon, G. 1997, 'Entering into a collaborative search for meaning with gay and lesbian youth in out of home care: an empowerment-based model for training child welfare professionals', *Journal of Child and Adolescent Social Work*, vol. 14, no. 6, pp. 427–44.

Mallon, G. 1994, 'Counselling strategies with gay and lesbian youth', in T. DeCrescenzo (ed.), *Helping Gay and Lesbian Youth*, Harrington Park Press, Binghamton.

Markus, A. 1994, *Australian Race Relations 1788–1993*, Allen & Unwin, St Leonards.

Marsden, S. 1986, *Business, Charity and Sentiment: the South Australian Housing Trust, 1936–1986*, Wakefield Press, Netley.

Marshall, M. & Dixon, M. 1996, *Social Work with Older People*, 3rd edn, Macmillan, Basingstoke.

Martin, E. & Healy, J. 1993, 'Social work as women's work: census data 1976–86', *Australian Social Work*, vol. 46, no. 4, December, pp. 13–18.

Martin, J. & A'Dugelli, A. 2003, 'How lonely are gay and lesbian youth?', *Psychological Reports*, vol. 93, no. 2, p. 486.

Martin-Baro, I. 1989, 'The psychological consequences of political terrorism', presentation made at the Symposium on the Psychological Consequences of Political Terrorism, 17 January, Berkeley, California.

Martinson, R. 1974, 'What works—questions and answers about prison reform', *In The Public Interest*, vol. 35, pp. 22–54.

Maslow, A. 1970, *Motivation and Personality*, Harper and Row, New York.

Mason, J. & Gibson, C. 2004, *The Needs of Children in Care, Social Justice and Social Change*, University of Western Sydney and UnitingCare, Burnside.

Mason, G. & Tomsen, S. (eds) 1997, *Homophobic Violence*, Hawkins Press, Sydney.

Mason, J. (ed.) 1993, *Child Welfare Policy: Critical Australian Perspectives*, Hale & Iremonger, Sydney.

Mason J. & Falloon, J. 2001, 'Children Define Abuse. Implications for Agency in Childhood', in L. Alanen & B. Mayall (eds) *Conceptualising Child-Adult Relations*, Falmer Press, London.

Mason, J. & Gibson, C. (in press), *Needs of children in care. A report*, Social Justice & Social Change Research Centre UWS & Social Justice and Research, Burnside.

Mason, J. & Michaux, A. (in press), 'Facilitating Children's Participation in Child Protection Processes', The Starting Out with Scarba Project, The Benevolent Society, Sydney.

Mason, J. & Noble-Spruell, C. 1993, 'Child protection policy in New South Wales: a critical analysis', in J. Mason (ed.), *Child Welfare Policy: Critical Australian Perspectives*, Hale & Iremonger, Sydney.

Mathews, R. 1999, *Jobs of Our Own*, Pluto Press, Sydney.

Maynard, M. 1985, 'The response of social workers to domestic violence', in J. J. M. Pahl (ed.), *The Needs of Battered Women and the Response of Public Services*, Routledge, London, pp. 125–41.

Mazibuko, F. 1996, 'Social work and sustainable development: the challenges of practice, training and policy in South Africa', in *Proceedings of Joint World Congress IFSW & IASSW: Participating in Change—The Social Work Profession in Social Development*, Hong Kong.

Meadows, G & Singh, B. 2001, *Mental Health in Australia*, Oxford University Press, Melbourne.

Mehraby, N. 1999, 'Revisiting a harsh place', *Transitions*, vol. 3, STARTTS, Sydney, pp. 13–15.

Meekosha, H. 2000, 'Political activism and identity making: The involvement of women in the disability rights movement in Australia', *WWDA News*, no. 18, September, pp. 26–34.

Merriam, S. B. 1995, 'Butler's life review: how universal is it?', in J. Hendricks (ed.), *The Meaning of Reminiscence and Life Review*, Baywood, Amityville, New York.

Metherell, M. 1999, 'Healthy and wealthy', *Sydney Morning Herald*, 24 July.

Meyer, C. 1995, 'The ecosystems perspective: implications for practice', in C. Meyer & M. Mattaini (eds), *The Foundations of Social Work Practice*, NASW Press, Washington DC.

Middleman, R. & Goldberg, G. 1972, 'A frame of reference for social work practice', in *Social Work Practice*, Columbia University Press, New York.

Midgley, J. 2001, 'Issues in international social work: resolving critical debates in the profession', *Journal of Social Work*, vol. 1, no. 1, pp. 21–35.

Midgley, J. 1990, 'International social work: learning from the 3rd world', *Social Work*, vol. 35, no. 4.

Millbank, J. 1999, 'The De Facto Relationships Amendment Bill 1998: the rationale for reform', *Australasian Gay and Lesbian Law Journal*, no. 1.

Millbank, J. & Gay and Lesbian Rights Lobby 2002, *Meet the Parents: A Review of Research on Lesbian and Gay Families*, Gay & Lesbian Rights Lobby (Inc), Sydney.

Miller-Perrin, C. L. & Perrin, R. D. 1999, *Child Maltreatment: An Introduction*, Sage, UK.

Millet, K. 1970, *Sexual Politics*, Avon, New York.

Minichiello, V., Alexander, L. & Jones, D. (eds) 1992, *Gerontology: A Multidisciplinary Approach*, Prentice Hall, Sydney.

Minton, H. & McDonald, G. 1985, 'Homosexual identity formation as a developmental process', in J. De Cecco & M. Shively (eds), *Origins of Sexuality and Homosexuality*, Harrington Park Press, New York.

Mitchell, D. 1996, 'The sustainability of the welfare state: debates, myths, agendas', *Just Policy*, vol. 9, pp. 53–7.

Moberly Bell, E. 1961, *The Story of Hospital Almoners: The Birth of a Profession*, Faber & Faber, London.

Moore, C. 2004, <www.clovermoore.com/idx.htm?www.clovermoore.com/issues/g+l/> (accessed October 2004).

Morgan, W. 1999, *Lesbians, Gay Men and Anti-Discrimination Law: The Problems in Practice*, Continuing Legal Education, University of Sydney.

Morris, A., Giller, H., Szwed, E. & Geach, H. 1980, *Justice for Children*, Macmillan, London.

Morris, J. 2001, 'Impairment and disability: Constructing an ethics of care that promotes human rights', *Hypatia*, vol. 16, no. 4, fall, pp. 1–16.

Morris, J. 1993, 'Gender and disability', in J. Swain, V. Finkelstein, S. French & M. Oliver (eds), *Disabling Barriers—Enabling Environments*, Sage Publications, London, pp. 85–92.

Morris, J. 1991, *Pride Against Prejudice: A Personal Politics of Disability*, The Women's Press, London.

Morrow, D. 1996, 'Heterosexism: hidden discrimination in social work education', *Journal of Gay and Lesbian Social Services*, vol. 5, no. 4, pp. 5–31.

Mowbray, M. 2004, 'Community development and the Third Way: Mark Latham's localist policies', *Urban Policy and Research*, vol. 22, no. 1, pp. 107–15.

Mullaly, B. 2002, *Challenging oppression: A critical social work approach*, Oxford University Press, Don Mills.

Mullaly, B. 1997, *Structural Social Work: Ideology, Theory and Practice*, Oxford University Press, Toronto.

Mullender, A. & Morley, R. 1994, *Children Living with Domestic Violence: Putting Men's Abuse of Women on the Child Care Agenda*, Whiting & Birch, London.

Mullender, A. 1997, 'Gender', in M. Davies (ed.), *The Blackwell Companion to Social Work*, Blackwell, Oxford, pp. 42–9.

Munford, R. 1995, 'The gender factor in care giving', in *Community Care: The Next Twenty Years: A Future Policy Conference*, Carers Association of Australia, Canberra, pp. 29–50.

Munro, E. 1998, 'Improving social workers' knowledge base in child protection work', *British Journal of Social Work*, vol. 28, pp. 89–105.

Murphy, J. 1995, *The Commonwealth-State Housing Agreement of 1956 and the Politics of Home Ownership in the Cold War*, ANU Urban Research Program Working Paper No 50, Canberra.

NACBCS, *see* National Association of Community Based Children's Services.

NASW (National Association of Social Workers) 1997, *NASW Policy Statements: Lesbian, Gay and Bisexual Issues*, NASW Press, Washington DC.

National Association of Community Based Children's Services 2003, *Submission to the Senate Inquiry into Poverty in Australia*, <www.cccinc.com.au/pdf/poverty%20submission.pdf> (accessed 28 March 2003).

Neave, M. 1995, 'Women, divorce and redistributing the cost of children', in A. Edwards & S. Magarey (eds), *Women in a Restructured Australia: Work and Welfare*, Allen & Unwin, in association with the Academy of Social Sciences in Australia, Sydney, pp. 223–43.

New South Wales Police Service 1995, *Out of the Blue: A Police Survey of Violence and Harassment Against Gay Men and Lesbians*, NSW Police Service and Price Waterhouse Urwick, NSW.

New South Wales Violence in Lesbian and Gay Relationships Committee 1995, *Selected Papers*, Lesbian and Gay Anti-Violence Project of NSW, Sydney.

Newell, C. 2002, 'Embracing life: ethical challenges in disability and biotechnology', *Interaction*, vol. 16, no. 2, pp. 25–33.

Newell, C. 1996, 'The disability rights movement in Australia: A note from the trenches', *Disability and Society*, vol. 11, no. 3, pp. 429–32.

Nguyen, T. & Bowles, R. 1998, 'Counselling Vietnamese refugee survivors of trauma: points of entry', *Australian Social Work*, vol. 51, no. 2, pp. 41–7.

Noble, C. & Briskman, L. 1998, 'Workable ethics: social work and progressive practice', *Australian Social Work*, vol. 51, no. 3, pp. 9–15.

Nolan, M., Grant, G. & Keady, J. 1996, *Understanding Family Care: A Multidimensional Model of Caring and Coping*, Open University Press, Buckingham.

NSW Department of Housing 2004, *Regional Strategic Plan*, Illawarra and South East Region, NSW Department of Housing.

NSW Ministerial Task Force of Affordable Housing 1998, *Affordable Housing in NSW: The Need for Action,* NSW MTFAH, Sydney.

NSW Ombudsman 2004, *Special Report to Parliament: DADHC—the need to improve services for children, young people and their families,* A report arising from the investigation into the Department of Disability, Ageing and Home Care, April, <www.nswombudsman.nsw.gov.au/publications/Publist_pdfs/reports/DADHC_April_2004.pdf> (accessed 14 June 2004).

NSW Refugee Health and STARTTS 2004, *Working with Refugees: A Guide for Social Workers,* Sydney.

Nunno, M,. Holden, M. & Leidy, B. 1997, 'Child maltreatment in loco parentis', in J. Garbarino & J. Eckenrode (eds), *Understanding Abusive Families: An Ecological Approach to Theory and Practice,* Jossey Bass, California.

NZH 2003, 'Old law leaves sperm donor dad out in cold', *New Zealand Herald,* 31 January.

Oakley, A. 1981, *Subject Woman,* Pantheon, New York.

O'Brien, L. & Turner, C. 1979, 'Hospital almoning: portrait of the first decade', *Australian Social Work,* vol. 32, no. 4.

O'Connor, I. 1993, 'Aboriginal child welfare law, policies and practices in Queensland: 1865–1989', *Australian Social Work,* vol. 46, no. 3, pp. 11–22.

O'Connor, I., Smyth, P. & Warburton, J. 2000, 'Introduction: The Challenges of Change', in I. O'Connor, P. Smyth & J. Warburton (eds), *Contemporary Perspectives on Social Work and the Human Services: Challenges and Change,* Longman, Australia, pp. 1–10.

O'Connor, I., Wilson, J. & Setterlund, D. 1995, 'Social work, welfare work and social arrangements', in I. O'Connor, J. Wilson & K. Thomas (eds), *Social Work and Welfare Practice,* 2nd edn, Longman Cheshire, Sydney.

O'Connor, I., Wilson, J. & Setterlund, D. 2003, *Social Work and Welfare Practice,* Pearson Education, Sydney.

O'Connor, I., Wilson, J. & Thomas, K. (eds) 1991, *Social Work and Welfare Practice,* Longman Cheshire, Melbourne.

OECD, *see* Organisation for Economic Cooperation and Development.

Office of the Status of Women 1995, *Community Attitudes to Violence against Women: Detailed Report,* Office of the Prime Minister and Cabinet, Australian Government Printing Service, Canberra.

Oliver, M. 1996, *Understanding Disability from Theory to Practice,* Macmillan, London.

Oliver, M. 1992, 'Changing the social relations of research production?', *Disability, Handicap and Society,* vol. 7, no. 2, pp. 101–13.

Oliver, M. 1990, *The Politics Of Disablement,* Macmillan, London.

Orbach, A. 1996, *Not Too Late: Psychotherapy and Ageing,* Jessica Kingsley, London.

Orchard, L. 1995, 'National urban policy in the 1990s', in P. Troy (ed.), *Australian Cities,* Cambridge University Press, Sydney, pp. 65–85.

Organisation for Economic Cooperation and Development 2003, *Transforming Disability Into Ability: Policies to Promote Work and Income Security for Disabled People,* OECD, Paris.

Osborn, T. 1996, *Coming Home to America: A Roadmap to Gay and Lesbian Empowerment,* St Martins Press, New York.

Osburn, L. 1999, 'Power to the Profession;, unpublished PhD thesis, University of New England, Armidale.

O'Shane, P. 1993, 'Assimilation or acculturation problems of Aboriginal families', *ANZ Journal of Family Therapy,* vol. 14, no. 4, pp. 196–8.

Owen, J. 1996, *Every Childhood Lasts a Lifetime,* Australian Association of Young People in Care, Australia.

Owen, L & Richards, D. 2002, 'Social work and corrections practice', in P. A. Swain (ed.), *In the Shadow of the Law: the Legal Context of Social Work Practice,* The Federation Press, Sydney.

Ozdowski, S. 2002, *Disability Discrimination Legislation in Australia from an International Human Rights Perspective: History, Achievements and Prospects,* Human Rights and Equal Opportunity Commission, <www.hreoc.gov.au/disability_rights/speeches/speeches.html> (accessed October 2004).

Pallotta-Chiarolli, M. 1998, 'Cultural diversity and men who have sex with men', *Monograph 3/1998,* National Centre in HIV Social Research, Macquarie University, NSW.

Palmer, G. R. & Short, S. D. 1989, *Health Care and Public Policy: An Australian Analysis,* Macmillan, Melbourne.

Parbury, N. 1986, *Survival: A History of Aboriginal Life in New South Wales*, Ministry of Aboriginal Affairs, New South Wales, Sydney.

Paris, C., Williams, P. & Stimson, B. 1985, 'From public housing to welfare housing', *Australian Journal of Social Issues*, vol. 20, no. 2, pp. 105–17.

Parmenter, T. R., Cummins, R., Shaddock, A. J. & Stancliffe, R. 1994, in D. Goode (ed.), *Quality of Life for Persons with Disabilities: International Perspectives and Issues*, Brookline Books, Cambridge, Mass., pp. 75–102.

Parsons, I. 1994, *Oliver Twist Has Asked for More*, Villamanta, Geelong.

Parton, C. 1990, 'Women, gender, oppression and child abuse', in Violence Against Children study group (ed.), *Taking Child Abuse Seriously: Contemporary Issues in Child Protection Theory and Practice*, Unwin Hyman, London, pp. 41–62.

Parton, N. 1991, *Governing the Family: Child Care, Child Protection and the State*, Macmillan, Houndmills, Basingstoke.

Parton, N. 1990, 'Taking child abuse seriously', in Violence Against Children study group (ed.), *Taking Child Abuse Seriously: Contemporary Issues in Child Protection Theory and Practice*, Unwin Hyman, London, pp. 7–24.

Parton, N. 1985, *The Politics of Child Abuse*, Macmillan, Houndmills, UK.

Parton, N. & Martin, N. 1989, 'Public inquiries, legalism and child care in England and Wales', *International Journal of Law and the Family*, vol. 3, pp. 21–39.

Parton, N. & Otway, O. 1995, 'The contemporary state of child protection policy and practice in England and Wales', *Children and Youth Services Review*, vol. 17, no. 5/6, pp. 599–617.

Parton, N., Thorpe, D. & Wattam, C. 1997, *Child Protection: Risk and the Moral Order*, Macmillan, Basingstoke, UK.

Pastor, S. 1997, 'The distinctiveness of cross-cultural training in the Northern Territory', *Northern Radius*, vol. 4, no. 2, pp. 3–8.

Patford, J. 1999, 'What's happening in health: progress and prospects for social work', *Australian Social Work*, vol. 52, no. 1, pp. 3–7.

Patmore, G. 1991, *Australian Labor History*, Longman Cheshire, Australia.

Patterson C. 2002, 'Lesbian and gay parenthood', in M. Bornstein (ed.), *Handbook of Parenting: vol. 3: Being and Becoming a Parent*, Lawrence Erlbaum Publishers, Mahwah.

Pauwels, A. 1995, *Cross-Cultural Communication in the Health Sciences. Communicating with Migrant Patients*, Macmillan, Melbourne.

Pawar, M. & Cox, D. 2004, *Communities in Formal Care and Welfare Systems: A Training Manual*, Centre for Rural Social Research, Charles Sturt University, Wagga Wagga

Pawar, M. 2000, 'Social development in the courses of Australian social work schools', *International Social Work*, vol. 43, no. 3, pp. 277–88.

Pawar, M. S. 1999, 'Social Work Schools and Social Development Prospects in the Asia-Pacific Region', *Social Development Issues*, vol. 21 (1), pp. 21–35.

Payne, M. 1997, *Modern Social Work Theory*, 2nd edn, Macmillan, London.

Payne, M. 1996, *What is Professional Social Work?*, Venture Press, Birmingham.

Peace, S. M., Kellaher, L. & Willcocks, D. 1997, *Re-Evaluating Residential Care*, Open University Press, Buckingham, England.

Pearlman, L. 1996, *Transforming the Pain: A Workbook on Vicarious Traumatisation*, WW Norton, New York.

Pearlman, L. & Saakvitne, K. 1995, *Trauma and the Therapist: Countertransference and Vicarious Traumatisation in Psychotherapy with Incest Survivors*, WW Norton, New York.

Pearson, N. 1999, 'Opinion', *Parity*, vol. 12, no. 4, p. 20.

Pease, B. & Fook, J. (eds) 1999, *Transforming Social Work Practice: Postmodern Critical Perspectives*, Allen & Unwin, Sydney.

Pelton, L. H. 1991, 'Beyond permanency planning: restructuring the public child welfare system', *Social Work*, vol. 36, no. 1, pp. 337–43.

Pelton, L. H. 1989, *For Reasons of Poverty: A Critical Analysis of the Public Child Welfare System in the United States*, Praeger, New York.

Pelton, L. H. 1978, 'Child abuse and neglect: the myth of classlessness', *American Journal of Orthopsychiatry*, vol. 48, pp. 608–17.

Penton, K. 1993, 'Ideology, social work and the Gaian connection', *Australian Social Work*, vol. 46, no. 4, pp. 41–8.

Perry, J & Henman, P. 2002, 'Welfare dependency? A critical analysis of changes in welfare recipient numbers', *Australian Journal of Social Issues*, vol. 37, no. 3.

Peterson, A. R. 1994, *In a Critical Condition: Health and Power Relations in Australia*, Allen & Unwin, Australia.

Petrie, C. C. 1904, *Tom Petrie's Reminiscences of Early Queensland*, Watson, Ferguson & Co, Brisbane.

Phillips, J. (ed.) 1995, *Working Carers: International Perspectives on Working and Caring for Older People*, Avebury, Aldershot.

Phillipson, C. 1982, *Capitalism and the Construction of Old Age*, Macmillan, London.

Phoenix, A. & Woollett, A. 1991, 'Motherhood: social construction, politics and psychology', in A. Phoenix, A. Woollett & E. Lloyd (eds), *Motherhood: Meanings, Practices and Ideologies*, Sage, London.

Picton, C. & Boss, P. 1981, *Child Welfare in Australia: An Introduction*, Harcourt Brace Jovanovich, Sydney.

Pilger, J. 2003, 'What good friends left behind', *Good Weekend*, October 18, pp. 34–9.

Pittaway, E. 2002, 'Refugees in the twenty-first century, a humanitarian challenge', *Mots Pluriels*, No. 21, May, <www.arts.uwa.edu.au/MotsPluriels/MP2102edito1.html> (accessed October 2004).

Pittaway, E. 1991, *Refugee Women—Still at Risk in Australia*, AGPS, Canberra.

Pixley, J. 1998, 'Social movements, democracy and conflicts over institutional reform', in P. Smyth & B. Cass (eds), *Contesting the Australian Way*, Cambridge University Press, Sydney, pp. 138–53.

Pollard, D. 1988, *Give and Take: The Losing Partnership in Aboriginal Poverty*, Hale & Iremonger, Marrickville.

Powall, M. & Withers, G. 2004, *National Summit on Housing Affordability* Resource Paper, <www.appliedeconomics.com.au/pubs/papers/gw03_house.htm> (accessed October 2004).

Pritchard, J. 1996, *Working with Elder Abuse: A Training Manual for Home Care, Residential, and Day Care Staff*, Jessica Kingsley, London.

Productivity Commission 2003, *First Home Ownership*, Productivity Commission Discussion Paper, Melbourne.

Pryke, J. & Thomas, M. 1998, *Domestic Violence and Social Work*, Ashgate, Arena, England.

Public Policy Research Centre 1988, *Domestic Violence Attitude Survey*, for the Office of the Status of Women, Department of the Prime Minister and Cabinet, Canberra.

Pugh, C. 1976, *Intergovernmental Relations and the Development of Australian Housing Policies*, Research Monograph No. 15, Centre for Research on Federal Financial Relations, Australian National University, Canberra.

Putman, R., Leonardi, R. & Nanetti, R. 1993, *Making Democracy Work*, Princeton, New Jersey.

Quadroy, A. 1989, 'A brief history of the Commonwealth-State Housing Agreement', *Shelter: National Housing Action*, vol. 6, no 1, pp. 34–5.

Ranald, P. 2003, 'Developing New Solidarities: unions', in Sheil, C. (ed.), *Globalisation: Australian Impacts*, UNSW Press, Sydney.

Randolph, B. & Holloway, D. 2004, *Shifting Suburbs: Population Structure and Change in Greater Western Sydney Urban Frontiers Program*, University of Western Sydney.

Randolph, B. & Wood, M. 2003, *The Benefits of Tenure Diversification*, Australian Housing and Urban Research Institute, University of NSW/University of Western Sydney.

Raper, M. 1999, 'Impact', *Journal of the Australian Council of Social Service*, July.

Raysmith, H. 1998, 'Facing the future: emerging models in community services', *Impact*, May, pp. 10–12.

Read, P. 1982, *The Stolen Generations: The Removal of Aboriginal Children in NSW from 1883–1969*, Occasional Paper No. 1, NSW Ministry for Aboriginal Affairs, NSW.

Rees, S. 1995a, 'Defining and attaining humanity', in S. Rees & G. Rodley (eds), *The Human Costs of Managerialism: Advocating the Recovery of Humanity*, Pluto Press, Leichhardt, pp. 285–300.

Rees, S. 1995b, 'Greed and bullying', in S. Rees & G. Rodley (eds), *The Human Costs of Managerialism: Advocating the Recovery of Humanity*, Pluto Press, Leichhardt, pp. 197–210.

Rees, S. 1995c, 'The fraud and the fiction', in S. Rees & G. Rodley (eds), *The Human Costs of Managerialism: Advocating the Recovery of Humanity*, Pluto Press, Leichhardt, pp. 15–27.

Rees, S. 1991, *Achieving Power: Practice and Policy in Social Welfare*, Allen & Unwin, St Leonards.

Refugee Council of Australia 2004, *Statistics*, <www.refugeecouncil.org.au/html/facts_and_stats/stats.html> (accessed October 2004).

Refugee Health Policy Advisory Committee 1997, *Strategic Directions in Refugee Health Care*, NSW Health, Sydney.

Refugee Resettlement Working Group 1990, *The Role of the Non-Government Sector in Refugee Resettlement*, RRWG, Sydney.

Reid, J. & Strong, T. 1988, 'Rehabilitation of refugee victims of torture and trauma: principles and service provision in NSW', *Medical Journal of Australia*, vol. 148, no. 7, pp. 340–6.

Reid, J. & Strong, T. 1987, *Torture and Trauma—The Healthcare Needs of Refugee Victims in New South Wales*, Cumberland College of Health Sciences, Sydney.

Rein, M. 1976, 'Social work in search of a radical profession', in N. Gilbert & H. Specht (eds), *The Emergence of Social Welfare and Social Work*, F. E. Peacock, Itasca, pp. 459–84.

Reiter, L. 1991, 'Developmental origins of antihomosexual prejudice in heterosexual men and women', *Clinical Social Work*, vol. 12, no. 2.

RHPAC, *see* Refugee Health Policy Advisory Committee.

Richardson, S. 1999, 'Regulation of the labour market', in S. Richardson (ed.), *Reshaping the Labour Market*, Cambridge University Press, Sydney, pp. 1–37.

Roach Anleu, S. 1998, 'The medicalisation of deviance', in J. Germov (ed.), *Second Opinion: An Introduction to Health Sociology*, Oxford University Press, Melbourne.

Roberto, K. A. (ed.) 1996, *Relationships between Women in Later Life*, Harrington Park Press, New York.

Roberts, R. 2001, 'Rethinking sex and gender in work with gay identified men', in B. Pease & P. Camilleri (eds), *Working with Men in the Human Services*, Allen & Unwin, Sydney.

Roberts, R. 1996, 'School experiences of some rural gay men coping with "countrymindedness"', in G. Wotherspoon (ed.), *Gay and Lesbian Perspectives III—More Essays in Australian Gay Male Culture*, Department of Economic History and the Australian Centre for Lesbian and Gay Research, University of Sydney, Sydney, pp. 45–69.

Roberts, R. 1995, 'A "fair go for all?": discrimination and the experiences of some men who have sex with men in the bush', in P. Share (ed.), *Communication and Culture in Rural Areas*, Charles Sturt University, Centre for Rural Social Research, Wagga Wagga.

Roberts, R. 1994, 'Challenging the uncritical application of urban HIV/AIDS politics to rural contexts', *Australian Social Work*, vol. 47, no. 4, pp. 11–19.

Roberts, R. 1993, 'Factors influencing the formation of gay and lesbian communities in rural areas', *National AIDS Bulletin*, vol. 7, no. 3, pp. 14–17.

Roberts, R. 1992, 'Men who have sex with men in the bush: impediments to the formation of gay communities in some rural areas', *Rural Society*, vol. 2, no. 3, pp. 13–14.

Roberts, R. 1990, *Lessons for the Past: Issues for Social Work Theory*, Routledge, London.

Roberts, R. 1989a, 'The influence of homophobia and heterosexism on social work education', *AASW Newsletter*, vol. 3, pp. 8–9.

Roberts, R. 1989b, 'Challenging heterosexist assumptions in social work education', in D. James & T. Vinson (eds), *Advances in Social Welfare Education*, The Heads of Schools of Social Work in Australia, University of NSW, Kensington, pp. 1–20.

Roberts, R. 1987a, 'Sexuality and social work', *AASW Newsletter*, vol. 2, pp. 3–4.

Roberts, R. 1987b, 'Social work control of sexuality', *AASW Newsletter*, vol. 2, pp. 5–8.

Roberts, R. J. & Maplestone, P. 2001, *The Age of Consent and Gay Men in New South Wales*, University of New South Wales, Sydney.

Roe, J. 1983, 'The end is where we start from: women and welfare since 1901', in B. Cass & C. Baldock (eds), *Women and Social Welfare*, Allen & Unwin, Sydney, pp. 1–19.

Roe, J. 1976, 'Leading the world? 1901–1914', in J. Roe (ed.), *Social Policy in Australia: Some Perspectives 1901–1975*, Cassell, Sydney, pp. 3–23.

Rofes, E. 1996, *Reviving the Tribe: Regenerating Gay Men's Sexuality and Culture in the Ongoing Epidemic*, Harrington Park Press, Binghamton.

Rogan, L. 1996, 'Tides of change in community services: the Industry Commission and COAG as case studies', in A. Farrar & J. Inglis (eds), *Keeping it Together: State and Civil Society in Australia*, Pluto Press, Leichhardt.

Rogers, C. & Wrightsman, L. 1978, 'Attitudes towards children's rights—nurturance or self-determination', *Journal of Social Issues*, vol. 34, no. 2, pp. 59–68.

Rolley, F. & Humphreys, J. S. 1993, 'Rural welfare—the human face of Australia's countryside', in T. Sorensen & R. Epps (eds), *Prospects and Policies for Rural Australia*, Longman Cheshire, Melbourne, pp. 241–57.

Rubin, G. 1993, 'Thinking sex: notes for a radical theory of the politics of sexuality', in H. Abelove, M. Barale & D. Halperin (eds), *The Lesbian and Gay Studies Reader*, Routledge, New York.

Ruthchild, C. 1997, 'Don't frighten the horses! A systemic perspective on violence against lesbians and gay men', in G. Mason & S. Tomsen (eds), *Homophobic Violence*, Hawkins Press, Sydney.

Rutter, M., Giller, H. & Hagel, A. 1998, *Antisocial Behaviour by Young People*, Cambridge University Press, Cambridge.

Ryan, M. & Martyn, R. 1997, 'Women writing on social work education: findings from a study of the content analysis of Australian journal articles 1983–1993', *Australian Social Work*, vol. 50, no. 2, pp. 13–18.

Rybash, J. M., Roodin, P. A. & Santrock, J. W. 1991, *Adult Development and Aging*, 2nd edn, Wm. C. Brown, Dubuque.

Salvaris, M. 1995, 'Jeff Kennett's anti-government', in S. Rees & G. Rodley (eds), *The Human Costs of Managerialism: Advocating the Recovery of Humanity*, Pluto Press, Leichhardt, pp. 145–58.

Santrock, J. 1985, *Adult Development and Aging*, Wm. C. Brown, Dubuque.

Saunders, P. 1996, 'Poverty in the 1990s: a challenge to work and welfare', in P. Sheehan, B. Grewal & M. Kumnick (eds), *Dialogues on Australia's Future*, Centre for Strategic Economic Studies, Victoria University, pp. 325–50.

Saunders, P. 1999, *Social Policy Research Centre Newsletter*, no. 50, winter.

Saunders, P. 2003, *Examining Recent Changes in Income Distribution in Australia*, SPRC Discussion Paper 130, October, UNSW, Kensington.

Savage, J. 1999, 'Reclaiming identity after torture', *Transitions*, vol. 3, pp. 24–5.

Sax, S. 1990, *Health Care Choices and the Public Purse*, Allen & Unwin, Australia.

Sayce, L. & Perkins, R. 2002, '"They should not breed": Feminism, disability and reproductive rights', *Off Our Backs*, vol. 32, no. 11/12, pp. 18–24.

Scheff, T. 1966, *Being Mentally Ill: A Sociological Theory*, Aldine, Chicago.

Schembri, A. 1995, 'To do more with less: hospital social work in 1995', unpublished paper presented at the centenary celebration of hospital social work, AASW (NSW Branch), October, cited in E. Browne 1996, *Tradition and Change: Hospital Social Work in NSW*, AASW, NSW branch, p. 71.

Schembri, A. 1992, *Off Our Backs: A Study into Anti-Lesbian Violence*, Gay and Lesbian Rights Lobby of NSW, Sydney.

Schlesinger, B. & Schlesinger, R. (eds) 1992, *Abuse of the Elderly: Issues and Annotated Bibliography*, University of Toronto Press, Toronto.

Schlesinger, E. G. & Devore, W. 1995, 'Ethnic sensitive practice: the state of the art', *Journal of Sociology and Social Welfare*, vol. 22, no. 1, pp. 29–58.

Schmidt, D. & Goodin, R. E. 1998, *Social Welfare and Individual Responsibility: For and Against*, Cambridge University Press, Cambridge.

Sedgwick, E. 1990, *Epistemology of the Closet*, University of California Press, Berkeley.

Segal, S. & Baumohl, J. 1981, 'Social work practice in community mental health', *Social Work*, vol. 26, no. 1, pp. 16–24.

Senate Economic Committee 1996, *Historical Perspective Industrial Relations In Australia*, <www.aph.gov.au/Senate/committee/economics_ctte/completed_inquiries/1996-99/workplace/report/e04.htm> (accessed September 2004).

Service for the Treatment and Rehabilitation of Torture and Trauma Survivors & Friends of STARTTS 2002, 'Trauma Changes Adults But Forms Children—Protecting and Healing Child Asylum Seekers and Refugees. Submission to the HREOC Inquiry into Children in Immigration Detention', STARTTS, Sydney, May 2002.

Shakespeare, T. 1996, 'Disability, identity, difference', in C. Barnes & G. Mercer (eds), *Exploring the Divide: Illness and Disability*, Disability Press, Leeds, pp. 94–113.

Shamgar-Handleman, L. 1994, 'To whom does childhood belong?', in J. Qvortrup, M. Bardy, G. Sgritta & H. Wintersberger (eds), *Childhood Matters: Social Theory, Practice and Politics*, Avebury, Aldershot, England.

Shannon, P. & Young, S. 2004, *Solving Social Problems: Southern Perspectives*, Dunmore Press, Palmerston North.

Sharland, E. 1999, 'Justice for children? Child protection and the crimino-legal process', *Child and Family Social Work*, vol. 4, pp. 296–304.

Shaver, S. 1998, 'Poverty, gender and sole parenthood', in R. Fincher & J. Nieuwenhuysen (eds), *Australian Poverty: Then and Now*, Melbourne University Press, Carlton, pp. 276–92.

Sheen, V. 1999, 'Policy step by step', *COTA News*, Council on the Ageing, June, pp. 10–11.

Sher, J. & Sher, K. R. 1994, 'Beyond the conventional wisdom: rural development as if Australia's rural people really mattered', in D. McSwan & M. McShane (eds), *Issues Affecting Rural Communities*, Rural Education Research and Development Centre, James Cook University of North Queensland, Townsville, pp. 9–32.

Shernoff, M. 2002, 'Body image, working out, and therapy', *Journal of Gay & Lesbian Social Services*, vol. 14, no. 1, pp. 89–94.

Sidoti, C. 2002, 'Refugee Policy: Is there a way out of this mess?', paper presented at Racial Respect seminar, Canberra, 21 February.

Sidoti, C. 1999, *Issues and Strategies around Couple Based Discrimination*, Human Rights and Equal Opportunity Commission, Australia.

Silove, D. 2002, 'The Asylum Debacle in Australia: A Challenge for Psychiatry.' *ANZJ Psychiatry*, vol. 36, no. 3, pp. 290–6.

Silove, D., Steel, Z. & Mollica, R. 2001, 'Detention of Asylum Seekers: Assault on Health, Human Rights and Social Development', *Lancet*, no. 357, 1436–7.

Silove, D., Steel, Z & Watters, C. 2000, 'Policies of Deterrence and the Mental Health of Asylum Seekers', *Journal of the American Medical Association*, vol. 284, no. 5, pp. 604–11.

Silove, D., Tarn, R., Bowles, R. & Reid, J. 1991a, 'Psychosocial needs of torture survivors', *ANZ Journal of Psychiatry*, vol. 25, pp. 481–90.

Silove, D., Tarn, R., Bowles, R. & Reid, J. 1991b, 'Psychotherapy for survivors of torture', in H. Minas (ed.), *Psychotherapy for Survivors of Trauma*, Cultural Values Mental Health, Melbourne.

Singh, R. R. 1995, 'Emerging partnerships in social work practice and education: development prospects in the Asia Pacific Region', in *Proceedings of Asia and Pacific Regional Conference of APASWE & IFSW Asia Pacific: Enhancing Social Integration, Structure Process and Intervention for Social Development*, Bangkok.

Skidelsky, R. 1986, *John Maynard Keynes*, Viking, New York.

Smith, B. 1993, 'Homophobia: why bring it up', in H. Abelove, M. Barale & D. Halperin (eds), *The Lesbian and Gay Studies Reader*, Routledge, New York.

Smith, B. 1991, 'Australian women and foster care: a feminist perspective', *Child Welfare*, vol. 17, no. 2, March–April, pp. 175–84.

Smyth, P. 1994, *Australian Social Policy: the Keynesian Chapter*, UNSW Press, Sydney.

Smyth, P. & Wearing, M. 2004, 'Towards a New Welfare State? Reflections on the British Social Policy legacy in Australia', unpublished paper presented at the Third British World Conference, 2–4 July, University of Melbourne.

Smyth, P. & Wearing, M. 2003, 'After the Welfare State? Welfare Governance and the Communitarian Revival', in Bell, S. (ed.), *Economic Governance and Institutional Dynamics*, Melbourne, Oxford University Press.

Snowdon, J. 1998, 'Management of late-life depression', *Australasian Journal on Ageing*, vol. 17, no. 2, pp. 57–62.

Sorensen, T. 1993, 'The future of the country town: strategies for local economic development', in South Australia Health Commission 1998, *A Social Health Strategy for South Australia*, SAHC, Adelaide.

South Australia Health Commission 1988, *A Social Health Strategy for South Australia*, SAHC, Adelaide.

Spice Consulting 1998, *The Kit—A Guide to the Advocacy We Choose to Do*, Mental Health Branch, Commonwealth Department of Health and Human Services, Canberra.

Starr, R. (ed.) 1982, *Child Abuse Prediction: Policy Implications*, Ballinger, Cambridge.

STARTTS, *see* Service for the Treatment and Rehabilitation of Torture and Trauma Survivors.

Steketee, M. 1999, 'Budgeting for a social conscience', *Weekend Australian*, 'Australia unlimited supplement, 8–9 May, p. 2.

Stewart, J. 1996, 'A dogma of our times—the separation of policy-making and implementation', *Public Money and Management*, July–September.

Stilwell, F. 1998a, 'Planning and Markets: An Urban Political Economy', in B. Gleeson & P. Hanley (eds), *Renewing Australian Planning? New Challenges, New Agendas*, Urban Research Program, Research School of Social Sciences, ANU, Canberra.

Stilwell, F. 1998b, 'Planning and Markets: An Urban Political Economy', in B. Gleeson & P. Hanley (eds), *Renewing Australian Planning? New Challenges, New Agendas*, Urban Research Program, Research School of Social Sciences, ANU, Canberra.

Stilwell, F. 1997, *Globalisation and Cities: An Australian Political-Economic Perspective*, Urban Research Working Paper No. 59, ANU, Canberra.

Stone, D. A. 1984, *The Disabled State*, Temple University Press, Philadelphia.

Stout, M. 2001, 'The influence of sexual orientation and gender on body dissatisfaction, self-esteem, collective self-esteem, and eating disorder symptoms', *Dissertation Abstracts International*, vol. 61 no. 12-A, p. 4684.

Strang, H. 2001, 'The crime victim movement as a force in civil society', in H. Strang & J. Braithwaite (eds), *Restorative Justice and Civil Society*, Cambridge University Press: Cambridge.

Strang, H. & Braithwaite, J. 2002, *Restorative Justice and Family Violence*, Cambridge, Cambridge University Press.

Strombeck, R. 2003, 'Finding sex partners on-line: a new high-risk practice among older adults', *Journal of Acquired Immune Deficiency Syndromes*, vol. 33, supp. 2, pp. S226–S228.

Stubbs, J. 2003, 'Battle for the Right to the City: Opportunities for an Emancipatory Social Practice in a Polarising Urban Landscape', unpublished PhD Thesis, School of Social Science and Town Planning, RMIT, Melbourne.

Stubbs, J., Richardson, R., Thorpe, D. Myers, S. and Berryman, C. 2004, *Enhancing the Role of Local Government in Affordable Housing: Options for Improving our Planning System*, NSW Affordable Housing Network and Shelter NSW, Sydney, www.shelternsw.net.au.

Studt, E. 1965, *A Conceptual Approach to Teaching Materials: Illustrations from the Field of Correction*, Council on Social Work Education, New York.

Sue, D. W., Ivey, A. E, & Pedersen, P. B. 1996, *A Theory of Multicultural Counseling and Therapy*, Brooks/Cole Publishing Company, Pacific Grove.

Summers, A. 2003, *The End of Equality*, Random House, Australia.

Summers, A. 1994, *Damned Whores and God's Police: The Colonisation of Women in Australia*, Penguin, Ringwood.

Swain, J., Finkelstein, V., French, S. & Oliver, M. (eds) 1993, *Disabling Barriers—Enabling Environments*, Sage, London.

Swain, S. 2002, 'Derivative and indigenous in the history and historiography of child welfare in Australia', *Children Australia*, vol. 27, no. 1, pp. 5–9.

Sweeney, T. 1983, 'Child welfare and child care policies', in A. Graycar (ed.), *Retreat from the Welfare State*, Allen & Unwin, Sydney.

Swift, K. 1995, 'Missing persons: women in child welfare', *Child Welfare*, vol. 74, No. 3, May–June, pp. 486–502.

Swift, K. 1991, 'Contradictions in child welfare neglect and responsibility', in C. Baines, P. Evans & S. Neysmith (eds), *Women's Caring: Feminist Perspectives on Social Welfare*, McLelland & Stewart, Toronto, pp. 234–71.

Swiss, S., Jennings, P., Aryee, G., Brown, G., Jappah-Samukai, R., Kamara, M., Schaack, R. & Turay-Kanneh, R. 1998, 'Violence Against Women During the Liberian Civil Conflict', *Journal of the American Medical Association*, no. 279, pp. 625–9.

Sydney Morning Herald 2004a, 'Boy's death vents despair over autism', 4 June, <www.smh.com.au/articles/2004/06/03/1086203567331.html> (accessed 13 June 2004).

Sydney Morning Herald 2004b, 'When love is not enough', 1 June, <www.smh.com.au/articles/2004/05/31/1085855494917.html> (accessed 13 June 2004).

Sydney Morning Herald 2003, 'Qld's foster care condemned', <www.gaiaguys.net/vic.qldchlsdcaresmh16.12.0.htm> (accessed 15 December 2003).

Sydney Morning Herald 2002, 'Lesbian mum kills son', 4 August.

Sydney Morning Herald 1999, 'Jobs revival for battling coast, west', 28 September.

Szmukler, G. 1998, 'Ethics in community psychiatry', *ANZ Journal of Psychiatry*, vol. 33, no. 3, pp. 328–38.

Tasker, F. 2002, 'Lesbian and gay parenting', in A. Coyle & C. Kitzinger (eds), *Lesbian and Gay Psychology: New Perspectives*, Blackwell, Malden MA, US.

Taylor, J. 1999a, *Community Services Development in Social Work Practice*, South Australia Centre for Rural and Remote Health, University of South Australia, Whyalla.

Taylor, J. 1999b, 'Rural social service provision and competitive tendering: against the heart', *Rural Social Work*, vol. 4, April, pp. 20–5.

Taylor, J. & MacDonald, H. 1994, *Disadvantage and Children of Immigrants: A Longitudinal Study*, Bureau of Immigration and Population Research, AGPS, Canberra.

Taylor, L., Lacey, R. & Bracken, D. 1980, *In Whose Best Interests? The Unjust Treatment of Children in Courts and Institutions*, Cobden Trust and MIND, UK.

Taylor, N. 1994, 'Gay and lesbian youth: challenging the policy of denial', in T. DeCrescenzo (ed.), *Helping Gay and Lesbian Youth*, Harrington Park Press, Binghamton.

Teshuva, K., Kendig, H. & Stacey, B. 1997, 'Spirituality, health and health promotion in older Australians', *Health Promotion Journal of Australia*, vol. 7, no. 3, pp. 180–4.

Tesoriero, F. 1996, 'Mental health services in multicultural Australia: a challenge of social justice', in *Proceedings Joint World Congress IFSW/IASSW: Participating in Change—Social Work Profession in Social Development*, vol. 11, Hong Kong.

Tesoriero, F. 1999, 'Will social work contribute to social development into the new millennium?', *Australian Social Work*, vol. 52, no. 2, pp. 11–17.

The Australian Collaboration 2001, *A Just and Sustainable Australia*, ACOSS, Redfern.

Thompson, D. 1985, *Flaws in the Social Fabric: Homosexuals and Society in Sydney*, George Allen & Unwin, Sydney.

Thompson, E. H. (ed.) 1994, *Older Men's Lives*, Sage, Thousand Oaks, California.

Thompson, N. 1998, 'Social work with adults', in R. Adams, L. Dominelli & M. Payne, *Social Work: Themes, Issues and Critical Debates*, Macmillan, London, pp. 297–331.

Thompson, N. 1997, *Anti-discriminatory Practice*, 2nd edn, Macmillan, Basingstoke.

Thompson, N. 1993, *Anti-Discriminatory Practice*, Macmillan, Houndsmills.

Thomson, J. 1996, 'Trained in life: material feminist work by women community workers', *Northern Radius*, vol. 3, no. 1, April, pp. 20–1.

Thorpe, D. 1994, *Evaluating Child Protection*, Open University Press, Great Britain.

Thorpe, R. & Petruchenia, J. (eds) 1985, *Community Work or Social Change*, Routledge & Kegan Paul, London.

Tikkanen, R. & Ross M. 2003, 'Technological tearoom trade: characteristics of Swedish men visiting gay internet chat rooms', *AIDS Education & Prevention*, vol. 15, no. 2, pp. 122–32.

Tindale, S. 1995, 'Sustaining social democracy: the politics of the environment', in D. Miliband (ed.), *Reinventing the Left*, Polity Press, Cambridge.

Touraine, A. 1985, 'Social movements and social change', in O. F. Borda (ed.), *The Challenge of Social Change*, Sage, London.

Trainer, T. 1998, 'Can permaculture save the world?', *Permaculture International Journal*, no. 68, pp. 14–17.

Trainer, T. 1995, *Towards a Sustainable Economy*, Envirobooks, Sydney.

Trainor, B. 1996, *Radicalism, Feminism and Fanaticism: Social Work in the Nineties*, Avebury, Aldershot.

Trattner, W. 1974, *From Poor Law to Welfare State: A History of Social Welfare in America*, The Free Press, New York.

Trotter, C. 1999, *Working with Involuntary Clients: A Guide to Practice*, Allen & Unwin: St. Leonards.

United Nations 2004, 'Secretary-General urges committee drafting disabilities convention to maintain momentum, understanding as it enters critical phase', M2 Communications Ltd, Presswire, Coventry, May 25, 2004 (full text article downloaded from Proquest).

United Nations 2003, *Agenda 21*, United Nations Department of Economic and Social Affairs, <www.un.org/esa.sustdev/documents/agenda21> (accessed 8 December 2003).

United Nations 1992, *Rio Declaration on Environment and Development: Agenda 21*, United Nations, Geneva.

United Nations High Commissioner for Refugees 2004, *Basic Facts*, <www.unhcr.ch/cgi-bin/texis/vtx/basics> (accessed October 2004).

United Nations World Commission on Environment and Development 1987, *Discussion Paper: Sustainable Development*, United Nations, New York.

US Committee for Refugees 2004, 'Worldwide Refugee Information', <www.refugees.org/world/statistics/wrs03_tableindex.htm> (accessed October 2004).

Valentine, B. 1999, 'National competition policy: legitimating economic rationalism', *Australian Social Work*, vol. 52, no. 1, pp. 26–31.

Van Krieken, R. 1991, *Children and the State: Social Control and the Formation of Australian Child Welfare*, Allen & Unwin, Sydney.

Vanclay, F. & Lawrence, G. 1995, *The Environmental Imperative*, Central Queensland University, Rockhampton.

Vardon, S. 1999, *Electronic Delivery of Government Services: The Centrelink Experience, keynote address to the Government of Alberta*, Internet Insight Conference, Edmonton.

Victorian Mental Illness Advisory Council 1997, *Report of the Lemon Tree Learning Project*, VMIAC, Melbourne.

Vinson, T. 1996, *Waterloo Estate Study, School of Social Work*, University of NSW, Kensington, with the NSW Department of Housing Better City Program.

Wald, M. S. 1982, 'State intervention on behalf of endangered children—a proposed legal response', *Child Abuse and Neglect*, vol. 6, no. 1, pp. 3–45.

Waldner-Haugrud, L., Gratch, L. & Magruder, B. 1997, 'Victimization and perpetration rates of violence in gay and lesbian relationships: gender issues explored', *Violence and Victims*, vol. 12, no. 2, pp. 173–84.

Warren, R. 1963, *The Community in America*, 1st edn, Rand McNally, Chicago.

Waters, W. J. 1976, 'Australian Labor's full employment objective, 1942–45', in J. Roe (ed.), *Social Policy in Australia: Some Perspectives 1901–1975*, Cassell, Sydney, pp. 228–45.

Watkins, R. J. 1992, *The origins and early development of social work in the Department of Social Security*, Master of Letters thesis, University of New England, Armidale.

Wattam, C. 1997, 'Is the criminalisation of child harm and inquiry in the interests of the child?', *Children and Society*, vol. 11, pp. 97–107.

Watts, R. 1989, *The Foundations of The National Welfare State*, Allen & Unwin, Sydney.

WCED, *see* World Commission on the Environment and Development.

Wearing, B. 1986, 'Feminist theory and social work', in H. Marchant & B. Wearing (eds), *Gender Reclaimed: Women in Social Work*, Hale & Iremonger, Sydney, pp. 33–53.

Wearing, B. M. 1984, *The Ideology of Motherhood*, Hale & Iremonger, Sydney.

Wearing, M. 2001, 'Risk, Human Services and Contractualism', *Law in Context* (Special Issue on Human Services and Contracts), vol. 2, no. 18, pp. 129–53.

Wearing, M. 1998, *Working in Community Services*, Allen & Unwin, Sydney.

Wearing, M. & Smyth, P. 1998, 'Working Nation and beyond as market bureaucracy: the introduction of competition policy in case-management', in P. Smyth & B. Cass (eds), *Contesting the Australian Way*, Cambridge University Press, Sydney, pp. 228–40.

Wearing, S. & Wearing, M. 1999, 'Decommodifying ecotourism: rethinking global–local interactions with host communities', *Leisure and Society*, (Loisir et Societe), vol. 22, no. 1, pp. 39–70.

Webster, T. 1995, 'Economic rationalism: the nature, influence and impact of the doctrine over the last decade in Australia', *Australian Social Work*, vol. 48, no. 4, pp. 41–7.

Weeks, W. 2003, 'Women: developing feminist practice in women's services', in J. Allan, B. Pease & L. Briskman (eds), *Critical Social Work: An Introduction to Theories and Practices*, Allen & Unwin, Crows Nest.

Weeks, W. 1996, 'Women citizens' struggle for citizenship', in J. Wilson, J. Thomson & A. McMahon (eds), *The Australian Welfare State: Key Documents and Themes*, Macmillan, Melbourne.

Weeks, W. 1994, *Women Working Together: Lessons from Feminist Women's Services*, Longman Cheshire, Melbourne.

Wesley Dalmar 2004, *Our year, your year*, calendar, Wesley Dalmar Child and Family, Sydney.

Westermeyer, J. 1991, 'Models of mental health services', in J. Westermeyer, C. L. Williams & An Nguyen (eds), *Mental Health Services for Refugees*, US Government Printing Office, Washington DC.

Wexler, D. B. 2002, 'Robes and rehabilitation', *Victorian Bar News*, vol. 123, pp. 27–31.

Wherrett, R. (ed.) 1999, *Mardi Gras True Stories: From Lock Up to Frock Up*, Penguin, Sydney.

White, R. & Haines, F. 2004, *Crime and Criminology: An Introduction*, Oxford University Press, Melbourne.

Whitelum, B. & Cheers, B. 2002, 'Globalisation and Local NGOs', *Asia-Pacific Journal of Social Work*, vol. 12, no. 1, pp. 6–20.

WHO, *see* World Health Organization.

Wiles, D. 1993, 'Ageing and reminiscence: some issues and implications', *Australian Social Work*, vol. 46, no. 1, pp. 4–12.

Wilkinson, K. 1991, *The Community in Rural America*, Greenwood, New York.

Wilkinson, M. 1993, 'Children's rights: debates and dilemmas', in J. Mason, *Child Welfare Policy: Critical Australian Perspectives*, Hale & Iremonger, Sydney.

Wilkinson, M. 1986, 'Good mothers—bad mothers: state substitute care of children in the 1960s', in H. Marchant & B. Wearing (eds), *Gender Reclaimed: Women in Social Work*, Hale & Iremonger, Sydney, pp. 93–103.

Williams, C. J. & McMahon, A. 1998, 'Ageing in rural North Queensland: planning and social justice issues', *Australian Social Work*, vol. 51, no. 1, pp. 27–31.

Wilson, A. & Beresford, P. 2000, 'Anti-oppressive practice: emancipation or appropriation?', *British Journal of Social Work*, vol. 30, pp. 555–73.

Wisniewski, J. & Toomey, B. 1987, 'Are social workers homophobic?', *Social Work*, vol. 32, pp. 454–5.

Wolfensberger, W. 1972, *The Principle of Normalization in Human Services*, National Institute in Mental Retardation, Canada.

Wolinsky, F. D. 1988, *The Sociology of Health: Principles, Practitioners and Issues*, Wadsworth, Belmont.

World Commission on the Environment and Development 1987, *Our Common Future*, United Nations, Geneva.

World Health Organization 2001, *International Classification of Functioning, Disability and Health*, WHO, Geneva.

Wotherspoon, G. 1991, *City of the Plain: History of a Gay Sub-Culture*, Hale & Iremonger, Sydney.

Yates, J. 2004, *Reviewing the Taxation Treatment of Housing*, Housing Australians Seminar, <www.shelternsw.infoxchange.net.au> (accessed October 2004).

Yates, J., Wulff, M. & Reynolds, M. 2004, *Changes in the Supply of and Need for Low-rent Dwellings in the Private Rental Market*, AHURI, Sydney Research Centre.

Yeatman, A. 2000, 'Who is the subject of human rights?', *American Behavioural Scientist*, vol. 43, no. 9, pp. 1498–514.

Yencken, D. & Porter, L. 2001, *A Just and Sustainable Australia*, The Australian Council of Social Service, Melbourne.

Yoon, G. 1996, 'Psychosocial factors for successful ageing', *Australian Journal on Ageing*, vol. 15, no. 2, pp. 69–72.

Zastrow, C. 1995, *The Practice of Social Work*, Brooks/Cole, California.

Zia-Zarifi, S. 2003, 'Losing the Peace in Afghanistan', *Human Rights Watch World Report 2004*, <http://hrw.org/wr2k4/5.htm> (accessed October 2004).

Zukin, S. 1982, *Loft Living: culture and capital in urban change*, John Hopkins press, Baltimore.

Index